EMPIRE CITY UNDER SIEGE

THREE DECADES OF NEW YORK FBI FIELD OFFICE MANHUNTS, MURDERS, AND MAFIA WARS

CRAIG McGUIRE
WITH ANTHONY JOHN NELSON

WILDBLUE
PRESS

WildBluePress.com

EMPIRE CITY UNDER SIEGE published by:
WILDBLUE PRESS
P.O. Box 102440
Denver, Colorado 80250

WILDBLUE PRESS is registered at the U.S. Patent and Trademark Offices.

ISBN 978-1-964730-93-6 Hardcover
ISBN 978-1-964730-94-3 Trade Paperback
ISBN 978-1-964730-92-9 eBook
Cover design © 2025 WildBlue Press. All rights reserved.

Interior Formatting and Book Cover Design by Elijah Toten
www.totencreative.com

EMPIRE CITY UNDER SIEGE

For Syndee, the wind beneath my wings.

Anthony John Nelson

For my sons Francis, Jace, and Antonio,
may these examples show you the world needs more men
who do the right thing when it costs them something.

Craig McGuire

CONTENT

AUTHOR'S NOTE

Real heroes are hard to find these days.

Real heroes never call themselves that.

Real heroes shun the spotlight, never grab for the mic, never take credit, and never complain.

Real heroes hold others up, hold things together, and above all, hold themselves accountable to their own highest standards.

I first met Anthony Nelson in a New Jersey bagel shop on a warm summer Sunday morning to discuss an entirely separate book project—different, but also about courage and law enforcement. I'd been referred to that project by former NYPD Detective Tommy Dades.

That project fell through, despite its merits, mostly due to my fumbling and bumbling.

In a last-ditch effort to salvage that endeavor, I met with Anthony and his lovely wife, Syndee, for breakfast at their home. I should note that Anthony had no vested interest in the success of that other project. With each clipping and grainy crime scene photo Anthony pulled from a pile, he made the case for forging ahead on this other doomed project. Yet every story was a highlight of someone else, some detective, some investigator, just some other hero—Anthony forever casting himself in a supportive role.

After an hour of being pummeled by story after story of shootouts, organized crime takedowns, celebrity abductions, hostage crises, and homicide investigations, I knew there was something there.

Even if Anthony did not see it.

Anthony didn't want credit, didn't want cash, didn't want to be front and center. And he certainly didn't want his name on the cover.

Still, for some time, Anthony just did not want anything to do with a book about all these amazing tales.

Even when Syndee and I were able to get him to entertain the remote possibility of publishing a book based on his stories (of course, with the urging of his family), it was a hard sell.

It took time. Eventually, though, Anthony came around. But there were conditions.

He wouldn't share stories that could impact victims, wouldn't include details that could compromise investigations, wouldn't divulge FBI techniques, and wouldn't participate in publicity unless absolutely necessary.

And more than anything, for Anthony to even consider this project, he had two deal breakers.

He did not want to share the spotlight.

He wanted to shine the spotlight.

Not on himself.

On those he considered the real heroes, his heroes. Those men and women he worked with during his lengthy career, many interviewed here, and most prominently Kenneth "Kenny" McCabe Sr., but also hundreds of others.

Apologies to nineteenth-century playwright Edward Bulwer-Lytton, as the pen may be mightier than the sword, but as I found on this journey with Anthony Nelson, the shield is mightier than all. A shield is not just a badge worn or a decoration borne, but the last line of defense of the defenseless held up by real heroes who uphold the law against the lawless, even when it is difficult, especially when it is dangerous.

I did my best to cast these heroes in the light they deserve. Though, ultimately, that was a fool's errand. There are limits to my abilities. I just hope this work reflects my well-meant intentions.

Secondly, more importantly—in fact, *most* importantly—Anthony did not want to get anything wrong.

Get it right. No matter what. No matter how long it takes.

I'm certainly no hero. I'm just a storyteller. And these sure are great stories. Stories of bravery, disaster, danger, and, well, heroic acts by everyday people. But I've never negotiated a hostage crisis, never been shot or shot at, never put my life on the line.

Therefore, any and all omissions, inaccuracies, or other issues with facts, writ large and small, are entirely my responsibility and my fault.

Understand, these are not *just* stories, not *just* crimes on a blotter. These are legacies of quiet courage in times of chaos. Pretending this work does them justice is a reach.

So, as I've come to learn on this journey, real heroes never call themselves that.

Real heroes shun the spotlight, never grab for the mic, never take credit, and never complain.

Real heroes are hard to find.

And the thing with our heroes is we never know when we'll ever encounter them, if we ever do—it could just be in a New Jersey bagel shop on a warm summer Sunday morning.

Enjoy the read.

— Craig McGuire

PROLOGUE

My name is Anthony John Nelson.

This story is not just *my story*.

This is the story of brave men and women in law enforcement with whom I had the great honor to serve alongside throughout my career at the United States Federal Bureau of Investigation, and later in the Special Investigations Unit of the Brooklyn District Attorney's Office.

This is the story of the few who stood against the many, who refused to stand by and watch their cities, their country, their way of life, be consumed by rampant corruption, violence, and the unraveling of it all.

I'm not a writer by trade. I never considered writing a book or assisting someone else to write a book about my experiences in law enforcement until recently.

So ... why? Why am I sharing this story ... now? Why should you, the reader, invest your time? What message should you take from these pages?

The real story behind *this story* started with a conversation at a dinner party, many years ago—a few moments that wedged this small nagging pebble in my shoe that over the years worked its way deeper and deeper into my being.

It was the late 1990s, a window of time that served as the bridge between our analog past and the rapidly approaching digital future of today's twenty-first century. I was attending a formal dinner party at a posh hotel in Manhattan with my lovely wife, Syndee, when I struck up a conversation with a neurosurgeon.

After learning that I was a Special Agent with the FBI, he confided in me that he would never be able to perform my job.

This caught me by surprise.

For one thing, doctors, especially surgeons, tend to be confident individuals, at times bordering on arrogant, but with good reason. After all, as children, we're drilled that the brain surgeon rests atop the apex of our species, possessing that rare genetic combination of intellect, aptitude, and dexterity to, essentially, play God.

Yet here was this accomplished neurosurgeon before me, likely with hundreds, if not thousands of surgeries under his stethoscope—insisting that I had a much harder job than he did.

Decades of interviewing some pretty exceptional liars teaches you things. You see, words lie. Bodies don't. It's the little things. The delayed answer. The slight wander of a gaze. The over explaining. The tightening of the voice.

But this was no self-effacing cocktail banter. This neurosurgeon was sincere; earnest, in fact. And I sensed something … else—a desire to dispel the skepticism on my face. And then I saw it, a quick flicker of emotion, a sense of … relief.

As our conversation continued, he spoke with purpose about how he held the lives of his patients in his hands, who could die on his operating table due to the natural complexity of their illnesses.

You see, playing God is not *being* God.

He shared how soundly he slept at night, sure that he performed his job to the best of his abilities, regardless of the outcome.

Despite the intricacies of these operations, he generally faced the same set of challenges. Sure, his work required exceptional skill and technique that few possess. But there was also a predictive nature to his work. His patients shared the same anatomical structures, their maladies known, familiar puzzles to piece together, but rarely surprises.

He said he doubted he could make the "split-second, life-or-death decisions" that police officers and FBI agents face. He questioned his ability to process so many random variables with so little time, or not enough time, to make the right decision.

These are decisions, he stressed, that the officer not only has to justify later in his own mind, but also in the minds of others who question his actions, and must live with their consequences.

This surgeon captured, quite eloquently, the crushing weight of responsibility members of law enforcement face when they pin on the badge and strap on the belt.

The topic of conversation changed. Yet that evening stayed with me, subconsciously, for many years, until I thought of it relatively recently.

Much has changed since the late 1990s.

Critics of law enforcement have the benefit of reviewing a police officer's actions with the luxury of hindsight.

However, more and more, influential people, some well-intentioned, too many not fully informed, began to demean law enforcement collectively, as a profession, to an extent I had never seen before. And I started at the FBI in the 1960s.

The criticisms took a darker tone, following in the wake of members of law enforcement being involved with tragic civilian deaths. Some critics even demanded that law enforcement in the United States be "reimagined" or "defunded."

They were using clever words and phrases to justify undermining law and order, casting aside the reputations and dedication of the heroic rank and file of law enforcement agencies across this great nation.

That is not to say the criticisms in some instances were unwarranted or unjustified. Sometimes change is needed. There is always room for improvement and innovation.

However, it was the misguided remedies and lack of understanding of the nature of police work that compelled me to assist in writing this book.

This work aims to cast light on the daily adversities faced by individuals who sacrifice their own comforts and those of their family members for the sake of others' safety and well-being.

The period covered in this work, spanning from the 1970s through the early 2000s, was transformative, affecting not just culture but also law enforcement and its symbiotic relationship across the criminal landscape.

I can say, having lived through this period, that there were times of misguided, extreme criticism of not just the wrongful, even criminal, actions of individuals who wear the shield, but a collective condemnation of law enforcement as a whole.

Where are their advocates? Why are they not heard just as loud, just as often?

Unfortunately, what rarely makes the front pages or fills the first few minutes of breaking newscasts is the tireless, thankless work done by law enforcement officers I personally knew, who withstood and overcame the difficulties of "The Job" in the face of such acrimony.

This is not my biography.

This is a homage to the unheralded men and women of law enforcement who step forward, step up, and dedicate their lives to making the world a better and safer place, despite the many dangers to their physical and emotional well-being.

They should be praised, and not just when they lay down their lives in the service of protecting us all.

I was fortunate to be in the company of courage throughout my career and there are many heroic men and women mentioned in this book. Still, I would like to call particular attention to the Special Agents of the FBI in the New York Office and detectives of the New York City Police Department, and in particular, NYPD Detective Kenneth McCabe, my dear friend, who was the most significant weapon the government employed to disrupt and dismantle traditional organized crime in New York City.

Though sadly Kenny is no longer with us, his presence casts a long shadow across law enforcement. He exemplified everything exceptional in what we do.

Kenny McCabe's intellect, aptitude, and dedication in the service of protecting and serving are legendary. His sacrifices, sense of fairness, and focus on justice not only place him at the forefront of the proud tradition of law enforcement in America, but in the annals of the NYPD Detective Bureau, he epitomizes the essence of their motto: "The Greatest Detectives in the World."

Ultimately, consider this book my testament to the relentless fight for justice, the vigilance needed to combat the ever-changing face of crime, and the legacy of those who dedicated their lives to defending the streets.

This is not just *my story*.

For Kenny, for those others mentioned in this work, for those I had the privilege of serving alongside, and for those who wear the badges and shields every day, and their families—*this story* is for you.

— Anthony John Nelson

TIMELINE

1969	
January	Hired by US Federal Bureau of Investigation for various duties on mostly 4 p.m.-to-midnight shifts (later assigned as radio dispatcher, electronics technician in 1972)
October	Enlists in Army National Guard; on active-duty military leave until February 1970
1970	
June	Graduates John Jay College of Criminal Justice with a BS in Criminal Justice
1975	
	Satisfies FBI requirements for Special Agent position, interviewed by legendary Special Agent in Charge Philip McNiff
August	Assigned to support team during kidnapping of Samuel Bronfman II, son of billionaire tycoon Edgar Bronfman of Seagram's fame
1976	
October	Sworn in as Special Agent in Washington, DC, enters FBI Academy in Quantico, VA
1977	
March	Graduates from FBI Academy
	Assigned to the FBI's New York Field Office, begins work undercover investigating hijacking
Spring	First meets legendary NYPD Detective Kenny McCabe in connection with an investigation into the theft of a tractor trailer load of electronics
Summer	Begins regular night rides with Kenny McCabe to surveil dozens of Mafia social clubs across Brooklyn and Queens.
1978	

	Begins long-term hijacking investigation with ATF, operating undercover out of a warehouse in Red Hook, Brooklyn
February	Part of FBI team that foils kidnapping of Marci Klein, the eleven-year-old daughter of famed clothing designer Calvin Klein
Spring	With Agents Jules Bonavolonta and Lewis Schiliro, posing as rival organized crime figures to bust Lucchese ring extorting Times Square topless bar Adam and Eve
May	Meets future wife Syndee during a chance encounter while investigating bookmaker and fence Harold Rothenberg, who is murdered soon after
1979	
	Assigned to FBI Organized Crime/Gambino Squad
February	Part of team that takes down Gambino crew running guns based on ATF plan, 15 Mafia associates arrested; arrest plan formulated by ATF
June	On arrest team that foils plot to rob $2 million money shipment, hatched by ex-con serving as on-set advisor to actor Peter Falk while filming *The Brinks Job*
1980	
April	Arrests con artist preying on Manhattan women, dubbed "The Romeo Barfly with a Sting" by *New York Post*'s Jerry Capeci
October	Captures "cop fighter" Victor Caruso, a Genovese associate terrorizing store owners, following a wild outdoor scene in Sheepshead Bay
1981	

	Walter Mack, Assistant US Attorney for the Southern District, launches new organized-crime task force, Nelson begins to supply intelligence
March	Posing as a Gambino family associate, fronts multi-kilo cocaine sting in South Florida
Spring	Begins manhunt for Mafia hitman Joseph "Mad Dog" Sullivan
Summer	Informants report Roy DeMeo henchmen Freddy DiNome threatens to "easily take them out," referring to Nelson and McCabe, DiNome later refers to targeting McCabe's home and family
1982	
June	Tip leads to Nelson recovering stolen Picasso and Matisse artwork in an abandoned car in Queens, masterpieces the thieves were unable to fence
July	Leads raid on Brooklyn Mob-frequented restaurant to apprehend fugitive Genovese associate Joseph "Joe Curly'" Taglianetti.
September	Raids Manhattan apartment, arresting Colombo associate Rocco Santarsiero, taking down massive credit card fraud ring
1984	
June	Helps bust Brooklyn Colombo mortgage scam defrauding senior citizens of their homes
1985	
May	Investigates and arrests a corrupt assistant US attorney for stealing $500,000 worth of heroin and cocaine from an evidence safe
1986	
July	Arrests Governor's Island resident for makeshift bomb based on Coast Guard tip the same week President Ronald Reagan visits island

December	Cuffs corrupt corrections officer attempting to smuggle veal parm sandwiches to Mob boss John Gotti jailed at the Metropolitan Correctional Center (MCC)
1987	
June	Leads dramatic rescue team to save three-year-old hostage at Fort Wadsworth Staten Island military installation
1988	
July	Investigates senseless murder of VA Policeman Ronald Hearn at Bronx VA Hospital
October	Investigates murder of NYPD Narcotics undercover Christopher G. Hoban. Later hunts down and captures one of the perpetrators in Puerto Rico
1989	
February	Justice Department colleague and friend, DEA Agent Everett Hatcher, slain by a Bonanno drug dealer, leading to a massive manhunt
June	Uncovers culprit in mass poisoning at FDA offices in Sunset Park, Brooklyn
December	Involved in shooting after suspect plows through Brooklyn Battery Tunnel tollbooth and strikes Port Authority officer
1990	
January	Involved in a fatal shootout with bank robbers in Bay Ridge, Brooklyn
February	Leads investigation to apprehend suspect who perpetrated inside job robbing Adams Guest House on Fort Hamilton base in Brooklyn
1992	
July	Responds to an armed robbery in progress that tragically claims the life of retired NYPD Lieutenant Robert Nesbitt
1993	

June	Investigates retired Navy SEAL, part of plot of rip off other servicemen at VA Hospital. Veteran later dies by suicide, Nelson's card found gripped in his hand
1994	
February	Apprehends fugitive in notorious Red Hook Houses complex, severely injures back during wild melee
1996	
March	Investigates deaths of multiple stowaways aboard a West African cargo ship docked in New York
1997	
	Appointed Acting Coordinating Supervisory Special Agent, reporting to New York Office ASAC Jack Slicks
1998	
January	Responds to Brink's bank robbery at the World Trade Center
Spring	Promoted to a Supervisory Special Agent and tapped to supervise Major Theft—Truck Hijacking (1998) squad
June	Provides logistical support to the NYPD to bring Colombo gunmen to justice for the assassination of Officer Ralph Dols
August	"Steals" merchandise (part of $2 million in jewelry heisted from a UPS shipment) from outside the ringleader's Mill Basin home
1999	
January	Leads FBI team investigating *Banner of October*, where captain died by suicide aboard freighter stranded in New York Harbor for months.
March	Leads bust of major hijacking ring, recovering massive haul abandoned railway yard out in Staten Island, based on tip from mob informant.

2000	
November	Investigates Bin Laden terrorist lieutenant jailed in MCC who stabbed and maimed prison officer
2001	
September	Responds to World Trade Center terrorist attack, spends next few months supervising multiple investigations and efforts in aftermath of tragedy
2002	
	Tapped to supervise FBI/NYPD Bank Robbery—Violent Crimes squads
October	Supervises team of FBI investigators sent to Maryland to help apprehend the Beltway Snipers
November	Named Acting Assistant Special Agent in Charge of the FBI's Violent Crimes Branch
2004	
November	Formally retires from the Federal Bureau of Investigation
2005	
August	Appointed as investigator in Kings County District Attorney's Office
August	Investigator on the Bones Case, a corrupt funeral home director illegally harvesting and reselling body parts for medical uses without permission of the deceased's' families
2006	
February	Kenny McCabe Sr. passes away after a heroic fight with brain cancer
2012	
December	Retires as the Assistant Deputy Chief of the Special Investigations Unit in the Brooklyn DA's Office

CHAPTER ONE

We begin *this story* on an unseasonably warm autumn morning long ago, the day before Halloween in the year before the turn of the middle of the twentieth century.

Anthony John Nelson was born in Long Island College Hospital in Brooklyn on October 30, 1949, a time and place that no longer exists.

These days, this bustling northwest corner of Cobble Hill is not unlike many Brooklyn settings: prime real estate, a quick commute from Lower Manhattan, overrun by realtors, and disputed by developers in a desperate battle of gentrification that has long since been lost.

But that morning in 1949, this was a very different place in a very different world.

Founded in 1858 as St. John's Hospital, LICH introduced bedside teaching to America. LICH later became the first US hospital to use stethoscopes and anesthesia, and in 1873, launched the first emergency ambulance service in this country.[1]

As the bones of the majestic Brooklyn Bridge rose in nearby East River harbor, LICH began its long maternal legacy, delivering generations of newborns to a Brooklyn forever bursting with

---

1. "History & Mission | Sesquicentennial." https://www.downstate.edu/about/our-history/sesquicentennial/history.html#:~:text=The%20Long%20Island%20College%20Hospital,clinics%20were%20used%20for%20teaching

young, fertile families. At its peak, the facility pumped nearly 1,500 new offspring annually into Kings County.[2]

LICH survived the New York Draft Riots, the Spanish Flu, the Great Depression, two World Wars, the Great Blackout of '77, and even the aftermath of a mid-air collision over Staten Island that sent a DC-8 crashing into the intersection of 7th Avenue and Sterling Place (tragically, not a single survivor). However, gentrification ultimately claimed LICH, and by 2014, with a monthly hemorrhage of fifteen million dollars, it was closed.

This work is a story of change, so befittingly, 1949 was somewhat of an inflection point in our culture for so much of what was to come.

1949 was the year the Cold War heated up, hysteria fueling the Communist witch hunts of Senator Joseph McCarthy's Red Scare. The North Atlantic Treaty Organization (NATO) created a military alliance between European and North American countries just as the villainous Soviet Union detonated its first atomic bomb and the People's Republic of China was created by proclamation of Mao Zedong.

Harry S. Truman was our president and delivered his Fair Deal speech on January 20, 1949, the first time a presidential inauguration was televised. The modem was invented, making way for the modern digital age, as the first commercial jet made its maiden flight and the first Volkswagen Beetles flitted onto American shores.

In popular culture, the first Emmy Awards ceremony was held. The National Basketball Association tipped off. They discovered another moon of Neptune and oil under the Caspian Sea. George Orwell haunted us with the totalitarian terror of Big Brother by publishing *1984*, Rodgers and Hammerstein delighted us by debuting *South Pacific*, and Arthur Miller disturbed us by staging his Pulitzer Prize-winning drama *Death of a Salesman*.

Back in Brooklyn, just weeks after Catherine and Edward Nelson brought home their newborn baby boy, those damn Yankees

---

2. "The Rise and Fall of LICH: America's First Teaching Hospital – Cobble Hill Association." https://cobblehill.nyc/knowledge_base/the-rise-and-fall-of-lich-americas-first-teaching-hospital/

defeated *dem bums* (the New York Yankees bested the Brooklyn Dodgers, four games to one, to notch their twelfth World Series title).

"My family resided on First Place in the Red Hook section of Brooklyn at the time," Anthony Nelson fondly recalls. "I lived there with my mother, my sister Linda, and my father, when he was not away on a military assignment."

This Red Hook of 1949 was a much darker place than it is today.

These were mean streets where, not long before, a pre-Chicago Al Capone was a leg-breaking bouncer along the waterfront saloons. In fact, the 1954 film *On the Waterfront*, starring a young Marlon Brando, immortalized that seedier side of Nelson's childhood neighborhood.

This was bloody lip, black-and-blue collar Brooklyn, overrun by crime barons and corrupt labor bosses who preyed upon the struggling Italian and African-American families, where the men shaped up at the crack of dawn at the nearby warehouses and docks.

The area was a hive of industry before it became Industry City, its factories spinning out everything from mattresses to cigarettes. Not even a decade before, in 1941, the Gowanus Expressway, designed by the ruthless Robert Moses, gashed the neighborhood in half, displacing thousands of residents.

"When I was five years old, my uncle Dominick 'Charlie' LoPresti purchased a four-story brownstone on 4th Street near 7th Avenue in Park Slope, and we moved into the top floor of that building," Nelson recalls.

In 2010, *New York Magazine* ranked Park Slope as one of New York City's most desirable neighborhoods, praising its quality public schools, luxury dining, popular nightlife, green spaces, safety, and creative atmosphere.[3]

This Park Slope *ain't* that; though for the Nelson family, it was an upgrade from crime-ridden Red Hook. Park Slope, circa 1950s, had a ragged edge blended with the urban working-class grit

---

3. Silver, Nate. "The Most Livable Neighborhoods in New York." New York Magazine. https://nymag.com/realestate/neighborhoods/2010/65374/

of post-war optimism and that downtown Romanesque-revival charm.

This was the original South Brooklyn, though far north of what is now considered the actual geographical south of Brooklyn (neighborhoods including Bensonhurst, Bay Ridge, Dyker Heights, Sheepshead Bay, and Gravesend).

Park Slope, lined with those famed Brooklyn brownstones and apartment buildings, took its name from the western embankments of neighboring Prospect Park to the east, along with its sibling Central Park. Created when Brooklyn was still its own city, these were among the first landscaped parks developed in the United States.

This was older-than-old-school stoop-culture Brooklyn, that sepia-steeped era when everyone knew everyone and knew their business. When the weather was warm, families gathered outside in the early evenings up and down your block.

These were the last days of the horse drawn carts and the ice lords, where an endless parade of grizzled vendors hawked everything from fresh fish to fowl, cream to crude coal, crying out offers to sharpen your knives, get your ice, or grab the ragman making his rounds. The wash still hung on lines strung between buildings. Milkmen still delivered glass bottles to homes with cold boxes on their porches. And Krueger's still brought you your daily bread.

Music poured from the windows, and grape vines crawled along the fences. Wine was made in bathtubs, and meals were cooked at home, healthy and hearty. Families gathered around the radio in the evenings, or if you were lucky, the TV, which was not flat and more like a piece of furniture. And most lived in multigenerational homes. In fact, Nelson's grandmother, Pauline, and Aunt Laura lived on the ground floor.

"My grandmother was the center of our universe, and each Sunday afternoon, she was visited, without fail, by at least ten members of our large Italian family," Nelson says.

Edward Nelson made a career in the United States Army and, at times, relocated his family to the military bases where he was assigned. One of his overseas assignments was Livorno, Italy, where the Nelsons lived for two years.

"But when he was on certain assignments, or sent to places where military dependents were not allowed to reside," Nelson says, "we always moved back into our apartment on 4th Street."

Boys like young Anthony Nelson would go down to the local corner store to pick up a newspaper for their parents and a nickel's worth of candy for themselves. Small mom-and-pop shops were staples, sitting beside soda fountains, hardware stores, green grocers, butchers, five and dimes, candy stores, and Italian bakeries. And every other corner had a church, a synagogue, or a saloon.

You got dressed up to go shopping on The Avenue or Downtown, maybe dropped in at the Tea Room on Flatbush. There were no Starbucks or McDonald's, and the closest thing to a big-box chain was Abraham and Straus (later Macy's) on Fulton Street, a classy store, sure, with its lovely garden-room lunch restaurant, only outdone by Martin's with its white-gloved elevator operators.

Sunday church services and feasts were intrinsic to family life, with Roman Catholic parishes serving as communal hubs. Boys and girls who did not go to public school attended parochial institutions, where discipline and uniforms were both strictly enforced.

"I attended Saint Francis Xavier grammar school on President Street, which segregated the boys from the girls, and my classes were taught by Franciscan Brothers," Nelson says. "There didn't seem to be any rules against corporal punishment at the time, and it was not unusual to get whacked by one of the Brothers with a long wooden pointer if you displeased them in some way."

Nelson grew up in a stable home environment, where he was instilled with values of honesty and integrity that later inspired the path he chose for his life.

"I had a stay-at-home mother who believed deeply in Catholic teachings and inspired most of my values," Nelson says. "My father was in the US Army for twenty-three years, so of course he contributed significantly to those values, but in different ways."

In the 1950s, Park Slope, even with more of an ethnic mix compared to other New York zip codes, was a predominantly working-class Italian-American neighborhood.

"Although my last name is Nelson, since my father was Irish, I'm half Italian on my mother's side," Nelson says. "Except for my father, I grew up in an exclusively Italian family in Park Slope, and I spoke Italian fairly well." Little did young Anthony know at the time, his retention of the mother tongue would come in handy years later, and not just to order the entrees at Bamonte's.

"While Red Hook was a mostly Italian neighborhood, Park Slope was a very ethnically mixed area. But most of my Italian relatives remained in Red Hook while I began to enjoy my life in Park Slope."

By the late '50s, enjoying life for Anthony meant Saturday matinees at local theaters, with Westerns, adventure serials, and early sci-fi films playing in the movie palaces along Flatbush Avenue, Church Avenue, and Utica Avenue, where, if you were lucky, you kissed your first girl in the back row.

Kids played together on stoops, on sidewalks, in schoolyards, in the street, and in Prospect Park. Stickball was the favorite, although other games, such as stoopball, punchball, and marbles, were also common. Prospect Park offered acres of open spaces for running, picnicking, and sledding in the winter.

During the hot months, the neighborhood boys would crank open the fire hydrants, which they called the Johnny Pump, as sort of a makeshift sprinkler. Ice cream trucks rambled by every hour on the hour, and you always knew they were close by the loop of metallic chimes plinking out of tinny speakers competing with the dull moan of traffic.

And when it got too hot at night and it wasn't raining, you slept beneath the Brooklyn stars on your fire escape.

As a boy of 1950s Brooklyn, Nelson chomped at the bit to roam, as long as his schoolwork and chores were done. "At the age of seven, I was already learning about life on the streets and how to avoid danger. My mother was very protective of me, yet it was impossible for her to prevent me from picking up some of the bad habits of my friends."

Nelson's childhood friends were not committing serious crimes per se, but some were engaged in behavior that Mrs. Nelson would never approve of.

Back then, all the cars parked on the street had metal extendable "whip" radio antennae.

"Some of the older boys who hung out on the block showed us how to break off a car antenna and remove a portion of it that could easily be fitted to hold a .22-caliber bullet," Nelson explains. "They'd use the antenna piece as the barrel and then build a 'zip gun' fashioned out of carved wood. A sharpened sliding door latch and rubber bands served as the firing pin and trigger. And they actually worked."

For even more *fun*, some of the kids would tie a steel wool pad to a long rope, set it on fire, and spin the rope in the air over their heads.

"During the summer, the sparks from the steel wool would make a mess of our T-shirts and we'd go home with dozens of holes in our clothing. I have no idea how none of us were ever blinded by the sparks from these contraptions or how we didn't maim ourselves from the M-80 fireworks that we'd set off all summer long."

Nelson also remembers another favorite pastime was building "go carts." "We built them out of wood beams," he says, "which we nailed to old wooden milk crates, and we used metal skates for the wheels."

As Nelson grew, he began to cross paths with that other Brooklyn archetype—the gangster.

While the neighborhood was primarily residential, its proximity to commercial districts with significant Mob infestations, such as Red Hook and Gowanus, brought a spillover of organized crime influence.

This was Gangland USA. In the early twentieth century, Irish mobs, such as the White Hand, held sway along the Brooklyn waterfront. While their rackets were concentrated in Red Hook, their tentacles extended into Park Slope, where residents had ties to the docks and factories.

During Prohibition, Park Slope, like much of Brooklyn, witnessed the rise of the speakeasies as bootlegging flourished. Local gangsters used the bathtubs to make rotgut gin, and the brownstone basements and back alleys for storing and distributing illegal booze.

Eventually, the Italian gangs, forerunners of the modern Italian-American Mafia, overwhelmed the Irish crews to dominate the local rackets.

"During my youth, I had several friends who chose to pursue 'that life,' an expression used on the street even back then referring to involvement with the Mafia," Nelson says.

By the time young Nelson was banging around, his neighborhood had become a stronghold for several Mafia families, especially the Gambinos, Colombos, and Bonannos. They maintained interests in gambling, loan sharking, and extortion, all with low-key operations throughout Park Slope.

Nearby Gowanus and Carroll Gardens were more notorious Mob strongholds. Figures like Joseph "Crazy Joe" Gallo, who hailed from Red Hook, occasionally operated near Park Slope. While Park Slope itself was not a Mafia epicenter, its relative affluence made it a target for extortion and other schemes.

Walking by all these local spots, little did young Nelson suspect he'd eventually be a crusader against the next generation of criminal elements on these very streets.

This was the era of the South Brooklyn Boys, that conglomerate of 1950s Italian-American greaser gangs from Carroll Gardens, Cobble Hill, Park Slope, Red Hook, Gowanus, and Boerum Hill. These were the roaming gangs of the South Brooklyn Devils, the Garfield Place Boys, the SB Angels, the Wanderers, the Degraw Street Boys, the Sackett Street Boys, the Butler Gents, the Gowanus Boys, the Kane Street Midgets, the Little Gents, and the Young Savages.

The leading group, simply referred to as the South Brooklyn Boys by many, raised hell in and around 3rd Street Park, which, back in the 1950s, was still predominantly Italian. And they were bitter enemies with the Puerto Rican gangs, like the Untouchable Bishops and the Apaches, as well as African American gangs, such as the Mau Maus.

The 1962 book, *All the Way Down: The Violent Underworld of Street Gangs*, by Vincent Riccio and Bill Slocum, featured accounts of the Gowanus Boys, one of the earlier neighborhood crews that evolved into the larger, more loosely affiliated South Brooklyn Boys.

Reputed Lucchese mobster Anthony "Gaspipe" Casso was a member of the early South Brooklyn Boys, as was Carmine Persico, future head of the Colombo Family.

When Anthony Nelson turned nine years old, he was permitted to cross the bustling avenues without the aid of a grownup, an important milestone for any Brooklyn kid. He'd join his friends going to candy stores in the area to get fountain sodas and some junk food.

One day, while Anthony was walking with a friend on 7th Avenue, the boys heard a gunshot and the screams of young girls.

"When we walked over to see what happened, a neighborhood kid, whom I'd seen before but didn't know well, was lying on the ground, unconscious with a bullet wound in the side of his head," Nelson says. "It was the first murder aftermath I ever witnessed."

And it was the first of many.

Once the shock subsided, the boy with Nelson said, "Let's see if we can borrow a dime to call the *Daily New*s. I heard that they'll give you a reward if you tip them off to a good story."

"Even at the age of nine," Nelson remembers, "I was amazed my friend had not first said, 'Let's call the police.'"

As Nelson grew into his teenage years, he became more aware of what was happening in the back rooms of the candy stores and social clubs cropping up in the area.

"Betting on the numbers and gambling in the clubs was rampant, but I'd never given much thought to the fact that these activities were illegal, even though I didn't participate," Nelson says.

Nelson, however, did engage in some harmless forms of wagering on the streets with his friends. "Quite often, we'd toss quarters against a wall to see who could toss them closer. If you tossed a quarter and it happened to land in a leaning position, upright against the wall, you were not only the winner of all the coins that were tossed, but also deserving of significant praise."

At the age of fourteen, Nelson would go with friends to a large supermarket chain on Carroll Street and 7th Avenue, called Bohack's.

Before limping through multiple bankruptcies and ceasing operations in 1977, Bohack's was one of the original neighborhood grocery chains, opening its first store on Fulton Street back in 1887. Before Bohack's, you'd have to shop at multiple stores. Bohack's, at least the larger stores, had separate meat and fish counters, sold Bohack's branded merch, and even had its own in-store bakery.

"We'd ask people leaving the store if they wanted help carrying their groceries home, even though the store operated an optional delivery service with a Hippie Van," Nelson says.

The guy who drove this Volkswagen Microbus, likely an iconic pastel-hued Vanagon Westfalia, sometimes asked if the boys wanted to help him. It was a quick way to earn some cash. In the evening, he'd park it on the street overnight.

"It didn't take long for one of my friends to learn that the Hippie Van had a primitive ignition switch and virtually any car key that fit the ignition could start the van.

"My friend Patrick wasn't someone easily deterred by rules or regulations," Nelson says. "He was also only fourteen and obviously too young to have a driver's license. But he liked telling me that 'the VW starts without a license, so why not use it without permission?'"

In those days, parking spots in Park Slope were far more available than they are today, and after a night of joyriding, Patrick simply returned the vehicle to the same spot by morning.

It was during this time hanging around Bohack's that Anthony Nelson met several New York City police officers patrolling the beat on foot each day.

Before 1968, there was no centralized or universal emergency phone number in the United States. If you had an emergency, you called the operator or the local precinct. If there was a fire, hopefully you had the neighborhood fire station's number on hand. And switchboard operators at local hospitals often reported being flooded with calls, especially during peak flu seasons.

The implementation of the 911 system led to a shift towards car patrols. However, back in the 1950s, community policing played a central role in maintaining order and addressing crime in neighborhoods across the five boroughs.

These beat cops were not just present; they engaged the community, checking in with shopkeepers, patrolling trouble spots, and providing a sense of security for their neighborhood.

"I grew to admire them," Nelson says. "They were always around, protecting and serving, and doing heroic work that was quite noticeable to me."

About this time, Nelson arrived at a crossroads that many boys in Brooklyn face—some of Nelson's friends began to emulate local mobsters, particularly those associated with the Colombo crime Family, then captained by Joseph "Crazy Joe" Gallo.

"One of the social clubs closest to me was The Nestor, which bordered Carroll Street and 5th Avenue," Nelson says. "A few of my friends hung out there, some associated themselves with neighborhood gangs like the South Brooklyn Boys. Some of them even began to get involved in non-violent criminal activities, collecting numbers or simple loan sharking. Although most of them knew I would not get involved, I never had any confrontations with them, nor arguments about the choices they made in life."

Then one day, young Anthony Nelson had an epiphany.

A friend nicknamed Bug Eyes had developed a drug problem. That day, after injecting himself with heroin, he fell into a stupor sitting atop the wall of a second-story building entryway and fell over the side.

"The police officers responding to the call, whom I knew and admired, really tried to help Bug Eyes, but they couldn't revive him," Nelson says. "The fall killed him instantly. However, their heroic efforts in those moments had a profound impact on me. They didn't stand by. They really tried. It brought to the surface my latent belief that I was born to spend my life as a law enforcement officer."

As time wore on, Nelson became more familiar with the South Brooklyn rackets. The wiseguys were much more brazen and unchecked. Nelson knew the operators and could recognize the regulars of the network of candy stores, car services, and social clubs that served as fronts for organized crime.

"Through my associations, my friendships, my mere presence, I saw how things worked on the streets, with both the street gangs and organized crime," Nelson says. "Just by frequenting these locations, overhearing conversations, seeing how people interacted, I put it together, picking up the nuances of how certain locations worked, at a time when some of my friends were becoming more involved.

"I also spoke Italian fairly well, which enabled me to create more of a rapport with them," Nelson adds. "For many of these wiseguys, Italian was their native tongue."

Sometime after Bug Eyes' death, Nelson came across a documentary on television about the United States Federal Bureau of Investigation.

"Instantly, I just knew that was the career I wanted," Nelson says, "especially once I learned it was one of the most difficult jobs to get."

Shortly after, now sixteen years old, Nelson penned a letter to the FBI requesting more information about becoming an FBI Special Agent. Imagine his surprise when, soon after, he received not just a response, but a letter signed by none other than J. Edgar Hoover himself, the legendary director of the FBI.

"I kept that letter to this day," Nelson says. "In all probability, the inked signature was signed with an automated pen, but for that sixteen-year-old boy growing up in Brooklyn, it sure meant a lot to me."

CHAPTER TWO

Around the time the handwritten letter from a boy from Brooklyn arrived at the US Federal Bureau of Investigation in Washington, DC, the agency was undergoing a transformation.

As America barreled into the second half of the twentieth century, it faced unprecedented waves of social unrest, political upheaval, and rampant corruption, attacked from within by increasingly sophisticated homegrown criminal organizations, and besieged from without by foreign threats.

You could even say the FBI was born in 1908 out of necessity to help cope with the unprecedented change facing America.

In the early twentieth century, this country faced challenges in urbanization, industrialization, and immigration, all plagued by shadowy crime syndicates, fueled by Prohibition. For these criminals, the Volstead Act, prohibiting the making, sale, and transportation of alcoholic beverages, was the gift that kept on giving until its repeal in 1933 by the 21st Amendment.

Criminal tentacles spread far and wide, choking the nation, exploiting law enforcement's inability to collaborate across state lines.

In an America where every jurisdiction was a silo, the FBI became that centralized agency to combat the interstate crime that local and state authorities were not equipped to handle.

Even before it was chasing gangsters and bank robbers, the early FBI was investigating anarchists and agitators. Violence-plagued strikes, political uprisings, and fears of communism underscored the need for this new federal agency to monitor and act on threats.

The country's cities had grown enormously by 1908—there were more than one hundred with populations exceeding fifty thousand—and crime grew right along with them. In these big cities, with their overcrowded tenements, clashes between striking workers and factory bosses were turning violent. Slums fast became breeding grounds for criminal gangs and the crime lords who led them.

In Brooklyn, a nine-year-old Al Capone set out on his life of crime. In Indianapolis, a five-year-old John Dillinger was growing up on his family farm. And in Chicago, Lester Joseph Gillis, aka "Baby Face" Nelson, was just a … baby.

Corruption was rampant coast to coast as crooked political machines had risen in Boston, Chicago, Cleveland, Kansas City, Philadelphia, St. Louis, Memphis, and more, the most infamous Tammany Hall in New York led by William M. "Boss" Tweed.

Big business was unchecked and underhanded, from the shoddy, even criminal, conditions in meat packaging plants and factories (as muckrakers like Upton Sinclair so artfully exposed) to the illegal monopolies threatening entire industries.[4]

At first, FBI agents mainly investigated civil rights and white-collar crimes, from racial violence and forced labor to banking fraud and graft. It addressed a few national security issues, including treason and some fringe anarchist groups. However, its jurisdiction would grow as Congress recognized the potential of this new agency.

By 1915, Congress had increased the Bureau's ranks tenfold from its original thirty-four Special Agents to three hundred and sixty, including support personnel.

It wasn't long before the Bureau got its first taste of national security work. Along the border with Mexico, the FBI opened several offices to investigate smuggling and neutrality violations.

With the outbreak of war in Europe in 1914, the United States initially avoided involvement. Then German submarines started sinking American ships, and saboteurs began planting bombs

---

4. "A Brief History." https://www.fbi.gov/history/brief-history

on US freighters while targeting munitions plants on US soil, provoking the nation to enter the conflict.

On November 24, 1932, this Bureau of Investigation (BOI) started the first national crime laboratory in the United States. Besides serving the BOI, the lab's mission was to assist local law enforcement agencies with ballistics testing and fingerprint identification. In fact, in his memoirs, Special Agent Melvin Purvis wrote that by 1936, the FBI had the fingerprints of six million criminals on file in Washington, DC.

On August 10, 1933, the BOI was officially renamed the Division of Investigation (DOI). And J. Edgar Hoover was determined to create a modern, sophisticated force that blended scientific methods with advanced police skills. Hoover implemented more stringent qualifications for recruits. They now required a college or law school degree, as well as a background in law enforcement. Forensic science training and the use of firearms also became mandatory.

On July 1, 1935, the DOI was renamed again—the Federal Bureau of Investigation (FBI). Today, in its modern form, the FBI is the domestic intelligence and security service of the United States and its principal federal law enforcement agency.

The Bureau has grown to more than thirty-five thousand. As of 2025 on the Bureau's public site, the FBI lists fifty-six field offices in major cities throughout America, as well as more than four hundred resident agencies (RAs) in smaller locales, with jurisdiction over two hundred categories of federal crimes.

Yet despite the FBI's constant reshaping throughout its formative decades, by the time young Anthony Nelson sent that letter, the Bureau *still* grappled with its approach to protecting an America under siege.

Up until that point, Americans felt secure behind their monopoly on the atomic bomb. Fear of a Russian bomb, though, came to dominate the American psyche once the Soviets detonated an atomic device in 1949, the same year Anthony was born.

Counteracting communism became a priority, expanding under the administrations of Presidents Harry S. Truman and Dwight D. Eisenhower. Any public or private agency or individual with information about subversive activities was urged to report it to the FBI.

The FBI was given more authority to investigate the backgrounds of federal employees, especially those with access to classified atomic energy information (powers granted by the 1946 Atomic Energy Act). Presidents Truman and Eisenhower tasked the FBI with investigating "disloyalty" among federal employees. Note that convicted spies, Julius and Ethel Rosenberg, were federal employees.

But the FBI's role in fighting crime also grew dramatically in the post-World War II period, from increased intervention to assist state and local law enforcement to expanding jurisdictional responsibility. However, in the years to come, the FBI would need to find a balance between when and where to allocate its resources, considering the vast scale of criminal activity across America.

Meanwhile, the law itself needed to evolve along with law enforcement to provide federal prosecutors with more effective legal tools to combat increasingly sophisticated criminals.

After Prohibition, Mob activities were generally local rackets. Even illegal interstate trafficking did not account for a significant volume of criminality. The Mafia? That was a myth perpetuated by overzealous investigators and headline writers.

Then, in 1957, Sergeant Croswell of the New York State Police stumbled upon a meeting of many of the best-known mobsters in America in Upstate New York. The FBI collected information on dozens of gangsters identified as attending the meeting, ripping the veil from this national organized crime network.

After an FBI agent persuaded mobster Joseph Valachi to testify before the United States Senate, the public learned firsthand of the insidious nature of La Cosa Nostra, the Italian-American Mafia.

In the years ahead, the FBI would contend with the constantly evolving, complex machinations of modern organized crime.

Meanwhile, more flashpoints drove periodic refinement of the Bureau's mandates.

The assassination of President Kennedy was, technically, a local homicide; no specific federal law addressed the murder of a president. But if there was ever a murder screaming for special treatment, this was it.

President Lyndon B. Johnson assigned the Bureau to conduct the investigation. And Congress then passed a new law making the assassination of a sitting president a federal crime.

President Kennedy's assassination was also a tipping point from the idealism of the early 1960s to a much darker, more violent period that lasted well into the mid-1970s, plagued by an increase in urban crime and a propensity to challenge "the Establishment."

Americans started decrying their country's involvement in Vietnam and other foreign and domestic policies. They boycotted, burned their bras or their draft cards, picked up their peace signs, petitioned, picketed, paraded, protested, counter-protested, sat in, loved in, locked themselves to things, barricaded themselves, and then they rioted, looted, and worse.

In 1970 alone, an estimated three thousand bombings and fifty thousand bomb threats alone occurred in the United States. And when America turned to Washington, Washington turned to the FBI.[5]

Then, suddenly, on May 2, 1972, J. Edgar Hoover died at the age of seventy-seven, just shy of forty-eight years as the director of the FBI. The next day, Hoover's body lay in state in the Rotunda of the Capitol, an honor accorded only to twenty one other Americans to that point.5

The following month, five men broke into the Democratic National Headquarters in the Watergate Office Building in Washington, DC, and were arrested.

Time and again, America called upon the FBI to protect it from the darker side of a modernizing society, forcing it to forge innovations in law enforcement, while in the heat of battle. To do so, the FBI needed to become a symbol of not just federal

---

5. "History - Federal Bureau of Investigation." https://irp.fas.org/agency/doj/fbi/fbi_hist.htm

authority, but adaptability, capable of the type of ingenuity that strikes fear and awe in criminals.

It was into this desperate, running war between good and evil that a young, idealistic Anthony Nelson set out to embark on his career in law enforcement.

CHAPTER THREE

Ever wonder *how* someone becomes a "Special" Agent in the United States Federal Bureau of Investigation?

And ... *why*?

The "how" is as easy to explain as it is difficult to attain.

The "why," though—that's more personal.

Let's start with what makes them so "Special."

Within the US government, the title of "Special Agent" may be applied to federal criminal or non-criminal investigator or detective roles assigned in the 1811, 1801, 2501, or similar job series, according to the US Office of Personnel Management (OPM) handbook.[6]

Agents are typically educated at least to the undergraduate level. They're usually armed and have the power to arrest and conduct investigations into the violation of federal laws. However, not all federal investigators are Special Agents. Different agencies have different titles.

Benjamin Franklin, when he was postmaster general, called his investigators "Surveyors." The US Postal Service nixed that in 1801, becoming the first federal agency to use "Special Agent," which it later changed to "Postal Inspectors."

The US Marshals Service refers to its investigators as "Deputy Marshals." Other agencies refer to their sleuths as "Criminal Investigators."

---

6. US Office of Personnel Management (OPM) Handbook.

But the designation "Special Agent" has been most closely associated with the FBI.

So how do you know you're *Special*?

Long before you arrive at the FBI training academy at Quantico, Virginia, you must meet specific criteria to be considered.

In the 1960s, applicants like Anthony Nelson needed a bachelor's degree and at least three years of full-time professional experience, or an advanced degree and at least one year of work experience.

Anthony needed a valid driver's license, had to meet rigorous physical fitness requirements, and, very importantly, he had to be able to obtain a top secret Sensitive Compartmented Information (SCI) clearance.

Additionally, Anthony needed to be at least twenty-three years old and have all of this confirmed when he entered duty, no later than the day before his thirty-seventh birthday, unless he had a veteran's exception or federal law enforcement experience, which he did not.[7]

But these were table stakes.

Anthony needed something more.

Something *Special*.

See, Anthony was competing for a limited number of slots that flexed based on the FBI's needs.

Some applicants gain an advantage coming in from law enforcement agencies or military operations. Some transition from national security, litigation, accounting, contract law, counterterrorism, counterintelligence, cybersecurity, and foreign intelligence.

To compete, Anthony Nelson gave himself a head start.

He graduated from New Utrecht High School early. This massive school in the heart of Southern Brooklyn produced a surprising number of well-known personalities, from comedian Buddy Hackett and record executive David Geffen to TV hidden-camera

7. "Eligibility and Hiring." FBI Jobs. https://fbijobs.gov/eligibility

funnyman Allen Funt and, of course, Gabe Kaplan of *Welcome Back, Kotter!*[8]

New Utrecht also gave us generations of gangsters, bank robbers, and assorted undesirables, many of whom Nelson later pursued, few who graduated.

Next for Anthony, it was on to Brooklyn College, where he spent two years before transferring to the prestigious John Jay College of Criminal Justice in Manhattan. John Jay made accommodations for law enforcement-related applicants, offering the same classes with the option to attend either daytime or nighttime sessions.

Anthony also knew needed relevant work experience. "One option was to gain three years of experience by working for the FBI in a capacity other than the Special Agent," he says. And here, he found an edge.

Modern technology.

Well, the term *modern* is relative. More like, mid-twentieth-century technology.

In the 1960s, computers were room-sized, expensive, and mainframes were mainly used by governments and large corporations. Phones were not smart, had dials, not buttons, and were not mobile at all, tethered to walls by winding curled chords. There was no email, just mail. No Instagram, just telegrams. We were not digital. We were all analog, all the time.

Music was pressed on vinyl records and played on turntables. Cameras needed to be loaded with film, then developed in dark rooms.

If you needed to find a fact, you couldn't ask Google. There was no Google. You physically visited the local library and combed through volumes using the Dewey Decimal System. Even the fax machine was still a couple of years away.

For driving directions, we used maps, not apps. Or you rolled down your car window by hand and asked passersby for directions.

---

8. New Utrecht High School Alumni. https://newutrechthighschool.org/

Anyone with any innate technical talent was not just admired, but revered, and indeed seen as useful for the investigative arm of the US Justice Department.

See, as far back as he could remember, Anthony Nelson had a knack for gadgets and gizmos. He tinkered and took things apart. Put them back together, not always successfully, but still. He didn't hit the wall. He persisted. He figured it out, by searching, without an engine.

And most importantly, what he found stuck. He clearly articulated technical concepts to others and worked well in team situations.

"The thing about Anthony is that he could take the most complicated matters, with complex facts and unusual circumstances and conflicting interviews, and be able to capture it all on paper in an understandable and clear format," says George Terra, who, years later, worked closely with Anthony Nelson.

George Terra knows a thing or two about investigating and reporting. He spent twenty years with the New York Police Department (NYPD), including five years with an FBI Task Force. Upon his retirement, he joined the Kings County District Attorney's Office as a supervising detective investigator, then rose to the rank of assistant chief investigator responsible for their Criminal Investigations Division.

"I always thought Anthony would be good as one of those guys who writes technical manuals for how to assemble and use complex machines and products," Terra says. "He could take the most complex cases and put them into a format any Joe Blow could understand. That was a rare talent, especially back then."

In 1969, Anthony Nelson applied for an electronics technician position at the FBI.

An interviewer told him that while he was qualified for the role, those positions were filled, but he'd be considered for the next vacancy. Days later, in a stroke of luck, a support role opened, enabling him to start the clock running on his three years of required service.

Anthony Nelson entered duty with the FBI on January 6, 1969. During those early years, he mainly worked the four p.m. to midnight shift on security patrol and then as a radio dispatcher, until a vacancy opened for an electronics technician in 1972, which he held for the next four years.

Once Nelson entered active duty as a support employee of the FBI in 1969, though, some friendship issues did develop. You see, the Bureau was just not that popular on the boulevards and in the backrooms of Park Slope. But it was not only uneasy racketeers who looked at him sideways.

"I started to notice some of my friends would no longer speak freely around me," Nelson says. "At least three of my friends had decided the Vietnam War was not for them. Two of the three failed to register for the draft under the Selective Service Act. The third friend, whom I'll call Tommy, actually registered and was drafted. However, within less than a month of Basic Training in the Army, he deserted and returned to the streets of Brooklyn."

Soon, all three of those friends were avoiding Nelson outright. At the time, the New York Office of the FBI was well-known for tracking down both Selective Service violators and military deserters.

"They were concerned that my employment with the Bureau was going to result in their arrest," Nelson remembers. "There had been two entire squads within the New York FBI Office that were devoted exclusively to the capture of military deserters. Whenever I spotted these three friends in the neighborhood, it was always from a distance. They would no longer hang out with me in a local candy store or attend any functions if they knew I was there."

He then noticed others, not necessarily friends, starting to keep their distance. "They were fiercely against the Vietnam War and I knew they were regularly attending anti-war rallies and I suspected their protesting may have even been more active than just mere attendance," Nelson says. "They crossed the street if they saw me and would not engage me in conversation."

To top it all off, Anthony Nelson also joined the Army National Guard in October 1969.

There was juggling involved, and he was stretched thin, but as ambitious young men do, he found a way to make it work.

"My service on active duty in the US Army temporarily interrupted my attendance at college, and I was also placed on military leave by the FBI through February 1970," Nelson says. "These life interruptions did not adversely affect me to any great degree because to become an FBI agent, I still had to reach my twenty-third birthday."

That is *how* Anthony Nelson set about joining the FBI.

Yet … *why*?

With his technical talents and his education, surely Nelson could have found far more lucrative, and certainly less stressful, career options.

So, *why* do people like that join the FBI?

Some of it had to do with that era. Anthony Nelson was among a generation of young Americans, aspiring to make a difference, who saw the FBI as a path to providing meaningful service to their country.

J. Edgar Hoover understood this, insisting that the FBI only be depicted in the media in a heroic, positive light, even adopting the slogan "Crime Doesn't Pay" in 1927, a mantra which then went into heavy rotation with comic-strip Detective Dick Tracy created by cartoonist Chester Gould in 1931.

And soon, in 1935, the FBI "G-Man" archetype was born, slang for "Government Man," and popularized in the James Cagney film, *G Men* (J. Edgar reportedly worked with Hollywood studios to shape the heroic image of the G-Men).

But did gangster George "Machine Gun" Kelly *really* shout, "Don't shoot, G-Men! Don't shoot!" when surrounded by FBI agents before he was arrested in 1933?

Does it matter?

Whether or not that quote is real, it seared into the pop cultural consciousness this heroic image of the G-Man as the federal government's answer to evil Depression-era gangsters. The G-Man was everything that crooked cops and bought-off politicians were not—disciplined, fearless, incorruptible … and well-dressed.

Instead of a uniform, he wore a dark suit and tie, carried a badge and a gun, and he was educated, projected a calm, methodical, and relentless pursuit of justice as he chased gangsters in trench coats, firing Tommy guns and clinging to the sides of black sedans.

The G-Man was the government's weapon against crime, corruption, and chaos—and for a time, he was one of the most respected figures in American law enforcement.

From *Mississippi Burning* to *The Silence of the Lambs*, the G-Man was readymade for reliable box office returns. And over the years, a parade of Hollywood heartthrobs has followed in the black-laced-up footsteps of Cagney.

In *Point Break*, Keanu Reeves posed as an undercover bank robber/surfer Special Agent (seriously). Bradley Cooper and Louis C.K. traded jabs as agents in *American Hustle*, a fictionalization of the ABSCAM operation. Johnny Depp did time in *Donnie Brasco*, based on the true story of undercover FBI agent Joseph D. Pistone's infiltration of the Mafia. Christian Bale (as Special Agent Melvin Purvis) even pursued Depp (as John Dillinger) in *Public Enemies*.

And it's not just dramas.

In *White Chicks*, African American comedy clan royalty Marlon and Shawn Wayans were Special Agents who went undercover as, well, white chicks. Pop megastar Beyoncé Knowles played Foxy Cleopatra, an undercover FBI Special Agent/love interest of that international man of mystery, Austin Powers, to take down the diabolic Goldmember.

On the small screen, the networks tossed the FBI baton back and forth over the years, using the Bureau as backdrop for some of the highest-rated shows in television history. *The F.B.I*, an ABC network crime drama series that aired from 1965 to 1974 starring Efrem Zimbalist Jr. as Inspector Lewis Erskine, not only featured storylines based on actual case files, but J. Edgar Hoover served as a series consultant until he died in 1972.

In fact, when word got around the neighborhood that Anthony Nelson was working for the FBI, more and more local fans of this genre stopped him.

"I began to be approached by several young, decent people who'd ask how to apply for a career in the FBI," Nelson says. "They'd been attracted to the Bureau by all these crime shows, especially the Efrem Zimbalist Jr. FBI series."

Nelson even volunteered at Police Athletic League functions to speak about employment with the FBI, showing an old grainy recruitment film named *The FBI Story*. "But there were no VCRs or DVD players in those days," Nelson says. "So I had to lug in a screen and use a projector to show them the film."

Much later, the series *Wiseguy* was a massive hit for CBS in the late 1980s as we followed Special Agent Vinnie Terranova's infiltration of the Mafia, a white supremacist group, the garment district, and the record industry.

Then it was on to *The X-Files*, a weird but compelling take on paranormal investigations performed by Special Agents Fox Mulder and Dana Scully. Next up, in the early 1990s, *Twin Peaks* dominated our Sunday nights as Special Agent Dale Cooper investigated the murder of small-town homecoming queen Laura Palmer.

Along the way, in the smash hit HBO drama, *The Sopranos*, the Bureau pursued the dreaded Dimeo (New Jersey) and Lupertazzi (Brooklyn) crime families, and FBI Special Agent Dwight Harris tipped off Tony Soprano about the location of rival gangster Phil Leotardo.

More recently, we had *FBI* (2018), *FBI: Most Wanted* (2020), and *FBI: International* (2021). From *Mindhunter* to *The Mentalist* to *Men in Black: The Series*, *Blindspot* to *Bones* to *The Blacklist*, dozens of television shows have prominently featured the FBI.

The Bureau even busted in on video games. In *Call of Cthulhu: Dark Corners of the Earth*, the protagonist assists J. Edgar Hoover and other agents in destroying the Cult of Cthulhu. And from *Counter-Strike: Global Offensive* to *Call of Duty: Black Ops II*, players can join the FBI as playable multiplayer factions.

In fact, not only does *Destroy All Humans!* parody 1950s-era FBI members, *Grand Theft Auto*, one of the best-selling video game series of all time, repeatedly features FBI characters. Even *Red Dead Redemption*, set back in 1911, features the BOI, the precursor to the FBI. In the game, mustachioed Bureau agents commit the "justified" murders of outlaws in order to "tame" the Wild West.

But was it just the G-Men phenomenon?

For Anthony Nelson, it was always something else, something more. "Even some of my friends with whom I grew up made bad choices by committing crimes proscribed by law and by society, crimes such as gambling and loan sharking," Nelson adds. "But the members of some of the Mafia's more violent crews, who I later encountered regularly, engaged in acts that we, as human beings, intuitively know are evil, rather than just proscribed by law."

As time passed, he noticed further changes in how he was perceived in the neighborhood. "The word had spread rather quickly that I had joined the FBI and they no longer trusted me," Nelson says.

One day, a local acquaintance Nelson did not speak with often began to frequent the Nestor Social Club. Nelson knew members of the Colombo crime Family operated the spot and that it was of interest to the FBI.

"He approached me, knowing I'd joined the FBI, and he asked me if I could talk to an FBI agent named Bernie Welsh for him," Nelson says. "He wanted me to ask Bernie to stop 'busting into the club and crashing their card games.'" This local guy claimed the card games were just innocent forms of entertainment for some of the neighborhood guys and they weren't operated as a source of income for the Mafia.

"I couldn't help but laugh in his face because I could picture Bernie Welsh raiding the games just as he described," Nelson says.

Bernard Welsh was a giant in law enforcement—literally, standing six feet six inches—before he retired from the Bureau and was appointed the police commissioner in the village of Lloyd Harbor, New York. In an account in *New York Newsday*, Jim Abbott, a retired FBI agent and one of Welsh's best friends for forty-seven years, remembered one particular stakeout with Welsh.

Assigned to the Bureau's Organized Crime Division, they half-jokingly asked Mob boss John Gotti and company if they could join the Bergin Hunt and Fish Club in Ozone Park—a longtime reputed hangout of the Gotti-run Gambino crime Family.

They were turned down, Abbott said, but Welsh would end up getting the last laugh.

Not long afterward, while on a different stakeout at the Belmont Park racetrack in Elmont, Welsh had security remove Gotti from the premises due to laws prohibiting felons from being there.

While with the NYPD, Welsh was assigned to the Tactical Patrol Force, although the neighborhood thugs would refer to them derisively as the "Trees, Plants, and Flowers." They were a mobile force deployed in troubled areas, with members trained to deal with neighborhood gang disturbances and riots.

"Bernie was a big guy and there were not too many, if any, wiseguys who would dare to give him a hard time," Nelson says of Welsh.

And so no, Anthony would not intervene on this guy's request.

For some members of law enforcement, such as Anthony Nelson, it's not just a career. Becoming a Special Agent is a deeply personal, philosophical, and even spiritual journey that begins long before Quantico.

"I don't know what makes some people grow up evil and others to become doctors, lawyers, sanitation workers ... or FBI agents," Nelson says. "I know that I was compelled to join the FBI because of a need to be needed. And I think most people who devote themselves to law enforcement share that same need to be needed."

For Anthony, it started on the streets of Brooklyn, watching local beat cops make a difference. "I always knew that in the sunset of my life I did not want to simply count how much wealth I had amassed," he says. "I wanted, and still want, to perhaps try to cheat death by doing things that will outlive me—things that will hopefully cause my family, my friends, my neighbors, and even strangers to remember that I tried, in some small way, to make our world a better place."

In some twisted ways, perhaps, even those most vile criminals Nelson describes share a parallel desire.

But instead of honor and righteousness, their aim is infamy, villains bereft of morality, bent on exploiting the vulnerable and victimizing the innocent with extreme ruthlessness.

And in dark times, *special* men and women will always be needed to protect the world from the wicked.

CHAPTER FOUR

Times change.

People change.

Even the FBI changed since a young Anthony Nelson joined its ranks in 1969.

"At the time I applied to become a Special Agent, thousands of people also applied for the same position," Nelson recalls. "Incredibly, from that enormous pool of applicants, only a few hundred, about three to five percent, were chosen to continue with the application process."

That part hasn't changed … much.

The FBI, on average, accepts fewer than twenty percent of all applicants to any position within the Bureau, according to a study by Tulane University. Moreover, the FBI itself reports that the rates of acceptance for the role of Special Agent are closer to five percent.[9]

Anyone applying to be a Special Agent undergoes a ten-stage process known as the Special Agent Selection System.

The list of disqualifiers is long. There are the usual dings, such as felony and domestic violence convictions, but also the more benign, like defaulting on government-backed student loans or delinquency on court-ordered child support—even failing to file income tax returns at any level.

---

9. "How Can You Become an FBI Agent?" Tulane University School of Professional Advancement. https://sopa.tulane.edu/blog/how-can-you-become-fbi-agent

You must still be a US Citizen in compliance with the FBI's drug policy and be able to obtain a top security clearance to be considered for any position with the FBI.[10]

However, the FBI has eased some of its entrance requirements.

For example, the FBI has made the drug-use requirement more lenient from the "zero drug use ever" standard Nelson needed to meet. Now, candidates must not have used marijuana or cannabis in any form within one year before the date of their application instead of three years. And marijuana use prior to your eighteenth birthday is no longer a disqualifier like it was back in the '60s.

In 1976, the New Agent Training program for candidates entering the FBI Academy at Quantico was twenty-one weeks long. It's since been reduced to sixteen weeks.

The Bureau also reduced the number of years of prior work experience from three to two, while lowering the physical fitness test (PFT) score required to enter Quantico from 12 to 9. And today's candidates only need to pass three of the four fitness categories. Additionally, candidates now have an unlimited number of attempts to pass the PFT for up to one year after passing the background check.

That was not the case when Nelson applied.

Still, many things are the same.

Today, as it was in 1976, to obtain a top security clearance, the FBI still requires candidates to undergo an invasive background investigation that draws conclusions on aspects of their person: Stability, Trustworthiness, Reliability, Discretion, Character, Honesty, Judgment, and Loyalty to the United States.

Background investigators will check records (e.g., credit, criminal, and civil), employment history, references, income tax filings, and driving history. Former employers, co-workers, neighbors, friends, and family may all be contacted during the process.

---

10. "Special Agent Overview." FBI Jobs. https://fbijobs.gov/special-agents?gad_source=1&gad_campaignid=22295396297&gbraid=0AAAAAD d8NODrELmFXMJh-q0T6u-w93hXC&gclid=Cj0KCQjwoZbBBhDCARIsA OqMEZW0gjqnAze4AIldRaB-TQ3w9m6oWgSSiEns3JAs68TUdjhww51Pb-UaAh42EALw_wcB

The FBI fitness standards are still strict. Unless you already have a background in the military, sports, or law enforcement, you should begin cardiovascular and strength training as soon as possible. Male and female applicants must perform a minimum of twenty push-ups and twenty sit-ups within a minute, as well as complete short- and long-distance running challenges.

Back in 1976, however, the background check, polygraph, and Quantico invitation were still ahead for Nelson.

First, he needed to clear Phase 1 testing, a combination of written and physical fitness testing.

"I was fortunate enough to pass that initial written general knowledge and law tests, and clear the interview," Nelson says.

More challenging was the FBI Phase 2 Test, the fourth stage of this ten-step process. This involved a timed written assessment, which requires the applicant to analyze given data, followed by a structured interview with veteran Special Agents.

During the interview, they ask why you want to become an FBI Special Agent and how you handle difficult situations, while also gauging your responses to hypothetical scenarios. The interviewers also drill down to ask about your qualifications, education, work experience, training, and certifications.

While the FBI Phase 1 Test assesses your cognitive ability, professional judgment, and personality, the FBI Phase 2 Test focuses on practical application.

And for Anthony Nelson, that meant passing muster with none other than an absolute legend at the Bureau. "My interview was conducted by then Special Agent in Charge of the New York Office Administrative Division Phil McNiff," he remembers.

Talk about setting the right tone at the outset of your career.

At the time of his passing in February 2015, per his obituary in the *Tampa Bay Times*, "Phil McNiff served the FBI, then George Steinbrenner's New York Yankees," and described the famed lawman as "tall, trim and with steely blue eyes, Mr. McNiff was a prototypical G-man, solving crimes with the same drive that had won him a basketball scholarship to George Washington University."[11]

As Special Agent in Charge of the Tampa office, McNiff took down an arson ring made up of corrupt Tampa businessmen and firefighters, busted a $7.5 million "daisy chain" price-fixing scheme that extended to the president of Florida Power Corporation, and monitored the activities of Mafia boss Santo Trafficante Jr.

Just weeks into his new post as head of the Tampa Field Office, McNiff led a takedown of a violent home invasion crew, orchestrating an undercover sting to purchase stolen paintings the gang had lifted during a recent robbery—then personally led the dramatic raid at a Treasure Island motel. "It was rare to see a field office chief out on the street, taking charge and knowing exactly what he was doing," recalled retired FBI agent Al Scudieri. "I watched him in action that day, and from then on, I was a Phil McNiff fan."[11]

McNiff served in the US Navy from 1945 to 1946. A natural athlete, he was offered a tryout with the Brooklyn Dodgers farm team. He was a four-year starter for the George Washington University Colonials basketball team and captained the team (after completing his military service, he attended GW on an athletic scholarship). Later, he became a YMCA national handball champion.

His professional career started by following in his brother Tom's footsteps, who was also a career FBI agent. Phil was first appointed as an FBI Special Agent in 1951 and served in Detroit, Knoxville, New York, and Cleveland, as well as in a supervisory capacity in the Fugitive Section at Headquarters. Phil was assigned to Tampa as Assistant Special Agent in Charge (ASAC) in 1970 and subsequently served from 1972 to 1980 as SAC in Mobile, New York, and Tampa.

---

11. Meacham, Andrew. "Phil McNiff Served the FBI, Then George Steinbrenner's New York Yankees." Tampa Bay Times. August 25, 2019. https://www.tampabay.com/news/obituaries/fbi-agent-phil-mcniff-worked-major-cases-then-helped-george-steinbrenner/2218046/

One of McNiff's first arrests was in Detroit. The suspect was a seven-year fugitive (military deserter) who had altered his name and appearance and was, at the time of his arrest, holding one of the county's top law enforcement positions in the area.

Another sensational investigation McNiff cleared was the December 1968 kidnapping of Barbara Jane Mackle, a twenty-year-old Emory University student in Atlanta, Georgia. The kidnappers, Gary Steven Krist and Ruth Eisemann-Schier, drove Barbara to a remote pine forest in Gwinnett County and buried her alive in a box. She had a small amount of food, water, and tubes to the surface for oxygen. The kidnappers demanded and received half a million dollars. After spending eighty-three hours in the box, Barbara Jean Mackle was rescued, and both kidnappers were arrested.

In 1969, McNiff and his team made national headlines by arresting Robert De Pugh in Truth or Consequences, New Mexico, after a massive manhunt. De Pugh was on the FBI Ten Most Wanted List and was wanted for bank robbery, weapons violations, and was a member of the notorious radical group the Weathermen.

"In 1971, I remember Phil McNiff chased after a fugitive member of the Black Liberation Army in Tampa, Florida," Nelson remembers. "As McNiff turned a corner on foot, the fugitive fired a shot from his handgun at him. McNiff could hear that bullet whizz past his head and then hit a drain pipe. A second FBI agent who had also joined the pursuit fired at the fugitive and killed him with a shotgun blast."

Then in 1972, McNiff was one of the lead agents in the investigation of Arthur Bremer, after Bremer's attempted assassination of presidential candidate and Alabama Governor George Wallace, who was left paralyzed from the waist down. Bremer also intended to assassinate President Richard M. Nixon.

After McNiff retired from the FBI, he was hired by George Steinbrenner, then the owner of the New York Yankees. Steinbrenner tapped McNiff as his head of security and his personal confidant.

So it was this absolute giant in law enforcement who loomed across the table from a young Anthony Nelson for the FBI Phase

2 Interview, the most critical step in the hiring process for FBI Special Agents and analysts.

Nelson knew he had to nail this interview to qualify for his Conditional Appointment Offer (CAO). "I certainly made sure that I was on time for my interview with SAC Phil McNiff," he remembers. "I definitely was nervous because the job I'd wanted since I was sixteen years old now depended completely upon me convincing McNiff that I was not only qualified for the position, but even more qualified than the scores of other candidates he was most likely to interview."

Nelson, though, had an inside track. Since he was an electronics tech for the FBI before the interview, virtually all his close associates on the job were already Special Agents.

"Many of them provided me with advice on what to expect during the interview and how to answer some of the questions I'd most likely be asked," Nelson says. "Just about all of the agents giving me advice stressed I focus on the obvious—God, Country, and Patriotism—as reasons for wanting to become an FBI Special Agent."

However, Nelson was floored by the very first question McNiff asked.

It was a "stress question," designed to see how fast Nelson would react and respond to an unexpected query that usually required prolonged thought.

That question?

"What is the greatest achievement thus far in your life?"

Without hesitating, Nelson responded as if he knew the question beforehand. "I said, 'Successfully making it through the FBI's initial recruitment process and now qualifying to be sitting here before you for this interview.'"

Satisfied, McNiff smiled at Nelson and said, "Don't forget that the salary isn't too bad either."

Nelson laughs. "Ironically, my agent friends preparing me for the interview warned that under no circumstance should I bring up the issue of salary as a reason why I wanted the position."

"I must have done well," Nelson says. "For I was then offered a probationary appointment as a Special Agent."

Specifically, Anthony Nelson received a letter from the FBI with an offer of promotion from Electronics Technician to Conditional Probationary Appointment as a Special Agent.

"I had several months' notice. They give you this time to get any personal affairs in order because all Special Agent appointments require you to agree to accept an assignment anywhere in the United States. At the time, I didn't know where my assignment would be."

Nelson's new agent class was required to report on October 18, 1976. And just like that, the dream that the young Brooklyn boy had was now becoming a reality.

Anthony Nelson was heading to the FBI Academy in Quantico, Virginia.

CHAPTER FIVE

Before Anthony Nelson's Conditional Probationary Appointment as a Special Agent, on August 9, 1975, he was dispatched by the FBI to discreetly report to a 5th Avenue penthouse in Manhattan to aid in the investigation of the kidnapping of the child of one of the wealthiest men on the planet.

This was a delicate situation.

Kidnappings are difficult crimes to investigate.

Speed is everything.

Kidnappings often must be solved within hours. The longer someone is missing, the harder it is to trace them and gather clues.

Kidnappings are usually premeditated. They happen quickly, often in isolated or concealed areas. Witnesses are rare, and physical evidence is minimal or nonexistent. And even if the *kidnappee* is not bound or gagged, they are tucked away, unable to communicate.

In fact, kidnappings are so problematic that following a landmark case in the 1930s—dubbed "the Crime of the Century" by the media—the US Congress enacted special legislation. Amidst the Great Depression, the toddler son of famed aviator and international celebrity Charles Lindbergh was abducted and murdered. Following the media circus, Congress adopted the Federal Kidnapping Act (popularly known as the Lindbergh Law, or Little Lindbergh Law), empowering federal authorities to pursue kidnappers once they crossed state lines with their victim.

Today, officially, the FBI has "original jurisdiction" for kidnappings where (1) the victim is transported across state or country lines; (2) it occurs at sea within US maritime and territorial jurisdiction; (3) committed in flight; (4) the victim is a foreign official, an internationally protected person; (5) the victim is a federal officer or employee; or (6) the crime involves international parental kidnapping and the victim is under the age of sixteen years.

The FBI will also automatically initiate a kidnapping investigation involving a missing child of "tender years" (generally twelve years or younger), even when there is no known interstate travel.

Otherwise, in most other cases, the FBI does not get involved. In actuality, state and municipal authorities often ask the Bureau to bring to bear its advanced forensics and profiling tech that few local agencies can muster.

On August 9, 1975, Anthony Nelson responded to the residence of Edgar M. Bronfman, the head of Seagram's multinational conglomerate and a titan of the business world.

This situation evolved rapidly.

Edgar Bronfman's son, Samuel Bronfman II, had been kidnapped. Samuel was the twenty-one-year-old heir to a Bronfman family fortune valued at $750 million (or $3.78 billion in today's dollars).

The previous day, the younger Bronfman dined at his father's home in Westchester County, north of New York City. He left alone in his car around 11:30 p.m. Samuel then called the Yorktown Heights residence shortly before two a.m. to say that he had been kidnapped.

"I was assigned to remain with the Bronfman family, including Samuel Bronfman's uncle, Charles Bronfman, who owned the Montreal Expos," Nelson recalls.

Nelson had no way of knowing he would stay on-site with the family for more than a week as the crisis played out.

"I even offered them money to get me some basic clothing when they went shopping," Nelson says. "But they bought clothes for me that cost hundreds of dollars, even in the mid-1970s. I would never have had enough money to repay them. They also introduced me to one of their servants, who took care of me and handled all my living arrangements.

"I don't think that I appreciated the magnitude of media interest in the Samuel Bronfman's kidnapping at the time I responded to the family's penthouse apartment on 5th Avenue in Manhattan. Of course I felt the importance and significance of a kidnapping, but I don't think I anticipated that it would become such an internationally significant case for the media," Nelson adds.

Nelson may not have known that Samuel's father, Edgar Bronfman, was one of the wealthiest men in the world at that time. But it became evident soon after arriving at the penthouse.

"After spending a couple of days at their penthouse, without leaving, I took a few moments during downtime to just go out on the balcony," Nelson remembers. "Minutes later, I heard the noise of a helicopter approaching the building."

The press was now hot on the case and trying to obtain information and photographs however possible.

"As I was standing on the balcony, this news helicopter approached and photographed me standing there," Nelson says.

The following morning, when Nelson awoke, both Edgar Bronfman and his brother Charles teased him by remarking how comfortable and calm he'd been. Nelson was puzzled by the comment.

"Charles Bronfman jokingly said to me that I could pass as a member of their family," Nelson says, still puzzled. "He then pulled out a copy of the [New York] Daily News, which had a photo of me standing on their penthouse balcony." He adds that Charles Bronfman continued to joke that it looked as though he was "impersonating a member of the Bronfman family."

As the situation wore on, these moments of levity were rare, with the victim's family beset with feelings of hopelessness.

A ransom note arrived claiming Samuel had been buried alive with only ten days of oxygen and warned that if the money wasn't delivered, his father, Edgar Bronfman Sr., would be executed with cyanide-laced bullets.

The kidnappers' demand of $4.6 million was the most-expensive ransom ever sought in a US abduction at the time.

The case drew more intense public scrutiny, as reporters, photographers, and gawkers crowded the gates of the sprawling 180-acre Westchester estate, while helicopters buzzed overhead in a circus-like scene.

This agitated the kidnappers, who were alarmed by the media frenzy and demanded that news coverage be halted. As such a request was obviously beyond the family's control, it only added to their anxiety.

In their desperation, the family brought a self-proclaimed psychic, Uri Geller, up to the apartment.

During the 1970s, Geller rose to prominence as a popular Israeli-British illusionist, magician, television personality, and self-proclaimed psychic. Geller claimed his abilities were the result of paranormal powers bestowed on him by extraterrestrials. He was particularly known for his trademark spoon-bending and other illusions, while also using tricks to pass himself off as telepathic (capable of transmitting thoughts to others and of even knowing their thoughts). Several magicians slammed Geller as a fraud.

Geller's career spanned nearly forty years, and for a time, he was a popular draw for live audiences and televised specials. However, he was dogged by skeptics throughout his career and pursued or threatened litigation in some instances.

Not surprisingly, enlisting the aid of a self-proclaimed psychic is not part of the FBI playbook.

"While he was in the apartment," Nelson says, "he took a heavy-duty FBI office key and bent it in half just by rubbing his finger back and forth on it."

Ability to perform clever parlor tricks?

Very impressive.

Supernatural capabilities to help solve the case?

Not so much.

"As far as any psychic ability to locate the kidnapped Samuel Bronfman, I remember him saying he believed him to be in a place that started with the letter B," Nelson says. "That wasn't of much use to us, but Bronfman *was* eventually rescued in Brooklyn.

"I don't personally believe in psychic abilities," Nelson adds, "but I have to say, I don't know how he did that key-bending trick."

Joining Anthony Nelson at the apartment were Special Agents Joseph Jackson and Phillip Sandidge.

"My assignment," Nelson recalls, "among other things, was to intercept and record all communications and demands from the kidnappers to the Bronfman family at their residence." He intercepted, monitored, recorded, and reported those conversations to the FBI Special Agent in Charge, who then made the tactical decisions about how to deal with the kidnappers.

More demands for news coverage to stop followed, which the FBI had little ability to affect. Then, as Nelson fielded the calls from the abductors, they began to issue bizarre sets of instructions.

Soon Bronfman Sr. spent days rushing in and around John F. Kennedy Airport in Queens to answer public payphone calls from the kidnappers.

This built up to a dramatic August 16 meet in Woodside, Queens, where Bronfman Sr. met with one of the kidnappers to deliver a $2.3 million ransom. Although FBI agents observed the exchange, they held off on making an arrest since the victim remained missing and at risk. However, agents managed to record the license plate of the getaway vehicle—traced to Mel Patrick Lynch, an Irish-born New York City firefighter—marking a pivotal breakthrough in the investigation.

The ordeal ended the next day, when FBI agents and NYPD detectives stormed Lynch's Flatbush apartment and rescued Bronfman, bound, gagged, and blindfolded. Lynch was arrested along with his accomplice, Dominic Byrne.[12]

---

12. Kihss, Peter. "BRONFMAN'S SON RESCUED IN CITY AFTER A PAYMENT OF $2.3 -MILLION; MONEY RECOVERED, 2 SUSPECTS HELD." New York Times. August 18, 1975. https://www.nytimes.com/1975/08/18/archives/broafmans-son-rescued-in-city-after-a-payment-of-23million-money.html

Lynch and Byrne were charged with kidnapping and extortion. They gave up the location of the ransom, then recovered from the apartment of one of Byrne's friends who, at the time, was hospitalized and not involved in the crime.

"I was thrilled when Samuel Bronfman was safely rescued from the Brooklyn apartment where he had been held captive," Nelson says. "After all, as I had previously noted, my desire to become a law enforcement officer had primarily been motivated by my 'need to be needed.'"

Following the rescue, both Edgar Bronfman and Charles Bronfman, greatly relieved, sent personal letters of thanks to Nelson. Charles Bronfman wrote in part, "Seriously, Tony, thank you for everything. During our week of hell, you were the calm and quiet one who kept a hold on things that were going on ..."

"He also invited me to contact him any time in the future if there was anything that I ever needed," Nelson adds.

For his part, Edgar Bronfman stated that "the happiness of the Bronfman family following the events of August" had been made possible by Anthony Nelson's efforts and those of his associates.

"The letters from both Edgar and Charles Bronfman are among many I received during my career and are more important to me than any of the financial incentive awards and commendations I received for successful cases over the years," Nelson says. "I think a simple 'thank you' is probably the greatest reward any law enforcement officer can receive for their performance."

However, the drama did not end with the rescue. At trial, Lynch's defense attorney, William K. Madden, mounted a defense that accused the young Bronfman of masterminding the kidnapping.

Then the case took yet another despicable twist when Lynch and Byrne copped to separate, fanciful versions of the crime.

The first version was that Byrne, who ran a limousine service, had been hired to take two unknown men to Westchester County, and Lynch had gone along for the ride. Supposedly, they were then held at gunpoint and forced to abduct Bronfman, turning Lynch and Byrne into unwilling kidnappers, he claimed.

The motivation? Bronfman and Lynch were lovers, with Bronfman intending to extort money from his family, in part, to aid Lynch in his support of a united Ireland.

Lynch told investigators he only went along with the scheme once Bronfman threatened to expose his gay lifestyle to the New York Fire Department, which would have threatened his job. Lynch testified in his own defense for four days.

Meanwhile, Byrne's defense attorney, Peter DeBlasio, later shared that his initial defense was to argue that Byrne had been dragged into the scheme by Lynch. But after Lynch testified, he decided to instead mimic Madden's strategy, even though he knew Lynch had been lying.

In his 2020 memoir, DeBlasio wrote:

I can look back now after a 50-year, 600-trial career and say that among the thousands of witnesses I observed, nobody approached the magnificence of Mel Patrick Lynch. He was the Arturo Toscanini and Enrico Caruso of witnesses. He turned a horror story into a tragedy of operatic dimensions. The jurors were mesmerized. If they could have, they would have exploded in applause and cried for an encore.[13]

"There was no evidence found by the FBI during the investigation, nor did any evidence materialize afterwards, to support that Bronfman had been involved," Nelson says. Bronfman family representatives even substantiated that Samuel had been away at college in Massachusetts during the time he was allegedly supposed to have been plotting with the co-conspirators.

Following the courtroom theatrics and media firestorm, Byrne and Lynch were only convicted of extortion and not the abduction.

DeBlasio's self-published memoir fell flat, although a *New York Times* obituary writer later used it as source material to research a feature piece on the abduction for the *Times'* Metro section.

By the time the book was released, Byrne and Lynch had died. DeBlasio set the record straight in the book that there was no

---

13. DeBlasio, Peter E. Let Justice Be Done: A New York Trial Lawyer's Odyssey Through the Last Half of the 20th Century. 2020

romantic relationship between Bronfman and Lynch and firmly denied that Bronfman had any role in orchestrating the kidnapping.

CHAPTER SIX

On October 18, 1976, twenty-six-year-old Anthony Nelson was sworn in as a Special Agent in the US Federal Bureau of Investigation in a ceremony in Washington, DC.

That same day, he was dispatched to the FBI Academy located within the Marine Corps Base in Quantico, Virginia. Quantico is a special place, synonymous with elite law enforcement and military training, conjuring images of discipline, national security, and high-stakes preparation.

In 1933, the US Marine Corps first allowed FBI agents to use its firing ranges for training. Today, the FBI Academy spans 547 acres on Marine Corps Base Quantico, just thirty-six miles outside Washington, DC. This is the birthplace of criminal profiling, home to the FBI's Behavioral Analysis Unit, the real-life inspiration for the hit TV show *Criminal Minds*.

There's Hogan's Alley, a full-scale training facility simulating a small town, built with the help of Hollywood set designers, complete with a bank, hotel, post office, and even actors posing as civilians and criminals.

There's the Forensics Command Center, which houses DNA Analysis Units and Evidence Response Teams, as well as the Explosives and Hazardous Devices School. Some of the most complex crime scene reconstructions and forensic breakthroughs originated at Quantico.

The FBI discourages family members from moving nearby for the eighteen-week training program. In fact, no major highways pass this small town with fewer than six hundred residents, according to the 2024 census.

To even reach Quantico—ringed by dense forest, the Potomac River, and a controlled-access military base—you must first pass through checkpoints heavily guarded by stone-faced US Marines.

Many brave men and women have passed through these proving grounds.

"I'd be willing to bet that for most people who've made it to the Academy, those weeks ranked among the most stressful times they've ever experienced," Nelson posits.

Nelson's classmates gave up careers as attorneys, accountants, teachers, and scientists when they came to Quantico. Some had families who counted on them for financial support.

"I was single at the time but still felt the pressure of possibly not achieving this goal I set for myself at sixteen years old," he says. "But I never even considered another career. Not ever. Not once.

"When you go through Quantico, you forge bonds with fellow future Special Agents, some of whom go on to accomplish great things," Nelson adds.

Trainees share college-style dorms. "We had adjoining rooms with each two rooms sharing a common bathroom. One occupant of my adjoining room was John Pritchard," Nelson says. "He'd been assigned to the elite NYPD Major Case Squad but, nevertheless, John desired to become an FBI agent. I drove my personal car to the Academy and would give John a ride back to New York City on rare weekends when we were able to go home."

That was some roommate assignment. John Pritchard went on to leave an indelible mark on the Bureau.

A detective with the NYPD from 1965 to 1976, before pursuing a career at the FBI, Pritchard served as a Special Agent, supervisory Special Agent, and inspector's aide in place until 1987. His career included the successful investigation of Genovese Family don Vincent "the Chin" Gigante, who for years avoided prosecution by feigning insanity by wandering the streets of Greenwich Village, disheveled-looking and in a bathrobe.

Pritchard also investigated organized crime's grip on professional boxing; the ABSCAM case that involved undercover agents posing as Arab foreign nationals bribing government officials that toppled a US senator and seven congressmen; rampant corruption among military contractors; the capture of Atlanta Child Murders fiend Wayne Williams; and many more landmark cases.

Following his successful career with the FBI, Pritchard was named the Metropolitan Transportation Authority's inspector general from 1988 to 1993 before returning to the NYPD, where Commissioner Raymond W. Kelly appointed him first deputy police commissioner, the department's second-highest civilian position after the commissioner. In fact, Pritchard was the first African American appointed to that position.[14]

John Pritchard had been recruited into the FBI by another legendary FBI agent named James F. Murphy. "I first met Jim Murphy while I was working for the FBI prior to my Special Agent appointment," Nelson says.

Murphy was assigned to the Bank Robbery Squad in New York at the time.

"I was working on a night shift and I drove him and his partner on two occasions to the Federal House of Detention, the old federal prison located on West Street in Manhattan in those days," Nelson remembers. "Each of the two times I drove him, Jim and his partner were dropping off bank robbers they had arrested. I became friends with Jim Murphy, and every time I was with him, I felt that sense that I was in the company of courage."

Special Agent Jim Murphy later risked his life during one of the more sensational episodes for the Bureau that unfolded the afternoon of August 22, 1972, when three armed, desperate men strode into a Chase Manhattan Bank on Avenue P in the Gravesend section of Brooklyn.

14. Roberts, Sam. "John Pritchard III, Tenacious Law Enforcement Leader, Dies at 75." New York Times. September 17, 2018. https://www.nytimes.com/2018/09/17/obituaries/john-pritchard-iii-tenacious-law-enforcement-leader-dies-at-75.html

In the annals of crime fighting, no two groups are as closely linked as heroic FBI agents doggedly pursuing bank-robbing outlaws across the dusty plains of Depression-era America.

In 1934, it became a federal crime to rob any national bank or state member bank that was a member of the Federal Reserve System. The law later expanded to include bank burglary, larceny, and similar crimes, all with jurisdiction delegated to the FBI.

The robbery team—consisting of John Wojtowicz, Salvatore Naturile, and Robert Westenberg—targeted $200,000 (equivalent to $1.5 million today) scheduled for armored-car delivery at 3:30 that afternoon.

Wojtowicz later divulged he'd been tipped off to the score by a Chase Manhattan employee he met at a Greenwich Village gay bar.

The modern-day bandits entered the bank at three o'clock, unaware that the money had been picked up earlier that morning at eleven.

Seizing $29,000 on hand at that bank that day, they ran for the exits.

Only Westenberg escaped.

With the robbery in progress, a bank employee triggered a silent alarm. Within minutes, the bank was surrounded by dozens of officers and FBI agents. Wojtowicz and Naturile were trapped, and the robbery descended into a hostage standoff.

If these events sound familiar to readers of a certain age, they should. This drama served as the source material for the wildly popular Hollywood film *Dog Day Afternoon*, directed by Sidney Lumet and starring Al Pacino, John Cazale, and Charles Durning.

After two tense hours of negotiations, Wojtowicz and Naturile presented their demands to the police: they wanted Elizabeth Eden (formerly Ernest Aron) released from Kings County Hospital, requested hamburgers and Coca-Cola sodas, and insisted on transportation—along with the hostages—to John F. Kennedy International Airport. They also demanded a qualified pilot to fly them out of the country.

In the words of Wojtowicz: "I want them to deliver my wife here from Kings County hospital. His name is Ernest Aron. It's a guy. I'm gay."

Wojtowicz later told Judge Anthony Travia that he planned to use the proceeds from the robbery to fund sexual reassignment surgery for Aron, who went by the name Elizabeth Debbie Eden.

During the standoff, Wojtowicz called local New York radio stations, fueling a circus-like atmosphere playing out in real time in Gravesend. At one point, Wojtowicz even ventured outside the bank to throw money at the large crowd.

Wojtowicz then selected Jim Murphy to be the FBI agent who would drive them to the airport.

"Despite the clear danger to himself and the probability that someone was going to die that day, Murphy didn't hesitate to drive the limousine," Nelson says. "Right there is what it means to be a Special Agent, to answer that call."

During this crisis, Nelson was assigned to operate the FBI's radio system and relay messages among all the agents engaged and following the limousine.

The bank robbers carefully searched Murphy for a concealed weapon.

"Unbeknownst to Wojtowicz, Murphy had secreted a handgun under a floor mat in the limo," Nelson says. "Then, throughout the ride to JFK Airport, Sal Naturile is actually holding a shotgun to the back of Murphy's head the entire time. That's about fifteen miles, and even without traffic, that could take half an hour.

"But it didn't matter," Nelson adds. "Murphy knew he could not allow these bank robbers to leave the country with a planeload of hostages, and he had to think fast in those moments, getting closer and closer to the airport."

When the limo arrived at JFK, Murphy struck up a conversation about food.

"That discussion turned into a distraction that gave Murphy the opening to act," Nelson says. "He turned, and in one swift, calculated move, he pushed Naturile's shotgun away from his neck while, at the same time, he grabbed for the secreted gun and shot Naturile in the chest, killing him."

In 2012, forty years after the events, Murphy was interviewed about his experience that day and told news channel NBC 4 reporters how, in the heat of those moments, he thought of his wife and child, realizing that he very well could be killed.[15]

In another interview, Murphy reflected on his experience watching the film in 1975 about the fifteen-hour crisis he ended with a bullet but could have easily ended with his demise. As the movie reached this climactic moment, when Naturile was shot, the audience booed. "They were upset by the fact that he had been killed," Murphy told reporters.

After a successful career, Jim Murphy rose to Assistant Special Agent in Charge at the FBI's Brooklyn-Queens Metropolitan Resident Agency. Murphy retired from the FBI to lead Sutton Associates, a global investigative and research firm based in New York.

Wojtowicz was convicted and served fourteen years in prison. He passed away in 2006 from cancer-related complications. Eden died of AIDS-related illnesses in 1987.

Dog Day Afternoon opened on September 20, 1975, at the San Sebastian International Film Festival. The film premiered in New York City on September 21, 1975, and was released nationwide in October. It grossed north of $50 million (equivalent to $300 million today).

"I saw the movie," Nelson says. "I liked it and I thought it was a realistic account of the robbery and the police actions. Of course, since it was a movie, the character personalities were a bit exaggerated."

There was, however, another "million to one" coincidence that Nelson later experienced, related to the filming of the movie, which took place two years later, between September and November 1974.

---

15. Dienst, Jonathan, and Valiquette, Joe. "Forty Years Later, FBI Agent Who Shot Bank Robber Recalls 'Dog Day Afternoon.'" NBC New York. August 23, 2012. https://www.nbcnewyork.com/news/local/dog-day-afternoon-forty-year-anniversary-fbi-agent-interview/1955404/

A close friend lived on Prospect Park West and 17th Street in Brooklyn. Nelson would meet him at times, along with several other friends, at Farrell's Bar located at Park Circle, just a few blocks away.

Farrell's had been well-known in the neighborhood as a bar frequented by many law enforcement officers and firefighters.

In 1974, scenes from *Dog Day Afternoon* were scheduled to be filmed right in front of this friend's residence. Several people associated with the upcoming filming came into Farrell's while they were there, looking to hire extras to appear as part of the crowd that had gathered in front of the bank during the actual robbery. One of Nelson's friends volunteered.

Nelson wanted nothing to do with it.

Each day and night for several days, while hanging out at his friend's apartment, Nelson listened to the loud noises and cheers associated with the movie filming, while his friends would comment, "Just think, you had a role working on the actual robbery, and here is the movie version being filmed right downstairs. What are the odds of that?"

"Of course, my role was only a peripheral one working as the radio dispatcher at the time," Nelson says.

The bravery, experience, and training of the FBI agents, particularly the heroic actions of Murphy, made the difference that day and had a lasting impact on Anthony Nelson.

Nelson occasionally thinks back to the early days at Quantico and the lifelong bonds forged among aspiring agents.

"Despite all the stress while attending the FBI Academy, I often felt comforted seeing Jim Murphy roaming the halls every so often," he says. "Later during my career, Jim not only became the head of the FBI's Brooklyn-Queens Office and my boss, but an even better friend. Jim supported his agents, as he did when he supported my attempts to obtain the phone records of former Attorney General Ramsey Clark during my hunt for Joseph 'Mad Dog' Sullivan.

"In 1984, I was devastated when Murphy told me he was leaving the FBI to start his own private investigation business," Nelson says. "The entire Brooklyn-Queens FBI Office was saddened by his decision to leave."

CHAPTER SEVEN

At Quantico these days, they have this test called "the Yellow Brick Road."

The Yellow Brick Road is a grueling 6.1-mile run through a hilly, wooded trail in the Virginia foothills built by the US Marines.[16] Along the way, you climb over walls, run through creeks, jump through simulated windows, scale steep rock faces, scurry under barbed wire—that kind of stuff.

Years ago, the Marines started using yellow bricks as trail markers. Today, applicants who complete this test receive an actual yellow brick to memorialize their achievement.

Those who don't?

They go home.

While the Yellow Brick Road was instituted after Nelson passed through Quantico, he faced his share of formidable challenges.

"When I went through the Academy, there was a two-mile run and the required time to pass was twelve minutes," Nelson says. That's a six-minute-mile pace.

"At least that was on a paved road. Then there was another off-road course we had to master that I found difficult. I studied it and finally mastered it, but it included climbing this rope that went

---

16. "The FBI National Academy's Yellow Brick Road — 40th Anniversary." FBI: Law Enforcement Bulletin. February 8, 2022. https://leb.fbi.gov/bulletin-highlights/additional-highlights/the-fbi-national-academys-yellow-brick-roads-40th-anniversary

straight up, probably the height of a standard flag pole; I'd say at least twenty feet up."

The instructors added extra motivation.

"We were told they would place our FBI credentials, not yet issued, at the top of that pole, and the only way we would receive them would be to shimmy up that rope to get them." Nelson laughs. "They never actually put the credentials up there, but it sure motivated us to make it up to the top."

Quantico's challenges are not just physical.

"During my time at the FBI Academy, they required us to pass all of our written tests with a minimum score of eighty-five percent," Nelson says. "You were only permitted to score less than eighty-five percent on one test and then retake it."

If you scored less than eighty-five percent on that second attempt?

"Your desk was emptied by the next morning, and you were on your way home, unemployed," Nelson says. He estimates that at least twenty percent of his class at Quantico never made it to graduation.

As the weeks wore on, training and testing weeded out candidate after candidate. Nelson, though, began noticing something else: some candidates struggled with a simple psychological challenge.

"There were some who could not answer, in the affirmative, a particular question when it was posed to them," Nelson says.

That question?

Are you sure that if you had to, you could pull the trigger on your weapon and take the life of another human being?

In 1934, Congress authorized FBI Special Agents to carry firearms under Title 18, US Code, Section 3052.

Having prior experience with firearms is helpful, but not required. The FBI will train you. But once you sign up for this, you better be ready.

Special Agents must be armed, or a firearm must be accessible at all times, unless there are extenuating circumstances.

Rhys Williams, a Special Agent and instructor with the Firearms Training Unit, explains in an FBI training video how and why new agent trainees achieve proficiency with their weapons during their time at Quantico. "If they come to us with experience, we make them better; if they come to us with no experience, we teach them everything on the fundamentals of the gun—how the gun works, how their ammunition works—and the fundamentals of marksmanship, and we get them to leave here being extremely proficient with that gun. So, when the new agents come to us, the Firearms Training Unit, we train them on three specific types of weapons.[17]

"Their primary weapon, their sidearm, is a Glock 19M; it's a brand-new weapon—that's predominantly what we're going to teach them with," Williams states in the video. "In addition to that, we're going to expose them to the Remington 870P shotgun, 12-gauge. And then we'll also have them qualify and we'll teach them on what we call the Colt Pattern Carbine, what most people would consider an AR-15 or an M-16 variant."

With their pistol, they're going to shoot approximately four thousand rounds of ammunition.

With the shotgun, they're going to shoot around 120 to 150 rounds through the 12-gauge shotgun.

And then with the carbine, they're going to shoot approximately 620 rounds.

"One of the best days I had ever experienced at that point in my life was successfully completing my training and receiving my FBI Special Agent credentials on graduation day," Nelson says.

That day, Nelson was issued those credentials along with a Smith & Wesson .38-caliber revolver.

Some law enforcement officers say it's rare that they discharge their firearms in the line of duty. Some say it's uncommon for them as they are not day-to-day first responders to crimes in

17. "Becoming an Agent: Firearms Training." Federal Bureau of Investigation. June 11, 2021. https://www.fbi.gov/video-repository/becoming-an-agent-series-firearms-training.mp4/view

progress. Some even say they've gone their entire careers without firing their weapons, except during training and qualification.

And sometimes, it depends on your assignment.

Even up to graduation, Nelson did not know to which FBI field office he would be assigned.

"At the time, most agents were required to accept assignments in other than large field offices or their hometown for at least two years," Nelson recalls. "This policy existed to provide new agents with experience investigating a variety of criminal activity in smaller offices before getting assigned to the more specialized large field offices with serious crime problems.

"However, very few agents wanted to be assigned to the New York Office," Nelson adds, "and those that were assigned had been on 'Office of Preference' lists to transfer out." As a result, the New York Office had staffing challenges.

"I believe that was the reason I had been allowed to transfer directly back home to New York, and I could not have been happier with my assignment," Nelson says. "But my happiness was not shared by some of my classmates who dreaded being assigned to the Big Apple."

It was March 1977, and there was no shortage of crime to investigate in New York. Upon Nelson's arrival at the New York Office, he was assigned to the Truck Hijacking Squad of the Criminal Division.

"Truck hijackings were among the most prevalent offenses committed by members of La Cosa Nostra at the time," Nelson says. "It was also an era of political unrest, somewhat like the current conditions of protest involving conflicts in the Middle East."

Meanwhile, the Black Liberation Army, which grew out of the Black Panther Party, was in the midst of a campaign of bombings and robberies, called "expropriations."

Also active was the FALN (*Fuerzas Armadas de Liberación Nacional Puertorriqueña*), a paramilitary organization seeking independence for Puerto Rico, responsible for over 130 bombings between 1974 and 1983. In March 1977, as Anthony Nelson was setting up his desk, the group claimed responsibility for bombings at the FBI's Manhattan headquarters and a foreign currency printing plant in the Bronx.

"I didn't work on counterterrorism matters, but these organizations, and others, gave rise to some tactical changes within the FBI," Nelson says. "And members of those and other terrorist groups, as well as criminals in general, were starting to carry more sophisticated weapons."

There were episodes that reminded FBI agents just how outgunned they were on the streets.

Nelson recalls vividly April 11, 1986, when two FBI agents were shot to death and five others were wounded during a wild shootout with two heavily armed armored-car robbers in Miami. "Both robbers were carrying weapons much more deadly than those of the agents who tried to arrest them," Nelson remembers. "During the shootout, several hundred rounds of ammunition were fired, and both robbers were shot and killed by the FBI arrest team."

According to a *New York Times* account of the tragic event, "The suspects, Michael L. Platt, 32 years old, and William R. Matix, 35, had no criminal records. In the exchange of gunfire, they killed the two agents, Gerald Dove, 30, and Benjamin Grogan, 53, and wounded five."[17]

The shooting began when FBI agents stopped a car linked to a man who'd been shot and left for dead weeks earlier near the Everglades. The agents were tracking a gang behind multiple armed robberies and shootings. As they pulled the suspects over, Michael Platt and William Matix jumped out and opened fire with an automatic rifle and shotgun.[18]

This incident, along with others, inspired the FBI to review its tactics and weapons policies.

"As a result, agents who were working dangerous criminal work were all issued their choice of a shotgun or an H&K MP5 rifle to supplement their handguns," Nelson says. "I chose the MP5

---

18. Shenon, Philip. "F.B.I., AFTER SHOOTOUT, ORDERS AGENTS TO USE VESTS." New York Times, June 16, 1986. https://www.nytimes.com/1986/06/16/us/fbi-after-shootout-orders-agents-to-use-vests.html

and kept it locked in my car trunk, even during day-to-day investigations.

"As the dangers increased," Nelson adds, "we were later also issued semi-automatic handguns to replace our six-shot revolvers. And as the FBI made these changes, many local police agencies also began to follow."

Meanwhile, although the first use of body armor can be traced back to the 1500s with Italian and Roman royalty experimenting with the idea of bulletproof vests, it was not until the late twentieth century that it saw widespread adoption in law enforcement in America.

In 1976, scientists concluded that Kevlar was bullet-resistant, wearable, and light enough for police officers to wear full-time. Interestingly, bulletproof vests had already become commercially available, even before the National Institute of Justice published these claims.[19]

According to the *New York Times* report on the tragic Miami FBI shootout, William H. Webster, the FBI director, indicated that an order to use the vests could prevent deaths in similar incidents. "The order will require FBI agents to wear vests when there is a reasonable assumption that they may encounter dangerous suspects," Webster said. "In the past, decisions about the use of vests were left to the Bureau's local supervisors."18

"I recall first being issued a ballistic vest in 1977," Nelson says. "Police officers today could probably not even imagine making dangerous arrests or knocking on suspects' doors without a ballistic vest."

Since that time, bulletproof vests have improved, according to manufacturer BulletSafe. Currently, a Level IIIA bulletproof vest weighs approximately 5.5 pounds and can protect the wearer from almost all handgun rounds. According to the International Association of Chiefs of Police, bulletproof vests have saved over three thousand officers' lives since 1987.[19]

19. BulletSafe Bulletproof Vests. "The History of the Bulletproof Vest." https://bulletsafe.com/pages/the-history-of-bulletproof-vests

CHAPTER EIGHT

Welcome to the Golden Age of Hijacking.

When Anthony Nelson landed at the FBI's New York Office in March 1977, he jumped into a variety of undercover assignments, focusing on tracking down stolen securities, credit cards, counterfeit and stolen checks, and fraudulent identification.

But nothing compared to the intensity of joining the FBI Criminal Division's "Truck Hijacking Squad."

By 1977, hijacking, particularly of trucks and cargo, had become a full-blown epidemic across New York and its surrounding areas. Skyrocketing hijackings, escalating homicides, and brazen armed robberies all fed New York City's 1970s' gritty reputation of lawlessness.

This was the decade of *Dirty Harry* (1971), *Death Wish* (1974), and *Taxi Driver* (1976), where rising crime rates and frustration with a perception of a revolving-door legal system inspired fear and vigilante justice.

However, there were brave men and women in law enforcement determined to turn back that dark tide.

The FBI began investigating hijackings back in the 1930s when organized crime started targeting trucks to steal loads of alcohol, cigarettes, and other high-value commodities. Interstate commerce was booming, and prime trucking corridors became targets for road bandits. In 1934, the passage of the Motor Carrier Act, regulating interstate trucking, gave the FBI jurisdiction over truck hijackings.

Yet those earlier crime waves were nothing compared to the 1960s and 1970s, when truck hijackings spiked, especially in large metro areas like New York, Chicago, and Los Angeles. Crime syndicates became more adept at targeting high-demand items, such as electronics, clothing, and jewelry, which can be easily resold on black markets.

This evolution made sense. Truck hijacking is way more lucrative and less dangerous than robbing banks. The 1990 movie *Goodfellas* depicts how 1960s gangsters so easily corrupted truckers, or just brutally seized vehicles. For once, this was no Hollywood over dramatization, as many truckers were easily threatened, especially those who gambled and borrowed from loan sharks and fell behind in payments.

Fencing the goods—selling the stolen merchandise illegally— never seemed to be an issue.

In 1970, a US Senate Select Committee estimated that $900 million was lost due to truck theft. In today's money, that's an eye-popping $7.5 billion.

Organized crime gangs had informants inside all the ports, airports, and warehouses to tip them off about what was coming in and where it was going. Their long incestuous partnership with (and control of) the International Brotherhood of Teamsters Union also enabled crews to corrupt drivers and dispatchers, so they knew when the truck was leaving, what route it would take, and even who the driver was in some cases.

To combat the surge in hijackings, federal agencies and municipal police forces in major cities formed specialized units.

In 1978, Special Agent Anthony Nelson was inserted by the FBI in an undercover capacity into a truck hijacking crew associated with both the Gambino and Genovese crime Families of La Cosa Nostra.

Back then, undercover work meant not only working without a safety net of sophisticated technology, but also required a ton of tedious legwork.

"We had no cellular phones at the time, no constant communications," Nelson says. "We were also conducting investigations without computers, so everything had to be manually, personally verified."

Still, for that era, the FBI was at the forefront of computerized crime fighting. The Bureau developed the National Crime Information Center (NCIC), the only national law enforcement computer system to check for stolen vehicles, stolen property, and wanted persons. Initially, fifteen state and city computers were connected to the Bureau's host computer in Washington, DC.

They call it a computer, but the cell phone device in your pocket right now has far more processing power. At the time, NCIC contained just over 350,000 criminal justice records across five different files—wanted persons, stolen articles, stolen vehicles, stolen license plates, and stolen/missing guns.

The very first NCIC hit came in May 1967 when a New York City police officer radioed in a request for a search of a license plate. In less than two minutes, he was informed that the car had been stolen the previous month in Boston.

"That doesn't seem like a big deal now, but back then, it was a seismic shift in how you could investigate these types of crimes," Nelson says.

By 1971, all fifty states were connected to NCIC. Over the next three decades, the database expanded and evolved as new technologies and information needs emerged. However, even with NCIC, there were limitations.

"In those days, to develop simple background information on suspects, or just to locate witnesses, we had to check huge, and I mean really huge, leased volumes of books," Nelson says. "There were books with telephone number subscriber information, real estate deed info, reverse telephone number lookups, and so many different printed background reference materials you had to pore over."

Today, investigators can obtain that information within seconds, even without the aid of artificial intelligence.

A 1974 *New York Times* article estimated that reported hijackings in New York City decreased from a high of 378 in 1971, involving $7.8 million worth of merchandise, to the comparatively low

1973 total of 127 hijacks (an average of slightly more than two a week), involving $4.2 million worth of merchandise.[20]

Sergeant Robert Chapman of the Safe, Loft and Truck Squad, stated in a 1974 *New York Times* article, that nearly ninety percent of hijackings reported in New York could be tied to organized crime. [20]

An FBI official involved with hijacking investigations observed that "by participating in a hijacking, a man on the fringes of organized crime can move closer to the inner network. The hijacker proves he can handle responsibility, that he can work with a team of men, and can make a big profit. Hijackings are stepping stones for the peripheral figures who hang out at these social clubs. If a guy can prove he has guts when he's in his twenties, he'll be a made man by his thirties."[20]

And just as Anthony Nelson was getting his bearings undercover, the criminal category rocketed through the early 1980s.

"Between 1978 and 1982, 586 trucks were reported hijacked in the city, though perhaps a third of the incidents were feigned by dishonest drivers. In the first nine months of this year, 37 trucks were hijacked and 63 trucks with loads worth more than $10,000 were stolen without the driver being taken hostage," according to 1984 *New York Times* coverage.

"Within a day last July, the police traced a load of hijacked radios from Manhattan to Brooklyn, back to an after-hours social club on the Lower East Side, and on to a warehouse in Staten Island. Inside the warehouse, the police said, were 500,000 counterfeit Sassoon and Jordache labels to be put on bogus designer jeans."[21]

Major transport hubs, such as John F. Kennedy International Airport, were frequent targets for theft, including hijackings of shipments before or after transport. Also vulnerable was the

20. "Truck Hijacking in City Is a $4.2-Million Business." New York Times. May 20, 1974. https://www.nytimes.com/1974/05/20/archives/truck-hijacking-in-city-is-a-42million-business-truck-hijacking-in.html

21. Farber, M.A. "TRUCK HIJACKING: A HIGHLY ORGANIZED AND SPECIALIZED CRIME IN NEW YORK." New York Times. December 16, 1983. https://www.nytimes.com/1983/12/16/nyregion/truck-hijacking-a-highly-organized-and-specialized-crime-in-new-york.html

sprawling Port of New York and New Jersey, as well as major highways connecting warehouses to distribution centers.

"During my time as an undercover agent, I operated on the front lines as the owner of a warehouse on Union Street in the Red Hook section of Brooklyn to store hijacked trucks," Nelson says.

By the 1970s, the declining inner-city neighborhood where Anthony Nelson first lived was an ideal setting for a Mob-friendly warehouse.

Once a bustling hub of shipping and industry, Red Hook's waterfront was in steep decline as container shipping largely relocated to port facilities in New Jersey. The loss of these jobs devastated the neighborhood. Empty warehouses, abandoned buildings, and crumbling infrastructure became common, just as the heroin epidemic of the 1970s slammed into Red Hook. Drug trafficking and addiction were rampant, with open-air drug markets operating in parts of the neighborhood. Violence related to the drug trade, including robberies and shootings, became commonplace.

The Red Hook Houses, one of the largest public housing complexes in the city, became a focal point for social issues such as unemployment, drug abuse, and inadequate services.

Poor transportation links (no subway stations accessible in Red Hook) further isolated this economic wasteland. Gangs controlled large swaths of Red Hook, clashing over territory, engaging in extortion, theft, and violent crime.

The NYPD had insufficient manpower to effectively police the entire Red Hook area. This absence of vigorous law enforcement allowed criminal enterprises to thrive, as burglaries, robberies, assaults, and murders became alarmingly frequent. This was an ideal backdrop for the FBI to rent the warehouse in 1978, allowing Special Agent Anthony Nelson to use it in a joint undercover operation with the Bureau of Alcohol, Tobacco, and Firearms (ATF).

The ATF was doing gun buys with multiple targets throughout this investigation. Nelson joined the undercover operation to investigate property crimes being committed by the same subjects, which was under the jurisdiction of the FBI. Posing as the "owner" of the large warehouse with a high front door that could accommodate full-size trailers, Nelson positioned himself as having connections to various organized crime factions.

"I only allowed a very select number of subjects to come down to the warehouse," Nelson explains. "It was not open to the public and was not operational every day of the week."

As the criminal activity increased at the warehouse, Nelson had to be very mindful of avoiding detection, from the way he dressed to the way he spoke, even the way he carried himself.

"You're engaging with criminals regularly and witnessing firsthand the trafficking of stolen merchandise," Nelson says. "It's a delicate tightrope, deciding not just when to make a minor arrest or instead let a situation develop, so you can later make a larger impact, maybe take down a ring, prevent the sale of weapons."

These were not dull thugs.

"These criminals have layers upon layers of complexity," Nelson says. "These are creative, highly paranoid, and volatile individuals. As an undercover, you develop sophisticated techniques in response to their behaviors, which are always evolving. And through it all, to them, you're not law enforcement. You're also a criminal. You're a potential threat or target, or someone to rip off, so you're always in harm's way."

Throughout much of 1978, Nelson engaged regularly with the ATF targets.

"I had 'first rights' to either buy the loads they'd bring in or else be paid to have stolen loads stored at my warehouse until they could be moved to a secondary location," Nelson says. "I also used the warehouse to accommodate some fellow agents in collateral matters."

Nelson allowed one subject to meet at the warehouse on several occasions to negotiate the purchase of several million dollars' worth of stolen corporate bonds, and another who told him he needed a drop for three days to store a hijacked tractor-trailer of dog food. Nelson also allowed another FBI agent to use the warehouse for a one-time criminal transaction.

One day, the targets claimed to the ATF agents that they were about to hijack an entire shipment of guns.

"They needed a reliable 'drop' to store the stolen tractor-trailer for a few days," Nelson says. "They also claimed they wanted to make sure that my warehouse had an entry door with enough clearance to accommodate the trailer they intended to hijack. I'm sure, however, that they also wanted to make sure I really even had a warehouse. With these guys, they're suspicious of everything."

In addition to illegal gun trafficking and hijacking, these crews were also dealing in stolen and counterfeit credit cards and American Express Traveler's checks.

"I intended to store the guns at my warehouse, but that transaction never happened," Nelson recalls. "However, during a meeting I had later with one of the subjects at a New Jersey restaurant, he told me he was ready to deliver a hijacked load of appliances.

"Then afterwards, I had this load brought to my warehouse by Huck Carbonaro."

Thomas "Huck" Carbonaro, a soldier in the Gambino Family, was serious business.

In his youth, Carbonaro met Gambino Family soldier Joseph D'Angelo, and through him got introduced to Salvatore "Sammy the Bull" Gravano, the Family's future underboss. Gravano took a liking to Carbonaro, helping him move out of his low-class neighborhood and relocate to Bensonhurst. Carbonaro then began working more actively for the Gambino Family as an associate in Gravano's crew, gaining a tough-guy reputation.

Carbonaro "made his bones" on November 2, 1987, by killing Gambino associate Michael DeBatt, who was targeted for death after developing a crack addiction. Carbonaro shot him in the head behind the bar of Gravano's former headquarters in Brooklyn, and afterwards became a made man.

Carbonaro later helped with the murders of two other Gambino mobsters: Edward Garofalo in 1990, shot to death as he and his roommate were walking to his car in Bay Ridge, and Frank Hydell in 1998, serving as a getaway driver after Hydell was killed outside a Staten Island nightclub.

Following Gravano's cooperation agreement with the government in 1992 and his subsequent testimony against boss John Gotti, the Gambino Family planned to have Gravano killed in 1999 after he left Witness Protection and began living publicly in Phoenix, Arizona.

Carbonaro led a hit team to kill Gravano on orders from acting boss Peter Gotti, and he and Gambino associate Salvatore Mangiavillano scouted Gravano's living area for over a year, acquiring surveillance and bomb-making equipment in Los Angeles as preparation for the hit. Their plans were only thwarted when Gravano was arrested on ecstasy trafficking charges in 2000, and Carbonaro was later indicted for this and other racketeering and murder charges, being sentenced to seventy years in prison in 2005.[22]

Carbonaro brought this stolen load to Nelson through the undercover agent's contacts with a group of fifteen other subjects who were targeted by and ultimately arrested in connection with this operation. Most of the subjects were arrested for illegal gun sales to ATF agents.

When Carbonaro arrived at the warehouse driving the tractor-trailer, he was instructed to approach Nelson with the code, "Huck for Tony."

"As soon as Carbonaro backed the tractor-trailer into my warehouse, he pulled out a revolver from his waistband and laid it on the fender of the tractor, pointed in my direction," Nelson says.

Carbonaro then exclaimed, "Okay, let's unload this thing!"

"I took Carbonaro's action with the handgun to mean that nothing better go wrong," Nelson says.

In the February 2, 1979, edition of the *Bergen County Record*, there's a photo of Anthony Nelson standing next to a partial load of portable refrigerators he stored in the FBI warehouse for Gambino Family associates.

"One of those fifteen subjects arrested was the second person who told me about this guy, 'Roy DeMeo,'" and his 'psycho crew of

22. Historica Wiki. "Thomas Carbonaro," https://historica.fandom.com/wiki/Thomas_Carbonaro

car thieves and killers,'" Nelson says. "Although I wasn't told if this specific load was going to anyone in DeMeo's Crew, one of the subjects asked me if I knew Roy DeMeo.

"Carbonaro was not initially arrested with the original group of fifteen subjects mentioned in the newspaper article," Nelson says. "However, we did arrest him for it about a year later. I believe he took a plea to the federal charge of Theft from Interstate Shipment and served time for the hijacking."

By the mid-1980s, law enforcement crackdowns, better security technology, and shifts in organized crime priorities led to a decline in truck hijackings. However, the crime remains a symbol of the broader challenges faced by New York during the 1970s. Nelson remembers Red Hook vividly, but it wasn't all bad. He remembers trips to longstanding local favorite DeFonte's Sandwich Shop on Columbia Street, just off the BQE, still serving mouthwatering heroes for over a century. Just get there before four p.m.

"I'd been buying sandwiches there for years, even beyond my undercover days," Nelson says. "I think they really are the best hero sandwiches in New York City. I'd stick around at times with Special Agent George Hanna, talking with the owner, Nicky DeFonte."

At the time of the undercover operation, Nelson had several uncles who worked on the nearby piers as longshoremen. "I'd go down to the docks to visit with them when I had some free time at the warehouse," Nelson says. "I remember my first visit to Pier 5 to visit an uncle," he adds. "After I drove through the front gates, there were two tractors parked off the side with their hoods up. I first thought they were having engine problems, but upon closer inspection, I noticed they were cooking breakfast on top of the hot engine blocks of their trucks."

CHAPTER NINE

With every criminal transaction, operating undercover posing as the owner of a Mob-friendly warehouse on Union Street was becoming more dangerous for Anthony Nelson.

But with his first right-of-refusal to fence the stolen merchandise, Nelson's daily interaction with Genovese and Gambino crews allowed him to gather invaluable intel on relationships, inner workings, distribution points, shot callers, and so much more.

Embedding undercover also enabled Nelson to start developing an expanding network of confidential informants. One day in late 1977, Nelson received a telephone call from an informant who tipped him off to a hijacked shipment of electronics stored on a rental truck in Sheepshead Bay.

It was always a challenge to act on tips in ways that did not implicate him, his CI, or other law enforcement operatives. One wrong move could undermine months or years of investigations, or even have lethal consequences.

"The informant told me that the hijackers would be returning to the truck later in the day and they were going to move it to a storage facility somewhere in Canarsie," Nelson says. "He also told me that part of the load was going to a guy who reported to a Roy DeMeo."

According to the informant, DeMeo had recently been "made" within the Gambino Family, as in formally inducted into La Cosa Nostra, or what some Italians would simply call Cosa Nostra.

It was not until 1963, thanks in part to the FBI, that the first major Mafia turncoat—Joseph Valachi—publicly testified before a Senate subcommittee about the Mafia's secret induction ceremony.

Yet the Bureau still needed legislative tools to connect all these lower-tier underlings with the barons of their borgatas. Congress delivered with new illegal gambling statutes that helped target the Mafia's financial networks, and other laws like the Omnibus Crime Control Act of 1968 and the Racketeer Influenced and Corrupt Organizations (RICO) Act of 1970.

This made undercover operations, such as the one in Red Hook with Nelson, not only possible but also essential in unlocking troves of intelligence to build larger cases.

"DeMeo was described by the informant as the leader of a violent and sadistic group of young thugs who had blind ambitions about becoming mobsters," Nelson recalls.

Today, DeMeo is one of the most notorious names in the annals of the underworld. But back then, he was just one of many wiseguys who happened to control a growing network of towing companies, junkyards, and car theft operations in Flatlands and Canarsie.

Also around that time, another name began to crop up in surveillance, Nelson says: Anthony "Nino" Gaggi. And there was a connection.

Gaggi, a soldier and later captain in the Gambino Family, first spotted DeMeo in 1966 when Roy was associated with the Luccheses. Gaggi told him that he could make even more money if he shifted his allegiance to the Gambinos.

By the late 1960s, DeMeo was making steady strides in the world of organized crime. He remained active in the loansharking trade alongside Gaggi while quietly assembling a tight-knit group of young thieves specializing in stolen cars. This growing network of criminals formed the nucleus of the infamous DeMeo Crew.

DeMeo was a hustler. Initially focused on clients in Brooklyn's auto industry, his loan shark operation quickly broadened to target a broader range of businesses, including a dental practice, an abortion clinic, several restaurants, and local flea markets.

On paper, DeMeo held a job at a Brooklyn firm called S&C Sportswear Corporation, but to his neighbors, he offered a rotating cover story—claiming at various times to work in construction, food sales, or the used car trade.

Despite Bonanno underboss Salvatore Vitale later telling the FBI that he had been instructed in 1974 to deliver a freshly killed body to a Queens garage for DeMeo to handle, Roy kept a relatively low profile with law enforcement throughout the mid-1970s, avoiding the spotlight until his rise later in the decade.

The DeMeo Crew developed a standardized method of execution designed for efficiency and secrecy—ensuring victims were swiftly eliminated and vanished without a trace. This technique became known as the "Gemini Method," named after the Gemini Lounge, a bar on Flatlands Avenue that served as both the crew's unofficial headquarters and the grisly setting for many of their killings.

That day in 1977 when the name Roy DeMeo first hit Anthony Nelson's radar, the informant also said that he saw some unmarked police cars in the area where that hijacked truck was being stored, and he had hoped that the cops were not watching the same truck.

"I was born at night, but I wasn't born last night," Nelson says. "I knew right away from his comments that I was being set up in some way."

After carefully scouting the area where the truck was parked, Nelson spotted a familiar face, a detective nearby whom he recognized from the Brooklyn District Attorney's Office. At the time, Nelson was unaware of the detective's name. So, he immediately set up a meeting with NYPD Deputy Inspector John Nevins in the Brooklyn District Attorney's Office.

During a meeting later that same day, Nevins introduced Nelson to this mysterious detective he had seen.

His name was Kenneth "Kenny" McCabe.

To say Kenny McCabe is a legend in law enforcement is an understatement, especially in the heroic battle to defeat the American Mafia in the latter half of the twentieth century. It is remarkable, stunning actually, that someone of McCabe's caliber and contributions has never been profiled in a significant way or received the Hollywood biopic treatment.

However, it's less surprising for those who knew the low-key, no-ego McCabe, who wrote no books, did not court politicians, and avoided those flashbulb-popping, publicity-grabbing interviews that were so common in that era.

In the US Attorney's Office in Lower Manhattan there hangs a memorial plaque to McCabe, who passed in 2006, honoring the federal investigator who was a key part of the government's most significant Mafia prosecutions—and whose role as an in-house investigator, after his illustrious career with the NYPD, makes him one of law enforcement's most unsung heroes.

McCabe was a member of the New York Police Department for eighteen years, most of that time as a detective assigned to the Brooklyn District Attorney's Office, and then for twenty years as an organized crime investigator for the United States Attorney's Office in Manhattan.

Among the elite investigators of the era, McCabe stands head and shoulders above all, known for his encyclopedic memory of complex intricacies of modern organized crime groups operating throughout New York and beyond, with photographic recall of their faces, having spent thousands of hours prowling the underworld.

In the digital age, where everyone has a high-definition camera in their pocket, it's difficult to appreciate the unique value Kenny McCabe lent to investigations, filling in blanks and connecting dots to help build cases that resulted in thousands of convictions and the dismantling of hundreds of crews.

Normally confident defense attorneys who knew McCabe, even by reputation, would cringe when the lawman strode into a courtroom to provide expert testimony. They knew he could reel off the names, ranks, and *family* ties of hundreds of mobsters without even referring to his extensive and detailed notes. Some defense attorneys began to decline invitations to cross-examine McCabe, fearing that his responses would introduce even more damning and certainly believable context to further incriminate their clients.

"Kenny knew all the wise guys, and they all knew," says George Terra, who often engaged with McCabe through his forty-five-year career in law enforcement, both during his twenty years with the NYPD as well as his time in the Kings County District Attorney's Office.

"And when I say he knew all the wise guys," Terra says, "he knew these guys' shoe sizes. Kenny knew who they partnered with on bank jobs years ago, who their siblings were, who their cousins were, who they were married to, and who their girlfriends were. He knew which clubs they frequented, what they were alleged to have done, and with whom they were associated. He knew who was made or not made, and just on and on and on. This is not an exaggeration: Kenny McCabe was the real deal."

It helped that McCabe was a force, physically, a towering, beefy man with a gentle manner and a Brooklyn accent, exuding confidence and integrity.

Regardless of agency, ask any member of law enforcement of that era involved in the epic battle against organized crime about Kenny McCabe, and they'll break into a smile.

Everyone seems to have a Kenny McCabe story.

Anthony Nelson just happens to have more.

That day in downtown Brooklyn, the two lawmen struck up a lifelong friendship.

They had much in common. Both hailed from the Park Slope section of Brooklyn, Kenneth James McCabe was born three years earlier on May 14, 1946. McCabe's father was an assistant district attorney in Brooklyn. They both shared a strong faith-based upbringing in hard-scrabble mid-century New York, both attending local Roman Catholic schools, McCabe later graduating from Loyola College in Maryland.

They both pursued careers in law enforcement in the 1960s amid major cultural upheaval, with McCabe joining the police department in 1968 (the same year he married Kathleen Moriarty), a year before Nelson entered service at the FBI.

Nelson soon joined McCabe on what became regular afterhours cruises across the vast plain of Brooklyn, after both lawmen had completed their respective tours during the day.

On those rides, McCabe took so many photographs (remember, using actual cameras, you had to load film into and then have it developed), including not just social club surveillance, but mobsters' weddings, wakes, and funerals, he received another nickname on the street: "Cosa Nostra's unofficial photographer."

In a 2003 trial, McCabe testified about a new edict requiring Cosa Nostra initiates to have both a mother and a father who are Italian.

McCabe was the one who revealed that the Bonanno Family had changed its name to Massino. And then, when Joseph Massino later went to prison for murder, and his successor, Vincent Basciano, faced murder and racketeering charges, his trial was postponed because so many law enforcement leaders attended McCabe's funeral.

Back in 1977, Anthony Nelson broke the ice by telling Kenny McCabe about the telephone call he received from the informant. "I also vaguely described the source, hoping that McCabe would acknowledge he had received his information about the hijacked truck from the same person," Nelson recalls.

McCabe didn't skip a beat.

"He even went a step further, identifying the informant by name," Nelson says. "I was really impressed from the start."

Nelson and McCabe not only decided to watch the hijacked shipment together, but also agreed to "stiff" the duplicitous informant out of any reward money for the return of the stolen merchandise.

Within a few hours, this new dynamic duo recovered a stolen shipment of electronics valued at eighty-eight thousand dollars and made a solid arrest for the hijacking. This case also yielded yet another cooperating witness, willing to wear a wire and testify, who shared more intel on this shadowy up-and-coming gangster named Roy DeMeo, and even connected him to Nino Gaggi.

"He told us that Roy was 'with' a Gambino Family capo known as 'Nino,'" Nelson remembers. "This was another partial name I had not yet heard while in my undercover capacity."

DeMeo was, once again, described by yet another informant as a vicious loan shark who was also dealing in stolen property and murder.

"We were told that he and his group of young car thieves and murderers were based at the Gemini Lounge in Flatlands," Nelson says. "So, my interest in Roy DeMeo was piqued at this point."

Roy DeMeo was now firmly on the radar.

"On a couple of occasions, I went into the Gemini Lounge just to look around," Nelson says. "Except for the hard stares that came my way, obviously intended to make me feel unwelcome, there was not much else to see."

Nelson, you see, was not invited to tour the apartment attached to the Gemini Lounge and had no idea of the awful atrocities committed there, which would later hit like a bomb.

CHAPTER TEN

It's so much easier to get caught today than when Anthony Nelson joined the FBI in 1969.

They don't even have to tail you anymore.

Did you know virtual assistants like Apple's Siri and Amazon's Alexa running on smart devices can do more than adjust lighting and play music?

They can listen to your conversations.

Sort of.

Sure, Alexa or Siri only record your voice when you speak directly to it.

Well …

With probable cause and a warrant, investigators can search your search history, tap into your GPS data, and *bingo*—place you at the scene of a crime or track your movements.

They don't even need the conversations. Call logs can connect you to co-conspirators.

Deleted those incriminating texts?

Sorry.

Depending on the device and time of deletion, that data may be retrievable with the right forensic tools.

Social media posts, pics, and check-ins contain timestamps, while WhatsApp, Signal, and Facebook Messenger back up message content.

They can just follow all your digital bread crumbs.

Checking Google Maps to plot the perfect escape route? Searching for advice on how to remove blood stains from a carpet? Maybe shopping at Home Depot for a shovel, some nylon rope, a large bag, perhaps throw in some lye?

Good luck with that.

None of this was available to a young Anthony Nelson in 1969, incidentally, the same year the first message was sent between computers at UCLA and Stanford University over the ARPANET network developed by the US Department of Defense.[23]

But it was coming.

This was the dawning of a new digital age in law enforcement.

"When I was an electronics technician for the FBI, I was involved in bug installations and maintaining electronic surveillance and radio equipment," Nelson says. "Sure, by today's standards, the tech was primitive. But back then, these were game changers."

In a world without smart devices or digital networks, to plant a bug, you needed to physically enter a premise, as in breaking and entering, but only within the bounds of the law.

So much could go wrong.

"I probably went on a dozen Title III installations, but I was not always on the entry team," Nelson says. "In most cases, I set up the receiving end, generally at a remote location."

In one investigation where Nelson did participate as part of the entry team, they were assigned to a construction trailer in Queens.

"I remember this entry mostly because our period to overhear conversations was during the day when the trailer had been occupied," Nelson says.

Nelson set up monitoring equipment in a rented apartment near the trailer.

Then the apartment was burglarized.

---

23. "How a Simple 'Hello' Became the First Message Sent via the Internet." PBS News. February 9, 2015. https://www.pbs.org/newshour/science/internet-got-started-simple-hello

And then it was burglarized again.

"We lost all of our electronic equipment in the apartment and had to have agents stationed in there twenty-four hours a day just to protect the equipment," Nelson remembers.

While most of the entries were reasonably safe, as the FBI had simultaneous surveillance coverage of the subjects associated with target locations, Nelson remembers one challenging instance.

He set up the monitoring end fine, but the agents attempting the entry had difficulty defeating the alarm system. "They set off the alarm several times and had to retreat because there was always a response to the location by the alarm company, whose personnel were armed," he says. "During the third attempt to enter, we were successful."

It didn't take long for the wiseguys to get wise to electronic surveillance techniques.

They thought they could limit the effectiveness of a bug by turning their televisions to a deafening volume. Then they began stepping outside their social clubs to discuss serious business. They started using code words, even covering their mouths when they got wind of FBI lip readers.

In that deadly cat-and-rat arms race, though, only one side had to follow rules. (Well, unless you consider the Mafia's Omertà code of silence, but the bad guys began to break that anyway, en masse.)

"There definitely were and are rules law enforcement must follow to protect privacy, taken very seriously," Nelson says. "You had a specific window of time from when you started listening and recording to determine if criminal activity was being discussed. Otherwise, you need to turn it off."

Pretty soon, the wiseguys wised up, counting down the exact time they now knew they needed to wait out Johnny Law, discussing the weather or whatever, before they could jump into their nefarious plotting.

"But some couldn't help themselves," Nelson recalls. "They'd say something like, 'Watch what you say,' start with a benign initial conversation, like discussing some spaghetti dish they'd eaten. But some couldn't wait, and sooner or later, the conversation shifted to criminal activity. And yes, they started using code words, but it was often so obvious they were discussing criminal acts."

Once the gangsters realized they were being watched, some carefully chose every word they said.

In the 1980s, Maria Scopello joined the FBI's New York Office in a support role, assisting Special Agents in locating records of closed cases to help build new cases and support prosecutions. Scopello also ran background checks using the NICS and pulled criminal history records.

Then, one day, while working with the NICS Indices (which contain information on people prohibited from receiving firearms by federal or state law), Scopello was approached by a Special Agent who needed immediate help with a live Title III recording— he knew that Scopello, born in Brooklyn to parents who emigrated from Italy to New York, was fluent in Italian and Sicilian.

"I never once imagined that my language skills would take me into the world of organized crime investigations," Scopello says.

Anyone can translate words. This Special Agent needed someone with an ear for dialect and meaning, like cultural references and context cues.

"You can't literally translate from Italian or Sicilian to English, word for word, especially not the thick dialects they were using," Scopello shares. "It won't make sense. And these targets speak in code, so you're not only translating, but deciphering, reading between the lines, listening with your gut, trying to figure out the meaning behind the words to find the clues to make the case agents aware of all these nuances."

This linguistic code-breaking, as much art as science, is intense, working side by side with agents on stakeouts, holed up in a seedy apartment or huddled in the back of a van, listening in on a live wire, or overseeing undercovers as they bug an office or a cigarette machine.

"We're capturing audio and processing it in real time, listening for clues, warning signs, anything we can pick up to make sure that covers don't get blown, doing what we can to try and keep agents safe," Scopello says. "You start to realize, this isn't a game. This is deadly business, and they're putting their lives on the line.

"Depending on what we pull off the wire, it could steer the investigation in a different direction, reveal a missing piece, and things could change speed very quickly," Scopello says. "I had a case where the person of interest sounded like he was saying 'Yes, yes, yes,' but he was actually saying 'Six, six, six.' When you're talking about drug transactions, kilos being exchanged, it's essential to catch those small differences."

This was not crisp, clear audio. The geographic range of the radio signals was limited. "So you needed to be close nearby, and that was a major challenge because they were very aware of their surroundings, especially in or near the clubs," Nelson says. "There was such misguided loyalty in the local communities, where residents, my neighbors, would tip off the wiseguys to the presence of an unusual van or new tenant in an apartment, making the job of law enforcement that much more difficult and dangerous."

Talk about high-stakes stakeouts.

"Remember, you break into a social club or a wiseguy's car at night," Nelson says, "their first reaction is not to think you're law enforcement. You're a threat, maybe some rival trying to blow up their club. So you have to be prepared for all possibilities."

Obtaining permission to place a device was painstaking. The law considers the interception of conversations within one's own home to be a significant intrusion on privacy. Under both federal and state statutes, law enforcement must follow stringent requirements before they can lawfully plant a bug inside a residence.

First, a court order is required to enter a home and install a listening device. The Court will only issue such an order if a law enforcement officer, under oath, swears there is probable cause (meaning a reason to believe) that someone is committing or about to commit a serious crime inside the house, that communications concerning that offense will be captured through recording the conversations, and that agents have unsuccessfully attempted to obtain information concerning such criminal activity through other means, or that it would be too dangerous to try.

Even then, when agents and prosecutors persuade the judge to authorize the placement of a bug, it's only for thirty days, unless the judge later extends it.

Conversations that do not involve criminal activity should not be recorded or listened to once their non-criminal nature is determined. Progress reports must be filed with the Court periodically. And bedrooms and bathrooms are rarely bugged due to the obvious enhanced privacy interests.

On rare occasions, the FBI leased direct phone lines from the telephone company and monitored conversations from a remote location. But for the most part, they had to rely on laughably archaic, battery-operated radio transmitters.

"These were analog devices, so basically, anyone could pick up on the surveillance with a scanner you could buy at Radio Shack," Nelson says.

Remember Radio Shack?

For anyone under the age of, say, forty, that once ubiquitous American electronics retailer, which peaked in 1999, may be unfamiliar. But back then, it was wildly popular with hobbyists, had a massive mail-order business, and more than eight thousand stores, seemingly on every other corner in Brooklyn that didn't have a pizzeria.

RadioShack drew ham radio enthusiasts, remote control racing fans, and, for a time in the 1980s, Brooklyn gangsters.

"Some of these wiseguys started figuring out the radio frequencies," Nelson remembers, recalling one series of events involving Frank Alphonse "Funzi" Tieri.

Funzi claimed to be an employee of a sportswear manufacturer. He lived in a modest home in the Bath Beach section of Brooklyn with his wife and two granddaughters. His mistress, a former Italian opera singer, lived in a house a few blocks away.

But by 1972, after the murder of Genovese acting boss Thomas Eboli, Tieri also became the don of the Genovese Family.

At that time, it was speculated that Gambino kingpin Carlo Gambino ordered the hit because Eboli owed him four million dollars. According to this theory, Gambino wanted Tieri to lead the Genovese borgata. However, most experts now believe Tieri was a front for the actual boss, Philip "Benny Squint" Lombardo.

Still, Tieri was a powerful presence in Southern Brooklyn. He operated out of several front businesses, including The Cotillion, a popular wedding hall located on 18th Avenue in the heart of the Mafia stronghold of Bensonhurst.

At the time, Tieri had Russell Benvenuto, an alleged soldier for the Genovese Family, as a driver.

That day, Anthony Nelson and Kenny McCabe tailed Tieri and Benvenuto to the Cotillion. As they idled outside in Nelson's FBI car, Nelson observed one of Tieri's associates noticing them, haunting the entrance to the hall, smiling. Then he began to make a motion with his hand as if holding something.

"This guy sees me and realizes that we're law enforcement," Nelson recalls. "He then points to a portable scanner he's holding, and I realize … he's taunting us, letting us know that he could listen to everything we were transmitting over our car radio. And you know, he was right, and at the time, there was no law against it."

Soon, more and more wiseguys started shopping at Radio Shack.

Some gangsters, like Frank "Beansie" Melli, identified in an affidavit as "a soldier in the Colombo organized-crime Family," took it to the next level.

"Beansie had this van he called the War Wagon that had all kinds of monitoring equipment, so he became very good at tipping the wiseguys off to radio transmissions and tracking devices on cars," Nelson says. "They were able to adapt and develop these capabilities because the technology was so primitive, not digitized, not encoded. But these were the tools we had to work with, and despite their limitations, they did work and did help us produce evidence and build cases."

Slowly, painfully, the pieces to the organized crime puzzle began to fit.

In 1981, the FBI bugged the Howard Beach, Queens, home of Gambino soldier Angelo Ruggiero. The plant was so successful, the FBI received multiple extensions and later wiretapped

Ruggiero's Cedarhurst residence when he moved in December 1981.

The Ruggiero bug picked up a conversation between him and Gene Gotti, a brother of John Gotti. In the conversation, they discuss how Gambino Family don Paul "Big Paul" Castellano had put out a hit on Roy DeMeo but was having difficulty finding someone willing to do the job.

Gene Gotti mentioned that John was wary of taking the contract as DeMeo had an "army of killers" around him. At that time, John had killed fewer than ten people, while DeMeo was involved in thirty-seven homicides that they knew about.

Later, Mob informant Sammy Gravano told the feds that the contract was given to Frank DeCicco, the Gambino soldier who later conspired with Gotti on the assassination of Castellano, as Frankie Cheech was named underboss. But even DeCicco and his crew could not reach DeMeo. DeCicco allegedly handed the job to DeMeo's own men.

With each conversation, the stakes increased.

"Compared to today's technologies, the tools we had were primitive," Scopello says. "But back then, it was state of the art. In fact, in some ways, I think it was easier to do my job with plain old telephones. It was much less complex than the technology they use today. I think it's more difficult now with encryption and the ability to capture content and cameras at every angle.

"As time went on, the high stakes started to get to me, more so as I got older," Scopello says. "There are real consequences here, and the pressure can be overwhelming, but you just focus and keep going."

CHAPTER ELEVEN

In the autumn of 1977, FBI Special Agent Anthony Nelson and New York City Police Department Detective Kenneth "Kenny" McCabe settled into a routine.

"I started to meet more frequently with Kenny and we very quickly became friends," Nelson recalls. "It turned out that we lived just a couple of miles from each other in Brooklyn. So we made time to socialize at least once a week and started comparing notes."

Soon, several nights a week, the two lawmen began prowling the vast network of social clubs, cafes, and bars that saturated Brooklyn and Queens, controlled by the families and factions of organized crime.

Nelson always drove. McCabe took the notes and snapped the pictures.

That first night, they received a tip from one of Nelson's growing portfolio of CIs. There was going to be a sit-down at an Italian restaurant, including key members of the Colombo Family, the most violent and unpredictable of New York's Five Families.

This was late 1970s Carroll Gardens, long before it became the gentrified district it is today. Not as beset by the blight besieging many New York neighborhoods during the period, Carroll Gardens was both a staunch Italian-American enclave and a stronghold of organized crime.

The decline of manufacturing, especially in nearby Gowanus and Red Hook, drove a general sense of economic dread, high unemployment feeding the local gangs a steady stream of neighborhood corner flunkies.[24]

Nelson navigated the narrow street clogged with late-model, gas-guzzling sedans, crossing over the polluted Gowanus Canal, which has been contaminated since the Civil War. He drove a Plymouth Gran Fury, a curious choice for a surveillance vehicle.

The Plymouth Gran Fury was popular with law enforcement during the 1970s and 1980s for its combination of performance, reliability, and cost-effectiveness, equipped with those powerful V8 engines. Reinforced suspension systems and heavy-duty brakes handled the punishing wear-and-tear of high-speed driving on New York's pot-holed blacktop. Plymouth even offered a "Police Package" for the Gran Fury featuring heavy-duty cooling systems to handle both extended idling and high-speed pursuits, upgraded electrical systems for sirens, radios, and emergency lighting, and, of course, heavy-duty tires and wheels.

But everything about the Plymouth Gran Fury screamed, "*Look at me, I'm a cop!!*"

So for surveillance?

Actually, the Plymouth Gran Fury gave Nelson and McCabe exactly the conspicuousness they wanted.

"We were surveilling locations frequented by organized crime figures, and we certainly were not hiding," Nelson says. "We wanted our presence to be known, to be felt. We wanted them to see us, so we could then see how they reacted to seeing us, how they behaved, who they spoke to, who they deferred to."

Sometimes later, but rarely, Nelson didn't drive the Gran Fury. The FBI gave him the even more obvious Ford Crown Victoria Police Interceptor, a formidable four-door, body-on-frame sedan Ford manufactured from 1992 to 2011, the first police car version of the Ford Crown Victoria.

Nelson knew what he was doing by slow-rolling that cop-mobile up Carroll Street eastbound toward 3rd Avenue with the instantly

24. Zukin, Sharon. 2011. Naked City: The Death and Life of Authentic Urban Places. OUP USA

recognizable Kenny McCabe riding shotgun with his notepad and camera.

"We heard that the dinner meeting of Colombo Family members was taking place at Monte's Restaurant on that block," Nelson recalls.

Monte's Venetian Room was one of dozens of Brooklyn restaurants favored by organized crime figures to take over a backroom for *"family"* gatherings. It was the type of place where they felt safe, in control.

Located a block away from the ancient Our Lady of Peace Church on Carroll Street, Monte's sits on a somewhat sleepy block lined with brick-front homes, the type where people used to sit out all night on their stoops. There are a couple of parking lots, some quiet, small-scale industrial buildings.[25]

They say Frank Sinatra used to sing at Monte's, and Joe Torre and Joe Pepitone were known to swing by. Leona "Queen of Mean" Helmsley brought her dog down one night (though it's not clear if it was the Maltese Trouble she left twelve million dollars in trust when she died). James Caan and Danny Aiello ate at Montes, and one night Sammy Davis Jr. showed up and showed out with a spontaneous concert that lasted well into the early morning hours.

Gotham's movers and shakers aside, ever since the notorious Gallo brothers became regulars (all three: Joe, Larry, and Albert), the spot had been a regular haunt for the Colombos. Monte's is so Brooklyn gangster authentic that it even served as the setting for not one but two Mob-themed movies: *Prizzi's Honor* in 1985 and the 1990 film *Men of Respect*, starring local legend John Turturro. In 2008, after more than a century in business, Monte's served its final cheesecake on Carroll Street.

With McCabe readying his camera, about a block away, Nelson stopped for the traffic light on the corner of 3rd Avenue, right in front of the Diplomat Social Club, another notorious Colombo Family hangout. In fact, for a time the Diplomat was the de facto headquarters for Carmine "the Snake" Persico, the Colombo

---

25. Justice, Peter. "The Life and Times of Monte's Venetian Room." Carroll Gardens-Cobble Hill, NY Patch. September 7, 2011. https://patch.com/new-york/carrollgardens/the-life-and-times-of-montes-venetian-roo

Family boss, after he was released from prison and assumed the throne.

On any given evening at the Diplomat, you could cross paths with a revolving cast of Colombos: Carmine, when he was out of prison; his brother Alphonse "Ally Boy" Persico; Gennaro "Jerry" Langella, future underboss; Hugh MacIntosh, one of the Family's primary enforcers; soldier Carmine "Turi" Franzese, nephew to former underboss John "Sonny" Franzese; and pretty much anybody who was part of the Persico faction or had dealings with them.

"Suddenly, I heard a loud bang on the rear passenger fender of my car," Nelson recalls.

Then someone yelled out, "Hey, *cazzo!*" an Italian expletive for a male body part (let's just say, not the thumb).

"I knew that word well," Nelson says. "And the first thought that popped into my head was that some brazen guy was giving us a hard time because he knew we were cops from the type of vehicle I was driving."

Instead, this guy, all smiles, brashly approaches McCabe on the passenger side, lets out a big belly laugh, and says, "Hey, Kenny, whatcha doin'? Who *youse* looking for? *Youse* looking for me?"

Nelson knew that laugh and that voice: Colombo enforcer Greg Scarpa, who'd just exited the Diplomat. Scarpa, also known as the Grim Reaper, was a murderous soldier and, by conflicting accounts, a capo in the Colombo Family or just the guy pulling the strings.

Born in 1928, Scarpa became infamous for his violent nature and his improbably long tenure in organized crime during which he suspiciously evaded lengthy incarceration (more than three decades active, he spent only twenty-five days behind bars).

Operating out of the Wimpy Boys Social Club on 13th Avenue, Scarpa had his hand in everything: extortion, racketeering, gambling, armed robbery, murder-for-hire, murder-for-revenge, murder-for-minor infractions, and even drug trafficking. Scarpa went on to be a central figure in the internal Third Colombo Family War. He is believed to have been responsible for dozens of murders, from rival mobsters to suspected informants to even an innocent cocktail waitress.

"If we were looking for you, Greg," McCabe quipped, "you'd already be in cuffs."

Scarpa let out another one of those big laughs just as the red light at 3rd Avenue turned green. Nelson drove on.

Then McCabe made a stunning revelation, one that would one day rock the organized crime landscape and inspire several books and a Hollywood film, *By Any Means*, with Scarpa played by Mark Wahlberg.

Kenny knew Scarpa had a big secret.

"I said to Kenny that Scarpa obviously knows you pretty well," Nelson remembers. "Kenny then replied that 'he should also know me pretty well because he's a high-level FBI informant.'"

This is what made Scarpa so successful—and so deadly: his double life as a confidential informant for the FBI, providing information about the Mafia while continuing his violent machinations within the Colombo Family. Scarpa's secret dealings with the FBI spanned back to his involvement in the investigation of the murders of civil rights leaders in Mississippi during the 1960s.

According to longtime Scarpa girlfriend Linda Schiro and other sources, the FBI enlisted Scarpa to help locate missing civil rights workers Andrew Goodman, James Chaney, and Michael Schwerner. Agents believed the men had been murdered but couldn't find their bodies. Scarpa, known for using tactics the FBI couldn't legally employ, was seen as a potential solution, according to the allegations.

Scarpa supposedly beat Lawrence Byrd—a TV salesman and covert member of the Ku Klux Klan—into revealing the location of the bodies.

The FBI has never officially confirmed this account.

"I was astounded," Nelson remembers. "First of all, I didn't know at the time that Scarpa was an FBI informant. But what really amazed me was that Kenny *did* know."

The true identities of FBI informants were so tightly guarded that even other FBI agents did not generally identify their informants in the office, Nelson explains. "I was learning that I was not the only agent who trusted Kenny," Nelson says. "Someone in my office had revealed Scarpa's relationship with the FBI to him. It was even somewhat embarrassing that Kenny knew more about certain secretive matters within the FBI than I did.

"I realized on that evening that Kenny McCabe and I were going to be really good friends," Nelson recalls. Nelson and McCabe resumed their ride to prowl multiple social clubs. "Kenny pointed out and named dozens of mobsters to me, most of whom I'd never seen or heard of before. He seemed to know every single one of them and could identify them at a distance."

McCabe carried binoculars with him but rarely used them.

"It didn't take long for me to also start to recognize them by name, although I could never master their personal and criminal histories as Kenny McCabe could, so easily," Nelson says.

Afterwards, Anthony Nelson became a regular presence at the McCabe household.

"My dad loved Anthony Nelson, which really jumps out if you knew Kenny McCabe because he wasn't like that, at all, with anybody," says Kenny "Duke" McCabe Jr. "My dad was different. He was very family-oriented, so his life was centered on both his job and his family. There were very few people in his life with whom he was close, and nobody was closer to him than Anthony Nelson.

"They had a powerful bond that was obvious. Anthony was like his right hand and vice versa. They just complemented each other so well."

One of Duke's earliest memories of Anthony Nelson, and certainly one that stands out from his childhood, has nothing to do with gangsters and stakeouts.

Nelson set up a home computer in the McCabe home.

"I would say this had to be about 1985, making me eight years old, and I have such a clear memory of that day," Duke shares. "Anthony not only set up a computer in my house, but he then showed me and my three sisters how to use it. So from very early on, I saw him as someone who had these special technical skills, always savvy with electronics, which of course as a kid I thought was pretty cool."

This was a big deal for the McCabe children. Nelson replaced the family typewriter with the Commodore 64, listed in the Guinness World Records as the highest-selling single computer model of all time, which sold upwards of seventeen million units.[26]

Outside the home, though, McCabe relentlessly stalked organized crime locations, even when Nelson was not around.

These ride-alongs sometimes coincided with Duke's basketball away schedule.

Duke was a star player for Xaverian High School in the 1990s, the perennial basketball powerhouse in Southwestern Brooklyn that is part of the competitive New York State Catholic High School Athletic Association. He is a member of the Xaverian Basketball Athletic Hall of Fame.

"So, every time I had a game or practice, anywhere, maybe in Harlem or out in Queens, I knew that we were going to swing by any of the organized crime social clubs and bars in the area," Duke remembers.

At times, Kenny McCabe would hand his son a pad and pen so that as he took the pictures, young Duke would write down the license plate numbers. "I got to know how valuable that work was because my dad would explain who was who and what was going on, whether he was doing surveillance for a case or preparing for an upcoming trial," Duke says.

"I remember one time, we were outside a club and I wrote down the license plate number and my dad took the pictures," Duke shares. "Then, when this guy, this member of organized crime, went to trial, he testified that he had no knowledge of this club, said he never even stepped foot in the club, and didn't have any connections to the criminals who frequented the establishment." Duke elaborates, "But at the trial, my dad was able to pull out the

26. Edwards, Benji. "Inside the Commodore 64." PCWorld. November 4, 2008, https://www.pcworld.com/article/531679/comm64.html

pictures that put him at that club, and put the others at the club. And then he also had pictures of the guy's car, with license plate and the front of the club clearly visible."

In fact, the first time a young Duke McCabe saw the inside of a courtroom was when his father testified.

It was for the Pizza Connection case.

"I was engrossed sometimes in what my father was doing, simply by riding along with him," Duke adds. "I was around that surveillance work pretty much my entire life, and I remember. I always knew how important my father's work was and how valuable the surveillance they did was to the war against organized crime."

CHAPTER TWELVE

"Coincidence is God's way of remaining anonymous," Albert Einstein famously said.

Anthony Nelson does not believe in coincidences.

For Special Agents, suspicious by nature, skeptical by necessity, coincidences are too … convenient.

So when the universe actually tries to tell them something, it takes a bit to sink in.

There was something in the air that summer of '77. Extreme heat and humidity plagued a New York City struggling with high crime, rising unemployment, and social turmoil.

Then, lightning strikes on Con Edison power lines in Westchester County, crippling critical power lines, plunged eight million New Yorkers into darkness on July 13. The outage lasted twenty-five unforgettable hours of widespread looting, arson, and civil unrest, particularly in the city's poorest neighborhoods.

During the blackout, more than 1,600 stores were looted and over a thousand fires were started, prompting the largest mass arrest in New York history, as roughly 3,700 people were detained. The Blackout of '77 only worsened spiking categories of crime, especially those with organized crime connections, such as armed robbery, hijacking, auto theft, and counterfeiting.

That same evening, Kenny McCabe was barreling headlong through Brooklyn with no streetlights, rushing to an emergency not related to the unfolding chaos.

"The night that big blackout rocked NYC, I was born," Duke McCabe says. "My father dropped my mother off at Methodist Hospital and left because he was concerned about all the trouble in the city. He also had to get back to my three sisters, who were eight, seven, and three years old at the time."

Less than a week after the city emerged from the darkness, the partially nude body of nineteen-year-old Cherie Golden was found stuffed under the dashboard of a stolen Lincoln Continental abandoned near the juncture of Louis Avenue and Fran Court in the Gerritsen Beach section of Brooklyn.[27]

Cherie, missing since the previous Wednesday evening, was discovered on July 25 with three gunshot wounds to the head. Her disappearance coincided with the murder of her boyfriend, John W. Quinn.

Of course, those homicides were connected.

According to law enforcement officials, Quinn, thirty-five, a resident of Farmingdale, Long Island, was under investigation by the Nassau District Attorney's Office in connection with a $52.5 million securities theft. He was married and the father of six children. His body was found near the Fresh Kills landfill on Staten Island, dressed in pajamas with his hands tied behind his back, approximately two and a half hours after he had picked up Cherie Golden. She was living with her parents in Brooklyn's Flatbush neighborhood.

Police reported that Quinn had been shot once with a handgun.

Piecing together the double homicides, investigators linked them as unsanctioned killings committed by the DeMeo Crew. Cherie was collateral damage. Quinn, her boyfriend, was the primary target.

Quinn's sin?

He ran a car-theft ring that competed with DeMeo's operation and was suspected of cooperating with law enforcement.

---

27. "BODY IN CAR IDENTIFIED AS BROOKLYN WOMAN, 19." New York Times. July 26, 1977. https://www.nytimes.com/1977/07/26/archives/body-in-car-identified-as-brooklyn-woman-19.html

Demonstrating just how brazen the DeMeo Crew was becoming, the bodies were discarded in locations where they were *meant* to be discovered, to send a message warning against cooperating with authorities.

During the 1985 murder and racketeering trial of Gambino captain Nino Gaggi, eight witnesses—including the prosecution's key cooperator, Dominick Montiglio (Nino Gaggi's nephew)—testified about how John Quinn was targeted for execution by Gaggi's faction after being summoned before a Long Island grand jury.

Joseph Bennett, a convicted car thief, testified that about a week before the day Quinn's body was discovered, Bennett was approached by members of the DeMeo Crew. They wanted his help in setting up Quinn. Bennett was Quinn's cousin.

Bennett said he was offered twenty thousand dollars to arrange the ambush—on the condition that he also lure Quinn's girlfriend. When prosecutors asked why they needed to die, Bennett explained bluntly that there were suspicions John Quinn was cooperating with law enforcement.

"John had gone before a Nassau County grand jury and wasn't in jail," Bennett said. "The rule of thumb is, if you weren't in jail, you had talked."

Montiglio also testified that Cherie Golden's murder had unsettled Gambino boss Paul Castellano.

"Mr. Castellano asked him why this girl Cherie was killed," stated Montiglio, later a witness for the federal government. "My uncle told him she was involved with Quinn and that Quinn was suspected of cooperating with the law—so they both had to be dealt with."

Before the murders, Nelson says, a great deal of the counterfeit and stolen New York State Motor Vehicle documents trafficked by Quinn had already been distributed to factions of several organized crime families.

"At one point in time, starting in 1977, several subjects from different OC families began using this fake documentation to rent storefronts," Nelson says. "They presented themselves as legitimate businesses they created using the DMV documents, and they also rented trucks, mostly U-Hauls, using counterfeit driver's licenses and registrations."

As Nelson explains, this not only signaled a move by several organized crime factions into lucrative "bust-out schemes," but also an escalation of violence, with the DeMeo Crew at the center of the action. "Instead of sticking a gun in the face of a truck driver, they ordered tractor-trailer loads of electronics, food items, and anything else of value," Nelson explains. "When the trailer loads were brought to these 'businesses,' COD, they used counterfeit bank checks to pay for them. Hours later, they would close up the storefronts and take off with the products."

By early 1978, Nelson was conducting surveillance almost daily on a suspected bookmaker and fence named Harold Rothenberg, who had phony DMV documents linked to Quinn. Nelson learned that he had already stolen, along with a group of others, several tractor-trailer loads of merchandise.

As Nelson tracked his target near a bus stop on Ocean Avenue and Avenue Y, he noticed a new pattern, something unrelated and out of the ordinary. "Each day I conducted surveillance, I saw a young woman several doors away exit her home and walk to work," Nelson says. "I became fascinated by her. I thought she was beautiful."

Not long after, on an evening in May 1978, Nelson went to meet and brief backup agents who were assigned to cover him at the undercover warehouse on Union Street in Red Hook. The agents met at a restaurant in Park Slope named Snooky's Pub.

Traffic was light at the bar about six p.m. at this 7th Avenue staple, famed for its reasonably priced 20-ounce "house special" steak dinner with German-fried potatoes.

Snooky's gained notoriety as one of the first establishments to have an integrated wait staff and to welcome gay couples. Sprinkled among the regulars said to have dined at the spot were New York City icons such as Shirley MacLaine, Paul Aster, Pete Hamill, Reverend Al Sharpton, Betty Shabazz, and former Governor Hugh Carey.

"I never usually had dinner at that time, nor would I ever normally be in a bar then," Nelson says.

That was when something happened that the suspicious and skeptical Special Agent could not explain.

A coincidence?

Perhaps.

"A few minutes after I arrived at Snooky's, which was on the complete opposite end of Brooklyn from where Rothenberg lived, that same woman from that same bus stop walked in to have dinner with a friend of hers," Nelson says. "And then, she sat down right next to me at the bar."

Adding to the mystery, Syndee Liemer says that it was highly unusual for her to be at Snooky's that evening, as she had only gone to restaurants in Park Slope on a couple of prior occasions. "I sat at the first vacant area of the bar to order a drink and to await my friend," Syndee says. Anthony Nelson was standing at the bar right next to where she ordered her drink.

"I was immediately attracted to him because he was so friendly and handsome," Syndee says. "I don't recall him telling me that night that he was an FBI agent. I did, however, get the impression that he was involved in something mysterious, but not illegal. It was just a feeling that I couldn't explain."

Nelson laughs. "She didn't know that she was the same woman I had seen, actually admired every day, watching Rothenberg's residence in Sheepshead Bay. We started talking and she gave me her telephone number."

This was not exactly standard operating procedure for FBI Special Agents conducting team briefings.

"I was glad that he asked me for my telephone number," Syndee says. "About two weeks later, he called me and asked me to go to dinner. That's when I learned he was an FBI agent and had been waiting for several of his agent friends to arrive at Snooky's on the night we first met."

At the time, Anthony Nelson was not on the market for a wife.

"Although I admired Syndee from a distance while conducting surveillance of Rothenberg, I was living through an exciting period of my life," Nelson says. "The notion of being married was so remote to me that I never even thought about it."

But that first brief conversation at Snooky's sparked something in the young Nelson. "After she left, I remember thinking that if I ever did decide to get married, she was exactly the type of woman I envisioned as being my wife," Nelson says fondly. Not long after, they had dinner.

At about the same time Anthony Nelson was getting to know his future wife, Harold Rothenberg and an individual named Artie Sonenshein were both shot to death and dumped in a car on the Belt Parkway in the 61st Precinct. These were just two of the many murders associated with the DeMeo Crew during its brutal run, a body count disputed to be between one hundred and two hundred victims.

That evening, though, was the start of something special. "It turned out that Syndee had similar interests to me," Nelson says. "Mainly, we loved to take long road trips up and down the East Coast, stopping to explore less-traveled areas. Our favorite state to visit was, and still is, Maine."

Syndee grounded Anthony and brought some normalcy to his often chaotic life in law enforcement. "Every moment I spent with Syndee was an escape from the world of evil in which I lived," he says.

After dating Syndee for a year, Anthony proposed, following a dinner along picturesque Sheepshead Bay.

The two were married on August 31, 1980, at the Chapel at the United Nations, a modernist space designed by William Lescaze on the east side of Manhattan, known for its stained glass and altar. Even today, it remains a popular venue for weddings, especially those with interfaith or international aspects.

"We both had large families but did not have a traditional wedding," Nelson says. "Still, a large number of family and friends joined us. My uncle, John Nocera, served as my best man."

Of course, the young couple honeymooned in Maine, with an itinerary featuring at least one activity not typical for newlyweds.

"I taught Syndee how to shoot a handgun on our honeymoon." Nelson laughs. "It wasn't exactly the most romantic thing."

The couple visited Old Orchard Beach and Anthony Nelson introduced himself to the town's chief of police. "He was gracious enough to show us areas on the outskirts of the town where we could shoot.

"I don't know how such a series of events could have occurred, but because of Quinn's counterfeit DMV documents and the DeMeo Crew's car theft operation," Nelson says, "I would not have met my wife."

The two have been happily married for more than four decades.

Coincidences sure can be funny things.

CHAPTER THIRTEEN

By 1978, Anthony Nelson and Kenny McCabe were more than just colleagues.

"Within a couple of months after first meeting Kenny McCabe, we'd become the best of friends," Nelson says. "I never met anyone who so closely shared my likes and dislikes, or a man with such high values. He impressed me like no one ever had with his honesty, integrity, and his love for his family.

"Kenny was like a brother to me when we were off-duty, and he was often my partner on the street."

At least one night a week, the two lawmen wound their way through the underside of New York City, shadowing as many LCN social clubs as possible. Even solo, Nelson and McCabe routinely cruised by Mob-infested locations on their ways home from work.

Soon, it was not unusual for them to prowl two or more nights a week, always in Nelson's Gran Fury, Nelson driving, McCabe riding shotgun.

It was like riding along with a seasoned play-by-play announcer.

"Kenny's ability to recall faces, names, dates, and details was nothing short of remarkable," Nelson says. "He also had the vision of an eagle, but surprisingly, he was somewhat colorblind."

Camaraderie is one thing. But collaboration like this was not commonplace among law enforcement agencies in previous decades.

This was changing.

The Department of Justice established Organized Crime Strike Forces nationwide in the late 1960s as part of a congressional effort led by Senator Robert F. Kennedy.

Formally, the Organized Crime Strike Force program of the Department of Justice Criminal Division empowered units across the country to pursue racketeering syndicates, including the Italian-American Mafia, major drug gangs, the Irish Mob, the Russian Mafia, and more.[28] These new partnerships combined representatives from multiple agencies invited to regularly scheduled meetings at the local US Attorney's Offices to share intelligence.

Kenny McCabe, assigned by the NYPD to the Kings County District Attorney's Squad, was designated as the Brooklyn DA's representative on the federal task force in the Eastern District of New York. The strike force was headed by Thomas Puccio.

Five years older than Nelson and also hailing from Brooklyn, Puccio was a successful trial lawyer who served in the Justice Department, notably as both investigator and prosecutor in the high-profile ABSCAM case—a late-1970s-to-early-1980s FBI sting that resulted in bribery and corruption convictions for seven members of Congress and several others. Puccio later became a prominent criminal defense attorney, representing notable clients like Claus von Bülow. Puccio passed away from leukemia in 2012 at the age of sixty-seven.

"Kenny and I had already been operating as partners on the street, even though we worked for different agencies," Nelson says. "However, his assignment to the relatively new US Attorney's Office Strike Force allowed me to work with him on a more formal basis."

By the latter part of 1978, Nelson began receiving intel from confidential informants about organized crime's involvement in the distribution of pornography, as well as its infiltration of topless bars. Investigations revealed organized crime generated substantial profits from blockbuster porn titles such as *Deep Throat*, *The Devil in Miss Jones*, and *Wet Rainbow*.

---

28. "Organized Crime: Issues Concerning Strike Forces." https://www.ojp.gov/ncjrs/virtual-library/abstracts/organized-crime-issues-concerning-strike-forces

Supposedly, on a production budget of only twenty-five thousand dollars, *Deep Throat* alone grossed six hundred million, a figure difficult to substantiate, as organized crime bagmen collected the box office receipts directly. However, adjusting for inflation, dollar for dollar, makes it the most profitable film ever produced.

More Mafioso followed, most prominently Robert DiBernardo, considered one of the rare individuals to have been inducted into the Mafia without committing a murder.

DiBernardo, aligned with the DeCavalcante crime Family, in the late 1960s, purchased the softcore pornography distributor Star Distributors. DiBernardo used Star as a front to sell hardcore pornography across various formats to adult entertainment businesses concentrated around Times Square. He played a central role in commissioning many of the hardcore films produced in New York during the so-called Golden Age of Porn. He maintained control over the industry by either coercing competitors into shutting down or absorbing them into his expanding network.

DiBernardo eventually became affiliated with the Gambino Family, mainly due to his connection with fellow pornographer and Gambino capo Ettore Zappi, who is believed to have sponsored his induction into the Family.

An investigation by the *New York Times* revealed that Mafia members and their financial backing permeated all levels of the porn trade, from funding the production and distribution of adult films to the distribution and ownership of theaters. In cases where organized crime figures didn't hold a direct financial stake in a film—such as *Behind the Green Door* and *The Life and Times of Xaviera Hollander*—they resorted to piracy, illegally duping and distributing films to make millions of dollars without investing a dime.[29]

"Some OC Families, as well as independents like the Westies [the Irish gang from Hell's Kitchen], were vying for control over this industry centered in and around Times Square," Nelson says.

29. Gage, Nicholas. "Organized Crime Reaps Huge Profits From Dealing in Pornographic Films." New York Times. October 12, 1975. https://www.nytimes.com/1975/10/12/archives/organized-crime-reaps-huge-profits-from-dealing-in-pornographic.html

"Linked to the Westies, you had Roy DeMeo's Crew involved, and of course, Genovese capo Matthew 'Matty the Horse' Ianniello was a major player in the porn rackets."

Nicknamed "The Horse" for his imposing build, Ianniello spent over fifty years shaking down bar owners, adult entertainment operators, and topless dancers for protection money. His influence was a driving force behind Times Square's descent into a seedy hub of peep shows and pornography throughout the 1960s and '70s.

The area became the center of American porn theaters starting in the late 1950s. Known as "the Deuce," the two-block stretch of 42nd Street between Broadway and 8th Avenue near Times Square, saw its old, lavish vaudeville theaters retrofitted into "porn palaces" like Peepland and Show World.

Droves of sex workers patrolled street corners and alleyways. The opening of the Port Authority Bus Terminal on 42nd Street and 8th Avenue attracted waves of wayward teenage boys and girls who crashed into the sex trade. Massage parlors, basically brothels, exploded, while camera shops and arcades transformed into pornographic book emporiums and sleazy video stores.

By late 1978, Nelson developed a cooperating informant named Robert Fimbel, who managed the popular topless bar Adam and Eve, located on East 45th Street and Lexington Avenue.

One evening, an individual who identified himself as "Joe Priest" appeared at Adam and Eve, along with his muscle, a thug named Georgie, Nelson recalls.

"Joe Priest told Fimbel that he'd be coming by every Wednesday night to collect three hundred dollars per week," Nelson says. "He warned if the money wasn't forthcoming, heads would be busted." Georgie flashed a handgun at Fimbel to let him know he meant business. Fimbel began making payments to this Joe Priest, and the extortion went on for months.

Eventually, Fimbel wanted out. He decided that testifying against Joe Priest and Georgie gave him a better future than continuing with the exorbitant extortion payments.

Nelson wired up Fimbel with a Kel transmitter and a Nagra tape recorder to monitor his conversations. "These devices were so primitive compared with current technology," Nelson says. "And they were risky, because they were so bulky and could easily be detected on one's person with just a quick pat down."

Nelson surveilled Adam and Eve, with the assistance of other FBI agents, on the days Joe Priest dropped by to collect the extortion money.

"But I still did not know the true identity of Joe Priest or that of Georgie," he says. He asked around, even discussed this case with Joel Cohen, the Eastern District Strike Force prosecutor.

Nothing. Nada. No one heard of this mysterious Joe Priest.

Then Nelson brought the name up in conversation with Kenny McCabe.

"In less time than it would take today to type the name into Google and click, Kenny told me that Joe Priest was most likely Joseph Calder, a Lucchese Family associate who lived on Carroll Street in Brooklyn," Nelson says.

Soon, Kenny joined Nelson and FBI Special Agent Arthur "Artie" Ruffels on regular surveillance at Adam and Eve, waiting for Joe Priest to return.

Ruffels was another legendary member of law enforcement from that gritty era. Nearly fifteen years Nelson's senior, Ruffels served in the US Navy before working as an art teacher for ten years, and *then* joined the FBI, where he logged twenty years of distinguished service. This included time as the case agent for the FBI's Organized Crime Unit, heavily involved with investigating the DeMeo Crew, among many other successful assignments.

In fact, investigating the Westies, Ruffels flipped high-ranking enforcers Francis "Mickey" Featherstone and Billy Beattie, who both entered witness protection and helped take down the gang.

The Westies were the most notorious and final generation of Irish-American gangsters in Hell's Kitchen, on Manhattan's West Side, peaking during the 1970s and 1980s. Unlike the Mafia with its rigid hierarchy and Omertà code of silence, the Westies were loose cannons, loosely organized, and followed no ancient rules.

Their penchant for brutality and wanton violence found a kindred spirit in Roy DeMeo while attracting media and law enforcement like flies.

"Kenny not only positively identified Joe Priest as Joe Calder, but also told me that Joe Priest had a brother known as Julius 'Red' Calder," Nelson remembers. "Kenny even told me he heard that Joe Priest got his nickname from the fact that he had attended a seminary and actually intended, at one point in his life, to become a Catholic priest."

With a positive ID linking the extortion plot to organized crime, the FBI set up an elaborate undercover sting. "We sent word back to Joe Priest and Red Calder that Adam and Eve was 'our' place," Nelson says, posing as a competing crew.

This ploy prompted sit-downs at both the Seafood Palace in Brooklyn and the 19th Hole Bar between undercover operatives posing as porn players to meet with Red Calder and Lucchese soldier Thomas "Big Tom" DiDonato.

The 19th Hole, located across the street from the Dyker Beach Golf Course (hence its name) was a notorious Mob bar for years run by Christopher "Christie Tick" Furnari, a Lucchese Family mainstay.

"During the sit-down at the 19th Hole bar, Big Tom warned FBI undercover agents Jules Bonavolonta and Lewis Schiliro that Adam and Eve already belonged to them and to stay away from the joint," Nelson says.

A native of Newark, New Jersey, Bonavolonta served more than six years as a Green Beret in the US Special Forces during the Vietnam War, returning to the States a highly decorated veteran. He was awarded the Silver Star, Bronze Star with V for Valor (1st Oak Leaf Cluster), Purple Heart, Air Medal (1st Oak Leaf Cluster), and the Vietnamese Cross of Gallantry.

Upon Bonavolonta's return, he began his twenty-three-year career of exceptional service to the FBI. As chief of the Organized Crime and Narcotics Division of the FBI's New York City Office, he played a pivotal role in securing convictions that made the 1980s the FBI's most successful decade in combating organized crime.

Likewise, Lewis Schiliro enjoyed a long, distinguished career at the FBI, ultimately retiring as the assistant director in charge responsible for the supervision, management, and leadership of over 2,300 Special Agents and support personnel in all areas of criminal, national security, and international and domestic terrorism. Schiliro went on to serve as a board member of the Hain Celestial Group, Inc. and as an adjunct professor of criminal justice at Wilmington College. He was also an adjunct professor at Fordham University Law School.

On October 31, 1979, after believing that Big Tom had resolved the dispute, Joseph Calder, aka Joe Priest, returned to Adam and Eve to resume collecting his extortion payments. After picking up another three-hundred-dollar payment, he was arrested by Nelson and other FBI agents as he exited the bar.

"At the same time, we also arrested Julius Calder, George Monge, and Thomas DiDonato, all organized crime associates who were waiting in a car outside the bar," Nelson says.

As FBI Special Agent George Hanna went to arrest Monge, he spotted Monge's hands on a gun tucked in his waistband.

"Hanna lunged at the loaded handgun in Monge's waistband so quickly, he tore part of Monge's pants off him," Nelson says. "A TV video crew began laughing hysterically as they were filming live coverage of a new disco grand opening a few doors away from Adam and Eve."

All four of the Lucchese crew members were convicted on federal charges related to the extortion.[30]

Red Calder was subsequently murdered in Dom Carbucci's social club on June 2, 1990.

According to informants, one of the shooters was Joseph "JoJo" Truncale. Calder had made the fatal mistake of breaking and entering the home of Robert "Bobby" Amuso, brother of Vittorio "Little Vic" Amuso, eventual boss of the Lucchese Family.

---

30. US District Court Federal Complaint – Joseph 'Joe Priest' Calder – Adam and Eve Extortion

CHAPTER FOURTEEN

A war is not won with a single battle.

But who knew crime fighting involves so little fighting?

The late 1970s marked a turning point in law enforcement's assault on the Italian-American Mafia.

But this was not glamorous work.

"When people think of the FBI, they picture agents kicking down doors," says Maria Scopello, a former FBI Language Specialist. "What they might not realize is there's a lot of hard, tedious work that goes into investigations."

During Scopello's time supporting the FBI's C-7 Squad, the organized crime drug enforcement task force, including the squad specializing in Sicilian heroin traffickers, she processed thousands of Title III interceptions to decipher thick-accented dialects (i.e., Sicilian, Neapolitan, and Calabrese).

"There were so many cases being investigated, so much important work," Scopello says. "We're helping prosecutors prepare for upcoming trials as we're already working on other cases. And all roles are important, because the break can come from anywhere. Even running a tag could change everything."

Scopello even obtained a New York State real estate license to reduce suspicion when leasing apartments and houses needed during a two-year sting operation. "Everything was moving so quickly, with agents often needing a location on the fly," she explains. "Agents and language specialists, including me, used one of the residences. We posed as tenants and gathered evidence of illegal activities. Some of these rentals were only a few blocks from my home in Bensonhurst, making it a bit uncomfortable."

Task forces were forming. Cross-agency collaboration was growing. Old homicides were being reexamined, predicates proven, and cases being built, sometimes one wiretapped tip or CI conversation at a time.

"I developed quality informants and had a virtually unlimited amount of FBI money to keep them actively reporting on criminal activity," Nelson says. "Kenny McCabe, on the other hand, lacked financial resources from the NYPD to maintain high-level informants, but he knew every wiseguy in New York City."

Slowly, the make-up of these complex underworld enterprises was emerging, knitting together hundreds of inducted members, thousands of street operatives, and even more unofficial associates.

And as if all of that were not hard enough to track, assassinations, hospitalizations, and incarcerations constantly reshuffled the deck as crews rose and fell across the five boroughs.

This incestuous web was woven through many clubhouses within close proximity of each other.

"That's why Kenny had such an impact, for so long," Nelson says. "He was like a personal computer which, by the way, was not even available to the general public at that time."

Nelson received informant tips about upcoming Mafia meetings, and he and McCabe would conduct less-than-discreet surveillance. "We quickly became an annoyance to members of all the Families," Nelson says. "But many wiseguys ignored our presence because they didn't appreciate the significance of the information we were gathering. And by then, they were accustomed to seeing us parked outside their meeting locations."

Maybe they'd cruise Paul "Paulie Zac" Zaccaria's social club at 7716 18th Avenue, make a stop by the Bonanno's Banner Social Club at 2009 72nd Street, before shooting over to scan for Colombo plates outside the Tazza Villa del Golfo at 7021 20th Avenue.

One evening, they parked outside the West Side Civic Club, a Gambino club at 8009 17th Avenue. From there, they tailed a

Cadillac full of wiseguys to a new social club, named Veterans and Friends, which had recently opened on 86th Street, just off Bay 7th Street in Brooklyn, and just a block and a half from the Luccheses' 19th Hole bar.

Before long, they noticed a new face outside this fledgling club, a middle-aged man not yet known to even the remarkable Kenny McCabe.

"This was very unusual since Kenny knew everyone, everywhere," Nelson says. "On those rare occasions when someone showed up that we didn't know, we'd just pull them over for a traffic infraction or some other offense to identify them."

That evening, the two lawmen noticed a few other interesting elements to the scene unfolding outside this new clubhouse.

For starters, this mystery man was in the company of Roy DeMeo and Dominick Montiglio, both Gambino operatives who were already on law enforcement's radar.

"More importantly, this middle-aged man we saw was being afforded a great deal of respect by the known wiseguys who were at the club that night," Nelson says. "But we really sat up when we saw that he was kissed on the cheek by Roy DeMeo and was ushered to a Cadillac that was parked nearby."

As the Cadillac door was respectfully opened for this enigmatic stone-faced player, Nelson and McCabe knew they'd stumbled onto a little-known power figure within the Gambino hierarchy.

Kenny jotted down the plate number. It was traced back to a company owned by Anthony Frank Gaggi, a Brooklyn businessman with operations throughout Canarsie and Southern Brooklyn.

It took some investigative legwork, but McCabe and Nelson uncovered the key. "It didn't take us long to put together that Anthony Gaggi, and Roy DeMeo's boss, 'Nino,' whom we had previously heard about, were one and the same person," Nelson says.

Moreover, Veterans and Friends was opened with the help of Dominick Montiglio, a former Green Beret in the United States Army, hence the "veterans and friends" moniker.

And Montiglio was actually Gaggi's nephew.

"At the time, many early events occurred involving Kenny McCabe and me, we had no idea of the magnitude of criminal activity that the DeMeo Crew was involved in and what was to ultimately follow concerning them. Therefore, when I first heard DeMeo's name, or Nino's name," Nelson says, "it was just another case to me and Kenny."

McCabe and Nelson were the first law enforcement officers to positively identify both Roy DeMeo and Anthony "Nino" Gaggi.

"In 1977, when I first met Kenny, he had already heard the name Roy DeMeo but didn't know much about him," Nelson clarifies. "He never knew the true identity of Nino until we observed Roy DeMeo and Dominick Montiglio kiss him and usher him to a Cadillac at Veterans and Friends that night. This encounter is well documented in *Murder Machine*, the genre-defining true-crime masterpiece penned by Gene Mustain and Jerry Capeci chronicling the DeMeo Crew's bloody reign.

The name "Nino" was known to some law enforcement entities, but no one knew his true identity until that evening, when Nelson and McCabe observed him and obtained his license plate number during surveillance.

"This was why it was so important to put that time in, work those clubs, develop informants and collect intelligence on the street. There was no other way but the hard way. We always went out in my FBI car. I always drove and Kenny always took photos and notes."

McCabe and Nelson disseminated the intel they gathered on the street to dozens of investigators and squads in their respective organizations, whether they were homicide details or FBI organized crime squads.

"But realize, Kenny and I didn't crawl under cars checking vehicle VIN numbers, collect physical evidence, or conduct interviews of homicide case witnesses," Nelson clarifies. "But the info we collected was used many times to associate people in criminal proceedings or in affidavits for search and wiretap warrants."

Very rarely was an arrest the result of a single person or informant.

"So, in many cases, I cannot tell you what statistical accomplishments resulted from our efforts," Nelson says. "Kenny also went out at times when I was not present. He would drive his personal Ford Pinto, which became very recognizable to most of the OC crews."

Nelson, while serving in an undercover capacity, was not always the case agent for the criminal transactions, so, in some instances, he was not involved in the outcomes. "I am humbled and proud to have served in the company of such courage and dedication during my years of service," Nelson adds. "These men and women made a difference, and far too many of them are not credited with their contributions."

Soon Nelson and McCabe's presence was definitely being felt on the streets, especially when the wiseguys spotted that damn Plymouth Gran Fury idling outside their clubs with a camera poking out the passenger side window.

Roland "Ron" Cadieux enjoyed a highly successful twenty-three-year career in law enforcement, including years as a high-profile NYPD detective. He worked his first organized crime case in Brooklyn's 10th Homicide in 1972.

Cadieux, along with Frank Pergola and his partner, NYPD Sergeant Joe Coffey, was part of the arrest team that put the cuffs on Gambino godfather Paul "Big Paul" Castellano in March 1984. That team also included Kenny McCabe. FBI Agents Artie Ruffels and Marilyn Lucht were also present.

Cadieux often accompanied Nelson and McCabe on their night rides.

"It wasn't just the rank and file; Anthony and Kenny were pulling over godfathers, rank didn't matter," Cadieux recalls. "And they'd always ask, 'What are you pulling me over for?' Kenny would say, 'Failed signal.' After a while, I said to Kenny, 'Do me a favor and tell them it's for speeding.'" Cadieux laughs. "C'mon, I'm embarrassed we're telling these wiseguys we're pulling them over just for signaling."

One early evening, the three lawmen driving in Nelson's FBI mobile cruised 86th Street between 14th and 15th Avenues, near multiple Mafia social clubs, when they stopped for a red light by a car dealership lot.

"We look over and you can see into the office of this dealership and it's crowded, like really crowded, just completely mobbed with all these wiseguys, who are clearly organized crime guys," Cadieux says. "All of a sudden, someone yells, 'McCabe!'"

"If I tell you all hell broke loose, maybe as many as fifty guys started tearing out of there, going out windows, side doors, back doors, running down side streets, jumping in cars, jumping over cars, jumping over fences, getting stuck, scrambling, and they're all trying to cover their faces." Cadieux laughs. "See, these guys know Kenny McCabe and they know Kenny McCabe knows them, and most of them are on parole," Cadieux says. "So just by being in the presence of other convicted criminals can easily violate their parole and send them back to prison."

Cadieux, Nelson, and McCabe exited the vehicle and walked over. McCabe then started loudly calling out name after name, while writing them down to later notify their parole officers.

"Anthony and I are just hysterical watching this scene play out, all these wiseguys tripping over each other and Kenny barking out their names," Cadieux says. "And he sure knew all their names. All of them. Every single one. What a scene."

"Kenny distributed our surveillance reports to a US parole officer named Mike Gillen, who started to violate the parole conditions for many of them for associating with known criminals," Nelson confirms.

Meanwhile, McCabe was also testifying at an increasing number of Fatico hearings. "The Fatico hearing is an opportunity for both sides, the prosecution and the defense, to present evidence that could influence the judge's decision on the defendant's sentence," Nelson explains.

"Kenny was an expert witness on so many trials, he became the go-to guy because he knew his way around that work like nobody else then or now," says retired NYPD Detective Tommy Dades. "Kenny singlehandedly did so much damage to organized crime, I don't think you could ever give him enough credit for his service."

Obviously, a Fatico hearing goes much differently when you can arm the prosecution with details that legitimately conflict with the mistruths presented by the defense.

"Kenny just had this photographic memory," Nelson says. "I know sometimes people say that and it's not entirely true. But I've seen it firsthand, over and over and over again. Kenny would never forget a face, or the time and the place that he had seen it.

"When they started realizing our surveillance was not so benign, more and more they'd scatter like bugs and hide their faces," Nelson says. "That day, we just happened upon an extraordinary number of them having a meeting at this dealership, but it became more frequent."

Cadieux recalls another episode driving with McCabe and Nelson. "We're driving and I spot this guy," Cadieux says. "I'm working a homicide that the guy's nephew committed. We pull him over. Kenny didn't know the other guy, so, of course, we stopped them for a failed signal.

"Kenny asks if we can look in the trunk, and he says okay," Cadieux says. However, the lawmen did not yet have probable cause to search this suspect. "So Kenny's bumping up real close to him with his body, I mean *real* close, using his body to feel him out and see if this guy's got a gun in the back of his pants," Cadieux says. "It was just so hilarious the way he was rubbing on him."

Occasionally, Nelson and McCabe attracted bigger fish.

"One day, Kenny McCabe and I were watching the Veterans and Friends club," Nelson recalls. "Unexpectedly, none other than the head of the Gambino crime Family, Paul Castellano himself, came over to my FBI car." He later learned that the club had been opened at the behest of Castellano, so the boss could assert more of a street presence in the heart of the Brooklyn faction of the Family, and with good reason.

By 1978, Paul Castellano had cemented his position at the top of the Gambino Family.

Born June 26, 1915, in Brooklyn's Bensonhurst neighborhood, Castellano joined the Mangano Family—the forerunner of the

Gambinos—in the 1940s. He climbed the ranks under boss Albert Anastasia, eventually becoming a caporegime. In 1932, his sister Catherine married their cousin Carlo Gambino, who later became boss.

In 1957, following Anastasia's murder and Gambino's rise, Castellano attended the infamous Apalachin summit, where police arrested sixty-one mobsters. He refused to testify before a grand jury and was sentenced to a year in prison for contempt.

Before Gambino died in 1976, he bypassed his underboss, Aniello "Neil" Dellacroce, naming Castellano his successor. Gambino believed Castellano's business savvy—particularly in white-collar crime—would take the Family to new heights. Dellacroce, jailed for tax evasion, was in no position to challenge the decision.

While Dellacroce accepted Castellano's succession, the deal effectively split the Gambino Family into two rival factions—Dellacroce's followers in Manhattan and Castellano's stalwarts in Brooklyn.

Although it was not a regular occurrence to see Castellano on 86th Street in Bensonhurst, he was making an effort to be more visible.

Throughout 1978, Castellano tightened his grip on the organization. He ordered the murder of Nicholas Scibetta, a volatile Gambino associate whose erratic behavior—fueled by drugs and alcohol—drew unwanted attention. Scibetta, the brother-in-law of future underboss Sammy "the Bull" Gravano, was killed with Gravano's reluctant approval after being warned by Frank DeCicco. That same year, Castellano authorized the killings of capo James Eppolito and his son after Eppolito sought permission to eliminate rival capo Anthony Gaggi. Castellano tipped off Gaggi instead, who, with DeMeo, murdered both men.

That February, Castellano secured a deal with the Westies, adding a stable of killers untraceable to the Mafia; they wanted Gambino protection. At a sit-down with Westies leader James Coonan, Castellano laid down the rules: "No more cowboy stuff. You're with us now. Any killings must go through us."

Castellano also formed a strategic alliance with the Cherry Hill Gambinos, Sicilian heroin traffickers in New Jersey, further bolstering his network of outside muscle.

McCabe quickly identified the Gambino kingpin to Nelson as the aging gangster approached the car.

"Castellano already knew Kenny from subpoenas Kenny had served upon him and Carlo Gambino," Nelson remembers. "Paul told us that it wasn't necessary to follow him. Rather than risk a traffic accident trying to conduct surveillance of him and his driver, Tommy Bilotti, he suggested we simply go to Ponte Vecchio, on 4th Avenue in Bay Ridge, where we would be able to find him within a few minutes." An overly confident Castellano smiled as he cut the curbside conversation short.

Soon, though, Castellano ceased being so smug, as more sightings of Nelson's Gran Fury filtered back to his table at Ponte Vecchio.

"Castellano's attitude changed when he started to realize how our seemingly benign observations were hurting his criminal activities," Nelson says. "And then he really didn't like it when word got back to him that we were having casual conversations on the street with some of his underlings."

The thousands of hours of surveillance by McCabe, Nelson, and hundreds of other agents and investigators began to knit together an unprecedented view of the vast interconnected web of organized crime.

Not solving for a single crime, but attempting to take down a series of massive criminal conspiracies.

To do that required work, hard work, tedious work to collect evidence and establish relationships, hierarchies, motives, plots.

A war is not won with a single battle.

And now, the tide was turning.

CHAPTER FIFTEEN

While car thief John Quinn had been murdered in 1977, well into 1978, many of his counterfeit Department of Motor Vehicles (DMV) documents were still being passed by organized crime figures. Moreover, legitimate DMV documents traced back to a burglary also started to surface in bust-out schemes.

"I had several open investigations alone, trying to determine where all these documents were being stored," Nelson says. "I was also trying to uncover who was printing the counterfeit bank checks that were an integral part of these bust-out schemes."

Through his confidential informants, Nelson learned some of the counterfeit bank checks were being distributed by a Genovese Family associate nicknamed "Fat Pete." Nelson believed that Fat Pete was the connection to the printer of the checks.

"As usual, no one on the street was able to positively identify Fat Pete for me, even though they had conducted criminal business with him," Nelson says. "The best I was able to piece together was his physical description and the fact that he lived on Bath Avenue in Brooklyn."

Of course, the one person able to identify Fat Pete was Kenny McCabe.

"Within a couple of weeks after Kenny gave me Fat Pete's last name," Nelson says. "His true identity was confirmed during a conversation intercepted in a vehicle bugged by the FBI."

After gathering enough incriminating information linking Fat Pete to the counterfeit checks and the bust-out schemes, Nelson obtained a federal grand jury subpoena ordering the gangster to appear at the FBI's Manhattan Office to provide his fingerprints and photographs.

Nelson and McCabe then headed over to serve Fat Pete at his residence on Bath Avenue in Brooklyn, which was a four-story brick building.

This is where things get a bit strange, even by South Brooklyn standards.

Nelson rang the bell at the apartment. After a few moments, he was greeted by an angry-sounding woman yelling out of the top-floor window in Italian, *"Cosa vuoi?"* or in English, "What do you want?"

"Siamo Poliziotti," Nelson responded. "I then explained to her in Italian that we were looking to speak with Pete."

He never got a chance to tell her that he had a subpoena before this belligerent woman shouted back at the top of her lungs, *"Pezzo di merda!"*

Apparently, she was not a fan of law enforcement. *"Pezzo di merda"* translates to "you piece of shit." The Italian insult was followed by a barrage of kitchenware raining down from a second-story window at the two lawmen.

With Nelson and McCabe ducking for cover, down came an avalanche of anything and everything this woman could get her hands on. When she ran out of pots and pans, the dishes, knives, forks, and spoons followed. Then, after a brief pause, a thick glass carafe exploded on the sidewalk.

"I'd never seen anything like it, and I responded to many, many calls," Nelson says. "I don't even know how she could have had so many kitchen items on hand to keep throwing at us. Neither Kenny nor I were hit, though now I don't know how we avoided being struck."

When both men managed to stop laughing, Nelson slipped a copy of the federal subpoena into the mailbox.

As they walked away, McCabe asked, "What the hell did you say to her?"

"I told him I simply said to her in Italian that we are policemen." Nelson laughs. "Although she deserved to be arrested for the assault on us, we had no desire to storm that apartment and forcibly put her in my FBI car and spend the remainder of the day dealing with her screaming at us," Nelson says.

Fat Pete failed to appear for the photographs and fingerprinting, as ordered by the subpoena. And he disappeared from his Bath Avenue residence and reportedly fled to Florida, supposedly never to be heard from in Southern Brooklyn again.

Meanwhile, auto theft continued to explode throughout the New York region, as hundreds of so-called chop shops sprang up from Brooklyn out to the Bronx, where stolen vehicles were dismantled, their parts stripped and sold for profit.

These operations catered to a booming demand for sourcing less expensive replacement parts, especially in areas where auto repair costs were high. Some vehicle owners even began colluding with thieves to have their cars stolen and stripped, allowing them to collect insurance money.

Mob-connected rings operated large-scale theft networks that controlled chop shops and corrupted dealers and officials. Stolen cars were either stripped, resold domestically, or shipped overseas, where they could fetch high prices.

Organized crime also engaged in car cloning, also known on the street as "tag jobs," where stolen vehicles were given fake identities by altering Vehicle Identification Numbers (VINs) to be sold as legitimate. Or VINs taken off wrecks were swapped with the tags on stolen vehicles to make them pass for legitimate.

Generally, though, auto theft by itself is not an overtly violent crime, and car thieves are not usually murderers. However, Mafia-backed auto crime rings are a different story.

As an FBI agent investigating organized crime, Anthony Nelson came into contact with some of the more notorious ring operators of the era in South Brooklyn.

This included Peter "the Pick" LaFroscia, a former member of the DeMeo Crew, dubbed the best car thief ever by NYPD investigators. LaFroscia is still alive today and one of the few remaining DeMeo Crew members.

"I first met Peter LaFroscia," Nelson says, "when I stopped him on Coney Island Avenue in Brooklyn while he was driving an older vehicle that did not have the proper license plates attached."

Since it was a minor motor vehicle offense, Nelson offered to release LaFroscia, provided he was willing to meet the agent for coffee at Bernie's Diner, located on Coney Island Avenue and Avenue U in Brooklyn. Nelson was hoping to develop LaFroscia as another confidential informant.

Car thieves are often easier to persuade to cooperate compared to more hardened criminals, such as armed robbers or enforcers. Car thieves more often have limited criminal histories, and if they get pinched, it's usually for property crimes rather than violent offenses. They're frequently outside the murderous culture of violence, and may have fewer psychological barriers to cooperating.

Mandatory sentences for auto theft are also less severe than for violent crimes tied to drug cartels and organized crime families. This creates a more favorable environment for plea deals to result in reduced penalties.

But this was not your usual encounter with a potential CI.

"LaFroscia showed up as scheduled at the diner, but he was accompanied by a woman he claimed was his mother," Nelson says. "Although I did not believe she was actually his mother, I later learned that he had a close relationship with his mother, and he did bring her with him to court proceedings whenever he was in trouble."

Nelson was unable to develop LaFroscia as a source, but his instincts proved accurate. In 1986, LaFroscia was one of five alleged Gambino Family members sentenced to the maximum penalty for their involvement in a global car-theft operation. Prosecutors said the ring stole thousands of vehicles from New York City throughout the late 1970s and early 1980s, dismantling them for parts or shipping them whole to destinations as far away as Kuwait.[31]

Two men received life sentences for conspiring in the murders of two rival car dealers who had threatened to expose the theft ring.

US District Judge Kevin Thomas Duffy sentenced sixty-year-old Nino Gaggi—identified by the Justice Department as the ring's second-in-command—to the maximum penalty of five years in prison and a ten-thousand-dollar fine for conspiracy involving stolen cars, altered vehicle IDs, and illegal overseas shipments.

DeMeo ring members and co-defendants Ronald Ustica and Henry Borelli were given life sentences for the 1979 murders of Ronald Falcaro and Khalid Daoud, killed in a Brooklyn garage. Borelli also received an additional 150 years for fifteen other convictions.

Others sentenced included Edward John Rendini, who received 165 years and an eighty-thousand-dollar fine, and Peter LaFroscia, thirty-six at the time, who was sentenced to five years for charges ranging from conspiracy and mail fraud to transporting stolen property.

LaFroscia was also arrested by the NYPD and tried in New York State Supreme Court in connection with the murders of John Quinn, the car thief who competed with DeMeo's ring, and Cherie Golden, Quinn's girlfriend.

Prosecutors maintained LaFroscia left Quinn's ring to join DeMeo's operation, which they characterized as being run by Paul Castellano. Prosecutors accused LaFroscia of setting up the couple. A witness, car thief William Kampf, who worked for Quinn, connected LaFroscia to Quinn.[32]

LaFroscia served prison sentences for vehicle thefts, but was acquitted of the murder charges related to Quinn and Golden and is currently a free man. He has, of late, been appearing in podcasts

31. "5 LINKED TO GAMBINO FAMILY SENTENCED IN a CAR-THEFT RING." New York Times. April 10. 1986. https://www.nytimes.com/1986/04/10/nyregion/5-linked-to-gambino-family-sentenced-in-a-car-theft-ring.html

32. Smothers, Ronald. "GAMBINO TRIAL HEARS CAR THIEF DESCRIBE WORK." New York Times. October 16, 1985. https://www.nytimes.com/1985/10/16/nyregion/gambino-trial-hears-car-thief-describe-work.html

and documentary YouTube videos about his days with the DeMeo Crew.

Through arrests, prosecutions, and the dismantling of networks, such as the DeMeo operation, the Bureau helped not only reduce auto theft but also sent a strong message about the federal commitment to combating organized crime.

These efforts laid the groundwork for improved collaboration between federal and local law enforcement in tackling organized criminal enterprises.

CHAPTER SIXTEEN

In 1978, someone was trying to come between the Calvins.

In the late 1970s, Calvin Klein debuted his iconic slim-fitting jeans with his name embroidered on the back pocket, transforming denim into high-end designer clothing. The jeans sold a stunning two hundred thousand pairs in the first week alone.

On February 3, 1978, his eleven-year-old daughter, Marci, was abducted.

FBI Special Agent Anthony Nelson was assigned to work on the kidnapping shortly after it was reported. He worked on more than a dozen kidnapping cases in his career, most of which were drug-related or parental kidnappings.

"I dreaded having to search for parents who kidnapped their own child," Nelson says. "These were always sad and problematic fugitive cases. In some instances, although custody was adjudicated by the courts, I was unsure which parent held the best interests of the child. But it was not my job to decide."

Nelson says it was also relatively easy to know when a kidnapping case was drug related. "In those cases, there'd be suspicious circumstances surrounding details of the kidnapping reports, and the ransom demands were often ludicrous," he explains. "In some cases, the drug kidnappers were only looking for thousands of dollars rather than millions of dollars, so that was a tip off."

Kidnapping is unlike any other crime. It's not one felony committed in a single moment, but a series of criminal acts unfolding over time—you're stealing something you can't fence, and you now must feed, care for, keep quiet, and keep from escaping. You can ask for a ransom, but you'll need to negotiate with experts. And you better be good with logistics, because so many things must go right, and so many things will go wrong.

And from the very moment you abduct a young innocent like Calvin Klein's daughter, you will be hunted.

Not every kidnapper is a master criminal. Many kidnappings are carried out by bungling opportunists who watch too many crime dramas.

Sure, they fool themselves into thinking they have a foolproof plan. In reality, they haven't thought things through. And as their flimsy plan falls apart, the kidnappers fall apart with it, becoming erratic, irrational, and desperate.

But this was not an abduction perpetrated by criminal masterminds.

Spoiler Alert! Yes, the babysitter did it.

Young Marci had been tricked into getting off a 3rd Avenue city bus at 7:30 a.m. while traveling from her home on East 76th Street in Manhattan to the prestigious Dalton School she attended on East 89th Street.

The abduction was easy. Marci knew and trusted her kidnappers. Her babysitter, Paule (Christine) Ransay Lewis, told her that her father was ill at Mount Sinai Hospital and she'd been sent to fetch her.

Instead of taking Marci to the hospital to see her father, she was brought, not to a secret, secure location, but to Lewis' home nearby on East 97th Street in Manhattan. Marci was then bound and gagged for most of the day.

Lewis had a plan. Not a great plan, not even a good plan. But it was *a* plan.

The first call came in at 8:15 a.m. The kidnappers demanded one hundred thousand dollars ransom in cash with further instructions to follow.

Each telephone call to Calvin Klein directed him to a different telephone booth. Undercover agents tailed Klein as he complied.

And so began the cat-and-mouse chase, much more challenging in 1978, without the "Ring of Steel" comprehensive surveillance cameras and plate readers that exist in Manhattan today.

"As the phone calls were being received, we traced the caller to various phone booth locations across the city," Nelson says. "I had been together in my car with a long-time fellow FBI agent and friend named Rodney Davis."

Following twenty-nine years with the Bureau that saw Davis rise to supervisory special agent, he retired in 2001. He founded XGCG, a private global investigative firm specializing in comprehensive due diligence checks, litigation support, civil/criminal investigations, as well as cybersecurity. Through Davis's leadership, XGCG is directly associated with approximately two hundred licensed PIs who collaborate with investigations and surveillance.[33]

"As Rodney and I raced from phone booth to phone booth with flashing red police lights and sirens operating, I slightly collided with another vehicle," Nelson remembers. "But the accident was so minor, I kept going to the next phone booth. When I checked for accident reports later, I learned that the driver of the vehicle I struck never reported the accident. I don't know if he didn't report it because it had been so minor or because he just didn't want his identity known for some reason."

In a scene that would play well in a Hollywood film, as instructed, Klein dropped the bag containing one hundred thousand dollars in cash near the top of an escalator in the Pan Am Building, behind Grand Central Terminal.

"For Marci's safety, we didn't stop the individual who picked up the cash, but rather attempted to follow him. Within an hour, another call from the kidnappers directed Calvin Klein to the East 97th Street address of their babysitter, where Marci was found in a third-floor apartment," Nelson says.

In dramatic fashion, Calvin Klein and investigators rushed to the apartment, and the designer shouted her name as he raced up the stairs.

33. "Rodney M Davis." FBIretired | Signature Directories. https://fbiretired. com/agent/xg-consultants-group

And here the kidnappers' master plan really started to unravel.

Lewis, who was in the apartment, claimed that she too had been kidnapped. She was taken into custody and later failed a lie detector test, then broke down and implicated her accomplices.

Lewis was arrested along with her half-brother, Dominique Placide Ransay, who was nineteen years old. The other perpetrator was identified as twenty-three-year-old Cecil Wiggins.

Police believe Ransay planned the kidnapping, recruiting his half-sister due to her relationship with the child, and adding his friend Wiggins, who happened to be there.

"This episode had been a poorly planned spur-of-the-moment kidnapping, with the babysitter first claiming that she had also been a victim of the kidnappers," Nelson says.

So though the plot was discussed beforehand, it was actually triggered on impulse after the group saw Marci boarding the bus.

Marci was kept blindfolded and bound for most of the ten-hour ordeal while the ransom calls were made from the apartment—all by Ransay.

Due to the celebrity connection with Klein, the sensational kidnapping story hit the front pages the next day. High bail was set by Acting Judge E. Leo Milonas after Assistant DA Thomas DeMakis stated that all three defendants had made complete, taped confessions.[34]

During the ten-minute arraignment, the defendants remained silent.

At FBI headquarters, Nelson and his fellow agents displayed the cash ransom—handled with gloves. "Except for a hundred dollars, which the kidnappers used to enjoy the day, all of the ransom money was recovered, some of which was in Wiggins' apartment," Nelson adds.

Despite the ordeal, Marci Klein went on to attend Emerson College before graduating from Brown University, and then

---

34. McFadden, Robert D. "Police Call the Klein Kidnapping Spontaneous and Poorly Planned." New York Times. February 6, 1978. https://www.nytimes. com/1978/02/06/archives/police-call-the-klein-kidnapping-spontaneous-and-poorly-planned.html

enjoyed a successful career as a television producer. Beginning in 1989, she launched a twenty-five-year run at *Saturday Night Live*, playing a pivotal role behind the scenes as a producer and the head of talent. She was instrumental in identifying and nurturing a new generation of comedic voices, future stars like Molly Shannon, Tracy Morgan, Jimmy Fallon, Seth Meyers, Will Ferrell, Fred Armisen, Chris Kattan, Darrell Hammond, Sarah Silverman, Jason Sudeikis, Bill Hader, Maya Rudolph, and Ana Gasteyer.

Klein's work earned her fourteen Emmy nominations and four wins—one for the *Saturday Night Live 25th Anniversary Special* and three for her contributions to *30 Rock*.

Not long after sentencing, in a stunning twist, Lewis, the bungling babysitter, claimed that Calvin Klein set up this abduction to get nationwide publicity.

She later retracted the statement.

CHAPTER SEVENTEEN

By 1979, the FBI's New York Office (NYO) had come a long way since the early days of the Bureau.

When Congress ended the practice of the Department of Justice and other agencies borrowing investigators from the Treasury Department's Secret Service, Attorney General Charles Bonaparte created the forerunner of the FBI, the Bureau of Investigation.

From the beginning, more agents were assigned to New York and Chicago because of the greater need for investigative support in those cities.

The New York Office had a special agent in charge and about six to eight field agents by 1911. Today, the FBI's NYO is assigned more than two thousand agents, support staff, and task force personnel.[35]

And by the time Anthony Nelson arrived in the 1970s, the NYO needed every agent it could field to work some of the most sensational cases of the era.

Federal investigators and prosecutors were rearmed with legislative tools like the Title III wiretap authority and the Racketeer Influenced and Corrupt Organizations (RICO) Act of 1970.

New York, with its sprawling underworld, served as a fertile testing ground. The groundwork was being laid for the epic Pizza Connection and Commission Trial prosecutions, as figures like

---

35. Federal Bureau of Investigation. "FBI New York History." August 8, 2016. https://www.fbi.gov/history/field-office-histories/newyork

Carlo Gambino, Paul Castellano, and Fat Tony Salerno were under investigation throughout the decade.

Meanwhile, the FBI began pursuing ties between Teamsters Local 560 (New Jersey) and the Genovese and DeCavalcante Families.

After the 1972 theft of heroin from NYPD evidence lockers, the FBI assisted in investigating whether organized crime or corrupt officers were behind it. The fallout disrupted multiple ongoing cases and prompted deeper collaboration between the FBI and federal narcotics agents.

In 1975, when John F. Malone retired as the longest-serving field division head in FBI history, the winds of change were stirring.

In the years ahead, the FBI overhauled its policies, revamped its national infrastructure, and the New York Office was at the heart of this transformation. New York scaled back its broad focus to concentrate on highly active left-wing radicals like the Weather Underground, which carried out several bombings in protest of the Vietnam War and racial injustice, including the 1970 accidental explosion of a Greenwich Village townhouse, as members were building a bomb intended for a military dance at Fort Dix.

The FALN (*Fuerzas Armadas de Liberación Nacional*, or Armed Forces of National Liberation) alone was responsible for over one hundred and thirty bombings in the United States, many in New York; its most infamous was the Fraunces Tavern bombing (1975), killing four and injuring dozens.

In 1972, a hijacker named Luis Armando Peña Soltren seized a flight from New York to Cuba. He evaded capture until 2009, when he surrendered.

New York was a frequent origin or destination of hijacked planes (1970-75)—often diverted to Cuba. As the term *skyjacking* entered the American lexicon, the FBI was establishing air piracy squads and coordinating with the Federal Aviation Administration and Port Authority to crack down.

The Cold War intensified, with New York a major battleground for counterintelligence, as the FBI monitored UN diplomats suspected of espionage, especially from the Soviet Bloc, as double agents and defectors flocked to the Big Apple.

The 1970s preceded the "junk bond" era of the 1980s, as the FBI began its assault on Wall Street corruption, launching probes into securities fraud, boiler room operations, and stock manipulation schemes.

The New York Office also helped pioneer the interagency task force approach to tackling crime problems. In 1979, the FBI/NYPD Joint Bank Robbery Task Force was established to stifle a resurgence in violent armed robberies. By April 1980, Bureau and NYPD counterterrorism investigators teamed up to form the nation's first Joint Terrorism Task Force, or JTTF.

Together, NYPD and FBI personnel took down major rings—from the deadly 1981 armored car robbery by a domestic terrorist group to foreign infiltrators, to the bombing of the World Trade Center in 1993 and the plot to bomb the Lincoln and Holland Tunnels. Following the September 11, 2001, attacks, all field offices that did not already have a JTTF were ordered to create one.[36]

Most of the fifty-five FBI field offices are led by a special agent in charge. The larger offices in Los Angeles, New York City, and Washington, DC, are managed by an assistant director in charge, reflecting the greater scope and complexity of operations in those cities. Within these field offices today are a total of about three hundred and fifty Resident Agencies (RAs) located in surrounding smaller cities and towns. Resident Agencies are managed by Supervisory Special agents.[37]

During this transformative period, in 1979, the New York Office opened a New York RA in Queens, the Brooklyn-Queens Metropolitan Resident Agency (BQMRA). Unlike a large field office such as New York, which is equipped to investigate all crime categories within a specific geography under the FBI's jurisdiction, Resident Agencies were staffed according to specific investigative programs.

---

36. Federal Bureau of Investigation. "Field Offices." June 27, 2025. https://www.fbi.gov/contact-us/field-offices

37. Maitland, Leslie. "3 Held as Brink's Plotters." New York Times. June 8, 1979. https://www.nytimes.com/1979/06/08/archives/3-held-as-brinks-plotters-assault-charge-possible.html

For instance, the "Gambino Family Squad" was placed in the BQMRA. Though New York's most prominent Family was active across the region, many of its operations and soldiers were concentrated in Brooklyn and Queens.

Shortly after the BQMRA opened, Special Agent Anthony Nelson was transferred from 26 Federal Plaza in Manhattan to the Gambino Squad in the newest Resident Agency.

In addition to the FBI's Gambino Squad, Nelson was assigned to the Major Theft—Truck Hijacking Squad, the Fugitive Squad, the Violent Crimes Branch (FBI/NYPD Task Force), all assignments that lasted through to his retirement.

"Before I even moved some of my official and personal property from Manhattan," Nelson says, "I was already being asked to participate in major ongoing investigations being handled out of the new BQMRA."

In June of 1979, the FBI received a tip that a group of professional thieves and bookmakers from Upper Manhattan was planning to rob a two-million-dollar Brink's money shipment.

This was a regularly scheduled Federal Reserve Bank cash delivery, transported every Thursday via an Eastern Airlines Shuttle from Logan Airport in Boston to LaGuardia Airport in Queens.

This case had a cinematic wrinkle.

Turns out, the prime suspect was an advisor on set for a new film in production starring actor Peter Falk.

The name of this film?

The Brink's Job.

According to the plot description:

On January 17, 1950, a group of unlikely criminal masterminds commits the robbery of the century. Led by Tony Pino (Peter Falk), a petty thief fresh out of prison, and Joe McGinnis (Peter Boyle), who specializes in planning lucrative capers, the gang robs Brink's main office in Boston of more than $2 million. However, things begin to go awry when the FBI gets involved, the cops start cracking down on the gang, and McGinnis refuses to hand over the loot.[38]

You see, while traveling back and forth to work on the film, one of these "advisors" hired to coach Falk and ensure authenticity, Spanish Eddie Colombani, noticed a pattern to those weekly Brink's money shipments.

Somehow, Spanish Eddie, boasting a lengthy rap sheet with convictions dating to 1955, got permission from his parole officer to participate in the film, later professing Falk to be "a natural" when it came to mastering lock picking and other criminal techniques he shared.

Nelson was assigned to assist in the arrests in the case, along with FBI Special Agents Bill Lynch and Tom Harrell.

According to a complaint filed on May 31 in federal court in Brooklyn, the conspirators were captured on tape planning the heist by FBI informant William A. Johnson, who was an accomplice.

A year after the film was released, FBI agents had gathered enough evidence on Colombani and two other suspects to arrest and charge them with conspiracy to rob the Brink's armored truck at LaGuardia during one of its regular pickups from the New York-bound shuttle from Boston.37

"We learned from that cooperating witness that Spanish Eddie would be at a restaurant named the Boat Yard on the night we had planned to arrest him," Nelson says. "The three of us were briefed about Colombani's extensive criminal record before we left to arrest him."

While the FBI agents were warned that Colombani was on federal parole and should be considered dangerous, the lawmen were not told that Colombani was also a professional boxer.

The Boat Yard was located on East 81st Street and 2nd Avenue in Manhattan, directly across the street from a bar/restaurant named O'Melia's. Tommy O'Melia, the owner of the restaurant, was a

---

38. "The Brink's Job DVD (1978)." Movie Buffs Forever. https://moviebuffsforever.com/products/the-brinks-job-1978-movie-dvd?_pos=1&_sid=5f78ba260&_ss=r

good friend to many FBI agents, and his restaurant was frequented by scores of off-duty agents just about any night of the week.

On that night, June 7, 1979, Special Agents Nelson, Lynch, and Harrell positively identified Spanish Eddie's car parked in front of the Boat Yard and concluded he was most likely inside. The three agents entered the Boat Yard, filled with unsuspecting diners, and began to search the crowd for Colombani.

"As my eyes scanned the bar area, I noticed Spanish Eddie sitting on a stool in the corner of the bar," Nelson says. "The suspect was surrounded by several people and engaged in conversation, including with a woman who we believed to be his girlfriend." As Nelson sized up Colombani, he pointed him out to Bill Lynch.

Colombani was built like a bulldozer.

"Can you imagine if he doesn't feel like getting arrested?" Nelson remembers remarking to Lynch.

Seconds later, all hell broke loose at the Boat Yard.

As the agents approached Colombani, they identified themselves, informing Spanish Eddie that he was under arrest.

"I ain't going nowhere," Colombani barked.

In the ensuing brawl, agents tumbled over barstools, knocked over dinner tables, and sent diners and wait staff scrambling.

"I was in excellent physical shape, as were the other two agents, but Spanish Eddie was in even better shape," Nelson says. "But he wasn't boxing or swinging at us. He just kept flailing his arms and hands, refusing to be handcuffed."

The scuffle spilled over onto the dining room floor, tables and chairs upending, dishes and glasses breaking. One of the women standing next to Colombani kicked Nelson, as hard as she could, in the side of his head.

"Next, the four of us went tumbling out the front door of the Boat Yard and onto the street outside," Nelson says. "Although Colombani was still not throwing punches, I was getting totally exhausted just trying, along with the other two agents, to get him handcuffed."

He turned to see one of the bartenders from O'Melia's watching the commotion on the sidewalk. "I told him to run into O'Melia's and get us some help from any agents that might be there," Nelson says. He also asked the bartender to call 911.

No help.

Not only did a NYPD cruiser fail to arrive, but this was the rare night when not a single FBI agent was in O'Melia's.

The agents, absolutely spent and panting, paused. Then Spanish Eddie relented, easing his arms toward his back, hanging his head, and signaling willingness to be taken into custody.

"The problem was that Eddie was massive and built so solidly that we couldn't get his arms close enough to each other to get him handcuffed," Nelson says. "Lynch, Harrell, and I had to link each of our handcuffs together just to make it work and take Colombani into custody."

Later, Colombani, along with John F. Mulligan and Thomas Murray, was charged with conspiracy in the two-million-dollar armed robbery of the Brinks truck. The FBI told the media Colombani was also likely to be charged with resisting arrest and assaulting a federal officer.

And so news of the chaotic arrest of Spanish Eddie's spread through BQMRA as sort of an informal welcoming for Anthony Nelson to the FBI's new satellite office.

CHAPTER EIGHTEEN

FBI agents deal with unsavory characters—informants, suspects, cooperating criminals, usually with baggage and hidden motives.

That doesn't mean they have to like it.

"I never moralized to anyone I arrested about the bad choices they made in life, except to a very few who morphed into pure evil, like members of the DeMeo Crew," Nelson says. "Even some of my friends who I grew up with made bad choices, committed crimes, such as gambling and loan-sharking."

But it's the illegal gambling and loansharking offenses, though, that are more likely to generate informants. They just scare more easily than leg-breakers and armed robbers.

"Degenerate gamblers would get themselves into trouble by losing tremendous amounts of money and then borrowing money from loan sharks, attempting to win back their losses," Nelson explains. "But as most people should know, that's usually a losing strategy.

"Over the years, I've seen many, many gamblers, loan sharks, and loan shark victims turn to the FBI for help and protection in exchange for their cooperation in criminal investigations," Nelson says.

An FBI Special Agent must be strategic, disciplined, and emotionally detached, knowing that even the worst person might help stop something even worse.

"Sure, it seemed unseemly to me to deal with some loan shark victims," Nelson says. "Many were con artists themselves. They'd get themselves into trouble because they suffered from the disease of a gambling addiction and then borrow money they couldn't repay."

In fact, it's not unusual for degenerate gamblers, jammed up, to seek help from the FBI by setting up their loan shark for an arrest.

"These loansharking 'victims' would borrow even more money from their loan shark," Nelson says, "knowing that he was about to be arrested by the FBI and wouldn't be around for a while to collect his principal or even the vig."

During the summer of 1983, Nelson slipped his FBI business card to a bookmaker associated with both the Colombo and Genovese Families.

Now, that bookmaker was calling him frantically from a payphone after fleeing from a Mob-controlled social club in Sheepshead Bay.

Basically, a bookmaker would, or should, try to balance his book—meaning he wants bets distributed in a way that ensures a profit no matter who wins. To do that, he could adjust odds to encourage or discourage bets on specific outcomes, or he could lay off risk with a hedge by placing bets with other bookies.

If a bookmaker balances his book right, he always profits, albeit modestly, on the vig (or vigorish), which is basically a built-in profit margin, like a small tax on top of every bet.

Not all bookmakers balance their books correctly.

"This bookmaker had taken the chance of pocketing some large-amount sports bets, placed by some really tough guys," Nelson recalls. "He'd hoped they placed losing bets, which he did not lay off. And he was wrong. These guys won big and now they wanted their money."

Running for his life, the bookmaker was being chased on foot across the Sheepshead Bay waterfront.

Hiding in a telephone booth, he paged Nelson and desperately waited for him to call him.

"We didn't have cell phones in those days," Nelson clarifies. "He was actually lucky to have paged me from a payphone that allowed incoming telephone calls."

When Nelson returned the call, he urged the bookmaker to call 911.

Not surprisingly, the desperate man did not want a police response since he had, in essence, stolen money as part of an OC-sanctioned gambling operation and was being hunted by Mob associates.

Kenny McCabe and Anthony Nelson had just finished having dinner at Brennan and Carr, a restaurant on Avenue U in Brooklyn that still serves some of the best hot roast beef sandwiches in New York City.

Since its opening in 1938 by George Brennan and Edward Carr, the iconic eatery is still going strong serving up thin-sliced, melt-in-your-mouth beef on a soft roll soaked in beef stock. Ordered either "Dingle-Dangle," which is just the beef of the sandwich dipped into the broth, leaving the roll dry; "Double Dip," where the entire sandwich is dipped into the broth; or the "K.F.J." or "Knife and Fork Job."

No offense to fans of roast-beef-and-cheese rival Roll 'n' Roaster located about a mile away on Emmons Avenue in Sheepshead Bay.

"We were relatively close, maybe ten minutes away," Nelson recalls. "But by the time we pulled up to his location on Gravesend Neck Road, he was getting hit by three guys who were using their fists and a baseball bat."

The two lawmen jumped out of Nelson's Plymouth Gran Fury and pretended to arrest the bookie for a robbery they claimed had just taken place.

Nelson laughs. "We played dumb and asked the guys beating him if they were also victims of a robbery by this guy."

Of course, none of the wiseguys cooperated. The gangsters must've known they were the law; Nelson had his emergency lights on and tooted the siren when they pulled up.

But in typical Brooklyn fashion, the thugs went right back to beating the bookmaker.

"We managed to handcuff the bookie and put him in my FBI car, but these guys were relentless," Nelson says. "They surrounded my car and swung the bat against my rear-side door, trying to hit him through an open back window."

In the process, they almost hit Kenny McCabe.

After threatening to arrest them, Nelson told them the guy they were beating was under arrest for robbery, and he was going to the 61st Precinct for processing, located nearby on Coney Island Avenue.

"Unfortunately, Kenny and I misjudged the determination of these guys to get at this bookmaker," Nelson says. "We thought they'd just go away. So we took the bookie for a long ride, debriefed him, and let him out of my car several miles away."

What they did not expect was for the wiseguys to head to the precinct station house to look for the bookmaker.

Then, after realizing he was not there and had never been there, they tracked him down again.

The next call Nelson received was from Coney Island Hospital, where the twice-beaten bookmaker was being treated for serious injuries.

Still, Nelson and McCabe had rescued him from the first beating.

That had to be worth something.

"Even though the ruse we used had not ended well for the bookie," Nelson adds, "Kenny and I had let him know in no uncertain terms that he now owed us a favor in the event we needed some investigative information."

So yes, Anthony Nelson has seen the darker sides of the dark side.

And like most members of law enforcement investigating organized crime, Nelson has files and folders full of bad guys and their bad behavior.

"In the late 1970s, I'd been acting in an undercover capacity and negotiating for fifty kilos of cocaine in Bernie's Diner on Avenue U and Coney Island Avenue in Brooklyn," Anthony Nelson recalls.

During the discussion, one of the subjects saw a truck that delivered bananas passing by the window. "His eyes widened and he said to me that he was thinking about hijacking that banana truck because he had seen it follow the same route a few times each week," Nelson says. "I told him we're discussing a deal for fifty keys here and you're looking to hijack a truck full of bananas that will rot in a few days.

"Sometimes I just couldn't relate to the mentality of some OC elements," he adds, "who would kill you if you owed them a nickel."

Then, an associate of the subject Nelson was speaking with came into the diner in the middle of this discussion about cocaine and bananas. He told his partner he had just come from a social club directly across the street from the diner.

"He said the club belonged to Charlie 'Moose' Panarella and that there was a party taking place," Nelson remembers. Panarella was a Colombo enforcer and captain of a crew that included a young Greg Scarpa, active in racketeering in both New York and Las Vegas. Panarella was alleged to have once forced a man to eat his own testicles before murdering him.[39]

"Then he remarked that they were about to cut a large cake for Charlie Moose," Nelson says, "that was inscribed with icing that read: *Whoever said that crime doesn't pay*." The three burst out laughing.

In many respects, it was easier to get away with bad behavior during that era, especially when it came to stealing someone else's identity.

New York State did not even have photographs on driver's licenses.

In fact, the only reliable way to validate a driver's license was to decode an algorithm embedded in the driver's license number. But there were no computers or apps to help. Most law enforcement didn't even know the decoding protocol.

---

39. "Old-school mob man may be headed back to a familiar haunt." Las Vegas Review-Journal

This made it relatively easy to counterfeit DMV documents, at least to the degree that the average person could not tell the difference.

"I started to notice a rise in more white-collar-type offenses being reported to the FBI, where counterfeit DMV documents and bank checks were used to commit the crime," Nelson says.

Nelson tried to determine if the documents were identical to those that had been distributed by John Quinn or were used by members of the DeMeo Crew, which were still in circulation.

In July 1979, Nelson investigated a scheme perpetrated by a neighbor who lived diagonally across the street from Kenny McCabe in Brooklyn.

"During the 70s, Kenny lived on a very interesting block," he recalls. "He had one neighbor I was investigating for his involvement in bust-out schemes, actually using Quinn's counterfeit DMV documents."

McCabe also had other organized crime associates who lived on his block, not particularly surprising considering that during the '70s and '80s, Brooklyn was infested with hundreds of the Mafias made members and thousands of their associates.

"However, this neighbor I was investigating didn't appear to have any connection to organized crime," Nelson says. "Yet here he was, using stolen and counterfeit IDs and bank checks."

Upon closer inspection, Nelson identified the suspect as thirty-two-year-old Jay Miller and learned that he was targeting singles bars in Manhattan to carry out his scheme.

"On several occasions, Miller connected with single women and led them to believe he fell in love with them," Nelson says. "After spending a night or two with them at their homes, Miller cleaned them out of their cash and jewelry and then disappeared."

Miller's victims variously reported that he used the names Michael Harris, Michael Margolis, and Gregory Scott. "While running his con games, he also posed as a US Customs Agent, an Immigration official, and a Naval intelligence officer," Nelson says.

In April 1980, the *New York Post* ran with a story warning women frequenting Manhattan singles bars to be on the lookout for Miller, dubbing him "the Romeo Barfly with a Sting." They announced that the FBI, as in Anthony Nelson and team, were on the hunt for a soft-spoken Brooklyn man accused of charming and defrauding lonely women in Manhattan's singles bars—stealing not only their hearts, but also their cash and jewelry.[40]

"By that point, I established that the suspect swindled more than a dozen victims out of upwards of $140,000 in scams that previous year alone. He targeted the more vulnerable divorced and single women at Manhattan singles bars, spent the night with them, and got close," Nelson explains. "With some of his victims, he even promised marriage. Based on interviews with these victims, I learned he was confident, intelligent, articulate, and knew what to say and how to say it to deceive these women. Then, once he had access to their valuables, he disappeared."

Miller stalked his victims mostly in East Side bars and upscale nightlife spots, but also Italian restaurants in Greenwich Village.

"Miller also developed another con scheme," Nelson says. "It was the one that caught my attention."

This is how the scheme worked. Miller searched "Car for Sale" ads in New York local newspapers for women who were selling their vehicles. After pretending to love the cars, he rendered stolen and counterfeit checks as payment and then immediately resold the vehicles before the checks bounced.

After identifying Miller, Nelson obtained a federal arrest warrant for him, charging him with Interstate Transportation of Stolen Property. Further investigation revealed that Miller was also wanted by New Jersey authorities for committing the same type of offenses in that state.

"Although he had an address on Kenny McCabe's block, Kenny never saw him after the warrant was issued," Nelson says.

One night during the winter of 1980, Nelson was driving down Kenny's block to pick him up in his FBI car.

"It was one of the nights that we were headed out to visit the OC social clubs in Brooklyn," Nelson says. As he approached

40. Capeci, Jerry. "The Romeo Barfly with a Sting." New York Post. April 22, 1980

McCabe's house, Nelson spotted a vehicle driving away from the front of Miller's residence.

The driver fit Miller's description.

"I followed the car, without stopping to pick up Kenny," Nelson says. "We didn't have cell phones in those days, so I couldn't call him. I was only able to use my FBI radio to request a backup unit."

As he tailed Miller, it began snowing fairly hard, so Nelson did not want to get into a chase. He followed the car into Bay Ridge, but still had no backup.

"When we arrived in the vicinity of 86th Street and 4th Avenue, I lost sight of the vehicle because of the heavy snow," Nelson says. "I turned on my emergency lights and siren momentarily, attempting to get within sight of the car."

As he drove through the intersection at 4th Avenue, the heart of a high-traffic commercial district, he was broadsided by a car heading east down 86th Street. The slickness of the snow caused Nelson's FBI car to lose traction. He whipped around in two complete circles, each time hitting another luxury automobile.

"It just so happened that several doctors, all driving expensive vehicles, had just had dinner at a local restaurant, and I struck their cars as my car spun around on the snow," Nelson says. "Luckily, no one was injured, but the vehicle I was following was now long gone."

Nelson entered Miller's information into the National Crime Information Center (NCIC) computer, and he was later stopped and arrested in New Jersey.

On March 26, 1981, Miller pled guilty to one count of Interstate Transportation of Stolen Property.

CHAPTER NINETEEN

Not all Brooklyn wiseguys ducked and covered when they spotted that damn Plymouth Gran Fury.

Roy DeMeo, by now accustomed to seeing the lawmen idling outside the Gemini Lounge, started to gesture at them sarcastically, in a somewhat joking manner. He would approach the car, act civil, and engage in meaningless conversations.

"During these little talks, I knew he was feeling us out, playing his little games to try and determine how much we knew about him," Nelson says.

DeMeo kept inviting the detective and the agent into the Gemini for a drink. But their answer never changed—they declined.

"Kenny and I were very careful about where we ate and drank, even off-duty," Nelson says. "If a place was suspected of having even a remote connection to wiseguys, the only thing we would order was a tightly capped bottle of beer."

DeMeo seemed to enjoy this game. He feigned innocence, insisting that he was legitimate, just a successful salesman who "buys and sells stuff."

On more than one occasion, he subtly claimed to have several business opportunities pending that could make McCabe and Nelson a lot of money, if they were interested.

His thinly veiled bribes always met the same response.

"We told him instead to come to work for us," Nelson says.

Then, those exchanges suddenly ended, though it took some time for Nelson to learn why. "It was not long before some informants told us that Nino Gaggi and Paul Castellano had warned Roy not to carry on any more conversations, specifically with us," Nelson says. Gaggi, according to these informants, believed that Roy had a big mouth and was developing a "Wild West cowboy attitude."

"Nino believed Roy was getting a little too cozy with us," Nelson adds, "and that he would unwittingly give us information that was going to get himself, or members of his Crew, in some serious legal trouble."

On another occasion, McCabe and Nelson dropped in on DeMeo at the Gemini Lounge, following up on an outstanding subpoena for Vito Arena, another killer in Roy's Crew who, along with his boyfriend, had been committing armed robberies of dentists' offices.

They found DeMeo sitting on an old wooden milk crate outside the door of the apartment attached to the lounge. Investigators later learned the crew used that apartment to drain, dismember, and package up the bodies of their slain victims for disposal. The apartment was usually occupied by DeMeo's cousin, Joseph "Dracula" Guglielmo.

Nelson knew enough of DeMeo's demeanor to sense something was definitely wrong with Roy during the visit.

"He was quiet, serious, and he would not look directly at us," Nelson says. "It became obvious that we were the last people he wanted to see at that moment." As the real purpose of the visit was some cage rattling, it was a success. "Of course, we didn't expect that he'd help us find Vito," he adds. "But we also didn't expect him to treat us like we had the plague. We knew something was up."

When the two lawmen got back in Nelson's Gran Fury, they surmised that DeMeo's attitude had something to do with the recent warning they knew he received from Gaggi and Castellano.

That was not the case.

"We later learned from a cooperating witness that Roy avoided us because, at that very moment of our visit, his crew was draining the blood of their latest victim inside the bathroom shower of the apartment."

DeMeo's ghouls were honing their skills, known as the Gemini Method, a sequence of techniques where they typically lured their targets to the lounge, shot them in the head, and then quickly wrapped the wound in a towel to contain the bleeding. Another crew member then stabbed the victim in the heart to minimize any further blood loss. The bodies were then drained, dismembered, and discarded—often in landfills—to reduce the chances of discovery.

Another night, not long after, Nelson and McCabe swung by Tomasso's Restaurant, a red-sauce classic on 86th Street on the edge of Dyker Heights deep in the heart of Mob-controlled Brooklyn.

Since 1971, owner and Chef Tommaso Verdillo built up a loyal following, as much for his *mozzarella Carrozza* as for his singing opera arias and classic Neapolitan songs. Glenn Rifkin wrote in the *New York Times* in 2006 that Tommaso's was the kind of place that elicits "a pang of nostalgia for the kind of restaurant that once defined many Americans' sense of what was Italian."[41]

Shortly after Verdillo debuted Tommaso's on 86th Street, the Gambinos opened Veterans and Friends one block over. Paul Castellano became a regular, along with his lieutenants and their underlings. Verdillo even catered food for events at Castellano's home on Staten Island.

Later, after Paul Castellano was assassinated outside another Mob-favored eatery, Spark's Steak House in Manhattan, Verdillo revealed he was far from a fan of his restaurant's notorious regulars.

One incident in particular soured Verdillo on Castellano and his crew. He recalled a night when members of the James Beard Society, the culinary arts organization, were dining at Tommaso's.

This was a big coup for Verdillo.

Until Castellano arrived with his entourage.

41. Rifkin, Glenn. "Thomas Verdillo, 77, Dies: Restaurateur Went From Red Sauce to Blue Ribbon." New York Times. January 11, 2021. https://www.nytimes.com/2021/01/11/obituaries/thomas-verdillo-dead-coronavirus.html

Before long, one of the wiseguys grew agitated, then accused someone at the Beard table of eyeing his girlfriend.

"In the middle of dinner, he got up, confronted the diner, and threatened him," Verdillo told reporters. "It felt like a scene from 'Goodfellas'—but the fallout was real: The Beard Society never returned."41

Verdillo reported after the 1985 slaying of Castellano that business tapered off.

But that night the restaurant was packed. Nelson and McCabe were surveilling Tommaso's after being tipped off by an informant of a "going-away party" for Gambino capo Nino Gaggi.

Nelson and McCabe recognized this rare opportunity to fill in some of the blanks in their Gambino hierarchy chart, for as flamboyant as fellow captain John Gotti was, Nino Gaggi was just as low-key.

Castellano expected a show of force.

Attendance was not optional.

Absences would be interpreted as disrespect or even disloyalty.

Gaggi was closely aligned with Castellano. In fact, the leadership meeting where Castellano was named Carlo Gambino's replacement was held at Gaggi's Bath Beach home. And Gaggi was promoted to capo of Castellano's old crew.

Gaggi even hoped to be promoted to underboss.

Then he got jammed up in a double homicide related to his association with none other than Roy DeMeo.

DeMeo had become a rising star and remarkable earner for Gaggi, with a stable of hitmen to call upon. In addition to stolen cars, DeMeo's Crew sold cocaine, marijuana, and pills in large amounts despite Castellano's prohibition on drug trafficking.

And that's what set in motion the sequence of events that led to Gaggi's going-away party.

Gambino capo James Eppolito ran to Castellano and accused Gaggi and DeMeo of trafficking in narcotics, knowing Big Paul had earlier proclaimed a death sentence for any Gambinos selling drugs. Eppolito also accused Gaggi of being a police informant.

Eppolito requested permission from his boss to whack Gaggi and DeMeo.

Instead, Castellano gave Gaggi and DeMeo permission to murder both Eppolito and his son.

On October 1, 1979, Gaggi and DeMeo fatally shot both Eppolitos. A nearby witness alerted an off-duty police officer, who arrived on the scene and spotted Gaggi leaving the area on foot. DeMeo slipped away and evaded capture. In the ensuing shootout, the policeman wounded Gaggi in the neck and arrested him.

Despite being charged with the murders and the attempted killing of a police officer, Gaggi was ultimately convicted only of assault. He received a federal prison sentence ranging from five to fifteen years.

Still, DeMeo knew he was despised by the don. And he must have known that his association with narcotics and the growing number of homicides attributed to his crew made him a liability.

That evening, the party for Nino was in full swing when a paranoid DeMeo exited his Cadillac and stopped cold when he spotted Nelson's Plymouth. He sprinted across 86th Street full speed, narrowly missing getting hit by cars whizzing by on that busy four-lane thoroughfare, running up to Nelson's driver's-side door.

"Roy was hot," Nelson remembers. "He starts screaming and cursing at us from the middle of 86th Street, yelling out loud that Kenny McCabe had just 'killed him.'"

DeMeo was referring to McCabe's testimony delivered at a recent sentencing hearing. The defense fought hard to exclude any evidence identifying their clients as members of organized crime and demanded that informants be identified. The federal prosecutors were reluctant to produce the CIs to corroborate, mainly because they did not want them identified and targeted.

Then the defense cried foul, arguing this violated their client's due process.

Kenny McCabe stepped into that breach, not only corroborating details but also going further by volunteering more information on relationships and associations, supported by photos to back up his assertions. Particularly, McCabe testified before a federal judge that a specific drug dealer reported to Roy DeMeo.

"Roy kept repeating that Kenny could falsely accuse him of anything he wanted, even 'killing little babies,'" Nelson remembers. "But he should never, ever falsely accuse him of dealing drugs. Roy told us that once Paulie [Castellano] heard about the drug-dealing story, [DeMeo] was 'going to be a dead man.'"

DeMeo then turned, leveled his venomous gaze at Nelson, and said, "And you, you're the FBI. You guys know everything that's going on everywhere. You know very well I'm not dealing drugs. Why would you let your partner say that about me?"

Note that as early as 1972, DeMeo finagled a position on the board of directors of a Brooklyn credit union in part to launder money earned through his illicit narcotics deals. By that night in 1980, the DeMeo Crew was trafficking large amounts of cocaine, marijuana, and methamphetamine pills.

"I told Roy to go back into the restaurant, or the club, and find even one, just one of his friends who will say that Kenny ever lied about them on a witness stand," Nelson says. "Of course he couldn't as every one of them knew that Kenny always tells the truth. He was even respected by them for that reason."

A stumped DeMeo stared at Nelson and said, "I wouldn't expect you to say anything else because he's your partner. You're both just trying to get me killed for no reason."

Keep in mind, DeMeo delivered his tantrum pacing back and forth, in and out of the path of oncoming cars, leaning in and out of Nelson's FBI car.

"I told Roy to 'get away from my car door before you get hurt,'" Nelson says. Roy's eyes widened, misreading the situation. "You could see it in his eyes—he thought I was going to hit him."

Nelson adds, "I said to him, 'No, you're not going to get hurt by me, Roy. You're standing in the roadway. You're going to get hit by a car.'"

"You'd be happy if that happened because you're both killers in your own way," DeMeo whined.

"Roy then slapped his hands down on the edge of my car window, shook his head in disgust, and then swung away and trudged back to his own car," Nelson says.

Nelson recalls McCabe laughing as he said, "Well, at least he's calmed down. Probably because he got to complain about us without getting locked up."

Years before, when Gaggi proposed that DeMeo be admitted into the Family, Castellano balked. He felt DeMeo was too violent and uncontrollable. Castellano eventually relented and allowed DeMeo to be inducted into the Family. DeMeo's proven value as a top earner and relentless enforcer for the Gambinos could no longer be denied. It also helped that DeMeo orchestrated an alliance between the Gambinos and the Westies.

In fact, once Gaggi was in prison, DeMeo became the acting capo of Gaggi's crew.

By 1981, Gaggi's sentence was overturned on appeal, and he was released from prison. Gaggi had bribed a juror to make false claims of government misconduct during the trial.

Sadly, Tom Verdillo succumbed to complications related to COVID-19, and on December 27, 2021, he passed away at Lutheran Hospital.41

On New Year's Eve, following fifty-five years in business, Tommaso's Restaurant closed its doors.

CHAPTER TWENTY

Over the years, organized crime has gotten some great publicity.

The myth that organized crime protected communities, somehow providing security and stability, is a fallacy that went Black Hand-in-hand with organized crime for decades.

"It was fairly common during the years I grew up in Brooklyn," Anthony Nelson remembers, "to hear people in Park Slope, Red Hook, Bensonhurst, and Bath Beach express admiration for mobsters who lived among them." He recalls neighbors, family, friends, others he'd meet, saying: "Well, they don't bother me," "They keep our neighborhood safe," "They keep the undesirables out of our area," "I look forward to playing the numbers with them every day."

In the early days of La Cosa Nostra, from the tenements of New York's Lower East Side to the row houses of Chicago's South Side, criminal gangs grew through the coercion of innocents, extortion of local businesses, and use of violence to maintain power.[42] Without exception, in every neighborhood in every American city where organized crime had a presence, extortion and violence created illicit pay-to-play monopolies, eliminating any chance of fair competition.[43]

And drugs?

42. Jacobs, James B. Mobsters, Unions, and Feds: The Mafia and the American Labor Movement. NYU Press. 2006.

43. Reuter, Peter. Disorganized Crime: The Economics of the Visible Hand. MIT Press (MA). 1983.

Don't believe Don Corleone that the Mafia dons forbade involvement with drugs, under penalty of death, because they knew they would lose all their connections to police and senators.

As far back as the 1950s, reports from the Federal Bureau of Narcotics tracked Italian-American crime syndicates importing heroin from Europe, often through Italian and Sicilian intermediaries.[44] By the 1970s, while Hollywood films like *The Godfather* perpetuated this false narrative, the Italian Mafia was flooding our streets with illegal drugs, fueling addiction and destabilizing neighborhoods.[45]

In 1975, researcher David C. Smith analyzed how the American Mafia consciously managed its public image, revealing how its leaders publicly condemned drug trafficking while profiting from it. Smith even documented multiple cases where Mafia figures were directly involved in drug trafficking operations, contradicting their claims to avoid such "dishonorable" activities.[46]

But somehow, the myth perpetuated ... but not for everyone.

"The platitudes about their presence were endless," Nelson says. "That is, unless you were a store owner, a successful local businessman, or a bar owner. The Mafia's presence for them was a cancer that was destroying their livelihood."

You're in business—they're either shaking you down, hijacking from your suppliers, laundering money through phony businesses, stealing from your union, forcing you to use their higher-priced vendors, adding a tax on everything from concrete to windows, and expecting you to turn a blind eye when they bang you out with stolen credit cards or walk out without paying.

Then, when all this underworld overhead becomes too expensive, you need a loan that the bank won't provide. Sure, the wiseguys will lend you money, but at rates that drive you into the street.

"So many businesses were being shaken down," Nelson says. "Many of them were forced to pay money for protection. You had

---

44. Federal Bureau of Narcotics (1950s-1960s). Reports on Organized Crime and Narcotics Trafficking.

45. Harrell, Adele, and Peterson, George E. Drugs, Crime, and Social Isolation: Barriers to Urban Opportunity. The Urban Institute. 1992.

46. Smith, Dwight C. The Mafia Mystique. 1975.

to 'be with somebody' to not be extorted or just plain taken over by factions of one organized crime family or another."

We're not talking 1930s Mulberry Street.

"Since the late 1970s, Kenny McCabe and I had been hearing constantly about this one Genovese Family associate and loan shark, named Victor Caruso," Nelson recalls. "This guy was wreaking havoc in shops and businesses throughout Sheepshead Bay and surrounding neighborhoods."

Caruso was a real piece of work, as they say in Brooklyn.

Nelson and McCabe were soon being bombarded with more reports. "Everyone from precinct detectives to informants began telling us how Caruso terrorized local store owners by walking into their establishments, taking whatever he wanted without payment, and attacking anyone who stood in his way," Nelson remembers.

Then Caruso's brutal attacks took a novel turn.

"Some detectives started describing him as a 'cop fighter' who, among other things, hung out in a deli across the street from the 61st Precinct station house and threw the gun of a patrol officer down a sewer after a confrontation," Nelson says. "I don't know if all the Caruso stories were true, and there were many reports, but he definitely seemed to have a screw loose."

One informant even warned Nelson and McCabe to be careful around Caruso because he was shooting bullet holes into his bedroom walls for fun.

One evening in October 1980, an informant tipped off Nelson that Caruso had arrived at The Barge, a restaurant at 2912 Emmons Avenue, with a woman.

He had a loaded gun strapped to his left ankle.

Nelson and McCabe set up surveillance near the popular eatery situated on an actual barge with waterfront views. Sheepshead Bay separates mainland Brooklyn from the eastern portion of Coney Island and the southern portions of Manhattan and Brighton Beaches, which were once the Outer Barrier Islands overrun by Coney rabbits but now form a peninsula.

At one time boasting the largest fishing fleet on the East Coast, by 1980, there were still dozens of boats moored along the piers on Emmons Avenue, offering a variety of fishing charters and party boat trips. Even in the autumn, the charming restaurant-lined boulevard was bustling with activity.

Before long, the two lawmen spotted the cop fighter himself as Caruso exited The Barge.

"We clearly saw the bulging outline of a weapon on his ankle," Nelson says. "When I pulled his car over and we got him out, his car windows were wide open." Kenny McCabe, without hesitation, bent over, reached in, and went directly for the gun on Caruso's ankle.

"As Kenny held him, I was cuffing him," Nelson says. "Then the female who was in the car with Caruso suddenly began screaming and cursing at us at the top of her lungs. She then reached out through the open car window and grabbed Kenny tightly around his waist."

McCabe slowly walked away from Caruso's car, dragging the screeching woman out of the window with each step he took. And as they muscled a resisting-arrest Caruso into the back seat of Nelson's Gran Fury, the woman still gripping McCabe's waist, a crowd formed on Emmons Avenue.

Then Caruso started yelling, "You fucking guys really think I'm stupid! That was some fucking act she put on. Some fucking act! She could have won an Academy Award. That was some fucking act. When I get outta here, you are never gonna see her again." Caruso paused, then added, "Oh, well … with me," avoiding self-incrimination before the fact.

"I told Caruso that she had nothing to do with his arrest and that she had better not get hit by a bus or die of natural causes because we would be coming for him," Nelson says. "But there was no way he believed me about her innocence, even though it was the truth."

The pair warned the woman about Caruso's suspicions and about his comments, but she chose to continue screaming and cursing anyway. "We also told her to call 911 immediately if he threatened her, but she didn't want to hear it," Nelson says. "It was just another night in Brooklyn with Kenny McCabe."

At the time, still posing as an associate of Gambino and Genovese Families, Nelson seriously considered winding down his undercover work, though not by preference, after these types of encounters. He was built for undercover work. He could not only walk the walk, but also spoke enough Italian to carry on a conversation with a Brooklyn wiseguy from overseas, though he did have trouble understanding some dialects, especially Sicilian variations.

"I had no problem getting vouched for by informants and, in one case, a corrupt lawyer with OC affiliations," Nelson says. "While I was undercover, if they started asking questions, I'd always be evasive and reprimand subjects who tried to get me to reveal names of my associates. But I'd give them enough first names and locations to convince them who I was with."

This work included drug deals in other jurisdictions he initiated through introductions made by informants. These cases originated in New York, with Nelson making connections, then flying south to execute deals with the drugs coming into Florida from South America and Cuba.

"Things really did start to get dangerous for me working these undercover operations, while I was also going out overtly on the street with Kenny," Nelson says.

For his undercover roles, Nelson swapped his Gran Fury FBI-mobile for high-end Cadillacs or Lincoln Town Cars.

Sooner or later, though, the more Nelson posed as a criminal (while at the same time cruising Mafia social clubs at night with Kenny McCabe), he knew someone somewhere would remember running into him in some hotel room or warehouse during a score. "It was just becoming too dangerous for me to be so visible on surveillance with Kenny McCabe while still conducting daily undercover operations," Nelson says.

CHAPTER TWENTY-ONE

By late summer in 1982, Special Agent Anthony Nelson and his squad were homing in on Rocco Santarsiero, a shadowy OC player behind multiple major credit card schemes.

Kenny McCabe confirmed to Nelson that Santarsiero was an associate of the Colombo Family.

"It started really in the early '80s, when some of the Five Families, especially elements in the Colombos and Bonannos, figured out they could earn more money stealing and counterfeiting credit cards than they could by dealing in narcotics," Nelson says.

The earliest schemes involved stealing physical credit cards from the mail, department stores, and unsuspecting victims. Mafia crews then corrupted employees in banks, post offices, and retail stores who provided them with lists of newly issued credit cards before they reached their legitimate owners.

Street-level criminals stole cards out of wallets and purses, raided mailboxes, even dove in dumpsters for discarded imprints of receipts run through knucklebusters, as the countertop credit card processing devices were known. Soon, they no longer needed to hit the dumpster. Employees sold them batches of the carbon copies.

Stolen cards (or pilfered numbers imprinted on blanks) were then either used directly or sold in bulk to fences.

As with all things organized crime, scams became more sophisticated over time. By the mid-80s, Mafia crews were even setting up fake businesses to process fraudulent credit transactions: they'd open a restaurant, jewelry store, or maybe an electronics shop, under a fake name, then install legitimate manual credit card processing devices with credit arrangements with banks. Eventually flagged for fraud, but weeks or maybe even months later, they'd simply abandon the business and move on to the next scam.

Credit cards also added a new wrinkle to the bust-out scams Nelson had been investigating since the 1970s. An inability to certify cardholders at the register allowed Mafia operators to make large purchases of high-value goods (luxury items, electronics, and jewelry). They'd then sell the goods for cash, usually at a deep discount, leaving banks and retailers to absorb the loss.

Mafia crews even paid off insiders at financial institutions to approve fraudulent credit card applications using fake or stolen identities, extend credit limits on existing cards controlled by the Mafia, and suppress fraud alerts or delay investigations.

Law enforcement, in general, was slow to react, and the courts did not mete out severe penalties.

"Even using multiple bogus credit cards and false identities at one time, they could still bring in thousands of dollars in profit every single day, and usually only risked an arrest on minor criminal charges," Nelson explains.

Comparatively speaking, if someone was caught selling a substantial amount of a controlled substance, such as heroin or cocaine, they faced lengthy prison terms, if not life imprisonment.

In fact, the Anti-Drug Abuse Act of 1986 included high mandatory prison sentences for cocaine possession, which were significantly different for powder cocaine and crack cocaine. Possession of five hundred grams of cocaine (equal to a standard bag of flour) triggered the same five-year mandatory minimum sentence as if you were busted with only five grams of crack.[47]

---

47. Madeo. "Anti-Drug Abuse Act Creates Racially Biased 100 to 1 Crack/Powder Disparity." https://calendar.eji.org/racial-injustice/ oct/27#:~:text=Oct%2027%2C%201986-,Federal%20Anti%2DDrug%20 Abuse%20Act%20Signed%2C%20Creating%20Racially%20Biased%20 100,people%20incarcerated%20in%20federal%20prison.

"But getting caught with one or two counterfeit or stolen credit cards would usually result in taking a plea to a misdemeanor with little or no resulting jail time," Nelson says.

In addition, the profits from the credit cards often outweighed those from drug sales.

By the late 1980s, the FBI, Secret Service, and NYPD Organized Crime Task Force, among other agencies, were struggling to derail this full-blown criminal epidemic as wiseguys from Brooklyn to Boston were trading credit cards like baseball cards.

In 1987, the FBI exposed a large-scale credit card fraud ring tied to the Gambinos, which racked up millions through counterfeit card transactions. Two years later, a takedown exposed a Lucchese-controlled scam using fake businesses and stolen credit card data to amass stunning profits.

Then, in the late 1980s, the feds brought a case against the Colombos, exposing how Mafia influence extended beyond cards and into bank fraud, including manipulating credit applications and laundering money.

Major credit card companies like American Express, Visa, and MasterCard hired private investigators to identify patterns to help staunch the bleeding. Many had prior law enforcement experience and began to work directly with the FBI.

One such ace investigator hired by American Express was Herbert "Herbie" Goldstein.

"Herbie had developed so much information and intelligence about illegal credit card activity that I gave him a desk in the Brooklyn-Queens FBI Office," Nelson says. The former Postal Police employee soon became a daily presence.

At each turn, criminals devised new schemes and tactics.

"At first, after the wiseguys banged out the stolen credit cards, they became useless because their loss had already been reported," Nelson says. "However, they learned a technique of melting a card in a particular way, and for a particular amount of time, to remove the numbers, while the remainder of the cards stayed intact." They then acquired embossing machines to place new numbers of valid credit cards onto the stolen ones.

"They could relatively easily obtain valid card numbers from a growing army of greedy waiters, waitresses, and gas station attendants who retained credit card receipts from their customers and then gladly sold the info to their Mob contacts," Nelson adds.

As the credit card crime problem grew, the wiseguys faced stunted industry opposition.

"The credit card companies, for some time, were reluctant to add security features to their cards that might discourage their use by legitimate customers," Nelson says. "There were no chips, photos, or other protections on the cards, except for a magnetic stripe that could easily be decoded."

Then Mob soldiers and associates took their show on the road.

Organized crime ring leaders were handing out prepackaged bags to their associates, containing not just stacks of counterfeit cards, but driver's licenses from all over the country. They were also given other forms of identification, even bogus Social Security cards.

"They then gave them airline tickets to fly to small-town malls and shopping centers all over America, including as far as Hawaii," Nelson says. "The counterfeit cards generally were embossed with valid credit card numbers, and the subjects would usually try to withdraw money by simply taking a guess as to the available cash balances of the legitimate cardholders. Others used the cards to purchase jewelry and electronics."

Nelson, along with Special Agent Gordon Strand, concentrated on tracking down the sources of the cards and checks flooding the market, then assigning the individual cases to other agents.

In addition to the counterfeit cards, American Express had suffered an enormous loss by theft of thousands of real cards that were called the "ML" cards, because those code letters were preprinted on the otherwise blank cards.

"I especially tried to get these cards off the street for American Express by having some of my informants seek them out and buy them using American Express funds," Nelson says.

American Express stood to lose millions of dollars just with the ML card scam alone.

"We made many buys of the ML cards and stolen AMEX Traveler's Checks with the help of American Express Investigator Herbie Goldstein," Nelson recalls. He, along with Goldstein and squad members, raided location after location across the city with federal search warrants. "We were very successful at recovering most of the ML cards as well as many counterfeit Visa and MasterCard cards. But the real target was getting to the source, the distributor of the genuine and counterfeit cards, as well as the printer of the fictitious identification.

"We had a federal prosecutor in the Southern District of New York who was assigned to help us obtain the search and arrest warrants for the counterfeit cards and stolen American Express Traveler Checks, which were as good as having US currency," Nelson reveals. "Traveler checks were guaranteed by American Express, so virtually every commercial establishment accepted them since they could not suffer loss, even if the checks were stolen."

By that summer in 1982, Nelson was closing in on one of those sources: Rocco Santarsiero.

"The investigation indicated Santarsiero was part of a sophisticated operation that used forged and stolen credit cards to rack up tens of thousands of dollars in purchases. And Santarsiero seemed to be the closest person to the subjects who had stolen the shipments of ML cards and traveler's checks."

On September 8, 1982, Nelson obtained a federal search warrant and led his team in a raid on an apartment occupied by Santarsiero on East 90th Street and 3rd Avenue in Manhattan. The apartment was littered with luxury products, designer clothing, and high-end electronics, most with price tags and packaging intact.

The arrest was based on evidence gathered by Nelson and fellow FBI investigators, including input from Goldstein at American Express, and carried out by Officer Marco Burdi.[48]

"Virtually every item we seized in the apartment had been stolen through the use of counterfeit credit cards," Nelson recalls. "We also recovered a quantity of the real cards that had been stolen from a shipment en route to American Express." Also recovered

---

48. Messing, Philip. "Cops Smash Giant Credit Card Ring." New York Post

were multiple fake IDs, forged credit cards, and several blank New Jersey driver's licenses. Authorities also confiscated credit card embossing machines.

Santarsiero's twenty-two-year-old girlfriend was questioned but released at the scene.

"The federal prosecutor assigned to these cases was none other than Paul Shechtman, one of the greatest federal prosecutors ever," Nelson says. "Although I have not seen Paul Shechtman in many years now, he had become a good personal friend of mine, and he had even been to my house in Brooklyn and to dinner with me and Syndee."

Shechtman served as the New York State director of Criminal Justice Services, taught law school, served as the counsel to former New York District Attorney Robert Morgenthau, and in private practice, represented famous clients, including hip hop megastar Lil Kim.

"It would take an entire chapter to list all of his prior positions and accomplishments," Nelson expresses. "Paul had also returned to the US Attorney's Office in the SDNY as head of the Criminal Division. Paul Shechtman and Walter Mack were two of the most respected prosecutors whom FBI agents sought for help with their cases. Shechtman also became an expert in prosecuting the credit card crime problem because he also led Secret Service prosecutions related to credit cards."

Soon, the problem of stolen and counterfeit credit cards had grown so enormously that Congress passed specific legislation to combat it. "They also delegated the investigation of these crimes to the US Secret Service if the offense was not organized crime related."

However, the determination of what was organized crime-related caused some conflict between the FBI and the Secret Service. "This was one of the rare times that I experienced conflict with another law enforcement agency," Nelson explains. "I didn't care about who led the investigations, but they were trying to identify and gain access to some of my informants."

Nelson received a letter of commendation from then US Attorney Rudolph Giuliani regarding the credit card cases and related theft of millions of dollars' worth of stolen Traveler's Checks.

It was a significant bust, but the case did little to stem the rising tide of financial crimes associated with organized crime. "The counterfeit credit card problem during Santarsiero's era had become so enormous and profitable that there were scores of subjects we identified who were involved in one part of the schemes or another," Nelson says.

By the 1990s, the Mafia had evolved its credit card scams, moving from physical theft and counterfeit cards to more sophisticated cyber fraud techniques. They began working with Russian and Eastern European hackers to commit large-scale identity theft, eventually laying the groundwork for modern digital credit card fraud.

Eventually, as digital technology progressed, the credit card companies added a number of security protocols, including computer "chips" to their credit card operations and the physical retail theft decreased significantly.

CHAPTER TWENTY-TWO

In the summer 1981, Nelson and McCabe made it a habit of surveilling RoSal's Restaurant.

In the early 1980s, underworld underlings were still under strict orders to shape up at whatever social club served as their crew's base of operations.

No excuses.

But showing respect was not the only reason to show up—there was crime to be organized.

Even with electronic surveillance a growing risk, face to face was still safer than phone calls for conducting Mob business. Receipts, ledgers, org charts—basically any documentation—could later implicate individuals in illegal activities. Crew members and associates also needed to hand over cuts of illicit earnings, known as tribute.

Mob-controlled social clubs and restaurants provided a somewhat controlled environment for gatherings. Over time, and with tips from informants, Kenny McCabe and Anthony Nelson developed a sense of when, where, and why they'd find the best surveillance opportunities.

Earlier that day, one of Nelson's informants tipped him off that crew members were to pass their thick envelopes of tribute to Genovese Family capo Ottaviano "Tommy" Lombardi. Within the Genovese hierarchy, Lombardi took over the DelDucca-Tieri Crew once Funzi Tieri was elevated to acting boss.

As they idled in that Plymouth Gran Fury, McCabe and Nelson observed a parade of Genovese racketeers marching in and out of RoSal's.

"To be even more obvious, I parked in a bus stop across the street from the restaurant," Nelson recalls. "Then a yellow Lincoln Town Car pulled up with none other than Anthony Casso and an individual we later identified as Thomas Capelli."

Now here was a rising star in the Brooklyn rackets.

Not Thomas Capelli.

Capelli was an alleged soldier, sure. And he was associated with one of the more twisted episodes in New York organized crime lore.[49]

Thomas Capelli was the first husband of Kimberly Kennaugh, unkindly dubbed by media as The Black Widow after her fourth husband, NYC Police Department Officer Ralph Dols, was shot to death in the summer of 1997—a hit ordered by Kennaugh's third husband, former Colombo Family acting boss Joel "Joe Waverly" Cacace, splashed across the front page of the *New York Daily News* and other tabloids.[50]

Cacace ordered the murder of twenty-eight-year-old Dols, driven by a sense of humiliation that his former wife had wed a member of law enforcement. (Kennaugh's second husband, mobster Enrico Carrini, was also murdered in 1987, but after they had separated.)

However, that day, Anthony Casso was by far the heavier heavy stepping out of that yellow Lincoln.

---

49. Mcphee, Michele. "She Married Three Mobsters and a Cop. Two Husbands Died Violently. Now the 'Black Widow' Breaks Her Silence. NOWHERE TO TURN FOR THE ex-MOLL Shunned by MAFIA – and NYPD." New York Daily News. April 9, 2018. https://www.nydailynews.com/2004/08/24/she-married-three-mobsters-and-a-cop-two-husbands-died-violently-now-the-black-widow-breaks-her-silence-nowhere-to-turn-for-the-ex-moll-shunned-by-mafia-and-nypd/

50. Marzulli, John. "Widow Seeks Vindication as 2 Mobsters Go on Trial in Murder of Her Husband, Officer Ralph Dols." New York Daily News. January 10, 2019. https://www.nydailynews.com/2012/03/19/widow-seeks-vindication-as-2-mobsters-go-on-trial-in-murder-of-her-husband-officer-ralph-dols/

By then, Casso, nicknamed "Gaspipe" for his penchant to beat people with, well, gas pipes, had risen dramatically in the Lucchese Family. Widely regarded as a homicidal maniac, Casso is suspected of committing dozens more homicides than the 15 he admitted to federal authorities.

"Kenny immediately recognized Casso sitting in the passenger seat of Capelli's car," Nelson remembers.

Then the two gangsters got out of the vehicle and headed toward the restaurant. Capelli appeared to have his hand inside a brown paper bag as they entered.

"Kenny and I both thought that Capelli had a gun in the bag and was going to kill someone inside RoSal's. We jumped out of my FBI car, but they quickly moved into the restaurant before we could get into position to intercept them."

They entered the restaurant, then paused. RoSal's was packed with diners. In an interesting twist, a live band was playing the haunting melody of "The Godfather Waltz" at that very moment. Not hearing gunshots, they retreated, deciding to wait outside out of caution rather than risk the possibility of causing a wild shootout inside.

Shortly after, Casso and Capelli reappeared, without incident, and drove away in the Lincoln.

Tailing the wiseguys for a bit, Nelson then turned on his police lights and siren and pulled them over a couple of blocks away on 86th Street, barking on his vehicle's loudspeaker to put the car in park.

"But as we approached the vehicle on foot, I saw that Capelli's reverse-gear white lights had not flickered," Nelson says.

In the 1980s, the transmission gear shift lever of the Lincoln Town Car, as in most vehicles, had to shift sequentially from drive, into neutral, then into reverse, before stopping in park. Whenever a driver shifted from drive into park, their rear lights would flicker on as the gear shift passed reverse.

Having pulled over hundreds of wiseguys, Nelson knew what to watch for to ensure safety. "If I didn't see the white reverse gear lights briefly flicker, I knew the transmission sequence was not right and the vehicle was not in park," Nelson says. "Whenever that happened, I knew I was probably going to face a pursuit. And that day, I knew he didn't put the vehicle into park as I ordered."

Sure enough, the Lincoln tore off at high speed.

"Kenny and I figured they didn't know we recognized Casso," Nelson says. "So, we set up surveillance at the corner of 86th Street and 14th Avenue, thinking that one way or the other, Casso was going to return to the 19th Hole bar."

The 19th Hole. That notorious Lucchese locale had become Casso's base of operations.

In 1974, at the age of thirty-two, Anthony Casso was officially inducted into the Lucchese crime Family. He became a member of Vincent Foceri's crew, which operated out of 116th Street in Manhattan as well as maintaining a strong presence along 14th Avenue in Brooklyn. Shortly after his induction, Casso became close to another rising star in the Family, Vittorio "Little Vic" Amuso, a partnership that lasted for two bloody decades. The two men committed scores of scores, trafficked in narcotics, ran a burglary ring, eliminated informants, and orchestrated untold mayhem across the underworld.

Casso and Amuso, solid earners for the Family, were moved to one of the more prominent crews operated by Casso's eventual mentor, Lucchese captain Christopher "Christie Tick" Furnari, the secret owner of the 19th Hole.

Within Furnari's 19th Hole Crew, Casso and Amuso led the Bypass Gang, a bank and jewelry store burglary ring with a knack for overcoming, or bypassing, security systems throughout New York City and into Long Island. Law enforcement officials estimated that throughout the 1970s and '80s, the Bypass Gang looted over one hundred million dollars by targeting bank vaults and safety deposit boxes.

Later, when Furnari was elevated to serve as the Lucchese Family's consigliere, he chose Casso to take his place as capo of the 19th Hole Crew. However, Casso turned down the promotion and recommended Vic Amuso for the role instead—solidifying a close alliance.

Nelson and McCabe staked out the bar. Sure enough, a few minutes later, Capelli's Lincoln rolled up.

"I pulled my FBI car right up to the grill of the Lincoln on 14th Avenue to block it in, but Capelli put his car in reverse and then forward onto the sidewalk," Nelson says. "He tore off speeding again. The escaping vehicle spun Kenny around like a top because he had just grabbed hold of the vehicle's door. I had to jump headfirst into my car to avoid getting hit."

Nelson took off after them and began transmitting the chase over the "citywide" law enforcement radio channel.

Several miles away on 86th Street, under the elevated train, 62nd Precinct patrol cars joined the chase. But instead of pursuing the Lincoln, they blocked the road and pulled over Nelson's Gran Fury, even though he had his emergency lights flashing and siren blaring.

"I was furious because Capelli and Casso got away, again, and I instinctively believed the 62 Precinct cars had pulled us over on purpose so that Casso could get away, even though that was unlikely the reason," Nelson says.

While cooperating with authorities, Casso revealed that highly decorated NYPD Detectives Stephen Caracappa and Louis Eppolito had secretly been on his payroll, carrying out contract killings at his direction. He also disclosed that the two detectives— who had previously served with the Federal Organized Crime Strike Force—had provided him with confidential information, including the identities of police and FBI informants, several of who were later murdered as a result.

The following week, Nelson and McCabe went out on the street on the same day of the week and at the same time of day. "We just played a long shot that maybe we would find the car again," Nelson says. "We then located it parked on 20th Avenue and 86th Street. We saw Capelli exit a building there and try to enter the Lincoln. This time, I had put my FBI car close enough to the Lincoln's driver's side door so he could not move."

Then, as McCabe pulled Capelli out of the vehicle, the Mafia soldier reached into his waistband and pulled out a handgun.

"I could not shoot because Kenny was right up against him and holding him by the collar," Nelson says. "Instead, I yelled out that he had a gun."

"This is just one of so many stories I remember clearly," recalls Duke McCabe. "My father actually broke Thomas Capelli's face with the butt of his gun. Capelli was pulling his gun, but Anthony couldn't shoot him because my dad was in between them. So, my father pulled his gun and literally broke his face with it." After McCabe hit Capelli with his weapon, Capelli's gun went flying into the Lincoln Town Car.

"This time we weren't about to notify the 6-2 of anything," Nelson says. "We just took Capelli to the Brooklyn DA's Office and then logged him into Central Booking."

They charged Capelli with Attempted Murder of Police Officers and Possession of a Loaded Firearm.

"But as usual within the justice system, even back then, I believe he was allowed to plead to something much less serious," Nelson says. "We didn't have enough evidence to go back out and get Casso since he wasn't the driver. Nor could we prove he had a weapon at the time of the vehicle pursuit. Again, after we arrested Capelli, I believe he pleaded guilty to a reduced charge."

After his arrest in 1993, Casso became one of the most senior Mafia figures ever to cooperate with the government. He entered a plea deal and was placed in the Witness Protection Program. Initially confessing to a dozen murders, Casso later acknowledged his role in several more when questioned further. However, his cooperation unraveled when authorities discovered he had concealed the extent of his financial assets and lied about key details. He also denied having any part in the murder of Peter "Fat Pete" Chiodo's uncle or the firebombing of Chiodo's elderly grandmother's home—claims investigators believed were false.

Gaspipe Casso ordered the murder of the four-hundred-plus pound Lucchese capo Chiodo, who had been the gangster's right hand for years and known as one of Casso's "angels of death." Facing indictments in multiple cases, Chiodo decided to plead guilty, angling for a reasonable ten-year incarceration. When he didn't clear his decision, Casso gave the order to "kill Fat Pete."

On May 8, 1991, at a service station on Staten Island, three hitmen shot Chiodo twelve times in the chest, stomach, legs, and arms, but he survived—due to his massive girth, according to doctors.

After surviving a second attempt by a Lucchese assassin disguised as a doctor sneaking into Chiodo's hospital room, Fat Pete agreed to serve as a key witness for the government in the Windows case. Chiodo's uncle was later murdered, and his sister was seriously wounded in a shooting.

In 1998, after several more infractions and a failed polygraph, Casso's plea agreement was rescinded and he was dropped from witness protection.

Later that same year, a federal judge handed Casso a sentence totaling 455 years behind bars for his involvement in racketeering, extortion, and multiple murders. Twenty years later, on December 15, 2020, Casso died in prison due to complications from COVID-19.

CHAPTER TWENTY-THREE

In 1981, the local tabloids in New York City ran a story about a threat made by a Genovese Family "associate" to shoot NYPD Detective Kenny McCabe and FBI Special Agent Anthony Nelson.

Such threats not only affected the agent.

But as they say, the heart wants what the heart wants … no matter what it gets.

"At the beginning of our relationship, I didn't dwell on the dangers of Anthony's job," Syndee Nelson reflects. "Anthony is quiet by nature and didn't tell me every detail of what he was doing. But several weeks after we met, he did confide that he had been watching one of my neighbors, who was shot to death with another individual shortly after we first met."

Syndee grew up in the Bensonhurst, where everyone knows someone who's connected or connected to the connected. As a teenager, she attended Lafayette High School in Bath Beach. Opened in 1939 in the shadow of the elevated BMT West End Line that runs out to Coney Island, Lafayette is a massive school, the first building of its type, designed to accommodate upwards of four thousand students. The school can be seen in several clips in the background during the harrowing chase scene from *The French Connection*.

Over the years, Lafayette produced its fair share of distinguished alumni, from sports (Sandy Koufax, Sal Campisi, John Franco) to the arts (Vic Damone, Paul Sorvino, Rhea Perlman, Maurice Sendak, Larry King). Yet there are likely just as many notorious as notable alumni. Though like Frank "Curly" Lino (former Bonanno captain turned informant), you won't find most of them on the graduate rolls. Lino never made it past the tenth grade at Lafayette, dropping out to run with a local Mafia farm team, the Avenue U Boys.

In unrelated alumni news, infamous financier and child sex offender Jeffrey Epstein skipped two grades before graduating in 1969.

Lafayette was always a tough Southern Brooklyn blue-collar school, even before it was tabbed "Horror High" by New York's tabloids in 2002 due to rampant violence. The school eventually closed in 2010, replaced by a collection of smaller institutions. Yet back in the 1960s, with Bath Beach predominantly Italian (and to some extent Jewish), Lafayette was a fertile OC breeding ground.

"Through Syndee's attendance at Lafayette," Nelson says, "she became acquainted with many of the future wiseguys that I would someday pursue with federal arrest warrants."

By all accounts, Syndee was a strikingly beautiful woman, and she later modeled, including posing in *GQ* ads.

"Syndee had to navigate the landscape of Italian social clubs on a daily basis," Nelson says. "She learned to ignore the constant whistling and lewd comments that came her way during her walks home from school and shopping."

But Syndee was no arm candy; exceptionally bright, not to mention savvy, she was well aware of the neighborhood's dynamics.

"As I began to get close with Anthony, I learned more about what his job entailed, and it made me much more aware of my surroundings and what I was doing," Syndee shares. "Although even at the early age of twenty, I'd already been cautious about the dangers growing up in Brooklyn."

Their courtship lasted two years. They were married on August 31, 1980.

Being married to an FBI agent—especially one investigating organized crime—can be emotionally and mentally taxing.

"After I learned more about his job and his associations with members of the Mafia, it gave me concerns about his well-being,"

Syndee says. "But I didn't, however, think too much about his job impacting me because I had been, and still am, a very independent person."

An agent's life is demanding, unpredictable, and often dangerous. But at least they have a line of sight into what's going on. For those who love them, there's always the fear that something could happen on the job, whether it's retaliation, an ambush, or a case going sideways.

"Anthony rarely brought the job home, but I always knew when he was facing stressful situations, particularly working undercover," Syndee says. "He'd be gone from mornings well into the night, sometimes unable to call me to let me know that he wouldn't be home."

Every time a member of law enforcement leaves for work, there's some level of uncertainty about whether they'll come back safely, which can easily tip over into dread in the darkness of night.

Or … if some of that madness will follow him home.

"Based on her life experiences and the way she met me, she was much more streetwise and acutely aware of the dangers I faced every day, especially during my undercover days," Nelson says. "But she had to also be concerned about her own safety, since it was widely known she was married to an FBI agent."

And Syndee's apprehension must have magnified once that cop party started breaking out in front of their home a couple nights a week.

Kenny McCabe and fellow NYPD Detective Ron Cadieux were now a regular presence at the Nelson's Mill Basin residence before embarking on their rounds.

And if that wasn't enough to draw attention, Detective John Murphy of the NYPD Auto Crime Unit soon began to accompany the lawmen once he began investigating a car theft operation controlled by Patty Testa, the brother of DeMeo Crew member Joseph Testa.

"John was also gathering evidence about all of the collateral criminal activities of Roy DeMeo, Nino Gaggi, and the rest of the Gemini Lounge Crew, including the murders they committed,"

Nelson adds. "In fact, like Kenny McCabe, John Murphy had become the institutional data bank for information about Roy DeMeo's activities."

By the way, the Gemini Lounge, the same notorious Flatlands clubhouse of the DeMeo Crew, where it was later learned dozens of victims "disappeared," was within walking distance of the Nelson home.

FBI agents can't and won't share much about their work with their spouses, especially cases involving organized crime. Still, Syndee couldn't help but overhear snippets of conversations here and there about the Gemini Crew's criminal activities and their indifference to the value of human life. However, most nights as the lawmen rolled out, she was left alone to deal with these concerns.

"Many of life's responsibilities, caring for our home and for our children, were left for me to handle," Syndee reflects. "Many of those responsibilities involved taking our children to school and sports events without Anthony." At one point, Anthony had missed so many functions with family and friends that some teased Syndee by saying they didn't believe she even had a husband. She shrugged it off.

"There were times, often not apparent to others, when Anthony did get away from work and we'd run away, get away, take these wonderful extended vacations with our children," Syndee fondly recalls. "These vacations and free weekends we took together whenever we could surely made up for the long periods when those luxuries were just not possible."

On these rare trips, the Nelsons never stuck to the typical itineraries followed by other tourists. "We always enjoyed places to visit, mostly in Maine, that were essentially off the beaten path and some places not even accurately mapped," Nelson says.

This has led to some interesting scenarios, like one trip to the far northern parts of Maine. Passing through a small town with a narrow border crossing into Canada, Nelson stopped to store his firearm in a hotel safe on the US side of the border.

"After I approached the Canadian border checkpoint in a Mercedes, a female border officer ordered me to pull off to the side of the road," Nelson says.

Canadian border officers instructed the Nelsons to wait in their office while they examined every inch of his vehicle, even removing the seats.

"At one point, a female officer approached me with two items in her hand," Nelson says. "I knew from the sound and manner in which she spoke that she believed the items were some sort of weapon or contraband."

These suspicious items?

Electric hand warmers.

"I couldn't understand, given such a cold climate, how she'd never seen or heard of hand warmers," Nelson says.

After about an hour and a half of being detained, Nelson spoke with a supervisor and revealed that he was an FBI Special Agent, verified by his credentials. The tense atmosphere relaxed, with the supervisor asking Nelson why he didn't identify himself earlier.

"I just told him that I didn't want to influence his actions by inferring that I should get special treatment," Nelson says. "He was so apologetic that he personally escorted our car onto the Canadian side of the border and then directed us to a nearby casino."

The supervisor explained that they were in such a remote part of Maine with a border crossing really only used by nearby residents, so they suspected Nelson was running drugs, especially since he was driving a Mercedes.

These escapes were few and far between.

"Both Anthony and I have very large families," Syndee says, "So I did have loving support when Anthony was out of town or involved in several critical incidents."

As the years wore on, Syndee, like Kenny's wife Kathy McCabe, could not attend certain social functions—weddings, funerals, or simple dinners with friends—if there were connections to La Cosa Nostra.

This is not much of a concern for the wife of an FBI agent in, say, Middle America. But in Brooklyn? That threat is real.

"I already knew the social clubs and places I should avoid," Syndee says. "However, it wasn't until I met Anthony that I realized there were so many more locations, restaurants, and catering halls that I had to steer clear of."

In the spring of 1981, Syndee was rattled by the murder of James Bennett.

On April 29, Bennett was slain outside the residence of his in-laws at Avenue N and East 59th Street in East Flatbush, Brooklyn. Bennett was a sixty-five-year-old Lucchese associate set to testify against DeMeo Crew member Richard Mastrangelo regarding a drug smuggling operation. He was shot twice in the head, allegedly by DeMeo Crew members Anthony Senter and Joseph Testa, known as the Gemini Twins for being nearly inseparable, as well as their mutual ultraviolent tendencies.

Bennett was shot to death not far from the front door of the Nelson home in Mill Basin on the same day he was to testify in the federal case.

Syndee was especially concerned about this murder because the assassination threats in the New York tabloids had hit just two weeks prior.

At the time of the publicized death threats, Nelson was in Fort Lauderdale, Florida, posing as a New York wiseguy conducting a multi-kilo undercover cocaine buy, while Syndee was home alone to read about it in the newspapers.

She called her lifelong friend, Grace Foster, to stay with her during Nelson's absence.

Although it wasn't meant to be funny, Syndee vividly recalls Grace, and her then husband, Doug, pushing her in front of them as they exited the front door of the Nelson home, telling her, "You go first!" and joking about dodging bullets that were surely going to start flying as soon as they stepped outside.

"Then, when Bennett was murdered, Syndee thought it had something to do with my undercover work, or whatever Kenny,

Ron, and I were doing concerning the DeMeo Crew," Nelson recalls.

She wasn't the only one speculating on a possible connection.

Other concerned FBI agents started dropping by Nelson's desk, asking whether Bennett was his informant and if he had been at Nelson's house just before the murder.

"I'd heard Bennett's name before, but he was not my informant and I'd never even met or spoken to him," Nelson confirms.

Then, to further heighten her anxiety, there were two attempts to steal Nelson's FBI car from in front of their home.

"I strongly believed that Peter LaFroscia had something to do with at least one of those two attempts," Nelson suspects.

Disturbed by death threats in the newspapers, incidents outside her home, and Bennett's murder, Syndee still soldiered on, dealing with the reality better than what could be expected of most people.

"I don't think there's anything I can do or say to make up for the depth of Syndee's profound sacrifice," Nelson says. "There's more than one individual behind the badge. I could not have done what I did without her support, and I deeply love and admire her for her strength and resiliency. You know, they don't award commendations to the wives and the families, but they really should."

CHAPTER TWENTY-FOUR

By the early 1980s, Special Agent Anthony Nelson, on occasion while working undercover, had to travel to Florida—Key West, Miami, and Fort Lauderdale—to participate in cocaine transactions related to organized crime narcotics investigations.

"These were deals in my cases and those of Special Agent Warren Flagg, put together by subjects I dealt with as an undercover operative in New York," Nelson says. "I went to Florida on these occasions because the New York subjects wanted me there to conclude the deals and pick up the drugs."

The Bureau increased its use of undercover agents significantly starting the decade prior in the wake of high-profile cases involving organized crime families, political corruption (e.g., Watergate), and drug trafficking rings.

Nelson knew to be ready to go at a moment's notice.

"There is no such thing as a typical day for a special agent," states the Special Agent Frequently Asked Questions on the Bureau's public site. "One day you could be executing a search warrant and making an arrest, while the next you could be testifying in court. Your morning could entail catching up on paperwork in the office, while the afternoon could bring a meeting with a high-level source. No two days are ever the same for an FBI special agent."[51]

In fact, a recent job ad on employment site Indeed.com states that as an FBI agent, you may be called upon to travel all over the country. "You may need to travel to conduct investigations and

51. FBI. "SPECIAL AGENT FAQ." https://fbijobs.gov/sites/default/files/2023-03/Special_Agent_FAQ.pdf

interview witnesses. While these are professional work trips, you might still see more of the country and work outside the office regularly."[52]

For Nelson, this usually meant slipping into an undercover persona to fly into Miami and execute a high-risk, high-volume narcotics transaction in a seedy hotel room.

Criminals are highly suspicious by nature, and the underworld is such an incestuous place, so this was hazardous undercover work.

Fortunately, Nelson just fit the part—not just because of how he looked, but how he carried himself: tall, dark, athletic, with a Mediterranean edge from his mother's side, always polished and composed. Calm and deliberate, he could turn on that slow-burning menace, command a space with silence and confidence. When he spoke, Nelson's voice had weight—a clipped, regional New York accent, thick-but-not-too-thick, like a Sunday sauce, with just enough Brooklynese or Italian inflections and dashes of street codes, spoken in a low, steady tone. Never cartoonish. Never loud unless it served a purpose.

Nelson learned to not posture or emote, blend but not disappear—leaning in just enough to earn trust, not attract suspicion. He acted without acting, lied without flinching, and listened without reacting.

A skilled mimic, Nelson studied the way others spoke, sat, and moved, then matched these mannerisms and made them his own. In criminal circles, standing out gets you killed. Fitting in meant being patient. Letting others talk. Waiting for the right moment to ask a question or catch a slip.

Cops rush.

Nelson didn't.

But even with seasoned undercover talent, this was always a high-risk proposition, especially when the targets were ultraviolent organized crime lords and their armed minions.

---

52. Indeed Editorial Team. "The Pros and Cons of Being an FBI Agent (Plus FAQs)." Indeed Career Guide. June 9, 2025. https://www.indeed.com/career-advice/finding-a-job/pros-and-cons-of-being-fbi-agent

In the early 1980s, no setting was more dangerous for undercover operatives than Miami.

Pablo Escobar and the Medellín cartel had established cocaine trafficking routes into the United States through South Florida, superseding the Cuban Mafia, who previously controlled drug smuggling into the Sunshine State. They were soon pouring hundreds of kilograms of cocaine into Miami every week via airdrops over the Everglades from small planes, pulling down millions per month.

Miami was ideal as a hub for cocaine smuggling due to its proximity to the Caribbean and the influx of Spanish-speaking immigrant populations from Central and South America. By 1981, Miami was responsible for trafficking seventy percent of the cocaine into America, seventy percent of its marijuana, and ninety percent of its counterfeit Quaaludes.

Other major traffickers in Miami at the time included the Falcon brothers and Sal Magluta, who smuggled in around two billion dollars of cocaine from Colombia alone, as well as Medellín traffickers Rafael Cardona Salazar, Carlos Lehder, Mickey Munday, Jon Roberts, Griselda Blanco, George Jung, Barry Seal, and Max Mermelstein.

With the drugs came the violence.

These were the days of the Cocaine Cowboys' drug wars, which burst onto the front pages across the nation following a shootout at the Dadeland Mall on July 11, 1979. Two members of a Colombian drug gang entered a liquor store and shot two men in broad daylight. Miami was soon anointed the "drug capital of the world."

How deadly was Miami?

In 1979, there were 349 murders in the city. The following year, Miami law enforcement recorded 573 murders. As Nelson was flying into Miami International in 1981, it topped out at 621 homicides. That year, the Miami City Morgue had become so inundated with dead bodies that it was forced to rent out a refrigerated truck, which remained in use until 1988.

Life was cheap in the Miami underworld that spring as FBI Special Agent Anthony Nelson flew down posing as a Gambino Family associate fronting a multi-kilo cocaine deal that took him from New York City to both Key West and Miami.

Much of Miami's significant drug trafficking activity was centered at the Mutiny Hotel in Coconut Grove's Sailboat Bay. Nelson's assignment was to orchestrate a risky undercover cocaine buy.

With the transaction being conducted at a second location, Nelson was held at gunpoint by a crew of nervous, dope-addled dealers in the nearby Kings Inn Motel, another notorious drug spot in Miami that had racked up its share of homicides.

"Two fellow FBI agents, Stephen Carbone and George Hanna, acted as my muscle and drug testers during the transaction," Nelson recalls.

This was good company for Nelson to entrust with his life. Both these exceptional agents went on to long, successful careers with the Bureau. Stephen Carbone was the FBI supervisor who led the federal probe into the Lufthansa heist. George Hanna would receive commendations for his work as the FBI supervisory special agent, including work on the Bonanno/DeCavalcante Squad, before leaving the Bureau, followed by a successful role as senior director of investigations for Major League Baseball.

In that seedy drug hotel along the outskirts of Miami, Anthony Nelson outwardly kept his cool—outgunned, outnumbered, nearly out of time.

"While Carbone and Hanna tested the cocaine at another location, I had to stay with six of the drug dealers inside this small hotel room until the money for the drugs arrived," Nelson says.

But there was a major snag in the plan that only Nelson knew in those critical moments.

"There was no money."

Facing down six trigger-happy Cocaine Cowboys expecting the delivery of a bag of drug cash that was not only late, but not even coming, presents a challenge for any undercover agent.

With the clock ticking down, no money in sight, tension escalating in that humid hotel room, Nelson knew he had to somehow talk his way out of that room.

They train agents at Quantico how to handle this type of work, but the exact scenario Nelson faced is one of the reasons the Bureau rarely uses early career agents for undercover assignments— criminals are easily provoked, overly suspicious, have no regard for human life, and, in that hotel room, are increasingly impatient. Not triggering a violent reaction takes more than bravery. It takes a level of self-control that is both innate and tempered through years of high-stress investigations.

And it also demands blind faith in the skill, discipline, and bravery of the members of the law enforcement you're depending on, just outside that door—some you've never met, let alone worked with.

That special bond was about to be tested.

"I was able to casually talk one of the drug dealers, named Richard Shubella, into accompanying me outside to the motel parking lot to supposedly await the arrival of the funds," Nelson says.

Shubella followed Nelson out the door into the parking lot, close, gripping a small-caliber handgun.

Nelson didn't see anyone, but he trusted that his fellow agents were in position when he suddenly dropped to the ground of the parking lot as part of a prearranged plan with the Miami Office of the FBI.

"So I drop and suddenly a team of Miami FBI agents swoop in to make the arrest of Shubella and the others inside the motel room," Nelson says.

A total of eleven drug dealers were arrested at the Kings Inn Motel and the location where Carbone and Hanna had tested the cocaine.

Just about every one of those arrested had been armed.

Unexpected travel is not the only challenging part of an FBI agent's job description. In fact, also listed in that recent job posting on Indeed is another you'll not find in advertisements for other types of careers: "Working as an FBI agent can sometimes put you in danger. Agents regularly search for those who have committed crimes, and some criminals may be aggressive. The FBI provides extensive training in topics such as defensive tactics. This helps to mitigate some of the danger and keeps FBI agents safer while they're working."[52]

So yes, there is no such thing as a typical day for an FBI agent.

When you join the Bureau, you never know.

One day, you could be executing a search warrant and making an arrest in New York, the next, you could be in a seedy hotel room on the outskirts of Miami, blindly trusting the agents on the other side of that door are ready when you step out, a gun at your back.

CHAPTER TWENTY-FIVE

Throughout the early 1980s, many agencies in New York were chasing the same bad guys.

The FBI was assigning squads dedicated to each of the Mafia's Five Families. The Department of Justice (DOJ) and the US Attorney's Offices were developing new prosecutorial strategies targeting organized crime.

The Drug Enforcement Administration (DEA) was investigating international drug trafficking rings, while the Internal Revenue Service's (IRS) Criminal Investigation Division was following money trails to build tax evasion cases targeting mob figures. The US Marshals Service was perfecting safeguarding cooperating witnesses and enforcing court orders while the Bureau of Alcohol, Tobacco, and Firearms (ATF) was working cases involving firearms trafficking and bombings linked to Mob enforcement operations.

And of course, at the street level, New York State and New York City police forces were investigating dozens of gangland homicides and rackets.

"I started to see I was constantly on the same path with the same detectives working the same hijackings and same organized crime cases," Nelson says.

Hijacking, long one of organized crime's bread-and-butter rackets, continued to be a common denominator for investigations; at one point, it was a $4.2-million racket, according to a report in the *New York Times*.

"Nearly 90 per cent of all the hijackings in this city can be tied to organized crime," says Sergeant Robert Chapman of the Safe, Loft and Truck Squad. Adds the squad's commander, Captain Paul Henry, "A significant number of these organized crime hijacks are planned at these two Queens clubs."[20]

Due to gaps in the law and the difficulty of prosecutors convincing juries that defendants were guilty beyond a reasonable doubt, upwards of ninety percent of hijacking charges were dismissed at trial.

Hearings held by the New York Joint Legislative Commission on Crime, headed by Senator Ralph J. Marino, concluded that at least "99.5 percent of [hijacking] arrests resulted in dismissed charges, fines, or probation."[54]

"I don't remember the first time I met Detective Frank Pergola, just that we crossed paths on many crime scenes, but had not actually conversed," Nelson says.

An NYPD detective for twenty-six years, working on the Homicide, Organized Crime, and Major Case squads, Frank Pergola already earned a reputation for his dogged pursuit of David Berkowitz, the Son of Sam, the serial killer who paralyzed New York City. He partnered with NYPD Sergeant Joseph Coffey, hunting down Berkowitz, even "ringing doorbells day and night," according to the *New York Times*.

Pergola later investigated dozens of homicides and cold cases intertwined with many of the landmark trials of the era, from the prosecution of Paul Castellano and the Commission Case to takedowns of Roy DeMeo's Gemini Crew to the Westies Irish gang on Manhattan's West Side.

"Being a homicide detective meant to me that everyone counted," Pergola says. "Homicide detectives do God's work and have to speak for the dead who can't speak for themselves. My reward for my investigation was the appreciation of victims' families, providing closure for their losses."

Pergola became a police officer in 1965 and in 1971, at the age of twenty-seven, was promoted to detective third grade, promoted to detective second grade in 1989, and promoted to detective first grade in 1991. Like Nelson, Pergola investigated hijackings, which were almost always connected to organized crime.

"I had a stolen truck taken from the Garment District in New York City," Pergola says. "I responded to 7th Avenue and conducted the canvas for possible witnesses. I entered the building in front of the location where the truck was taken and heard a voice behind me say, 'Frank, what the fuck are you doing here?'"

Pergola turned around to find the son of his neighbor from 16th Avenue in Bensonhurst within spitting distance from multiple Mafia social clubs. The young man was the son of a made member of the Colombo Family.

"I explained to him that a truck full of women's dresses was stolen," Pergola says. "He said, 'Forget about it, Frank. I'll take care of it.' The next day, I get a call at my office from the owner of the truck who informs me that his driver was unharmed and all his goods were on the truck when it was returned."

This was such a transformative period for the New York Office, forcing law enforcement in general to evolve.

"Remember, in that era, even with RICO on the books, it was very new, often shunned," Nelson explains.

The Racketeer Influenced and Corrupt Organizations (RICO) Act of 1970 gave the federal government powerful tools to prosecute criminal organizations rather than just individual members. Before RICO, organized crime leaders were insulated from prosecution by layers of underlings. Allowing prosecutors to now charge individuals involved in a criminal enterprise for a pattern of racketeering—even if they didn't directly commit every crime within the enterprise—was a seismic shift.

"However, until the 1980s, the federal government was reluctant to use it except for very select prosecutions," Nelson says. "They were often afraid it might be misunderstood by juries or seen as abusing prosecutorial powers. And they were concerned that some provisions in the actual RICO statute would lead to reversals on appeal."

Back in the early 1980s, before the Commission Case (1985–1986), before the Pizza Connection Trial (1985–1987), before the

Gambino Family Trials and the prosecution of John Gotti (1990s), even before the Windows Case (1990–1994), this was all still very new.

"Even some judges were uncomfortable with RICO, and there was not much precedent for the legal issues it presented in case law," Nelson says. "So what you had was separate groups of law enforcement investigating different crimes perpetrated by the same crews, or other members of the same crews, at the direction of their bosses. Even when individual prosecutions were successful, the organizations remained intact.

"This was real life and the stakes were high, a real battle between good and evil, with hundreds of homicides and thousands of victims, innocent people just preyed upon daily by these organizations," Nelson adds. "As law enforcement gained experience, it slowly became evident that you could look at predicate crimes together as operating parts of a larger organization. However, that was still years away."

Today, RICO is a weapon wielded widely by law enforcement, so feared by organized crime that it has entirely reshaped the way they operate.

The Venditti Case comes to mind for Frank Pergola.

NYPD Detective Anthony Venditti was just thirty-four years old when he was gunned down in 1986, the victim of a targeted Mob hit tied to his relentless pursuit of illegal gambling operations in New York City. Venditti joined the force in 1974 and was soon assigned to high-stakes duties, including protecting witnesses set to testify against powerful Mob boss Paul Castellano of the Gambino Family.54

In 1985, he was assigned to the Joint Organized Crime Task Force under the NYPD's Organized Crime Control Bureau, where he took a deep dive into the Genovese Family's illicit gambling activities, particularly in Queens. His investigation made him a target of the very criminals he was trying to dismantle.

On January 21, 1986, while stopping for a meal with his partner, Venditti was ambushed and fatally shot outside a diner by three alleged Genovese associates. His partner, Detective Kathleen Burke, was also wounded in the ambush. Burke later testified she saw three men outside a restaurant with their guns aimed at Venditti before the shooting erupted.

Even following multiple arrests and trials, no one was ever convicted of his murder. Contradictory witness testimony, Mob intimidation, and critical gaps in evidence combined to deny justice for the young detective whose work brought him too close to the truth.

Federico Giovanelli, a reputed mobster, *was* charged. Despite four separate trials—two State cases ending in hung juries and a federal racketeering conviction later overturned on appeal—Giovanelli was ultimately acquitted. He passed away in 2018.

"They worked with us, but they missed a lot of opportunities, and as a result, defendants walked on murders," Pergola says. "The Venditti case was an instance where they had information on this murder that was not brought to trial during the Castellano case. So you had twenty-five defendants, and the State could have walked in and brought charges and built these cases, but did not."

Many of the challenges with applying RICO stemmed from the fact that law enforcement was segmented and siloed.

"The focus at that time, in most cases, was on a particular crime and apprehending and prosecuting the perpetrators of that crime," Nelson explains. "And then, move on to the next case. You did not yet have that emphasis on targeting the hierarchy of criminal organizations. RICO was a complex, sophisticated prosecutorial tool, and applying it required a much more involved investigative process."

During this time, though, organized crime was getting more, well, organized.

Instead of the rudimentary crimes of the past, criminal organizations were concocting sophisticated, multifaceted schemes.

"You would have detectives, like Frank Pergola, working homicides or me investigating truck hijackings, and we were locking up perpetrators and moving on to the next case," Nelson says. "However, you had the Paul Castellanos, the Nino Gaggis,

Roy DeMeos, who were reaping the benefits of these criminal activities, regardless of who was being locked up at a lower level."

But law enforcement was circling the wagons, and as the war on organized crime raged, Nelson forged strong bonds with more detectives. "I actually met Ronnie Cadieux in '78 through Kenny McCabe," Nelson says. "And like I said, Ronnie was an exceptional NYPD detective who started joining us when we went out surveilling social clubs and organized crime spots at night. Soon, Ronnie was involved with whatever we were doing."

"Back then, it was all about wearing out that shoe leather," Ronnie Cadieux says. "I go back further than Anthony, and I was a foot cop. We didn't have radios. Sometimes, you had to run three or four blocks to find a police phone. Back then, they trained you to bang your nightstick in a way that would hopefully alert other cops nearby. But then again, you may be on your own because you're working a precinct that may be ten square miles, and you've got five cops working that beat."

The early 1980s saw the New York US Attorney's Office take aggressive measures to combat organized crime activity. At the time, Walter Mack was an assistant US attorney for the Southern District of New York. In 1980, he was tapped to lead a new organized crime task force by then US Attorney for the Southern District John S. Martin Jr.

For Mack and the investigators he corralled and collaborated with, this was a crusade.

Walter Mack was the product of an affluent Upper East Side upbringing, with degrees from Harvard and Columbia Law School. In fact, his father, Walter Mack Sr., the former president of Pepsi-Cola, is credited with being the first to put soda in cans and advertising jingles on national radio. But Mack showed no interest in the family business.

Instead, shortly after his graduation from Harvard in 1965, Mack signed up for officer candidate school in the Marine Corps. In typical fashion, he found his way to one of the most challenging assignments in Vietnam: a captain leading a rifle company through the treacherous highlands of the former demilitarized zone between North and South Vietnam, an area filled with

North Vietnamese troops. It was there, he said, he learned the rudimentary lessons that were to serve him well in his later career: to be exhaustively, even overly, prepared.

Following law school, Mack joined a prestigious law firm in New York. Three years later, he signed on as an assistant US attorney in Manhattan.

With the nation's leading prosecutorial office poised to launch a massive offensive against the Mafia, Mack joined a team of prosecutors that included future FBI Director Louis Freeh and Homeland Security Secretary Michael Chertoff.

In his official capacity, he served as an AUSA in the Southern District of New York, where he held multiple senior roles, including deputy chief of the criminal division, chief of the organized crime unit, and senior litigation counsel.

The primary mission of the Organized Crime Strike Force was to identify, investigate, and dismantle large-scale criminal enterprises—including the Mafia and other syndicates involved in narcotics trafficking, extortion, and racketeering.

Mack directed his focus toward the Gambino Family, widely recognized as the most powerful of New York's Five Families. By the 1980s, the Gambinos had built a vast network with hundreds of inducted members and over three thousand associates, including loan sharks, bookies, crooked union officials, pimps, drug traffickers, and street enforcers. At the height of his dominance, John Gotti reportedly oversaw thirty captains, each commanding their own crews.

As the strike force methodically connected a string of homicides to the organization, Mack homed in on some of the Gambinos' most violent and high-profile crews, determined to take them apart from the inside out.

"After developing a significant amount of evidence about the DeMeo Crew's car-theft operation, Detective John Murphy presented this case to Walter Mack, who decided to take down the crew rising under Roy DeMeo," Nelson recalls.

"There were a lot of OC hits in those days, and we're working all those cases with the Major Case squad, working with John

Murphy before the Strike Force was even formed, including seven cases alone that later were linked to the DeMeo Crew," Pergola says.

"Based on my experience with OC, the chief of detectives transferred me there, right as I was working on the Rosenberg and Katz cases," Pergola adds. "And even in my downtime, I'm reading all these murder files. DeMeo always stuck in my head, so when I caught the Rosenberg case in 1979, it all started to fall into place."

Andrei Katz was a young auto repair shop owner who partnered with DeMeo in a stolen car ring in the early 1970s. In January 1975, Katz provided evidence to the Brooklyn District Attorney that Rosenberg was heavily involved in car theft. DeMeo was tipped off about the meeting from a corrupt NYPD auto crimes detective on his payroll. In May 1975, Katz appeared before a Brooklyn grand jury and testified about what he knew about the DeMeo Crew. The following month, Katz was abducted by DeMeo Crew members and murdered in a supermarket in Rockaway Beach, Queens.

Chris Rosenberg first crossed paths with Roy DeMeo in 1966 while selling small amounts of marijuana and hash from a gas station in Canarsie. DeMeo quickly took notice. Rosenberg, still a teenager, was fearless, explosive, and brutally loyal—traits that would make him not only DeMeo's favorite but also one of his deadliest enforcers. Although Chris Rosenberg wasn't Italian—and thus ineligible for formal Mafia induction—he was every bit a trusted member of Roy DeMeo's Crew. Fiercely loyal and ruthlessly efficient, Rosenberg was deeply involved in loan sharking, drug trafficking, and a string of violent hits.

By the late 1970s, Rosenberg had expanded into larger drug operations, dealing in marijuana and cocaine. Some ventures were backed by DeMeo's protection, others he ran on his own. In 1979, Rosenberg traveled to Florida to arrange a cocaine deal through a loan shark client of Roy DeMeo's—Charles Padnick—who had turned to drug trafficking in a desperate bid to pay off his debts.

Padnick had ties to a Cuban, William Serrano, who in turn had access to two Cuban drug suppliers known only as "Pedro Paz" and "El Negron," says Frank Pergola. Padnick told Serrano that a group of Italians was looking to buy a large quantity of cocaine. After meeting with Rosenberg—who introduced himself as Chris DeMeo—Serrano relayed the offer to his Cuban contacts and helped broker the deal.

Unbeknownst to Rosenberg, however, Serrano never disclosed the trustworthy source of the drugs when setting up the meet in New York.

Within hours of the four drug traffickers arriving in New York City, all four were murdered and dismembered by Rosenberg and members of the DeMeo Crew.

"Two of the four dealers were Charles Padnick and a William Serrano," Nelson says. "The other two were related to El Negron, a cousin of his, and actually El Negron's girlfriend. It was believed that Rosenberg was also wounded during the murders because he showed up at a hospital with a gunshot wound."

Again, with the Jewish Rosenberg so enamored with fantasizing that he was Italian, he used the name Chris DeMeo. And this enabled El Negron to trace Rosenberg back to Roy DeMeo.

Through Dominick Montiglio, El Negron delivered an ultimatum—he wanted proof that the Gambino Family killed Rosenberg, and the homicide had to be covered in the newspapers. Otherwise, El Negron vowed to unleash a war.

Castellano and Gaggi sent word to DeMeo ordering the hit on Rosenberg.

The Cuban threat sent Roy DeMeo, already paranoid, off the deep end.

"Roy started suspecting anyone around him as a Cuban assassin," Nelson says. "This then led to an incident at Roy's house when he and Joseph 'Dracula' Guglielmo chased down an innocent eighteen-year-old salesman named Dominick Ragucci by car for several miles and then shot him to death in broad daylight."

Ragucci, a student and door-to-door vacuum cleaner salesman, had just finished a sales meeting when he unknowingly parked outside Roy DeMeo's residence. DeMeo, paranoid and drugged up, spotted the unfamiliar car and, suspecting a hit, approached with his associate, Guglielmo. Startled, Ragucci fled in his vehicle. DeMeo and Guglielmo gave chase in DeMeo's blue Cadillac, with DeMeo unleashing a hail of gunfire—firing approximately twenty shots—during a reckless pursuit that stretched more than seven miles.[53]

The chase ended when Ragucci collided with another vehicle and came to a stop. DeMeo exited his car, approached, and fired the fatal shots at point-blank range, killing the innocent young man on the spot.

Gambino Family capo Nino Gaggi was reportedly furious over DeMeo's mistake, and sources reported DeMeo privately expressed remorse.

According to an article in *Newsday*: "Homicide Capt. Al Hordoff said Ragucci's body was riddled with bullets. Three windows of the car were shot out, there were bullet holes in the passenger side of the car, and spent shells littered the street. Hordoff said the police knew of no motive for the slayings and had no suspects."[53]

It was around this time Castellano and Gaggi then ordered DeMeo to kill Rosenberg.

Roy was backed into a corner. He had mentored Rosenberg since he was a teenager—considered him like a son. But under growing pressure from boss Paul Castellano and the prospect of an all-out war with a Cuban drug cartel looming, DeMeo made the fateful decision.

On May 11, 1979, Rosenberg was summoned under the pretense of a meeting—perhaps believing he'd have a chance to explain or make amends. Instead, he was executed, shot multiple times in the head and chest by fellow Crew members Anthony Senter, Frederick DiNome, and Henry Borelli.

In a break from their usual protocol, Rosenberg's body was dumped in the open, left on the street to ensure the media coverage El Negron mandated.

53. O'Neill, Jim, and Williams, Stephen. "Death on Rte. 110: A Chase, Bullets." Newsday, April 20, 1979

Investigating the crime scene, Pergola noticed Anthony Senter, Frederick DiNome, and Henry Borelli—the actual murderers and core members of the DeMeo Crew—nearby.

He trailed them to the home of Rosenberg.

They were consoling the victim's wife.

"Just by the way we found the body of Rosenberg, we knew the murder didn't occur at that location," Pergola explains. "And that scene, at the Rosenberg home, didn't sit right with me. I remembered Tester, Senter, and Borelli from reading the Katz murder file while assigned to the Son of Sam case in 1975. I knew enough of these guys to suspect they were involved, which we proved in '83 when [Dominick] Montiglio flipped.

"After the Rosenberg murder followed more homicides which were just so depraved. And the other side of that you don't see is the victims' families, all the wives, the mothers, crying in front of you."

"It was when Frank [Pergola] was assigned to Walter Mack's task force in the Southern District that we started to engage regularly and developed a friendship," Nelson says. "I'd run into him on crime scenes, and then, certainly, more regularly, we would see each other related to the DeMeo case crimes. Ron Cadieux then became part of Walter Mack's task force and became Frank Pergola's partner."

Pergola and Cadieux would undertake the laborious effort of reopening cold cases, attempting to establish them as predicate crimes that furthered the criminal enterprise to qualify for RICO.

While not formally assigned, Nelson regularly contributed intelligence to Mack's new task force, helping Pergola and Cadieux fill in some of the gaps based on the FBI's own investigations, case files, and the stream of tips flowing in from his network of confidential informants.

"Anthony was a great street investigator and undercover agent," Pergola says. "We worked together from 1983 to 1989 on the DeMeo Crew investigations and then again in 1989 through 1999 on the Hijacking Task Force, where we made many arrests of Ecuadorian perpetrators.

"Anthony was a hero, an FBI agent and a good friend, born and raised in Brooklyn, like me, and like me, familiar with that life."

As dozens of cases and investigations unfolded, Mack made the bold decision to expand the scope to directly target Gambino boss Paul Castellano, confident he could prove in court that the boss benefited from DeMeo's crimes.

Working in tandem with the FBI's Gambino desk—then the Bureau's largest—and in partnership with district attorneys and investigators from NYPD squads, Mack's unit leveraged wiretaps, surveillance, and RICO statutes to build solid cases.

For all agencies involved, investigating the DeMeo Crew was different.

"Roy DeMeo was a psychopath," Cadieux says. "You know, people throw that word around. But Roy was a true psychopathic killer, with absolutely no regard for human life.

"And DeMeo's Crew was different from any other crew," Cadieux explains. "In any crew in any of the Five Families, you had different guys who did different things. So, when it came to violence, you'd have your button man or a couple of guys who do the murders. And the orders come from the captain. But with the DeMeo Crew, they were all hitmen, up and down the line. Roy DeMeo had twenty guys on the street who were cold-blooded killers. These were bad, bad men. Vicious, violent.

"When you're working cases like these, uncovering this kind of evil walking among us, it adds deeper meaning for an investigator," Cadieux adds. "You're not so much thinking about the violence, just working the case. And these nut jobs are running around killing people while you're investigating, so the stakes are high. But they didn't give us any shit, and they knew we wouldn't take any shit."

"Kenny, Frank, Ronnie, and so many others did all of that day-to-day legwork behind the scenes, and they were the best of the best," Nelson stipulates. "My role was providing intelligence."

And as investigators dug deeper and deeper, they found bodies that had been piling up for years.

"All those RICO cases from 1983 to 1989 actually involved cold case murders that had files that had to be searched for and found; in some cases, the murders going back twenty years," Pergola says. "Old witnesses had to be located and re-interviewed, some prepped for trial to provide testimony. Evidence had to be established and informers had to be identified and located."

The Strike Force employed a variety of strategies—including undercover operations, wiretaps, and informant testimonies— to gather evidence and build strong cases against key figures in organized crime.

The investigations gained momentum and the scope ballooned to not just target DeMeo and his many crew members, but also threatened Gambino captain Nino Gaggi and eventually Family don Paul Castellano. Ultimately, this avalanche of case work was organized into two significant prosecutions, including the legendary Commission Case.

"As we dug in with the task force and engaged with the detectives, FBI Special Agents Arthur Ruffels and Marilyn Lucht were formally assigned to debrief cooperators and witnesses," Nelson says. "They, along with the other members of the joint agency task force, began preparing witnesses and evidence for the trials.

"I knew from the beginning this was different, this was special, this level of collaboration, across the board. They were relentless, doing the hard work and putting in that exhaustive effort to bring these criminals to justice. I'd go down to the SDNY and sit in on some meetings in Kenny McCabe's office."

Law enforcement was closing in, and things were heating up in the underworld, which would have explosive consequences.

CHAPTER TWENTY-SIX

By the mid-1980s, the Mafia's aura of invisibility was cracking.

Intrafamily hits and street-level beefs became more frequent and public, drawing headlines and political pressure. Bosses became more reclusive, more insulated, and less accessible to their own crews. Some mobsters even started suspecting FBI infiltration in their own ranks.

Beginning in the 1970s, the FBI launched a sweeping surveillance campaign targeting New York's five Mafia Families. Through covert bugs placed in social clubs, restaurants, vehicles, union halls, construction offices, and even fishing boats, agents gathered audio evidence that would ultimately dismantle much of the Mafia's power structure.

The Ravenite Social Club in Little Italy and an upstairs apartment used by boss John Gotti were bugged. Similar surveillance at Café Giardino in Howard Beach and in Gotti's and Gravano's cars, including a transmitter hidden in Gravano's seatbelt, helped expose the inner circle. The FBI also bugged Gravano's construction office, which later supported his cooperation with authorities.

The Genovese Family was targeted at the Triangle Social Club, where boss Vincent "the Chin" Gigante was infamously evasive, and at the Palma Boys Social Club, where boss Tony Salerno was regularly recorded. Other sites, including restaurants in the Bronx and union offices in Manhattan, revealed key details about labor racketeering and the so-called Concrete Club, which controlled lucrative construction contracts.

One of the Lucchese Family's headquarters, the 19th Hole and additional sites like Club Capri and the 101 Club were bugged during the reign of Vic Amuso and Anthony Casso. These recordings exposed internal rivalries and ties to union corruption, including bugs in Plasterers Local 530 that revealed contractor shakedowns.

Colombo Family factions were tracked through bugs at the Brunetta Social Club and the longtime Persico base on President Street, helping the FBI navigate the Family's internal war in the 1990s. The Bonanno Family, infiltrated during the Donnie Brasco operation, was monitored at the Motion Lounge and Toyland Social Club. The FBI even bugged their boats—the *Left Hand* and the *Sea Trek*—to monitor drug deals in Sheepshead Bay.

Beyond the clubs and meeting spots, the FBI planted bugs in Mob-run businesses', like Ray's Trucking in Canarsie, union offices like Teamsters Local 282 and Carpenters Local 608, and nearby restaurants and streets when access wasn't possible.

Together, these surveillance operations gave prosecutors unprecedented insight into the Mafia's operations, alliances, and crimes. The tapes formed the foundation for major RICO indictments and helped dismantle the Five Families' decades-long grip on New York's underworld.

With Walter Mack's strike force gaining momentum, Anthony Nelson, assigned to the FBI's Violent Crimes branch, redoubled his efforts.

"I was going out on the street now twice a week with Kenny McCabe to develop additional organized crime informants, collect intelligence, and investigate collateral criminal matters," Nelson says.

Most Thursday or Friday afternoons, Nelson and McCabe met at Mama Tury's Restaurant on 86th Street and 15th Avenue in Brooklyn, often accompanied by NYPD Detectives Ronnie Cadieux and Frank Pergola, as well as a revolving cast of crime fighters.

"We started these working lunches, guys from different agencies, where we'd exchange intelligence, informant information, photographs of subjects," Nelson remembers. "We knew the owners of Mama Tury's, and it was one of the few restaurants that we completely trusted."

In a scene you'd only see in a Brooklyn Italian restaurant, the lawmen sometimes arrived for lunch at the same time as members of the Gambino Family.

"It became apparent to us that they believed our arrival was not by coincidence," Nelson says. "On several occasions, they simply walked out of the restaurant without paying their tabs."

Distractions aside, the group had much to discuss.

"I remember I was asked by the head of the Southern District to try and find a witness who had skipped, who was an eyewitness in the Galante homicide," Pergola says.

Carmine "the Cigar" Galante, the powerful Bonanno Family boss, was assassinated on July 12, 1979, while dining at Joe & Mary's Italian-American Restaurant in Brooklyn.

The hit, believed to be ordered by the Mafia Commission, was carried out by several gunmen who entered the restaurant's patio and opened fire. Galante, along with restaurant owner Giuseppe Turano and his bodyguard Leonardo Coppola, were killed in the attack. Galante's son, John, was also shot but survived.

"By the time the case went to trial, the witness had moved to Puerto Rico, was living in a rainforest; so with another detective, we found her living in a concrete hut, and she was pregnant," Pergola adds. "I talked her into coming back to New York, and I did take care of her." He met the witness at the airport, taking her to his own home to safeguard her for the trial. "She testified in the Galante case, and I stayed with her, drove her, took her back to my house, my wife prepared a suitcase of clothes, and put her back on a plane."

But then, federal prosecutors needed her to testify again. "So then we did the same thing all over again. She ID'd the three shooters; two had not previously been identified—Baldo Amato, Ceasar Bonaventura, and Bruno Indelicato.

"That series of events caused a war," Pergola says. Bruno Indelicato later went into hiding, with soldier Tommy Pitera, in Fort Lauderdale, Florida, after his father, Alphonse "Sonny"

Indelicato, was murdered. The murder was orchestrated by John "Johnny Boy" Massino, who also wanted to kill Bruno, but missed the meeting. Instead, Massino had Philip "Phil" Lino killed, but Lino survived and flipped to Massino's side.

Thomas "Tommy Karate" Pitera, a soldier and feared hitman for the Bonanno Family (and later a captain of his own crew in Gravesend), was suspected by law enforcement of as many as sixty murders. A skilled martial artist, the sadistic Pitera approached murder like a craft—precise, impersonal, and deliberate. He disposed of many of his victims in a remote patch of Staten Island wetlands, where he believed the damp soil would hasten decay and the protected wildlife area would shield graves from construction crews and curious eyes.

"Pitera would also dress as a woman, or even a Hasidic Jew, to commit murders," Pergola adds.

Pitera studied dissection guides and carried a customized toolkit designed for cutting bodies apart. He buried his victims deep— beyond the reach of cadaver dogs—often wrapped in plastic or sealed inside old suitcases. His only indulgence was morbid: he kept trophies—rings, chains, and keepsakes from the dead.

On June 25, 1992, Pitera was convicted of six murders and running a sprawling drug operation out of Brooklyn. "Pitera gets bored and he goes to his captain, Anthony Spero, and he goes to the Commission; they have a sit-down and agree not to hurt Bruno as long as he doesn't have to have revenge," Pergola explains.

It wasn't just the Mack strike force. Around this time, Nelson also began providing intelligence to various FBI and NYPD squads.

George Terra joined the FBI/NYPD Auto Crime Task Force started by Jim Murphy. He was in the BQMRA (Brooklyn-Queens Metropolitan Resident Agency) with Anthony Nelson, but assigned to different squads.

"So, I worked in the Auto Crime Division until about 1980," George Terra remembers. "Then, when they started the Joint Task Force with the FBI, they asked Danny Pisculli and me if we wanted to join, so we went out to the BQ [Brooklyn Queens] Task Force and worked there for several years.

"I don't think enough is said about the impact of these joint task forces," Terra says. "They got this idea to get different agencies to work together, which was the start of the task forces, and I had the pleasure to be asked to work with the FBI/NYPD Task Force out of BQ.

"You have to remember, especially back then, before the task forces, in law enforcement, all over the country—and I worked cases outside New York—everyone in law enforcement had the same general opinion about the FBI," Terra says. "Nobody liked the Bureau because the Bureau didn't discuss investigations or share information for so many years, until these task forces came together.

"Anthony was at BQ, and I got to meet and work with a lot of fantastic FBI agents, and I was impressed with them. The first day I got to BQ, they put five of us PD guys with five agents. We had a PD supervisor and an FBI supervisor. First, it was Jim Murphy, an outstanding individual, and then Steven Carbone, also a unique and excellent supervisor.

"One thing that I did notice right away was that the FBI, they were all better educated than the fellas from the NYPD," Terra says. "For the police department, back then, you just needed a high school degree. They didn't have the requirement yet for an associate's or bachelor's degree. I earned my bachelor's degree through the VA after leaving the service, and the military covered my college expenses.

"So, the fellas in the Bureau were all better educated," Terra adds. "It didn't make them better investigators, but it was definitely a positive because they had these different skills and understanding, like some had accounting degrees, others had law degrees. However, not even a week later after we all got there, you put us all in that room, and you couldn't pick out who were the agents and who were the NYPD detectives. We all just melded and were all focused on the same priorities and interests, and we all just worked together very well.

"Have to be honest, though, I did break their shoes all the time, telling them that they should thank God for television and all the money they gave those FBI guys, because if it wasn't for all that, the Bureau never would've been able to find anyone," Terra laughs. "But it was all in good fun. They were dedicated and hardworking, just remarkable individuals, and bottom line, that's what matters, and that's why it worked."

"One of the biggest misperceptions I've heard repeated over and over is the assertion that there was always conflict among all the different types of law enforcement agencies," Nelson says. "Yes, there definitely was conflict at times, but more often than not, these conflicts were driven by personalities.

"I remember when I started reading about these so-called conflicts between the FBI and the New York Police Department. Now, there were different ways we operated, different methodologies, but I would not characterize this as conflict. I honestly never experienced this conflict."

This interagency camaraderie not only spilled over into his personal life but also extended well into retirement. "To this day, I probably only speak to one retired FBI agent," Nelson laughs, "but I can rattle off the names of a dozen former members of the New York City Police Department that I still speak with to the present time."

Nelson has a wall filled with awards and pictures from major cases, many of which were worked jointly with the NYPD, that were resolved because of this level of cooperation.

Where Nelson did see conflict, it was more with prosecutors and among federal agencies. Sometimes, the lines of jurisdiction are not clear enough. Sometimes you have concurrent jurisdiction.

"Just look at the shooting of President Donald Trump and the second assassination attempt on his life," Nelson says. "Secret Service agents are throwing their bodies on him and risking their lives to protect him. But if the president or vice president is assaulted or killed, the FBI will enter the investigation and have exclusive jurisdiction over the matter. So, with both agencies involved, you can start to see where issues and animosity can arise."

Going back to the 1980s, the federal government gave the Secret Service jurisdiction over counterfeit and stolen credit card crimes, but not when they related to organized crime.

"So we would jump into a credit card case, and then there was the opportunity to have an issue with them," Nelson says. "Except for one or two individual personalities, I never had problems, and that was usually due to jurisdiction, in credit card cases. In New York, often the trucks would be hijacked in New Jersey and then driven into New York, so the FBI usually had a head start on these investigations because we immediately received the initial local theft reports in New Jersey."

From time to time, you hear stories about quotas.

"The men and women of law enforcement have a very difficult job, and the reality is, it is a very statistically driven occupation," Nelson says. "You need to be able to measure impact to be able to assign and deploy resources, so, despite the terminology, it often resulted in judging police officers by the use of quotas.

"Sometimes there would be tension when someone wanted to claim an arrest," Nelson clarifies. "Personally, I never had a strong feeling about who claimed an arrest, so there were many times I gave them up."

Despite this, Nelson states that throughout his career, he never experienced a systemic pattern of conflict between the NYPD and the FBI. Though he concedes there had always been some individual arguments or personality clashes. But such arguments were not unique to the FBI or the NYPD.

"On an individual and personal level, there were certainly people who absolutely hated the FBI as an agency," he says. "Likewise, there were many agents, again on a personal level, who distrusted and disliked the NYPD."

CHAPTER TWENTY-SEVEN

In 1981, there was a Mad Dog on the loose, and Special Agent Anthony Nelson was sent to hunt him down.

When it comes to fugitives, they don't get more dangerous than Joseph "Mad Dog" Sullivan. Wanted by New York State authorities for multiple murders, Sullivan was a cold-blooded contract killer estimated to have killed between twenty and thirty people, mostly on behalf of the Genovese and Gambino Families.

The FBI is uniquely equipped to handle high-profile manhunts. It has federal jurisdiction to operate across state lines. The FBI's profilers are experts at analyzing criminal behavior to predict movements and motivations. The FBI also has access to state-of-the-art forensic labs for analyzing evidence, including DNA, fingerprints, and digital forensics, and can deploy specialized units like the Hostage Rescue Team (HRT) and SWAT teams.

By all accounts, Sullivan was desperate and cagey. In fact, ten years earlier, he held the distinction of being the only inmate ever to escape from the notorious Attica Prison.

At the time, Sullivan was incarcerated in a maximum-security facility in rural western New York, serving a sentence for fatally beating a Queens man—reportedly a father of eight—during a barroom altercation in 1965, according to prison authorities. In April 1971, he managed a bold escape by hiding beneath a stack of empty flour sacks in the rear of a departing delivery truck. His freedom was short-lived; authorities tracked him down in Manhattan six weeks later and returned him to custody.

Paroled in 1975, Sullivan relocated to the New York City area, where he increased his notoriety as a contract killer.

His release from prison was credited in large part to the advocacy of his attorney, Ramsey Clark, a former US Attorney General. Their bond was so strong that Sullivan later named one of his sons Ramsey in Clark's honor.

It didn't take long for Sullivan to return to his life of crime, and he was soon wanted by New York authorities for several murders. "I became the affiant of the federal criminal complaint charging Sullivan as a federal fugitive," Nelson says.

Sullivan was somewhat of a freelance agent in the underworld, not only tight with the Italians, but also had ties to the Westies Irish Mob in Manhattan's Hell's Kitchen.

Sullivan was suspected, along with members of Roy DeMeo's Crew, of two murders of members of Mickey Spillane's crew during the internecine conflict among those two Irish gangs in New York City. (Joseph "Mad Dog" Sullivan is not to be confused with another Mad Dog, Vincent Coll, the Irish-American Mob hitman for Dutch Schultz in the 1920s and early 1930s in New York City.)

On the run, Sullivan partnered up with an ex-NYPD police officer named Steven Catalonotte, who'd become addicted to drugs and committed armed robberies to support his habit. During one of the robberies, Catalonotte engaged in a shootout with members of the NYPD. He was shot and wounded during the encounter but escaped.

"Due to his association with Joseph Sullivan, I contacted Sergeant Steve Marks, who was in charge of the NYPD Brooklyn Central Robbery Squad," Nelson says. "Marks assigned a team of his best detectives to work with me and the team of FBI agents who were assisting me to locate and arrest both Catalonotte and Sullivan."

During Nelson's routine nights on the street with Kenny McCabe, they made spot checks of known organized crime hangouts to smoke out Sullivan. One of those locations was a social club on Stillwell Avenue in Brooklyn, allegedly controlled by Steven Catalonotte's brother, Bart.

If there is a last exit to Brooklyn, it's Stillwell Avenue. It's a desolate stretch of road pitted with junkyards and auto shops overrun with feral dogs that runs into a dead end at Riegelmann Boardwalk on Coney Island, with massive residential towers and the brooding subway terminal in the background.

While working alongside members of the Central Robbery Squad, Nelson learned that Sullivan had developed a romantic relationship with Steven Catalonotte's sister-in-law, Theresa Palmieri.

Palmieri lived on Avenue X in Brooklyn, just a couple of blocks away from RoSal's Restaurant, the Genovese Family hangout Nelson and McCabe shadowed for years.

"So, we tried through sources at RoSal's," Nelson says, "to determine if any Genovese crew members were in some way assisting Sullivan and Catalonotte while they were on the run.

"During my time pursuing fugitives in the FBI, it was not uncommon to hear that guys on the run had made statements that they'd 'never be taken alive,'" Anthony Nelson says. "But the more we learned about Joseph Sullivan, the more we came to believe that he really meant it.

"We started to go out together both days and nights in a joint effort to apprehend both fugitives. Through it all, we became close friends. Our team consisted of FBI Agents Steven Braus and Michael Francis, who were two of the most experienced agents with whom I ever worked," Nelson says. Steven Braus enjoyed a distinguished thirty-year career as an FBI agent, including twenty-seven years in the New York Office, mainly in the Brooklyn-Queens office, and three years stationed at JFK Airport, before transitioning to a career in corporate security.

"NYPD Detectives Louis Randazzo, Carl Schroeder, Saul Rodriguez, and Joseph Sciarrino were likewise a team of the best detectives in the New York City Police Department," Nelson says.

"It became apparent during our investigation to locate both Sullivan and Catalonotte that the Palmieri sisters were most likely in contact with them," Nelson says.

Love is a powerful thing, and when fugitives are cut off from everyone else, they crave a safe harbor in the storm, damn the risks of capture.

Yet this was no romance novel, but a real-life manhunt. And in one of those South Brooklyn-style cosmic coincidences, it turned out that Agent Nelson's wife, Syndee, had known one of Steven Catalonotte's sisters, whom she really liked.

"The team of agents and detectives concentrated extensively on the movements of Theresa Palmieri, to the point that she developed a hatred of our presence," Nelson says. "For some reason, she seemed to particularly dislike me and Detective Carl Schroeder."

In addition to a long, accomplished career as an NYPD detective, Schroeder is also known for his help in organizing a boxing team for New York City police officers in 1983. The primary purpose of this team was to conduct boxing matches with teams from other New York City agencies and with other police departments throughout the United States and Europe.

In 1984, Schroeder requested the NYPD recognize his team officially and permit it to post notices of scheduled boxing matches on police premises. Today, the traditional feud between the Fighting Finest (NYPD) and the Battling Bravest (FDNY) is settled in boxing showdowns exhibiting the best in the rivalry while raising money for charities.

One afternoon, by chance, Nelson was driving with Syndee along Flatbush Avenue in Brooklyn. They were about to get on the entrance ramp to the westbound Belt Parkway when suddenly, Nelson spotted a familiar Volkswagen Beetle swerve in front of him with the windows open.

"It was Theresa Palmieri," Nelson says. "For the few seconds it took me to enter the ramp to the parkway, Palmieri cursed at me."

Palmieri then added, "You and that scrotum," a nickname she coined for Detective Schroeder.

As the hunt for Sullivan intensified, investigators followed up leads suggesting the career criminal may have contacted Ramsey Clark and may have reached out to Hollywood actor Jon Voight.

"I attempted to obtain a federal grand jury subpoena for Ramsey Clark's telephone records to determine if he was in recent contact with Sullivan and may have been aiding or abetting his status as a fugitive," Nelson says.

After considerable heated debate with the hierarchy and the legal counsel of the FBI's New York Office, Nelson's request for the subpoena was turned down because of Clark's status as a former attorney general of the United States.

Another FBI agent, Edward Woods, who was also assisting in the investigation, did, in fact, obtain a grand jury subpoena for actor Jon Voight.

Voight, and a co-producer, had been considering making a movie about Sullivan's life in which Voight would portray Sullivan. The film, supposedly titled *Tears and Tiers*, was never produced. Voight's cooperation, however, did confirm one thing. "In my personal opinion," Nelson attests, "Jon Voight was, and still is, a great actor, a decent person, and a patriotic American."

The manhunt succeeded in driving Sullivan out of the New York City area.

In December of 1981, while the lawmen were still hunting the two fugitives, Sullivan committed his last murder. He was hired to kill a Teamster's Union official named John Fiorino in Rochester, New York. Sullivan, along with one of his criminal associates, shot Fiorino to death outside a Rochester restaurant.

The night of December 17, 1981, during their escape from the scene of the shooting, their vehicle was pursued by a local rookie police officer, Michael DiGiovanni, of the Irondequoit Police Department because Sullivan's associate was driving their black Cadillac erratically with the headlights off.

DiGiovanni became engaged in a shootout with Sullivan.

"The first round he shot, he shot high and he took the light out on the top of the patrol car," DiGiovanni told local news channel 13 WHAM's Jane Flasch. "Something didn't feel right when I saw that car come at me, and I said, 'I'm going to see where this goes.'"

During the chase on snowy roads, DiGiovanni says the Caddy spun out of control and the driver took off on foot. The passenger, Joseph "Mad Dog" Sullivan, stood his ground.

"He gets out and he starts leveling the gun at me, and I remember thinking, 'You're going to get me? Well, I'm going to take you with me,' I just kicked open the door of the car and drew my weapon. I kicked open my car door and as I came out, he was firing at me," DiGiovanni, now a lieutenant, told the Rochester newspaper. He attested that Sullivan fired three shots. The first one took out the red light on top of the patrol car. The others were lower and bounced off the hood and into the windshield. DiGiovanni returned fire and wounded Sullivan, who fled on foot and managed to elude police.[54]

Sullivan and his accomplice were fleeing from a Mob-style execution at the Blue Gardenia Restaurant on Empire. They had been hired to kill John Fiorino, a suspected figure in the Mob turf wars that pitted the A Team against the B Team.

In an hour-long interview in the Monroe County Jail, Sullivan would deny his crime and have some choice words for his accomplice, who later became an informant for the police and agreed to testify. "This isn't even a stool pigeon," Sullivan said. "This is the lowest form of life in my eyes. It isn't even a rat who knows something."

Two months later, Sullivan returned to the Rochester area to presumably collect the remainder of the money owed to him for killing Fiorino. During that visit, the local FBI office received information that Sullivan was staying at a motel and was driving a vehicle that had been registered in Kings County, New York.

The FBI set up surveillance of the vehicle and managed to arrest Sullivan, who was accompanied by Theresa Palmieri.

Although Sullivan was captured by the FBI without further incident and did not get a chance to go out in a blaze of glory, he was prepared to do so. He was armed with an AR-15 rifle at the time of his arrest.

54. The Associated Press. "Ex-mob Hit Man 'Mad Dog' Sullivan Dies in NY State Prison." The Seattle Times. June 16, 2017. https://www.seattletimes.com/nation-world/ex-mob-hit-man-mad-dog-sullivan-dies-in-ny-state-prison/

Theresa Palmieri was also arrested by the FBI and was charged with harboring a federal fugitive. Steven Catalonotte remained a fugitive but was ultimately tracked down and arrested by the FBI in Virginia.

Joseph "Mad Dog" Sullivan was convicted in November 1982 for the Fiorino murder and the two others on Long Island. He was sentenced to three life sentences and was not eligible for parole until 2061, when he would have been one hundred and twenty-two years old. He was held in Fishkill Correctional Facility in Dutchess County, where he died of lung cancer in June 2017.

"My friendship with the members of the Brooklyn Central Robbery Squad continued for many years to come," Nelson says.

CHAPTER TWENTY-EIGHT

In 1981, when one of Roy DeMeo's disciples bragged to informants that he could "easily take them out," referring to Anthony Nelson and Kenny McCabe, the two lawmen took notice.

Then it took a more sinister turn.

Supposedly, organized crime will not target law enforcement because of the intense heat it generates.

However, according to a report by the US Department of Justice, agents and their families are, at times, surveilled and even threatened by criminals, who gather personal information about them, including addresses and daily routines.[55]

"There were incidents at my home," says Duke McCabe. "Someone once threw a Molotov cocktail. Another time, a homemade device was detonated outside. And whenever anything went down at my home, Anthony was usually the first one to respond."

"Just the fact he was there when things happened, and we knew he was with the FBI," Duke adds, "it brought Anthony closer to my family, not just my dad. We became very comfortable with him being around."

In the shadows, Roy DeMeo henchman Frederick "Freddy" DiNome was taking notes of how often Kenny McCabe and Anthony Nelson were conducting surveillance at the Gemini Lounge.

DiNome was one of those colorless, idiosyncratic losers the underworld is so good at producing.

---

55. Office of the United States Inspector General, 2017

In *For the Sins of My Father*, Roy's son Albert DeMeo described Freddy as a greasy, tattooed, rough-looking man with dirty blond hair, a crooked smile, and stained teeth.

One of three brothers born to Italian-American immigrants in Canarsie, Brooklyn, Freddy followed his older brother Richard—who worked at a Staten Island chop shop—into a life of crime. A fourth-grade dropout, DiNome grew up alongside future DeMeo Crew members Chris Rosenberg, Anthony Senter, Joseph Testa, and Henry Borelli. Though he had early ties to Lucchese figures Clyde Brooks and Paul Vario, Freddy's erratic behavior and bizarre tendencies—including keeping a pet monkey named Susie trained to pump gas—kept him from being taken seriously for Mafia membership.

In the late 1960s, DiNome tried to go straight, investing money from car theft and drag racing into a gas station and body shop he called "Broadway Freddy's Diagnostic Center." But after a near-fatal racing accident—witnessed by DeMeo—he abandoned that life.

DeMeo later recalled that crash, saying, "He climbs out on fire, waving and smiling like it was nothing. Don't tell me Freddy is crazy—I know he's fucking nuts."

Impressed and amused, DeMeo hired Freddy as a chauffeur and even got him much-needed dental work and a new wardrobe.

Although Freddy couldn't get a driver's license due to dyslexia, he had a remarkable memory for directions. He soon became involved in truck hijackings at JFK Airport while learning the notorious Gemini Method of dismemberment under DeMeo's personal tutelage.

Freddy DiNome had a violent side. After a dispute with a neighbor on Long Island, he decapitated the man's dog and left the head on his porch. According to later court testimony from fellow crew members Henry Borelli and Vito Arena, DiNome played a central role in the gruesome murders of Khaled Daoud and Ronald Falcaro, going so far as to mutilate Falcaro's body postmortem.

The homicides resulted from the DeMeo Crew's involvement in exporting stolen late-model American cars to Kuwait. Falcaro and Daoud operated a competing, but legitimate, venture of exporting cars to that same Persian Gulf country. Noting the astonishing availability of vehicles sourced by competitor Ronald Ustica, Daoud came to suspect that the DeMeo operation involved stolen cars. He began copying down vehicle identification numbers from cars in the DeMeo inventory.[56]

This was a fatal mistake, one witnessed by Ustica, the operations leader of the DeMeo stolen-car scheme.

In October 1979, Falcaro and Daoud were lured to a garage in Brooklyn by DiNome, who offered to sell them a portion of his excess inventory. Once inside the garage, Falcaro and Daoud were murdered by a group of men that included Joseph Testa and Anthony Senter.[56]

In later testimony, DeMeo associate Vito Arena told a federal jury that on the night of the killings, he waited outside the building as the victims walked in, unaware of what was coming. Moments later, he heard panicked screams, followed by muffled gunshots and low, pained moans. When the noise died down, Arena stepped inside, flipped on the light, and was met with carnage—bodies sprawled on the floor, blood smeared across the walls and pooled underfoot. Roy DeMeo and Henry Borelli stood over the scene, guns still in hand.

"They said the Arab [referring to Daoud] went down right away," Arena recalled. "But Ronnie [Falcaro] tried to bolt for the door."

Then came the order. "'We've got to cut them up,' Roy said."[56]

According to Arena, Borelli and Senter retrieved boning knives and set about dismembering the bodies, methodically breaking them down for disposal.

In 1981, Anthony Nelson and Kenny McCabe first learned of DiNome's boast to an informant that he could "easily take them out." At first, they were reluctant to act on DiNome's reckless bravado, for good reason.

---

56. United States v. DiNome, Salvatore Mangialino, Anthony Senter, Joseph Testa, Ronald Ustica, Carlo Profeta, Douglas Rega, Judith May Hellman, Wayne Hellman, and Sol Hellman: Docket Number: Nos. 9, 7, 8, 11, 10, 15, 13, 12 and 14, Dockets 89-1458, 89-1459, 89-1527, 89-1537, 89-1550, 89-1556, 90-1229, 90-1230 and 90-1263

"Kenny and I ignored this initial threat since it might have placed an informant in jeopardy if we confronted Freddy about it," Nelson says. "This was the kind of tough guy talk that Freddy thought might enhance his position with Roy, Nino, and the Gambino Family. But Freddy thought wrong."

Then Freddy kept running his mouth.

An undercover Nassau County detective reported that DiNome claimed to not only know where Kenny McCabe lived, but that he also knew some of his family members, including McCabe's wife, Kathy, and his young son, Kenny Jr., known as Duke.

And there was more.

"Freddy also supposedly knew that Kenny stored photographs of Crew members, as well as police reports, in the basement of his house," Nelson says. "This was the kind of information that suggested Roy may have had some cops in his pocket." This type of specific, tactical information, which could be used to target McCabe's family, was no idle boast that could be ignored.

Throughout his career, McCabe went to great lengths to stay out of the spotlight and shield his family. He also commanded a grudging respect from wiseguys for his even-handed treatment and integrity—something rare for criminals to acknowledge. The gangsters may have hated Kenny McCabe for his photographic memory and uncanny ability to undermine their defense strategies, but they knew he was honest to a fault and would never lie on the stand or use underhanded tactics to undo their underhanded schemes.

This hit too close to home.

"When Kenny heard this new threat, he went ballistic," Nelson says. "There was nothing more important to him than the safety of his family. Kenny immediately called me and asked me to pick him up in my FBI car. He wanted me to go with him and pay a visit to Freddy DiNome."

Nelson's Plymouth Gran Fury no sooner arrived at the Gemini Lounge when they saw DiNome slip away in a Jeep. They tailed him as he drove on Flatlands Avenue, heading east away from the Gemini.

Once DiNome was about a mile away from the lounge and out of DeMeo's sight, Nelson flipped on his police lights, sounded the siren, and pulled him over.

"At this point, I wasn't sure if Kenny wanted to follow up by filing criminal charges against him," Nelson says. "I told Freddy that we needed to speak with him and simply wanted him to accompany us."

Nelson handcuffed DiNome and put him in the back seat of the FBI vehicle.

Kenny McCabe sat in the back seat right beside DiNome.

They drove around for a short time in ominous silence.

"When I didn't drive directly to the 6-3 Precinct or to an FBI office," Nelson says, "it was obvious Freddy started to suspect that we were going to kill him."

Nelson parked on a desolate side street behind a movie theater located near Flatbush Avenue and Kings Highway.

As soon as Nelson parked the car, McCabe shoved his finger up to Freddy's nose and told him, "I am about to forget that I'm a cop, so you better listen to every word that I'm going to tell you."

"Freddy started whining that he was sorry for shooting off his mouth by making threatening comments and begged that we not say anything about the incident to Roy," Nelson recalls. "He said that he would never actually try to hurt anyone in Kenny's family, nor would he try to hurt either one of us." Freddy said that Roy had already warned him several times not to give us a hard time.

"Freddy believed Roy was going to make him 'disappear' if he found out about us taking him for a ride or about the threatening statements he'd made," Nelson says. "He then thanked us for picking him up out of Roy's sight because he also worried that Roy would've suspected he was a rat if he saw him getting into an FBI car."

Nelson then sternly told DiNome that if he made any further threats against anyone in law enforcement, they would be coming back to get him, the next time in front of Roy.

McCabe opened the back door and told Freddy to walk back to his Jeep, which was parked miles away.

McCabe's son recalls the incident. "For the past twenty years, I've been gathering information and case histories related to my father's career, and have conducted many interviews," Duke McCabe says. "I spoke to a couple of guys in the DeMeo Crew, and they told me they were furious at DiNome for threatening my father and his family. The Mafia did not mess with cops and certainly did not mess with their families, out of self-preservation."

Yet in this instance, it was even more than that long-standing tradition.

"My father had integrity, and he was not underhanded, and he was respected for it all around," Duke adds. "So Freddy threatening my father and his family created a mess for him. Those I spoke with later said that Roy was in such a rage, he was going to kill him over this, and probably some other things. And then sure enough, Freddy flipped."

With the DeMeo Crew throwing off so much heat, as federal pressure mounted on the Gambino Family—now with multiple investigations into drug trafficking, stolen vehicles, and murder—DiNome felt the noose tightening. In late 1982, DiNome agreed to flip and testify in exchange for protection, including entry into the federal Witness Protection Program.

It was only after DiNome cooperated with the government that Nelson learned Freddy had a loaded machine gun in the Jeep when they had pulled him over, and DiNome was panicking at the time that the lawmen would search the vehicle and find it.

"Kenny McCabe and I just had to exercise caution in everything we did together, and that caution also extended to our home life, especially if it had something to do with the Gemini Crew," Nelson says.

Mafia figures like Paul Castellano and Carlo Gambino were killers, but they generally played by unwritten rules with respect to law enforcement officers. However, Roy DeMeo and his crew were a different story.

"Roy didn't necessarily play by the rules, but even if he had, the younger psychotic members of his crew might not," Nelson says. "So Kenny and I were always extremely mindful of the threat posed by the Gemini Crew or any other crew for that matter."

Later, on February 11, 1986, McCabe called Nelson to catch him up, telling him he was in San Antonio, Texas, with DiNome, who was, by that time, cooperating with the government. DiNome's testimony backed up key details provided by other cooperating witnesses, including Vito Arena and, later, Dominick Montiglio.

DiNome offered prosecutors a firsthand account of how the DeMeo Crew operated—from their methodical approach to murder and body disposal at the notorious Flatlands Avenue chop shop to the internal hierarchy that kept the crew running.

His cooperation gave federal prosecutors critical credibility, strengthening the RICO cases that targeted not only the DeMeo Crew but the broader Gambino crime family network.

On that call, McCabe shared that DiNome was emotionally unstable, in a terrible mood, and was giving him and FBI Special Agent Artie Ruffels a hard time.

"My father and Artie Ruffels met Freddy DiNome at a diner in San Antonio to go over the trial," Duke McCabe confirms. According to Duke, at that encounter, DiNome became agitated and stormed out of the diner. When McCabe followed him into the parking lot, DiNome jumped into a car and tried to run the lawman over. "My father and Ruffels let DiNome go and expected to meet up with him a few hours later," he adds.

The following day, McCabe called Nelson again.

Freddy DiNome was just found dead.

DiNome had by then not only testified to help take down the international car-theft ring, but he was set to testify in at least four upcoming Gambino trials while he personally awaited sentencing for his role in seven murders.

News of DiNome's suspicious death made national headlines.

Authorities confirmed that the cause of death for the forty-five-year-old DiNome was suicide by hanging.

Sheriff Harlon Copeland of San Antonio said he never suspected foul play in DiNome's death. However, he kept the case open for nearly a week while pursuing three individuals believed to have looted DiNome's money and jewelry after discovering his body in a rented two-bedroom house.[57] According to the sheriff, the three claimed DiNome had left a suicide note addressed to his wife and children. Investigators were skeptical, especially since DiNome had previously testified that he was basically illiterate.

DiNome, found hanging from the canopy frame of a waterbed, had been living under the alias Fred Marino since June that year.

At the time, William M. Dempsey, spokesperson for the Marshals Service—which oversees the Witness Protection Program—stated that no participant who followed the Program's guidelines had ever been murdered. Still, he acknowledged there had been fifteen suicides among the more than 4,800 individuals who have entered the program since its inception in 1970, fifteen years prior.[57]

However, the media didn't have access to some of the key details.

"Kenny said that Freddy had been in a rage earlier about everything, especially unspecified issues concerning his wife," Nelson says. "I remember Kenny saying that Freddy was wound so tight that day that he even hit him (Kenny) with his open car door as he drove away. In fact, he had almost run Kenny over.

"Kenny's description, to me, of Freddy's emotional state was one of extreme anger rather than depression or thoughts of suicide," Nelson adds. "Although I suppose those outward behavioral qualities can coexist or be misinterpreted."

Then McCabe dropped a bombshell.

"Kenny seemed convinced that Freddy's death was the result of autoerotic acts he engaged in after leaving Kenny and Artie Ruffels," Nelson says. "It is not that unusual for people who engage in that form of sexual activity to not be capable of releasing themselves from the bonds they fashion to deprive themselves of oxygen.

---

57. Smothers, Ronald. "A PROTECTED WITNESS IN THE GAMBINO TRIAL IS TERMED a SUICIDE." New York Times. February 19, 1986. https://www.nytimes.com/1986/02/19/nyregion/a-protected-witness-in-the-gambino-trial-is-termed-a-suicide.html

"I had investigated many deaths that occurred on federal reservations such as federal prisons, military bases, and VA facilities," Nelson says. "But I had never personally experienced a death investigation involving autoerotic death.

"Although it wasn't the case with Freddy, sometimes family members who find their loved ones dead from this type of sexual behavior are embarrassed, and they will hide the items of evidence associated with the behavior before they call for medical help or the police," Nelson explains.

"These items may include things like pornographic magazines, ligatures, and sex toys. I don't recall the specific information that Kenny told me about what types of evidence were found at the scene of Freddy's death, but I remember him telling me he had believed the death was autoerotic in nature. Kenny was rarely, if ever, wrong when he drew conclusions," Nelson adds. "But I believe the medical examiner in Texas had simply classified Freddy's death as a suicide."

"My father had a feeling Freddy was going to kill himself to avoid trial," says Duke. Though only nine years old at the time, Duke later discussed the DiNome suicide. "My father always would tell me the knot Freddy tied was tied incorrectly. As he reached a certain point, he was to pull the line, and the knot would release. Freddy tied the knot backwards, so the knot never slipped, and he died."

Federal agencies have implemented various programs to address threats, but family protection remains challenging.

As of 2022, the Federal Law Enforcement Officers Association (FLEOA) has called for increased funding and resources to protect agents and their families in response to an uptick in violent threats and incidents against law enforcement personnel.

These days, the rise of online platforms has introduced new risks in the form of doxxing, where personal information is published publicly to intimidate or harm agents and their families. Threat actors may release an agent's home address, phone number, and other personal details, which increases vulnerability to harassment and potential attacks. The Government Accountability Office (GAO) reported in 2020 that federal agents face increased risks of doxxing by individuals upset by high-profile cases or groups aiming to disrupt federal operations.

CHAPTER TWENTY-NINE

In mid-1982, one of Anthony Nelson's confidential informants tipped him off to a sensational crime that would captivate New York headlines.

"He'd been present in a gambling location in Midtown Manhattan that was operated by associates of the Colombo Family when two wiseguys came in with stolen paintings that they were trying to unload," Nelson recalls.

By then, Nelson's stable of CIs was flowing in a steady stream of intel, with tips resulting in arrests and recoveries. They all had their motivations. Some were angling for rewards while others sought to jam up their rivals. "But honestly, many provided information to me simply because I had treated them decently during a previous arrest," Nelson says.

Managing informants is a complex business.

While informants provide crucial assistance in solving serious crimes, the method raises ethical concerns about exploitation, fairness, and the potential for harm.

The concept of using individuals to gather information for law enforcement is not new. In Ancient Egypt, Greece, and Rome, rulers employed spies to detect treason, corruption, and criminal activities. In medieval Europe, kings relied on networks of informants to gather intelligence about potential threats to their rule. In England, the "thief-takers" of the early eighteenth century were private citizens who captured criminals for a reward.

By the early twentieth century in the United States, the use of informants expanded alongside the rise of organized crime. Law enforcement agencies, including local police and the newly established FBI, used informants to infiltrate the Italian Mafia, the Irish Mob, and Jewish gangs.

The 1970s, in particular, saw a rise in both the use of informants and complexity in how they were recruited, handled, and compensated. The FBI's New York Office's Criminal Division also instituted an annual, office-wide "inspection."

"It was a review of overall office performance and adherence to guidelines," Nelson recalls. "But it was also a review of our individual performance, conducted by agents assigned to FBI Headquarters in Washington, DC.

"The operation of informants is one of the primary reasons the FBI has been so successful in the war on crime and counterterrorism," Nelson adds, "and is often characterized in the media as the premier law enforcement agency in the world."

"There is no doubt that this emphasis on informant development is of paramount importance because informants make significant contributions to investigations," he continues. "However, there are often difficulties and unseemly qualities inherent in their use."

And herein lies the moral dilemma of using informants, balancing the pursuit of justice with ethical concerns, especially as informants are often embedded in criminal organizations and participating in illegal activities to maintain their cover or gain access to information.

There are two types of criminal informants.

A confidential informant (CI) is an individual who provides information to law enforcement on an ongoing basis and whose identity the law enforcement agency will try to protect.

"CIs were generally developed because they may have once been subject to, or faced, criminal prosecution, but subsequently continued their relationship with an agent either for financial gain or because they had developed a rapport," Nelson says.

The second type of informant is a cooperative witness (CW). This individual agrees to testify, and the law enforcement agency will attempt to protect their identity for the duration of their cooperation in a criminal investigation. CWs are generally individuals who have committed serious offenses and have agreed to plead guilty to certain criminal charges, thereby helping the government achieve its prosecutive objectives. In exchange, they're usually angling for a recommendation from the prosecutor to help get a reduced sentence.

"Occasionally, a concerned citizen may come forward as a CW to volunteer information of value in a criminal investigation, and their motive for doing so may simply be patriotism," Nelson says. "But this type of CW is rare. During my entire time as an FBI agent, I had never encountered one such person. Most confidential informants and cooperative witnesses are generally people who are, or were, involved in some type of criminal activity."

Though it may seem antithetical, CIs are the more problematic and difficult to control, Nelson says. "Since they are neither under indictment nor otherwise facing criminal charges, greater effort and diligence are required to properly manage them," Nelson explains. "Some CIs will continue to engage in unauthorized criminal activity without the knowledge of the FBI. After all, that is why they are of value as an informant in the first place."

Nelson had a clear strategy for managing informants.

"I operated most of my informants as long-term CIs, and to the best of my knowledge, they adhered to the attorney general guidelines that I ingrained in them," he says. "That is not to say that I operated all of them without issues. There were times when local and federal prosecutors, as well as other law enforcement agencies, wanted to identify my CIs. Some, even worse, demanded that I produce them to testify in open court."

So in the summer of 1982, a Nelson CI provided the hot tip on Colombo associates, who swiped rare, expensive pieces of fine art. "The person who called me said he had followed them to a location in Elmhurst [Queens]," Nelson says. "They parked a car they had rented with fraudulent identification and simply abandoned the vehicle, along with the paintings, since they'd been unable to sell them through local art dealers."

Unlike high-end automobiles, electronics, and jewelry, fine art is hard to fence.

Rare art is, by nature, well-documented, distinctive, and often famous. Each piece is typically cataloged in museum records, art registries, auction house archives, and databases like the Art Loss Register. This makes it nearly impossible to sell the work openly without raising red flags.

And the legitimate art market is small and elite. Most collectors, dealers, and institutions won't touch a piece without verifying its provenance (history of ownership). If the art is listed as stolen, it becomes radioactive—no reputable buyer or gallery will go near art they can't display, insure, or resell.

Nelson responded to the location and recovered three stolen paintings.[58] "One of the paintings was a 1964 Picasso entitled *Homme et Femme*, and the other two were etchings by Henri Matisse entitled *Woodcut of a Nude* and *Nude on a Sofa*," Nelson says. "All three paintings had been stolen from a Beverly Hills, California, art dealer who was thrilled to get them back."

For comparison's sake, Christie's estimates on its site that Picasso's 1967 *Homme et Femme* would fetch upwards of $750,000 at auction. And while generally, the highest prices are commanded by Matisse's charcoal drawings from the 1930s, such as *Etude pour La Dormeuse (Le Rêve)* and his works made with sweeping lines of Indian ink, his etchings and lithographs regularly sell for tens of thousands of dollars, notes Christie's.

There's a human factor to consider when managing CIs.

Nelson developed such a good rapport with most of his CIs that some of them checked in daily.

"Two of them, who were probably twenty years older than me, would speak to me as though I was their father, even looking for help or guidance in their personal affairs," Nelson says.

As tough as these two hardened criminals were, they sometimes exhibited levels of naiveté, bordering on a gullibility that was challenging for Nelson to process. "One of the two, at one time, had been shot in the nose and stabbed several times in his back,"

58. Capeci, Jerry. "Hot Art from Coast Turns Up in Queens." New York Post. 1982

Nelson says, "but still had a childlike quality about him and a level of ignorance that astounded me."

This particular cooperating witness, who agreed to testify, was being sent by members of the Genovese Family to Fort Lauderdale, Florida, to do a job, with no additional details. And he was given a one-way train ticket to Miami.

"He was going to be told what he was needed for after he arrived in Florida," Nelson says. "I'd been suspicious of what he faced during the trip, and I believed he was going to be killed." Just in case, he decided to accompany his CI, joined by FBI Special Agent Rick Lahey, and the three boarded the same train bound for Florida.

"I was amazed to learn, while on the train, that he'd never been outside of New York City before in his entire life, even though he was close to fifty years old," Nelson says.

Although he gave firm instructions for the wiseguy to not acknowledge either lawman, the wide-eyed CI began to laugh loudly, to the dismay of the other passengers. To make matters worse, the aging gangster turned around, looked directly at Nelson and Lahey as the train departed Penn Station in New York City, and barked, "What day is it in Florida?"

It was Wednesday. Same day, same time zone as New York.

"Once the other passengers heard his intimidating laugh and that question, they began to move their seats away from him," Nelson says. "He also believed you had to take a trip 'across the ocean' to get to Staten Island. It was easy to see why some wiseguys manipulated him into criminal activity. Yet he had a certain innocence about him that made him likable."

Later, Nelson heard this same CI was arrested for assaulting cemetery staff who tried to stop him from mowing the grass at his mother's gravesite.

"I almost miss his daily telephone calls, which ceased after he suffered a stroke and passed away in his fifties," Nelson laments.

CHAPTER THIRTY

The walls were closing in on Roy DeMeo.

As more victims disappeared at the Gemini Lounge, multiple law enforcement agencies were either investigating or suspecting the DeMeo Crew of dozens of homicides, not to mention myriad crimes and capers. Meanwhile, the Brooklyn Central Robbery Squad focused its resources on tracking down DeMeo Crew member Vito Arena.

"Arena and his boyfriend, Joey Lee, had been suspected in a pattern of armed robberies at dentist offices," Nelson says. "Kenny McCabe and I had also been trying to locate Arena prior to him becoming wanted for the robberies in order to serve him with a federal subpoena."

It was not long after that Sergeant Steve Marks, the keen-eyed supervisor of the Brooklyn Robbery Squad spotted, and arrested, Arena inside a Long Island restaurant.

The June 4, 1982, arrest of Arena marked the beginning of the final act in the Roy DeMeo story.

By then, Arena had become a major problem for DeMeo.

A seasoned car thief and armed robber, Arena linked up with Roy DeMeo in 1978, shortly after killing a former criminal associate. But by 1980, Arena had begun pulling away from the increasingly ruthless crew—motivated by both fear and mounting tension within the gang over his openly gay identity. While lying low in Suffolk County with his partner, Joey Lee, the two were apprehended by authorities.

Facing serious charges and terrified of DeMeo's reprisal, Arena agreed to cooperate. He disclosed that he had been feeding information to the FBI since the spring of 1980 under the alias "Harry," offering intelligence on the killings of Khaled Daoud and Ronald Falcaro, along with details about the gang's stolen vehicle operation.

Although he pledged cooperation with the NYPD, Arena was released on bail and quickly disappeared.

In a strategic move to rattle DeMeo, the FBI subpoenaed him in connection with the car theft ring and informed him that Arena had flipped—though DeMeo denied any knowledge of the man.

By early 1982, both law enforcement and members of DeMeo's Crew were scrambling to locate Arena. A joint task force comprising the FBI, NYPD, and the US Attorney's Office pursued multiple leads in their effort to track down Arena and Lee.

NYPD Detectives Frank Pergola and Roland Cadieux were assigned to manage homicide investigations resulting from leads from Vito Arena. They pursued connections to the old cases and sought new witnesses, including a woman who had previously testified in a murder trial and was reluctant to do so again.

During the summer and fall of 1982, fearing arrest as a result of Arena's cooperation, DeMeo and members of his crew went into hiding. DeMeo eventually resurfaced to meet with attorneys, anticipating an indictment as the Southern District of New York closed in on his crew's criminal operations.

Nino Gaggi and Paul Castellano also became alarmed upon learning that Arena had turned State's evidence. Castellano then began conspiring to have DeMeo killed.

"Walter Mack obtained a writ for State prisoner Arena," Pergola says. "We responded to the Brooklyn House of Detention and kidnapped Arena, who immediately confessed to the murder of John Scorney and told us his body was in a barrel in the water off Long Island, where it was recovered." Joseph Scorney, a childhood friend of Vito Arena, was murdered on September 28, 1978, shot and bludgeoned with a sledgehammer by Arena and Richard DiNome after refusing to join DeMeo's auto-theft operation.

Arena was questioned during the 1985 Mafia Commission Trial and testified that he and DiNome stuffed Scorney's body into a fifty-gallon oil drum, filled it with cement, and dumped it off a pier in Center Moriches, New York. The barrel was recovered in 1982.

Arena was sentenced to eighteen years in prison in 1985 for this murder.

In 1991, Vito Arena, having been released from federal prison in 1988 upon his cooperation with the government, was shot and killed during the commission of an armed robbery in Texas.

In addition to Scorney, Arena confirmed more of the DeMeo Crew murders.

One was the 1982 murder of Constance Burke, a thirty-three-year-old confidential informant. She vanished after leaving the Gemini Lounge on April 4, 1982. More than two months later, on June 9, her remains were found in Canarsie, Brooklyn, following a tip from another informant to federal authorities.

Arena's cooperation triggered panic within the DeMeo Crew and, by extension, the Gambinos.

In the winter of 1982–83, Roy DeMeo was paranoid and withdrawn. According to an account later provided by his son Albert, DeMeo rarely left his home without a shotgun hidden under his jacket and even considered faking his own death. Roy knew his days were numbered.

During that winter, Anthony Nelson and Kenny McCabe were staking out a holiday get-together of Gambinos at the Veterans and Friends Social Club in Bensonhurst.

"Roy was walking up Bay 7th Street around the corner from the club," Nelson remembers. "He was most probably walking there to avoid having criminal conversations inside the club since he believed the club was bugged.

"We teased Roy about possibly being lost and asked him if he was looking for his car," Nelson says. "We jokingly told him where he had parked the car and we offered to give him a ride back to it." Letting members know they knew where their cars were parked was one of many methods Nelson and McCabe used to keep them off balance.

DeMeo brushed it off with a sarcastic comment, as much to demonstrate to his criminal companion that he was not intimidated as it was to reinforce that he was not cooperating.

"We teased Roy in front of his associate," Nelson clarifies. "But we did not warn him about him possibly being targeted or try to solicit his cooperation until he was alone later that night and was walking back to his car."

This was all part of the game. And Nelson and McCabe knew exactly the consequences DeMeo faced if they even jokingly referred to the gang boss as a cooperator in front of another Gambino associate.

After a time, as the lawmen watched from afar, DeMeo parted ways with his associate and walked silently to his car, the bravado gone, the crushing weight of his world clearly etched on his anguished face. Then the cagey DeMeo passed Nelson's Plymouth Gran Fury without responding with his usual sarcasm.

"He seemed sullen, as though he knew his days were numbered and he didn't need us to confirm his suspicions," Nelson recalls.

Nelson remembers that night Kenny McCabe voiced his belief that at that point, Roy DeMeo knew he was nearing the end and that he might just finally agree to cooperate.

Nelson was less optimistic that Roy would ever cooperate.

"Only because he had committed so many murders, and so many other crimes, that he probably figured anything he could tell us, or more importantly, a jury, would pale in comparison to the crimes he personally committed," Nelson says. "There were too many victims. He'd gone too far, done too much harm. There was no coming back from that, and he knew that better than anyone."

Then a major break came.

By 1983, Dominick Montiglio, nephew of Nino Gaggi, was a full-blown gangster, out of control, with a drug problem, and trying to collect on an old loan.

"The police department got lucky," Frank Pergola says. "A victim of extortion, by the name of Winick, reported that Dominick Montiglio attempted to extort twenty thousand dollars from him in New York City."

The borrower, Jeffrey Winick—now CEO of the commercial real estate firm Winick Realty Group—refused to repay the debt and reportedly orchestrated a setup that led to Montiglio's arrest. Montiglio had a falling out with Gaggi and left the state. He was arrested upon his return while trying to collect on that old debt.

"We wired Winick and he went to meet Montiglio in the Hickory Pit Restaurant in Midtown Manhattan," Pergola tells. "During that encounter, where Montiglio incriminated himself, an arrest was made. However, it turned out that the tape recorder didn't work. But Dominick never knew."

Montiglio was pressed for information and shown photos of the DeMeo Crew. He said he would consider cooperation if he was protected.

By then, the Gambino Family had put out a massive contract on Montiglio.

Pergola says, "I told Montiglio, 'Don't wait for the other shoe to drop. You know about all these murders, and your Uncle Nino has a contract out for you for the $250,000 that you stole in loan-sharking money from him.'"

At the arraignment, an inexperienced prosecutor made the mistake of saying in court that Montiglio was the nephew of a capo in the Gambino crime Family named Nino Gaggi," Pergola remembers. "The judge looked at me and thought I was a lawyer until I put my shield on. She said, 'You dress very well. Sorry for the mistake.'

"Next day, Montiglio gets a visit from an attorney his uncle sent," Pergola adds. "He immediately calls me and agrees to cooperate. I had already reviewed the possible two hundred murder cases and disregarded a hundred of them. We took Montiglio to a safe house in Lake George, and he confirmed seventy-nine of those murders and identified the perpetrators from information he got from Roy and Henry Borelli.

"My relationship with Dominick Montiglio began with his arrest and cooperation in 1983 and continued for the next thirty-eight years, up to Dominick's death following a stroke in 2021," Pergola explains. "His cooperation resulted in two major trials in the Southern District of New York and twenty-five convictions, closing seventy-nine cold-case murders.

"In my opinion," Pergola says, "Montiglio was always reliable and truthful and knowledgeable of murder investigations, which I verified by case facts and testimony of other witnesses, and my personal assignments to some of these murders in the US."

Debriefings of Montiglio were under the supervision of the Marshals' Witness Protection Program and conducted all over the United States, which required separation from an agent's family.

There's an interesting side story here.

"There was nothing funny in these investigations over all these years," Pergola says. "But I do remember an incident while we were up in Lake George, debriefing Montiglio and providing security for him and his family. We were living in two trailers. Our trailer had no heat, and the family trailer did. It was the middle of winter, and there was heavy snow on the ground. Me and my partner Ronnie [Cadieux] had the trailer with no heat. We spent ten days working ten hours a day, debriefing Montiglio, and he gave us information that corroborated seventy-nine murders."

On the weekends, Kenny McCabe and Artie Ruffels drove up to Lake George.

"One weekend, we said we needed a break, and you have to watch the family," Pergola says. "We were heading into town. So we left and we went to Lake George and went to the actual hotel that Kenny McCabe and Artie Ruffels were staying in, and we found their room." Pergola picked the lock on the door. Hotels had keys in those days, not plastic access cards.

"Turned the thermostat in the room completely off, put corn flakes under the sheets on the bed, and went downstairs to the lounge and had a couple of drinks," Pergola says. "Ronnie celebrated because he was getting even, and he bought a cigar.

"Sure, when Kenny and Artie came back and saw what I did, they were not happy and complained for a long time," Pergola laughs. "But if you ask me, they deserved it. It was Ronnie and me that were freezing our asses off in the trailer for ten days in the middle of winter with no heat. And then Ronnie got sick from his cigar and drinking. And we never heard the end of that too."

On January 10, 1983, Roy DeMeo arrived at Patty Testa's home for what was supposed to be a routine meeting with his crew.

Ten days later, DeMeo's Cadillac Coupe DeVille was found abandoned in the parking lot of the Varuna Boat Club in Sheepshead Bay. The vehicle was towed to a nearby NYPD precinct, where detectives from the Organized Crime Control Bureau made a grim discovery—in the trunk, beneath a chandelier, lay DeMeo's partially frozen body. He'd been shot multiple times in the head. A bullet wound to his hand suggested he had tried to defend himself when the shooting began.

Investigators quickly theorized that DeMeo was lured to his death in much the same way he ambushed victims himself. They believed his murder was orchestrated by his own Crew—specifically Nino Gaggi, Joseph Testa, and Anthony Senter. DeMeo's son, Albert, also came to believe his father had been betrayed by his closest associates.

In April 1984, Colombo soldier Ralph Scopo was caught on a wiretap telling an associate that DeMeo's murder had been sanctioned by his own Family. They feared he wouldn't withstand the legal pressure stemming from his massive stolen car operation. Scopo claimed Paul Castellano gave the final order, calling DeMeo "crazy" and saying he had "cast-iron balls"—a dangerous combination.

Anthony "Gaspipe" Casso, the Lucchese underboss who later turned government witness, offered another version. He said Castellano first tasked John Gotti and Frank DeCicco with the hit, but they couldn't get close. DeCicco then suggested Casso handle it, given his ties to Senter and Testa. Casso agreed, assuring them there'd be no consequences and promising them a place in the Lucchese Family. According to Casso, DeMeo stopped by Patty

Testa's home to collect a debt. While he waited for a cup of coffee, Senter and Testa opened fire, killing him on the spot.

Ironically, Casso claimed that by eliminating DeMeo, Castellano sealed his own fate. Gotti and DeCicco, already eyeing a power play, moved forward with plans to assassinate Castellano—something they may not have attempted if DeMeo had still been alive.

Castellano was gunned down outside Sparks Steak House on December 16, 1985.

"After Roy was murdered and the witnesses began cooperating," Nelson recalls, "FBI Agents Arthur Ruffels and Marilyn Lucht were assigned to Walter Mack's organized crime task force. I wasn't part of the formal team, but I stayed in the field, continuing to work with informants and sources, and gathering intelligence with Kenny McCabe."

After testifying, Montiglio entered the Witness Protection Program with his wife and children. Over the years, he and his family were relocated repeatedly—reportedly to more than a dozen different places—and lived under multiple aliases. Montiglio battled addiction, struggling with cocaine and alcohol before eventually getting clean.

In Witness Protection, Montiglio had a new identity, but he struggled to adjust to new areas and lifestyles, eventually abandoning his family. He left the Program and returned to Brooklyn, where he reinvented himself as an artist. In his final years, Montiglio lived quietly near Albuquerque, New Mexico.

"He drifted from state to state," Pergola says. "We visited and kept in contact by phone for many years. Later on, on the phone, he was obviously under the influence of alcohol and drugs, always finding criminal groups to associate with, motorcycle gangs, Samoans, etc., looking for protection from organized crime. He made little sense, was confused and delusional, and drifted away from family and Marshals, moving from state to state, finally ending up in New Mexico with his half-sister D, where he expired from three strokes in 2021."

Before he ended up in New Mexico in 1995, Montiglio returned to Park Slope, and lived with artist and producer Ross Brodar from 1992 to 1995. With the assistance of Brodar, Montiglio sold paintings in the East Village. Brodar also produced a podcast with Montiglio, aptly named *My Hitman Roommate*, as well as a 2021 documentary, *Lynchpin of Bensonhurst: The Dominick Montiglio Story*.

Still, it was dangerous for Montiglio to be in Brooklyn.

His uncle Nino Gaggi had a contract out on him for testifying and for stealing $250,000 of loan-sharking money from him when he ran to California.

"Montiglio separated from his wife and children, and also lost his youngest daughter, hit and killed by a train in Little Rock, Arkansas, in 2019," Pergola says. "He now called me less frequently, and when he did, he made little sense.

"While living in Brooklyn, he became more delusional from drugs and alcohol," Pergola adds. "He made many podcasts recorded by Brodar for *My Hitman Roommate* in which he was obviously under the influence of drugs and alcohol. He was rambling and delusional, bragging about fictional criminal activity, embellished, invented, and imagined stories from over thirty years ago about his close friend Danny Grillo committing suicide, while he and others testified that Grillo was murdered by the DeMeo Crew.

"Montiglio now stated he killed Governero and never told me," Pergola continues. "When he testified that Gaggi and DeMeo killed Governero, he had been present for the murder and carried a .22-caliber handgun, but didn't fire it. But Governero was killed by a .380-caliber, and no .22-caliber was used in the murder. That case would set in motion Montiglio's decision to cooperate with authorities, ultimately providing key testimony against Gambino crime Family captain Nino Gaggi, who later died in prison."

These inconsistencies were recorded on the podcast *Mafia Tapes* by journalist Celia Aniskovich while Montiglio was intoxicated and delusional, discussing events that occurred more than forty years ago.

On June 27, 2021, Montiglio died at the age of seventy-three in Albuquerque, New Mexico.

"Dominick's body was cremated and his ashes returned to his family in Little Rock, Arkansas," Pergola says. "And he never did get a military funeral."

CHAPTER THIRTY-ONE

It was just another night in 1982 when Anthony Nelson and Kenny McCabe set out to visit as many Brooklyn social clubs as they could, then get at least some sleep. Remember, they both had day jobs.

The American Mafia did not invent the Italian social club. But like so many other things in the community, organized crime corrupted it to serve its ends.

The first Italian immigrants arrived en masse in New York City in the 1840s, settling in the Five Points neighborhood of Lower Manhattan. The area around Mulberry Street became known as Little Italy. After World War II, a new wave of Italian immigrants settled in the outer boroughs, especially Brooklyn, Queens, and the North Bronx, a migration following the transit lines that extended across the city. Bensonhurst soon became the largest Italian community in New York City.

Italian immigrants formed mutual aid societies, cultural clubs, and religious organizations. They created theater clubs and coffee houses to share their culture through light comedies, tragedies, and vaudeville. These neighborhood fixtures often lay behind understated storefronts marked only by an Italian name or maybe a small Italian flag, where mostly men gathered to play cards, sip espresso, smoke cigars, and discuss local and international news. The clubs typically had unassuming interiors, furnished with tables, folding chairs, a television set, and framed pictures of Italian saints or famous Italian-American icons. The scent of espresso and De Nobili cigars hung in the air, a quiet hum of conversation punctuated by occasional bursts of laughter or heated arguments.

On the one hand, these were safe places of tradition and camaraderie, card games and celebrations tied to Italian heritage. On the other hand, more and more fell under the control of factions of powerful Mafia families. These clubs became informal offices where Mob bosses and underlings could plot schemes, resolve disputes, and conduct business, such as loan sharking, gambling, and racketeering.

And by the early 1980s, these clubs were everywhere in New York City.

There was Anthony Spero's Bath Beach Social Club on Bath Avenue, William Cutolo's Wild Bill's Friendly Bocce Club on 63rd Street and 11th Avenue, Colombo stronghold Neddy's Bar on 13th Avenue in South Brooklyn and across the street from Greg Scarpa's The Wimpy Boys Social Club.

Further down 13th Avenue, you had The Flip Side. There was Gambino hang-out Veteran's & Friends Club on 86th Street, a bit more than a block away from Christi Tick's 19th Hole across from Dyker Park. You had Sammy the Bull's 2020, Carmine Sessa's Occasions, the Gemini Lounge on Flatlands Avenue, the Bonanno's Motion Lounge in Williamsburg (made famous in *Donnie Brasco*), and the Lucchese's Bamboo Lounge (made famous in *Goodfellas*), and dozens more clubs and even more restaurants—in fact, far too many to surveil in a single night.

Perhaps not as well known (well, by civilians) were the Caravella Social Club, (Bensonhurst) tied to the Gambino Family, Café Giannini (East New York), a regular haunt for the Bonannos, the Marlboro House Social Club and the Wrong Number (both in Gravesend, both associated with the Colombos), and the White House Social Club in Canarsie (Luccheses).

And then there were those they didn't bother naming, the 15th Avenue Social Club (Colombos), the 20th Avenue Social Club (Colombos), the 24th Avenue Club (Colombos), the Bay Parkway Social Club (Gambinos), the Flatbush Avenue Social Club (Luccheses), and even the Mulberry Street Social Club (Bonannos and Gambinos), located in Brooklyn Heights and not be confused with the Ravenite Social Club, located on the more famous Mulberry Street in Manhattan and perhaps *the* most notorious Italian social club of them all due to its association with Gambino Teflon Don John Gotti.

That's a lot of ground for two men to cover in a conspicuous Plymouth Gran Fury.

"I'd usually arrive at Kenny's house in Brooklyn to pick him up; he'd already be standing outside waiting for me, his son Kenny Jr., Duke, would be standing by his side, holding his hand," Nelson says. "This is the scene I remember from so many evenings—Duke, not much taller than my thigh at the time, standing by his dad, getting ready to wave goodbye to us.

"And as I remember this scene now, it's hard to believe how quickly the years have passed since Duke was that size," Nelson recalls. "Today, I'm six feet and he makes me look small in comparison, taller and even more muscular than his dad, who stood at six-four."

"Throughout much of my earlier life, I just remember Anthony always being around my dad," Duke McCabe says. "They'd have those lunches together on Fridays and compare notes and cases. My dad would take me to those lunches every now and then, starting when I was nine or ten years old, all the way up to when I was in college … and then my dad passed away.

"They had a very strong bond, that was obvious," Duke adds. "Anthony was like his right hand, and vice versa. They just complemented each other so well."

That night, the first stop for the two lawmen was dinner at Collaro's Italian Restaurant, located at 1939 McDonald Avenue off Quentin Road, right near an old city cemetery.

In one of those bizarre twists you only see in Brooklyn, Sonny's Collaro's McDonald Avenue spot had no relationship to the other Collaro's red-sauce joint on Coney Island Avenue, or a third Collaro's on Ocean Parkway and Avenue L.

"Collaro's was one of just a handful of restaurants where we felt comfortable enough to eat the food," Nelson remembers.

The lawmen were particular about where they eat—to avoid confrontation as well as food contamination.

After dinner, they headed over to idle at a bus stop across the street from RoSal's Restaurant on McDonald Avenue. While the intent was to gather intel and snap some pics, both McCabe and Nelson knew they could be pressed into action at any moment.

McDonald Avenue in Gravesend is one of those real gritty Brooklyn locales, the perfect setting for a Hollywood gangster flick, long shadows cast by the elevated subway *tha-thunking* overhead barreling out to Coney Island. Late at night, it really does give you that feeling of Hubert Selby's *Last Exit to Brooklyn*.

BINGO.

Sure enough, as they sat parked there, they spotted Genovese Family associate Joseph "Joe Curly'" Taglianetti, then a fugitive wanted by the Bureau of Alcohol, Tobacco, Firearms, and Explosives (ATF). Like the FBI, the ATF is a domestic law enforcement agency within the Department of Justice, so there's a kinship between the two.

Taglianetti was wanted on a federal arrest warrant for conspiracy. As he walked toward the entrance of the restaurant, Nelson and McCabe jumped out of that Plymouth Gran Fury. Spotting the lawmen approaching, Taglianetti ran through the front door of RoSal's.

At the time, there was a formal function going on inside the restaurant that may have been a wedding.

This was a delicate situation.

Generally, the FBI, like other law enforcement agencies, needs a warrant to enter a private home or business.

There are exceptions. If the FBI is in immediate pursuit of a fleeing suspect and that suspect enters private property, agents may follow them inside without a warrant. This is also known as "fresh pursuit." If the owner or someone with authority over the property voluntarily allows the FBI to enter, no warrant is needed. However, this consent must be freely given, not coerced or tricked.

But to justify a warrantless entry under exigent circumstances, the FBI must have a reasonable belief that the situation requires immediate action, such as an imminent threat to public safety (e.g., sounds of a struggle or cries for help), a risk of evidence being destroyed, or a suspect's potential escape.

"So, at first," Nelson says, "we went inside discreetly and told Tommy Lombardi to send Joe Curly out or we were coming in." Ottaviano "Tommy" Lombardi ran the Genovese crew based out of RoSal's.

In typical whatta-you-want-from-me wiseguy fashion, Lombardi feigned ignorance, insisting Joe Curly wasn't there, had not been there, and was not expected. He then turned, ignoring the lawmen's protests.

The situation escalated rapidly. Nelson used his FBI radio to call for backup. Within minutes, two FBI agents armed with Heckler & Koch MP5 submachine guns were on the scene. They'd been passing nearby, returning from a SWAT training exercise that evening.

"We entered the restaurant, armed like the military," Nelson says, "while this formal function was taking place."

Following a search of the first floor of the premises, Joe Curly was nowhere to be found. He just had to do things the hard way. Guns drawn, the lawmen cautiously headed downstairs to flush him out.

"As Kenny and I descended into the dark, unlit basement of the restaurant, I heard Kenny yell out in a loud voice, 'Cuff him!'" Nelson says. "Kenny then dragged Joe Curly by the neck out of a dark closet. While I was placing handcuffs on him, he said to us, 'I wasn't hiding from you guys. I was just going to the bathroom.'"

That was the wrong thing to say.

"Kenny got so mad at him for that statement because he was in an unlit closet of the basement that had no toilet bowl or sink," Nelson says. "I rarely saw Kenny get genuinely angry. But I really think that he was upset by the way Tommy Lombardi had ignored our demand to surrender Taglianetti."

McCabe, holding Joe Curly firmly by his collar, dragged the wanted fugitive up to the dance floor, crowded with a group of slow-dancing women, oblivious a takedown was taking place.

According to Nelson, the towering McCabe then literally shook Joe Curly inches off the floor while yelling to Tommy Lombardi, "'So, he's not in the restaurant, Tommy? You lying bastard!' Unfortunately, this was all happening while people were enjoying their wedding or whatever they were celebrating."

Then, suddenly, despite the music continuing to play, some partygoers noticed the armed agents, the struggling fugitive, and the irate McCabe shouting down Lombardi. Loud screams set off a panic, people running in different directions, some taking cover, just chaos, as they dragged Joe Curly outside in cuffs.

When the lawmen stashed Joe Curly in the back seat of Nelson's FBI mobile, the gangster exclaimed, "Holy shit, I guess I won't be going into RoSal's for fried calamari anytime soon. Tommy is gonna kill me."

Several months later, Nelson and McCabe were summoned to Atlanta, Georgia, to offer testimony against Joe Curly. Upon arrival, they checked into the Peachtree Plaza Hotel.

"Oddly, as soon as we checked in and turned on the television, Sergeant Joe Coffey from the NYPD Chief of Detectives Office was on the news briefing the media about an arrest he had just made," Nelson remembers. Coffey was a media favorite who happened to be in charge of the NYPD's detective personnel assigned to Walter Mack's DeMeo Crew task force.

Joe Curly was convicted on federal charges and remanded to prison. Upon release, presumably, he was persona non grata at Rosal's Restaurant after that fiasco.

CHAPTER THIRTY-TWO

By 1983, Special Agent Anthony Nelson continued his undercover work for the FBI, again requiring trips to South Florida to participate in drug transactions orchestrated by New York organized crime figures under investigation.

As the decade wore on, all of New York's Mafia Families had moved into narcotics trafficking in a big way. That pipeline flowed through South Florida as the Cocaine Wars raged in Miami and spread to surrounding areas like cancer.

In February 1982, US President Ronald Reagan declared that "epidemic drug smuggling" created a "serious problem" in South Florida. He set up a Florida task force with agents from the DEA, US Customs, FBI, ATF, and the US Department of Justice, which began work in March 1982.

This time, instead of Miami, Nelson was headed to Fort Lauderdale.

Named after a series of forts built by the United States during the Second Seminole War, Fort Lauderdale has its own sordid history with vice. Back in the 1920s, during Prohibition, so much smuggled alcohol flowed through the city, it earned the nickname "Fort Liquordale."

When Nelson arrived in 1983, that flood of illegal booze had long since been replaced by an avalanche of cocaine.

Fort Lauderdale in the 1980s was in crisis. Fort Lauderdale Beach was spring break party central since the 1960s, ushered in by a clarion call heard on campuses nationwide when Connie Francis and George Hamilton starred in the wildly popular film *Where the Boys Are*.

Oh, the boys and the girls sure came.

But by the 1980s, the city was overrun every vacation season by rowdy hordes of drunken spring breakers packing and trashing hotels, fighting in the streets, and generally doing everything they could to drive away peaceful, more profitable, family vacationers.

It was still a few years until a massive Fort Lauderdale zero-tolerance crackdown and PR makeover, and the underground drug trade spilled over into the city, darkening the debauchery.

Nelson was asked by FBI Special Agent Warren Flagg to assist him and Special Agent George Hanna in a particular undercover case, with Flagg negotiating with the targets, who were dealing in large quantities of cocaine, as well as stolen rental vehicles.

Flagg distinguished himself during his twenty-two years as a Special Agent with the FBI and, before his appointment, an additional five years as a fingerprint filing clerk and FBI Headquarters tour guide. In retirement, Flagg launched a successful private investigation firm called Flaggman, Inc., and later consulted on television projects, including *Sleeper Cell* in 2005. More recently, he made headlines when he was hired by Mark Cuban to investigate the Dallas Mavericks' 2014 loss in the NBA Finals. Later, in 2018, he commented for CBS News, explaining how the FBI would investigate allegations made of then Supreme Court nominee Brett Kavanaugh.

As previously noted, Nelson had worked with Hanna on a major drug sting in Miami in 1981 that originated from organized crime investigations in New York.

During Flagg's negotiations with the subjects, a couple of the major car rental companies provided the three agents with high-end luxury vehicles to use in an undercover capacity.

"We were posing as drug-dealing mobsters from New York City," Nelson recalls. "As the deal unfolded, we had to drive the rental vehicles to Fort Lauderdale to pick up five kilos of cocaine."

When the lawmen arrived in Fort Lauderdale, they met for dinner with several targets to negotiate the final details for the delivery of the cocaine, as well as for the sale of several stolen vehicles. It was agreed that both the cars and the drugs were to be delivered to the undercovers at a Marriott Hotel in Fort Lauderdale.

To support the meetings with the drug dealers, the Miami Office of the FBI dedicated a squad of professional surveillance agents to follow the New York team and provide backup if needed.

However, unlike today, there was no direct communication between the undercover agents and their backup. Remember, this was 1983, so the undercover cocaine buy was being conducted at a time when both law enforcement officers and drug dealers were all carrying pagers, commonly referred to as "beepers."

Then, there was a complication.

At the time of the cocaine delivery, the principal drug dealers controlling the operation dispatched two "mules" (expendable members of their operation) to the Marriott parking lot. But they delivered only three of the five kilos of cocaine negotiated, in addition to two stolen rental cars.

Both drug mules were carrying pagers, only capable of receiving telephone numbers.

"When they delivered the three kilos of cocaine and the stolen cars," Nelson says, "the Miami FBI Special Operations team backing us up, as well as Flagg, Hanna, and myself, swooped down on them and placed them under arrest."

The mules claimed to have no idea where the other two kilos of cocaine were, and, not surprisingly, they did not provide much information of value.

Then their pagers began furiously beeping with the same callback number.

"It was obvious to us that their boss was trying to find out where they were with either the money or the drugs," Nelson says.

In an unbelievably bold move, while the agents were arresting the two subjects, which attracted scores of onlookers, a car thief, totally unrelated to the drug dealers, stole Warren Flagg's undercover Lincoln Town Car right from the arrest scene. The car contained personal property belonging to Flagg, including all his clothing.

But the stolen car issue had to wait.

Flagg, Hanna, and Nelson secured the two mules and then called back the phone number from the pager.

"We told the subjects who answered," Nelson says, "that we had their two delivery boys and we were going to keep them unless our other two kilos of cocaine were delivered." In reality, the two arrestees were already being fingerprinted, photographed, and processed by Miami FBI agents.

"We then negotiated a time and location for the drug dealers to deliver the remaining two kilos of cocaine," Nelson says. "We were hoping this tactic would help us both seize the additional cocaine and draw their bosses out from the shadows."

Unfortunately for the agents, the dopey drug dealers reported their delivery mules as kidnapped to the Fort Lauderdale Police Department. In turn, the FLPD notified the FBI about the kidnapping in progress.

"We caught a break," Nelson says. "The Miami FBI Office assigned the same special operations team that had been backing us up during the undercover operation to also cover the site we had designated for the remaining two kilos of drugs to be delivered."

The Miami agents immediately realized what Nelson and team had done, although they were just about to notify them anyway.

"We needed them to cover our drop site," Nelson says. "However, when they realized we were also the 'kidnappers,' our plan was aborted."

The head of the Miami Office then sent word to Flagg, Hanna, and Nelson that they were to take the next flight out of Florida and get back to New York City.

The following day, back in New York, the special agent in charge of the Criminal Division questioned the three agents about their actions.

"Although our plan may have made him feel uncomfortable because it was somewhat unorthodox, I don't think he or anyone else could put their finger on exactly what was wrong with it." Nelson laughs. "The only justified criticism might have been more timely communication with the Miami agents before we initiated the 'kidnapping' plan."

Nevertheless, not another word was heard about the case.

CHAPTER THIRTY-THREE

So much for flying the friendly skies.

One late night in 1983, Special Agent Anthony Nelson was notified by FBI command that an American Airlines flight, en route from Los Angeles to John F. Kennedy International Airport in Queens, declared an onboard emergency.

The FBI office located at JFK Airport had jurisdiction over crimes that occurred aboard aircraft in flight. This obligated Special Agents from all Brooklyn-Queens FBI squads to assist the Bureau's JFK Office agents as needed.

"There were criminal incidents constantly occurring aboard aircraft, happening day and night," Nelson recalls.

An assault on a plane in flight was one of those offenses that are under the "exclusive jurisdiction of the United States" that the FBI had to investigate. Like crimes on the high seas, federal property, military bases, and at veterans' hospitals, the FBI could not defer to local authorities.

This was not always the case.

In the mid-1970s, the FBI recognized that with its limited resources, it could never adequately investigate *all* crimes within its jurisdiction.

"The FBI traditionally managed its investigative resources based on caseload and accomplishments, giving equal weight to all crimes within its jurisdiction," Nelson explains. "In 1975, realizing the limitations of this method, the FBI implemented a quality over quantity concept in case workload to eliminate marginal investigations on matters not warranting federal attention."

To achieve its strategy of concentrating on quality cases, the FBI must rely on state and local police and prosecutors.[59] Basically, offenses that could be investigated equally well by federal or local authorities were to be left to local law enforcement agencies.

"When I was first appointed as an FBI Special Agent in 1976, and assigned to the New York Office Truck Hijacking Squad, I was given cases that the Bureau would not even consider investigating today," Nelson recalls.

This changed dramatically, as at that time, the General Accounting Office conducted a far-reaching assessment across multiple FBI field offices: "In its study of six FBI field offices, GAO concluded that the FBI's investigations of property crimes in fiscal year 1978 were mostly unproductive." Based on its findings, the GAO recommended that the attorney general direct attorneys to change their prosecutive policies for property crimes to agree with the FBI's stated criteria, emphasizing quality over quantity of prosecutions.59

This fundamentally changed how FBI squads operate.

"We started to concentrate more on the use of the RICO statute and employed sophisticated investigative techniques such as more undercover operations, consensual monitoring of cooperative witness conversations, and Title III wiretapping," Nelson says. "We began to respond only to armed bank robberies. We gave the 'note jobs' to the Major Case Squad of the NYPD. Instead of tracking down all federal fugitives, we gave over escaped federal prisoners to the US Marshals Service and instead went after mostly murderers and mass murderers."

To employ this strategy, FBI agents were also pulled away from a significant amount of street crime.

"Most FBI criminal squads had myriad crimes they handled even though their main emphasis may have been on truck hijackings,

59. U.S. GAO. "From Quantity to Quality: Changing FBI Emphasis on Interstate Property Crimes." https://www.gao.gov/products/ggd-80-43

major theft, bank robberies, or auto crimes," Nelson explains. "So we started setting higher standards for initiating investigations."

This deferment to local authorities, though, did not extend to crimes aboard airliners, even as the volume of incidents at times could overwhelm the JFK FBI agents. That meant each squad had to pitch in on a rotating basis to share the load.

This was not glamorous work, more like a glorified bar bouncer wrestling with drunk and unruly passengers flying back on the red eye.

"I remember pitching in and responding during late-night hours, and it was usually because of alcohol-fueled fights with flyers assaulting members of the flight crews," a less-than-thrilled Nelson recalls.

This incident was a bit more involved than most of the others.

The initial report was that a passenger on board was assaulting other passengers and flight crew members. The suspect, Doctor Lee Kim (name changed to protect the identity of those involved), was a pathologist at the Manhattan Psychiatric Hospital on Ward's Island.

That night, though, he was entirely out of control, as an argument escalated into Dr. Kim throwing punches and food at other passengers. He then began spitting food and wine at them.

And then Dr. Kim turned his attention to the crew members who tried to intervene.

A radio message from the cockpit of the plane reported that the belligerent must be well-versed in martial arts and was now demonstrating his techniques, striking and kicking the unfortunate flight crew.

And then, as if this situation was not wild enough, the karate-chopping, food-throwing, wine-spitting Dr. Kim threatened two passengers with a butane lighter. Then he set fire to the hair of stewardess Cathie Braun. She managed to beat out the flames and escape serious injury.

The next day, the Jerry Capeci bylined article with a classic New York Daily News headline read: "STEWARDESS' HAIR SET ON FIRE AS DOC GOES BERSERK."

"I immediately responded to JFK Airport, along with my partner Leo Farrell, and we waited for the plane to land," Nelson recalls.

Nelson would often refer to Leo Farrell as a "diamond in the rough," tough as nails, and the type of agent who always said whatever was on his mind. "Leo would never hesitate to break down a door with you to capture a fugitive," Nelson recalls fondly. "But he was also gentle and caring about everyone. He was literally one of those people who'd give you the shirt off his back. But he was also someone you did not want to tangle with."

Agent Farrell went on to a distinguished career at the Bureau, including being awarded the FBI Shield of Bravery, given to FBI agents who demonstrate courage while performing their duties, such as assisting a task force or undercover operation, confronting grave situations or crises, and working on high priority cases.

After the plane landed, the injured flight attendant was removed by EMTs to Jamaica Hospital, where she was treated for her injuries.

At the same time, Nelson and Farrell cornered Dr. Kim, who was now sitting down and appeared relatively calm. Nelson identified himself and Farrell and sternly told this mental health professional, in the middle of a mental breakdown, that he was going to put handcuffs on him.

At that point, Dr. Kim's nose began to twitch. Then he started rolling his eyes around in his head.

"Leo and I both knew he was getting ready to attack us," Nelson recalls. "I told him, 'Don't do it! You will be sorry.'"

Dr. Kim's nose stopped twitching. The calm look returned to his face as he turned and very politely said to the lawman, "Okay, Mr. Nelson."

"He was then completely relaxed and cooperative, almost sedated," Nelson says. "In my FBI car, he was a perfect gentleman. I told him it was hard for me to believe what he'd done on the plane because he was so polite."

Nelson and Farrell lodged Dr. Kim in the Metropolitan Correctional Center (MCC) on Park Row in Manhattan, where he was placed under psychiatric observation.

"As I left the jail, I told Dr. Kim I'd pick him up in the morning and take him to court," Nelson says. "He then said, 'Goodnight, Mr. Nelson, and thank you.'"

The FBI agents did not even make it over the Brooklyn Bridge nearby when they received an urgent radio call to return to the MCC immediately: Dr. Kim had barricaded himself inside a holding cell with other overnight prisoners and went absolutely ballistic. He ripped a bench off a wall in the cell and used it to batter the cell door. In fact, he hit the cell door so hard that it was now jammed, and the corrections officers could not enter.

As the FBI agents rushed back and returned to the jail, the MCC Special Reaction Team was trying to make a forced entry into the cell. Such teams are specially trained in responding to major disturbances, riots, cell extractions, mass searches, and other dangerous situations in prisons or jails involving uncooperative or violent prisoners.

But curiously, once news of Nelson's impending return reached Dr. Kim, that team was no longer needed.

"When Dr. Kim learned I was back at the jail, he calmed down again," Nelson says. "I told him again that I'd be back to pick him up in a couple of hours, since it was now close to morning. Once again, he thanked me by my last name. I just couldn't believe he'd barricaded the cell yet had been a perfect gentleman every time he was around me."

Fortunately, there was no recurrence.

At least not that evening.

Nelson and Farrell picked up Dr. Kim at sunrise. They lodged him in a jail cell in the basement of the Brooklyn Federal Courthouse with the Marshals and then Nelson went a few floors up in the building to write the federal arrest complaint charging him with Crime Aboard an Aircraft—Assaulting a Flight Crew.

"I was not upstairs even a half hour when I received a message from the US Marshals Service that Kim had now barricaded himself in their jail cell," Nelson says. "He then used his extraordinary strength to rip out the water pipes and tear the toilet bowl and sink from the walls of the cell."

To make matters worse, the entire basement of the courthouse was now flooding due to the broken pipes.

Amazingly, once Nelson responded and went down into the basement, Dr. Kim said, "Hello, Mr. Nelson," and once again immediately calmed down.

"I told the Marshals that I can't believe he is the same person," Nelson says.

Amazingly, since responding to the airport, and despite multiple violent outbursts, Nelson and Farrell had yet to see Dr. Kim in an agitated state.

Next, the agents brought Dr. Kim up to the courtroom of Judge Simon Chrein, who was conducting arraignments. The judge requested that Nelson uncuff Dr. Kim; it was the usual procedure to uncuff prisoners when they appeared before a judge.

Nelson suggested to the judge that Dr. Kim remain cuffed because of his overnight behavior. But the judge declined the warning and insisted that he believed Dr. Kim would behave.

Sure enough, as soon as Nelson uncuffed Dr. Kim, the defendant took a run at the judge while screaming incoherently.

"Luckily, a couple of deputy Marshals had also come up to the courtroom with us and helped Leo and me cuff Dr. Kim again," Nelson says.

At which time Dr. Kim said, again, "Thank you, Mr. Nelson."

A native of Korea, Dr. Kim, forty-seven, had been a US citizen for ten years and was married and the father of two.

After his arrest, officials estimated Dr. Kim caused six thousand dollars in damages at the MCC and the federal courthouse at Cadman Plaza. His lawyer, Milton Schachter, told reporters that he had "a past history of problems" and had been under a lot of pressure.

Dr. Kim's wife said in court that her husband "should be hospitalized immediately. He has to get Thorazine. He has had such problems for the last ten years. Two or three times, he has attempted suicide."

At his arraignment on assault charges before Judge Simon Chrein, prosecutor Harvey Golubock said a psychiatrist had diagnosed Dr. Kim as having had "an acute psychotic episode."

Kim asked, "What's a psychotic?" and started rambling about wanting to return to Korea.

At a second hearing, when Dr. Kim began rambling, Judge Eugene Nickerson ordered him committed to Kings County Hospital for fifteen days' observation and set bail at ten thousand dollars.

"Although Kim could have caused serious injury or death aboard the aircraft, I felt sympathy for him since he suffered from mental illness and could not help himself," Nelson says. "It was just another story of the insufficient attention that was, and still is, given to the problem of mental illness in New York City."

Meanwhile, the quality over quantity initiative continued to face stiff headwinds internally, meeting resistance from many FBI agents to the quality case concept.

"I, myself, had serious concerns that agents would no longer be able to develop quality informants and cooperative witnesses since many agents were assigned to monitor wiretaps rather than work the street," Nelson reflects. "But in the long run, the new strategy resulted in dealing irreparable harm to all five organized crime Families in New York and elsewhere."

CHAPTER THIRTY-FOUR

In February 1984, Walter Mack's strike force scored a significant victory by arranging the high-profile arrest of Paul Castellano. Mack helped bring federal racketeering charges against Castellano in what became known as the Castellano-Ruggiero indictment. The case was part of a broader strategy of using RICO statutes to connect Castellano to a vast network of criminal activities, even if he didn't personally commit the crimes.

Key allegations included running a criminal enterprise that involved violent enforcement of Gambino interests and ties to the Concrete Club, a Mafia-controlled cartel that rigged bids and extorted developers in New York City's booming construction industry.

Charges also featured control over labor unions, especially in the meat industry and construction trades, used to extort businesses and extract bribes, as well as Castellano's oversight of narcotics trafficking despite the Mafia's supposed ban on drug dealing (which ultimately helped justify his assassination by rivals).

Mack worked closely with FBI agents, NYPD detectives, and informants, including wiretaps and surveillance, to build a detailed case that showed Castellano as more than a figurehead—he was a micromanaging boss who approved murders and profited from the Family's rackets.

The government built RICO cases as it sought to authorize wiretaps, convene grand juries, and offer protection to those willing to testify.

Simply being affiliated with a criminal organization could carry harsh penalties, even without direct involvement in specific crimes. Between 1983 and 1985, Paul Castellano faced a string of indictments.

One by one, informants began to flip. Vito Arena—the enforcer tied to the DeMeo Crew—broke ranks and cooperated with authorities following the lead of Dominick Montiglio. Freddy DiNome and others soon folded and flipped, bolstering the government's growing list of insiders.

In 1984, US Attorney Rudolf W. Giuliani filed a seventy-eight-count indictment against twenty-four defendants, including Paul Castellano, Nino Gaggi, and remnants of the decapitated DeMeo Crew. The charges ranged from car theft to racketeering to narcotics trafficking. Due to the sheer volume of charges, the presiding judge, Kevin Thomas Duffy, split the case into two distinct trials to make it more manageable.

The first trial, which commenced in October 1985, resulted in convictions for six of the eight defendants, who were found guilty of operating an extensive car-theft operation across New York.

In a stunning development, Castellano was out on bail awaiting trial in December 1985 when he was assassinated outside Sparks Steak House in Manhattan on December 16, 1985—a hit orchestrated by Gambino captain John Gotti, who feared Castellano would leverage his edict against drug dealing to justify eliminating Gotti and members of his crew.

Specifically, Castellano earlier declared that any Gambino Family member initiated after 1962 would face death for involvement in drug trafficking. He pushed the Mafia Commission to adopt the same policy across all Families.

The move was a direct shot at John Gotti, Gotti's lieutenant Angelo Ruggiero, and Gambino underboss Aniello Dellacroce, who Castellano increasingly suspected of covertly backing and profiting from Gotti's drug business. With this and other calculated political maneuvers, Castellano aimed to halt the rapid rise of Ruggiero and Gotti within the Family ranks. Castellano, presenting himself as a more sophisticated wiseguy, loathed the streetwise Gotti.

Nino Gaggi became the lead defendant after Castellano's death, though Castellano's murder effectively ended the first trial.

Then Nino Gaggi died in the Metropolitan Correctional Center (MCC) on April 17, 1988, while awaiting the second trial in federal court. "I was assigned as the case agent in charge of the investigation into the circumstances of Gaggi's death," Nelson recalls. "The autopsy concluded that Gaggi died of natural causes."

"However, his wife sued the government for failure to assist her husband during a heart attack," Pergola adds.

Gaggi's widow, Rose Gaggi, successfully sued the prison system for negligence.

As per the case file, while incarcerated at the MCC awaiting the second trial, Gaggi supposedly told a guard that he was experiencing chest pains. According to reports, the guard allegedly dismissed Gaggi's symptoms and failed to provide timely medical attention. Rose Gaggi's negligence case was reportedly aided by testimony from several other inmates.

The second trial stretched over seventeen months and focused on a sweeping racketeering probe targeting the DeMeo Crew. Central to the case were five homicides allegedly carried out by members of the violent faction. The second trial featured nine defendants, including Ronald Ustica, Carlo Profeta, Ronald "Bulldog" Turekian, Salvatore Mangalino, Douglas Rega, Wayne "Sol" Hellman, Anthony Senter, and Joseph Testa.[60]

"I was assigned as the case agent in charge of the investigation into the circumstances of Gaggi's death," Nelson recalls. "The autopsy concluded that Gaggi died of natural causes."

In March 1986, six DeMeo Crew members—among them Henry Borelli—were convicted on multiple charges, including the murders of Ronald Falcaro and Khalid Daoud, both of whom had threatened to reveal the inner workings of the Crew's car-theft operation.

---

60. "Daily News From New York, New York." June 12, 1990. https://www. newspapers.com/newspage/406768394/

Through it all, federal prosecutor Mack shaped a new legal blueprint for dismantling organized crime. By leveraging the enterprise theory under RICO, enlisting the cooperation of former insiders, and plumbing financial records to tie top bosses to violent street crimes, Mack laid the groundwork for future upper-echelon prosecutions—most notably the landmark Commission Case later that same year.

In January 1988, longtime DeMeo enforcers Anthony Senter and Joseph Testa stood trial following a five-year investigation into Mob-related killings linked to the Gambino Family and, in particular, the DeMeo Crew.

Over the lengthy trial, Mack presented disturbing evidence to the jury—including graphic testimony and forensic findings—illustrating how the DeMeo Crew had systematically murdered and dismembered dozens of victims. Altogether, prosecutors introduced evidence connected to twenty-five homicides, though they maintained that the actual number of victims was likely far higher. Many of the bodies have never been recovered.

The Court heard testimony from 207 witnesses to substantiate that five homicides were directly tied to the operations of a sprawling car-theft enterprise.

The Crew stole thousands of vehicles across New York City throughout the late 1970s and early 1980s, many of which were dismantled and sold off piece by piece for greater profit. Others were shipped overseas to markets such as Puerto Rico and as distant as Kuwait.

At trial, Vito Arena—already serving an eighteen-year sentence for the murder of Joseph Scorney—took the stand as a cooperating witness. He hoped that his testimony might earn him favorable consideration on unresolved State charges still hanging over him. Arena, in particular, delivered for the prosecution, shocking jurors with his play-by-play, blood-soaked walk-throughs of multiple homicides.

"Retired NYPD Detective Frank Pergola is in possession of the specifics of approximately seventy-nine murders committed by the DeMeo Crew," Nelson says. "However, for practical and evidentiary reasons, they were not prosecuted for all seventy-nine of the homicides.

"That doesn't mean those homicides did not occur and those family members don't feel that pain to this day," Nelson regrets. "Pergola can provide all those details and data on crimes committed by all members of the DeMeo Crew. The exact number of homicide victims killed by the DeMeo Crew will never be known, but is estimated to be between one hundred and fifty and two hundred people. Think about that; all those innocent people and all their families."

A federal court jury found nine defendants in a racketeering case involving the Gambino Family guilty on all counts, including murder, narcotics, loan sharking, and pornography. The verdict came after a fifteen-month trial, one of the longest Mob trials in history, before Judge Vincent Broderick in US District Court in Manhattan.

Mack depicted the DeMeo Crew as one of the Mafia's most violent, relying on strong-arm tactics and murder to control its widespread interests. He successfully linked the defendants to twenty murders, and there was testimony from some of the two hundred witnesses about eighteen murders. Five of the seven defendants who were charged with racketeering were also charged with taking part in eleven murders.

During the latest trial, three informers who appeared as witnesses admitted to twenty murders. DiNome alone admitted to eight murders before he was found hanged to death in a Texas safe house.

Another witness was Francis "Mickey" Featherstone, an admitted killer who was a member of the Westies gang on Manhattan's West Side. Prosecutors said the Westies and the Gambino Family had an agreement to commit crimes for each other.

In June 1989, nine additional members, including Anthony Senter and Joseph Testa, were convicted. At sentencing, Senter and Testa were given life sentences for murder with an additional twenty years tacked on for racketeering.

Prosecutor Mack said, "The Roy DeMeo Crew is the most violent crew ever prosecuted in federal court, as far as my knowledge," adding that DeMeo "engaged in wholesale slaughter."

Under Walter Mack's direction, the strike force delivered devastating body blows, damaging the leadership of multiple crime families, crippling their operations, and weakening their strangleholds on the streets. By forming a focused task force that combined federal muscle, cross-agency collaboration, and tenacious legal strategy, he was instrumental in taking down major Mafia players in 1980s New York—reshaping the landscape of organized crime enforcement and setting precedents for future RICO-driven efforts.

"The DeMeo Crew engaged in acts that we, as human beings, intuitively know are evil in and of themselves rather than just proscribed by law," Nelson says.

"So, these were not just criminals, but evil men, presenting a clear and present danger to society," Nelson continues. "The many men and women who worked to bring them to justice were not just doing a job, but fighting for a cause, and they made a difference. I just think much of that has been lost."

After the shocking assassination of Gambino crime boss Paul Castellano in December 1985, Anthony Nelson and Kenny McCabe started to go out less often to cruise Brooklyn at night.

"Roy DeMeo had also been murdered and despite Castellano's death, Kenny was heavily involved in Walter Mack's task force and the ongoing federal prosecutions of La Cosa Nostra's hierarchy," Nelson says.

The winds of change were stirring in gangland.

After orchestrating the unsanctioned killing of Castellano, John Gotti installed himself as the leader of the Gambino Family as the captains fell into line, either out of loyalty or fear.

Yet this marked a turning point.

The audacity of that murder, brazenly committed on a December evening in 1985 as Big Paul stepped out of a limo in front of Sparks Steak House in Midtown Manhattan, captured the attention of a nation already infatuated with the American Mafia.

The murder itself seemed like something out of a Puzo plotline. The four assassins who gunned down Castellano donned trench coats and Russian fur hats in a ruse to throw off suspicion. Gotti himself sat in a car nearby to make sure his rival was dead.

The federal government indicted and prosecuted Gotti three times in the late '80s in trials that were as much media circus as courtroom drama, failing each time to get a conviction. Gotti's bravado and seeming inability to be convicted exasperated prosecutors, frustrated investigators, and earned him the nickname the Teflon Don.

Then in December 1990, the FBI again arrested Gotti, this time with underboss Salvatore "Sammy the Bull" Gravano and consigliere Frank Locascio, all on racketeering charges.

By the following year, Gravano flipped and became a federal witness, in part motivated by self-preservation after hearing taped recordings of Gotti implicating them both while also disparaging his underboss. Eventually, in 1992, the government finally convicted Gotti on numerous charges, including Castellano's murder.

The New York City underworld was roiling in turmoil. Law enforcement raids were common, and many of the streetside social clubs were becoming inactive or shuttered altogether.

"So, our nighttime rides began to subtly wane, but not our relationship," Nelson says. "Kenny and I still managed on most Friday afternoons to have a working lunch and trade intelligence and updates related to informants. There was still much work to be done. Mostly by Kenny and the traditional FBI organized crime squads, but many of the social clubs and surveillance targets were dying off from federal prosecutions and natural causes."

Keep in mind, La Cosa Nostra was losing its luster, though still intact.

And there is another, more recent footnote to the DeMeo Crew saga.

"Testa and Senter were sentenced to life without parole," Frank Pergola says. "But they were released in 2024, after serving thirty-five years, by federal parole, even though in my estimation, both Testa and Senter were involved in over seventy murders from 1970 to 1988."

CHAPTER THIRTY-FIVE

In 1984, though the upper echelon of multiple Mafia Families faced an unprecedented assault from law enforcement, on the streets, it was business as usual.

One day, NYPD Homicide Detective Ron Cadieux came to FBI Special Agent Anthony Nelson with a case involving organized crime victimizing Brooklyn residents.

Not just any case.

And not just any victims.

"I'm working in the 60th Precinct, and back then, the Homicide Squad was situated all the way in the back, so you had to go through the Detectives Squad," Cadieux says. "So I'm walking in and I see there's this old man, and he looks like he's been crying, like he really needs help. So I stop, I ask him, 'What's the matter?' and he says he can't find someone to help him. I told him to go downstairs to the desk, and he said he did, and they sent him up here.

"So, I got to do something," Cadieux remembers. "I take him to the interrogation room and we talk. It turns out there were some Colombo gangsters going around with these phony stamps as part of a real-estate scam to cheat senior citizens out of their homes."

The wiseguys would gather information about the property and its owner(s) from publicly available records. They would then doctor up documents, create a fraudulent deed, and forge the homeowner's signature. This involved the use of fake notary stamps, where the gangsters would either create a phony notary seal or enlist an unethical notary to notarize the forged deed, making it appear legitimate. This step was crucial, as the county recorder's office should theoretically verify the notary stamp number, but this process can be vulnerable to forged documents.

The scammers then filed the fraudulent deed with the county recorder of deeds or registrar of deeds and claimed ownership. Once the fake deed was recorded, the scammers presented themselves as the legitimate property owners and sold the property out from under these unsuspecting elderly victims.

"I said, 'This is your lucky day, I'll have the FBI look into this,'" Cadieux says. At the time, Anthony Nelson was heavily involved in multiple investigations into organized crime.

"So I meet with Anthony and Anthony reaches out to Washington," Cadieux says. "If you want to start investigating a case like this, you need money and resources. But for whatever reason, they would not take the case. So, Anthony says, what if Kenny, who is a detective in the Brooklyn DA Squad, was able to get all of these poor seniors their homes back?"

The FBI agent and the NYPD detective met with Brooklyn DA Investigator Kenny McCabe, who agreed to look into the matter.

"So then, I'm in the strike force and I get called by my chief in Brooklyn and I go down to meet him," Cadieux says. "I walk in and he throws a newspaper in my face, and he's raising his voice. I say, 'Wait a minute, I'm not some hobo. I don't care if you're a chief and I'm a detective. You better give me the same respect I give you.'

"He asks, 'Did you read the story?'"

Cadieux responds, "How could I read the story when you just threw the newspaper in my face?"

Sure enough, the paper, the *New York Post*, included an article written by Jerry Capeci on the same case Ronnie Cadieux, Anthony Nelson, and Kenny McCabe put together, and the Brooklyn DA Squad followed up.

"Anyway, I read the story, and it says the case was started by three agencies—the FBI, Brooklyn DA Squad, and Brooklyn South Homicide," Cadieux says. "The article says the reporter went to the FBI, and no comment. Then he went to the Brooklyn DA; no comment. But he then did get a comment from a third party close to the case. So this chief says that's got to be me, accusing me. I said, 'Obviously, Chief, you've never been an investigator, to be making those accusations against me.'"

The chief was confused.

After a long pause, where it was clear the chief did not understand, Cadieux added: "The reason I know you've never been an investigator is because that's the one thing an investigator never does."

And he still didn't get it.

"An investigator never gives up his sources," Cadieux explains. "Once you start giving up your sources, you're done. I said, sure, the investigation started with me and Anthony and Kenny, but that third party was definitely not me. And by the way, not only would an investigator never give up his sources like that, a reporter would certainly not give up his source because that would be the last story he'd ever get out of that source."

The Colombo ring was busted, and the senior homeowners were saved.

"With Anthony, we did a lot of work together on organized crime cases like that," Cadieux says. "It's no secret, anyone in law enforcement will tell you, and generally speaking, those guys in the FBI look down their noses at everybody. I say you're a federal police officer, and I'm a state police officer, and we're not that much different. But they still have this air about them. And it's not just with everyone else. They even look down their noses at other federal agencies. There's definitely a pecking order, with the FBI at the top, followed by the DEA second, down to the ATF, and so on.

"But not Anthony," Cadieux says. "Anthony was always willing to provide help; he'd come in with his guys, and he covered that whole area in Brooklyn and Queens. Anthony would come down, and together we'd go out to check locations working active cases. We got nine guys to flip in the Gambino Family, so we knew a lot about what was going on spread all over the place."

CHAPTER THIRTY-SIX

On the evening of May 26, 1985, a Sunday, Special Agent Anthony Nelson responded to US Attorney Rudolph Giuliani's office in the Southern District of New York (SDNY) to investigate a serious crime.

Nelson did not know what to expect when he arrived at the SDNY, other than it was likely a case involving someone who lied, manipulated, cheated, or worse.

"By 1985, though early in my FBI career, I'd already investigated so many cases involving organized crime murders, extortions, truck hijackings, robberies, narcotics trafficking, and just unchecked greed," Nelson says, "that it was hard for me not to be jaded about any prospect there would ever be a significant reduction in crime in New York City. I saw the dark side every day, interacting with so many bad people and groups, such as the Roy DeMeo Crew, who just seemed to be so inherently evil."

But not everyone Nelson investigated was as obviously wicked as Roy DeMeo.

Meeting with US Attorney Giuliani and an assistant US attorney assigned to his office, Nelson was informed that drug evidence from a major ongoing narcotics trial and another upcoming trial was missing from a safe in the US Attorney's Office. This was a serious security breach that could have far-reaching implications.

"The missing drugs consisted of a large quantity of heroin and cocaine," Nelson says, "and the loss of the evidence created a grave possibility that it could adversely affect these prosecutions of major drug dealers."

The following day, Nelson requested several other FBI agents from his squad to assist with interviewing employees in the SDNY Narcotics Unit to determine which individuals had the combination to the narcotics safe, and who would have been in position to swipe 8.7 ounces of heroin and 29 ounces of cocaine. He then assigned an agent to inventory the contents of the drug vault, who determined that there was also forty-one thousand dollars in cash missing from the safe.

After assigning a round of interviews, Nelson then had an unusual request.

"The one thing to know about Anthony Nelson, no matter what kind of case he got, he always seemed to come up with imaginative ways to get to the core of the resolution," says Special Agent Jason Randazzo, a former member of multiple FBI squads managed by Nelson. "A perfect example is the Perlmutter investigation. Anthony gets the idea to test the filters in the air conditioners for traces of cocaine. I was like, wow. I never would have thought of that. Who would have thought of that?"

At Nelson's behest, FBI Special Agent Leo Farrell removed all the air conditioning filters from the offices of every narcotics prosecutor. Needless to say, this was a bold ask, sure to ruffle some feathers.

Among those interviewed was twenty-nine-year-old Assistant US Attorney Daniel Perlmutter, a Narcotics Unit prosecutor.

With the interviews wrapped, within hours, the investigation team determined that Perlmutter had recently lied to both his supervisors and FBI agents concerning his whereabouts on specific occasions.

Nelson immediately requested a special detail of FBI surveillance agents to tail Perlmutter. The FBI surveillance team reported back that Perlmutter met with a girlfriend, Stacy Honeycutt, and that she was suspected by two of her acquaintances of abusing cocaine.

"I also determined from the FBI Laboratory that only one of the air conditioning filters examined by them contained a residue of cocaine," Nelson recalls.

Guess which office.

That tainted filter from the office of Daniel Perlmutter provided enough circumstantial evidence to justify a search warrant. Nelson knew he had to act quickly.

In the early morning hours of May 30, 1985, Nelson instructed FBI agents to lock Daniel Perlmutter out of his apartment, located on Park Avenue in Manhattan. "At the same time, I applied to US District Court Judge Harold Raby for a warrant to search Perlmutter's apartment," Nelson says.

These actions incensed Perlmutter, who placed a call to a fellow narcotics prosecutor and left a message on his answering machine stating in substance that "the assholes from the FBI think they're going to get a warrant to search my apartment," Nelson recalls.

Judge Raby granted Nelson's request for the warrant.

The search of Perlmutter's apartment resulted in the seizure of narcotics evidence bags, powder residue, and labels from narcotics prosecutions. One evidence bag also contained a quantity of lactose, often used as a drug-cutting agent, added to increase the volume of the narcotic and improve profitability.

The apartment raid also yielded used pipes, filters, a propane torch, and a freebasing bowl—all standard drug paraphernalia generally used to consume cocaine.

"Lastly, we seized a piece of paper from his wastebasket upon which was written the current combination to the narcotics safe in the US Attorney's Office," Nelson remembers.

Upon further investigation, it was established that Perlmutter was not one of the four prosecutors in the Narcotics Unit authorized to have the safe combination. "So he apparently had copied it down after seeing it on the desk of one of the authorized prosecutors," Nelson says.

The freestanding safe, seven feet by seven feet, was in a locked room, but not guarded.

On May 30, 1985, Nelson entered the Tivoli Restaurant on 3rd Avenue and East 35th Street in Manhattan with a team of FBI agents and loudly proclaimed to Daniel Perlmutter, "Guess what? The assholes from the FBI got the search warrant for your apartment, and you are now under arrest."

Stacy Honeycutt, the girlfriend with whom Perlmutter was having coffee at the restaurant, was also placed under arrest.

Shortly after, the story was splashed across New York newspapers and nightly news. Perlmutter was charged with stealing up to five hundred thousand dollars' worth of heroin and cocaine from a secure evidence safe in the US Attorney's Office. Both faced charges of possession and intent to distribute.[61]

Perlmutter was held without bail pending treatment. Honeycutt was released on her own recognizance, with her parents posting $25,000 in bail.

The missing evidence impacted up to five drug cases, including two that Perlmutter was prosecuting. While disruptions are expected, Giuliani said the cases were still viable.

At a press conference, Giuliani stated the arrest of Perlmutter, one of 131 assistant attorneys, marked the first time that serious criminal charges had been brought against a prosecutor in the Southern District's Office.

At trial, Daniel Perlmutter was convicted and sentenced to three years in prison. He was released after sixteen months.[62]

The federal prosecution against Perlmutter and Honeycutt was handled by Eric Holder and an associate who were sent to New York by the Justice Department in Washington, DC, to oversee this matter. Holder, later in his career, was appointed by President Barack Obama as the Attorney General of the United States.

Despite Perlmutter's disrespectful behavior toward him, Nelson held no grudge. "It ultimately turned out to involve an otherwise decent human being who made some bad life choices," Nelson reflects.

"I did not, however, consider him to be among the inherently evil," Nelson says. "The stresses of life that we all experience

61. Blair, William G. "A FEDERAL ATTORNEY HELD IN DRUG THEFT AT NEW YORK OFFICE." New York Times. May 31, 1985. https://www.nytimes.com/1985/05/31/nyregion/a-federal-attorney-held-in-drug-theft-at-new-york-office.html

62. UPI. "Former Federal Prosecutor Sent to Hospital for Psychiatric Evaluation." June 5, 1985. https://www.upi.com/Archives/1985/06/05/Former-federal-prosecutor-sent-to-hospital-for-psychiatric-evaluation/5680486792000/

apparently caused him to spiral out of control and into his own fantasy world involving the use of heroin, cocaine, and theft, which destroyed both his promising law career and most likely his personal life. He was simply a flawed human who had lost all self-control of his life."

Unlike investigations into organized crime, he points to the Perlmutter case as a cautionary tale.

"The more devastating consequence of Perlmutter's punishment was that he had embarrassed his colleagues and had earned the infamous distinction of being the only prosecutor in the prestigious Southern District of New York US Attorney's Office to ever be convicted of a serious felony offense. He also lost his law license and a promising career."

CHAPTER THIRTY-SEVEN

During the summer of 1986, one of Anthony Nelson's cooperating witnesses was at a Gambino social club in Queens when he overheard a plan to transfer four stolen submachine guns and a large quantity of cocaine. The deal was supposed to go down later that day on a street corner in the vicinity of the Cross Island Parkway and 150th Street in the Whitestone section of Queens.

Within just a few hours of the planned transfer, Nelson assembled a team of FBI agents to help intercept the shipment. He also enlisted the aid of Kenny McCabe to remain with the informant to obtain up to the minute details about the unfolding plan.

Why not assign the role to another member of the squad?

"During times when I was not available, that particular informant only wanted to meet with Kenny as my backup," Nelson says. "That's it; no one else, no matter what. And I also needed Kenny to help me identify any unknown subjects that showed up on the scene."

Managing a confidential informant is one of the most challenging aspects of an FBI agent's work. Every interaction is a calculated risk. It's a transactional relationship, but a relationship nonetheless that develops over time. CIs are almost always criminals, so not the most forthcoming individuals. They're often unreliable, manipulative, cagey, maybe drug-addled, possibly deluded that they're now an informally deputized extension of law enforcement.

Except in limited circumstances, pursuant to law or the attorney general's guidelines, FBI Special Agent Anthony Nelson would never reveal the identity of a CI to anyone.

Well, almost anyone.

"Kenny had an aura about him that made most people instantly like him," Nelson adds. "With informants, he was always able to develop an instant rapport and a sense of trust. Many of my informants had agreed, by their own volition, to meet with Kenny McCabe. And with this deal about to happen within hours, we had to get these guns off the street."

With McCabe retired from the NYPD and now working as a criminal investigator with the US Attorney's Office in the Southern District, he was debriefing federal informants and cooperating witnesses in connection with some of the most high-profile organized crime cases ever prosecuted. During this time, McCabe accompanied Nelson to meet with many of the FBI agent's informants.

Later that evening, an FBI Special Agent, in position to observe the location of the meeting of McCabe with the CI, advised Nelson over the radio that the subjects had just arrived in a 1982 Cadillac.

But there was a problem.

An innocent child wandered into the street near the Cadillac and was now in harm's way should the situation go south. The child was unknown to the informant.

Within moments of arriving, the two suspects (alleged organized crime associates Frank Cirri and Joseph Artino) noticed the presence of law enforcement.

One of the suspects grabbed the child and shoved him in the car. They then took off at a high rate of speed.

"Had it not been for that child, we probably would've let them escape because of the dangers to innocent people inherent in any car chase," Nelson says. "However, we didn't know if the child had been randomly kidnapped in order to deter us, so we were suddenly engaged in a high-speed vehicle pursuit flying down the Cross Island Parkway."

Nelson pursued the suspects, on and off the highway, for several miles until their vehicle blew a tire.

During the pursuit, one of the pursuing FBI vehicles, driven by Joseph Koletar, head of the Brooklyn-Queens FBI Office, observed the subjects toss a briefcase from the Cadillac onto the highway at 150th Street.

Born in Pennsylvania, Koletar distinguished himself throughout serving twenty-five years as a Special Agent and senior executive in the FBI, holding positions as special agent in charge, inspector, and section chief. At the time of his retirement, Koletar was the national program manager with responsibility for the Witness Protection Program and informant operations, criminal undercover operations, surveillance and aviation operations, the strategic intelligence operations center, and White House background investigations.

Prior to joining the FBI, Koletar was an intelligence officer in the US Army Special Security Group. After his career in the FBI ended, he worked as an executive director, principal, and director in the fraud and investigations practices of Ernst & Young, LLP, and Deloitte & Touche, LLP.

Sadly, Joseph Koletar passed away in November 2023 after years of declining health.

As the chase continued across Queens, the suspects flung yet another briefcase from the car, this one near Linden Place along the Cross Island Parkway.

Driving on a flat tire, the suspects were overtaken by FBI agents and heeded commands to pull off the road. They were arrested at gunpoint where Cross Island Parkway meets the Van Wyck Expressway.

"With the help of the NYPD Emergency Services Unit, which conducted an exhaustive search, we were able to recover one of the briefcases on the Cross Island Parkway at 150th Street," Nelson says. The recovered briefcase had broken open when it was thrown from the car and much of the narcotics were lost.

"However, we were able to retrieve the machine gun and enough cocaine residue to charge them both with federal narcotics and gun charges," Nelson says.

The child in the vehicle was unharmed.

The informant later requested that Kenny McCabe drop him off at an intersection in Queens.

"At that time, the informant met with a woman who walked him to her car," Nelson says. "Although the woman was visibly sober, Kenny McCabe was able to smell that she reeked of heroin and he warned the informant not to let her drive."

The woman then admitted that she had been "chipping," a street expression common among drug users that meant that she considered herself only an occasional user.

"It was just another day that Kenny McCabe surprised me," Nelson says. "I was unfamiliar with the term chipping. I also had no idea, until then, that Kenny McCabe had an unusual ability to recognize the smell of heroin in such small quantities."

With the stolen submachine guns secured, Nelson then received a call to respond to a bomb threat unfolding, unaware he was about to be thrust into the spotlight and onto the front page of every major newspaper in America.

Governors Island is a 172-acre island in New York Harbor, just eight hundred yards from Lower Manhattan and minutes by ferry from Brooklyn. Today, it draws nearly a million visitors each year with its award-winning park, historic buildings, cultural institutions, and a monument managed by the National Park Service. It's now a peaceful retreat—but it wasn't always.

The island's military history dates to 1776, when Continental Army forces built defenses there during the Revolutionary War. From 1783 to 1966, it served as a US Army post, primarily for training and coastal defense. From 1966 to 1996, Governors Island was a major Coast Guard base. Though its strategic importance declined by the 1980s, it remained active until its closure. The island was transferred to public ownership in 2003 and opened to the public in 2005.

On July 16, 1986, Special Agent Anthony Nelson was notified by the Coast Guard that they received a tip about an Island resident who wanted to kill his mother.

Military installations are federal property. While they have their own criminal investigative services, the FBI is often called in to investigate certain crimes.

But there was one complication.

"It just so happened that President Ronald Reagan had been on Governor's Island during the week of July 4, 1986, to celebrate Operation Sail, and the renovation and centenary of the Statue of Liberty," Nelson says. This detail would come into play soon.

With Nelson en route to Governors Island with FBI Special Agent Joseph Phelan, the Coast Guard shared new intel indicating that they had located what appeared to be an improvised explosive device (IED) in a storage bin in one of the resident buildings. The Coast Guard identified the suspect who allegedly built the device as nineteen-year-old John Atkinson, the stepson of a coastguardsman stationed on the base.

Nelson immediately notified the NYPD Bomb Squad and requested that they meet the agents at the location of the explosive.

"Upon arrival on the island, we located Atkinson, who admitted to me that he constructed the bomb days earlier and had intended to detonate it with a radio signal," Nelson recalls.

The NYPD Bomb Squad safely removed the device to deactivate at their explosives range.

Alarmingly, Atkinson's device had been in place in a building near the grandstands while President Reagan was giving his speech on the island.

"However, I personally do not believe that the President was ever in any danger of injury from such a low impact explosive device," Nelson says.

In an article the next day's edition of the *New York Daily News*, featuring Nelson and Phelan, reporter Willie Anderson confirmed that the device "allegedly was a .50-caliber machine gun shell stuffed with gunpowder and nails and had explosive power of two M-80 firecrackers."

Hardly a weapon of mass destruction.

Nevertheless, Nelson arrested Atkinson for possession of an explosive and arraigned him before Judge James Francis in the Southern District of New York, who set conditions for Atkinson's bail.

Then came the nationwide media storm.

"When I arrived at my office the following morning," Nelson says, "a fellow agent, who had performed a personal security job for the OpSail events and had been part of Whitney Houston's security detail, told me that a number of entertainment executives were upset by Atkinson's arrest because their TV appearances had been preempted in favor of the Reagan Bomb Story."

Although the celebrations on Governor's Island were over, some performers were still scheduled for media appearances related to the event that had cost millions of dollars to produce. However, the TV networks were giving more coverage to the story that President Reagan had been on the island speaking while a bomb was nearby.

"It was really a media exaggeration since Atkinson had not intended to hurt Reagan nor anyone other than his own mother," Nelson says. "In addition, as I had noted, the explosive was a very primitive, low-impact device that contained gunpowder and nails packed into an expended ammunition shell."

The story ran its course in the news cycle.

But then later in 1986, Nelson was involved in yet another sensational case, again tipped off by one of his many confidential informants.

In December, Nelson began to receive information from well-placed sources, as well as from officials at the Metropolitan Correctional Center, about a pattern of corruption at the federal lock-up located in Manhattan.

Combatting public corruption at all levels is the FBI's highest criminal investigative priority, and its fourth highest priority overall.[63]

Sure, local law enforcement agencies and federal Offices of Inspectors General also investigate corruption involving employees of their respective agencies. However, the FBI has the overall authority to investigate corruption across all levels of government (local, state, and federal) and across all branches (legislative, executive, and judicial).

---

63. FBI. "A New FBI Focus." https://archives.fbi.gov/archives/news/testimony/a-new-fbi-focus

Throughout his career, Anthony Nelson has seen more than his fair share of bribery, illegal gratuities, contract extortion, bid rigging, collusion, conflicts of interest, outright theft, diversion of goods, and individual and corporate conspiracies on every level of government operations. However, that day, Nelson was not responding to your run-of-the-mill pay-to-play public corruption scheme.

In fact, nothing tears at the fabric of the public trust as harmfully as corruption involving … veal cutlets?

Seriously.

Sort of.

Inmates at the MCC, including Gambino boss John Gotti, were reportedly bribing federal correction officers to get contraband into the prison.

Allegations also included a plot involving an attempt by an inmate to escape from the prison. An inmate allegedly planned to pay twenty-five thousand dollars to a prison official if she removed a "detainer card" from his files. Removal of the detainer card would have allowed him to be released when he was eligible for bail since there would have been no indication he was wanted by other authorities.

Shocking?

Sure.

And certainly newsworthy. But that wasn't the corruption scandal that grabbed the media spotlight in the next news cycle.

"Based on information I developed while working with the prison's Special Investigations Section," Nelson says, "I arrested a corrections officer for smuggling a veal cutlet sandwich into the prison that was ultimately intended for John Gotti. Additional information was developed that the corruption at the prison also involved sex and drugs, though not related to Gotti."

The story recalled the famous prison scene in the Mob-genre classic film *Goodfellas*, with Mob boss Paulie slicing the garlic "so thin it melted in the pan with very little oil," Vinnie prepping the *ragu* with three varieties of meat, and everyone complaining about too much onion.

In fact, this MCC veal cutlet smuggling caper, relatively minor in the grand scheme of Gotti's murderous mob career, became a footnote filler across hundreds of Gotti accounts over the years.

Innocuous as a few slabs of veal slathered between semolina may seem, still, it alluded to a larger pattern of corruption that investigators sank their teeth into during the months ahead.

In other words, where there's smoking veal, there's usually fire.

In January 1987, Nelson says, additional investigation determined that a corrections officer identified as Kim Gettys, who was implicated in the earlier alleged escape plot, also accepted a thousand-dollar bribe to smuggle in contraband.

This time it was not Italian delicacies, but instead something larger.

"Gettys accepted the bribe from a woman who attempted to smuggle a television into the prison for her inmate boyfriend, John Caruso," Nelson says with a head shake. "As a result, I arrested the woman, identified as Deborah Napoli, as well as Gettys."

This chapter in the MCC investigation had another interesting layer of corruption for Nelson to unwrap.

While Nelson attended a meeting in the US Attorney's Office regarding this case, he was accompanied by Kenny McCabe, who paused to say hello to a man who was also present at the meeting on behalf of Napoli.

"I asked Kenny who the man was and he told me that it was Napoli's grandfather, James 'Jimmy Nap' Napoli," Nelson recalls. "Kenny knew Jimmy Nap to be a semi-retired Genovese Family capo who supposedly ran the largest gambling operation in the New York area during the 1970s."

An amazed Nelson turned to ask McCabe, "Is there anyone that you don't know?"

CHAPTER THIRTY-EIGHT

On June 26, 1987, an aggravated individual later identified as Tony Caridi (name changed to protect surviving family members) entered the US Army Base at Fort Wadsworth in Staten Island. Within minutes, Caridi shattered the tranquility of this scenic place nestled along the Staten Island coastline in the shadow of the Verrazano Bridge.

Before closing in 1994, Fort Wadsworth was the longest continuously garrisoned military installation in America. Today, it's part of the Staten Island Unit of Gateway National Recreation Area, maintained by the National Park Service.

More widely known as the starting point of the annual New York City Marathon, it still houses a sizable population of military personnel, mostly members of the Coast Guard and the Army Reserve. And their families.

This is federal land, so the FBI in the local field office is called in to investigate serious crimes, like reports of domestic violence that, unfortunately, when involving current and former military personnel, have a higher propensity to spin into hostage crises.

"For those agents who worked cases at military facilities, at our army forts, VA hospitals, these can be really sad cases," retired FBI Special Agent Jason Randazzo says. "The Department of Veterans Affairs hasn't always done the best for veterans of foreign wars and their care, physically and mentally. As an agent, it can be pretty tough to respond. They're damaged, frustrated, angry, hopeless, and then one day, they just break, and then you have to respond to the aftermath."

At approximately nine that morning, Caridi, agitated, went to the home of his wife, Linda, from whom he was separated. He viciously assaulted her.

Beaten and bloody, Linda managed to call Military Police, who responded quickly and removed Caridi from the base while trying to sort out the details of what had happened. She was taken to nearby Saint Vincent's Hospital and treated for her injuries.

Then the situation started to spiral.

With Linda being treated at the hospital, an enraged Caridi returned to the apartment on Fort Wadsworth and forcibly took his three-year-old son away from a family member of Linda's who had been caring for him until she could return from St. Vincent's. The family member called Military Police just in time to prevent him from getting past the exit gate of the military base.

However, attempting to flee, Caridi revved the engine of his vehicle and drove it directly at one of the officers.

A Military Police officer drew his gun.

Caridi then picked up his young son and held him up in front of him as a human shield, preventing the officer from firing. Caridi repeatedly shook his son violently against the steering wheel of his car and dared the officer to shoot, vowing that he was ready and willing to kill his own son.

To protect the child's safety, the Military Police backed down. Caridi fled the scene as the FBI was notified.

FBI Special Agent Anthony Nelson fielded the call and was soon able to track Caridi to another home on Staten Island.

Racing to the address, Nelson knew he needed to think fast and establish contact. In a crisis, every second mattered.

"Remember, this was before the days of cellular phones, but we obviously didn't know what we didn't know," he explains. "So, we didn't consider the lack of a cell phone as an impediment, since that technology had not even been invented.

"When I think back to the 1970s and 1980s, it's hard to believe that we were fighting crime and solving cases with such primitive tools. It wasn't until 1981 that I was even issued a pager, and then it was tone only." There were no telephone numbers to alert Nelson about the identity of the individual paging him. Its only value was to alert him to call the office.

Nelson was eventually upgraded. "Sure, the new pager displayed the caller's number, but I still had to find a working payphone to return a call. That's not always as easy as it would seem, especially when responding to a hostage crisis."

There were many, many times when Nelson scrambled to find the nearest working payphone, a store owner's phone, or a private citizen's residence during emergency situations. But he knew that the sooner he could make telephonic contact with his office and the hostage taker, the better the likelihood of a non-fatal outcome.

"This most often happened during arrests of dangerous fugitives or while executing arrest warrants for subjects who were deemed to be armed and dangerous," Nelson says. "Today, that's something I would be able to do easily when arriving at the front door with a cell phone."

That wasn't the case in 1987 as Nelson raced across Staten Island.

Arriving on scene first, Nelson approached the next-door neighbor, who agreed to let him use her home as a command post and her landline to try to make contact with the subject, who was holding the child hostage inside.

As Nelson's FBI squad members arrived at the building to back him up, he had already established a conversation with Caridi.

Caridi told Nelson he would kill his own son if the FBI entered the premises.

"These situations were among my worst nightmares," Nelson says, himself a father of young children at the time. "I'd already had enough critical situations weighing on my mind that were keeping me awake at night. I dreaded the thought that I could now become responsible for the death of a three-year-old child just by making an incorrect tactical error."

But there was nothing to do but handle the crisis and trust his training and his colleagues.

"During my telephone negotiations with Caridi, I gave him enough time to calm down and to think more clearly about what he was doing."

Nelson relied on his training to de-escalate the tense hostage standoff with a mentally unstable Caridi, who had already proven incapable of controlling his violent impulses. But one thing was sure—he had to keep Caridi talking to avoid a tragedy.

Hostage negotiators are specifically trained to keep the hostage taker on the line, to build rapport, understand motivations, and diffuse some of the tension by actively listening and engaging in compassionate dialogue rather than taking immediate action.

"I asked him to think about how he would be forever remembered by people who cared about him if he were to end his life and the life of his son," Nelson says.

By listening attentively and showing empathy, negotiators like Nelson can establish a connection with the hostage taker, making them more likely to cooperate.

"I told him that he could correct whatever he was upset about," Nelson says.

Despite all that, Nelson knew the situation could take a deadly turn at any moment. The only thing he could do was to keep talking.

And hope.

"I told him I would listen to him for as long as he wanted, and I would try to help him with whatever issues existed."

After a tense pause, everyone's fears heightened, Caridi agreed to surrender himself and his child to Nelson.

Caridi's son was brought to Saint Vincent's Hospital and was found to be unharmed.

"I then placed Caridi under arrest," Nelson says. "At his arraignment in Brooklyn federal court, I suggested he be sent for a psychiatric examination while in federal custody."

Today, virtually everyone has a sophisticated cellular telephone, but they give little thought to the level of technology they hold in their hands.

"Technology like that would've been invaluable during my early years in the FBI," Nelson says.

Phones that would have provided law enforcement with the ability to instantly track the location of fugitives, provide calendars and diaries containing their activities, data concerning what types of information they were searching for, access to financial records, and an accounting of their movements and activities—all these advancements were years away.

"The technology of today is the reality that had only been imagined during the vast timeline of my career," Nelson says. "Technology that had only been envisioned in comic strips like *Dick Tracy* and *Batman*. I did have the luxury of using these tools, as well as information databases such as Lexis-Nexis. But these investigative tools came late in my career.

"As valuable as these tools are today, they are also sometimes used against well-meaning, honest law enforcement officers who are the heroes of our current generation," he laments. "Everyone has a cell phone and every cell phone has a camera. Sometimes those devices are used to show manipulated or partial stories that can destroy the lives and careers of today's generation of police officers, most of whom often want no more than to be appreciated for the job they perform.

"The police officers themselves are also wearing body cameras that record all of their actions during critical incidents," Nelson adds. "As I look around at the officers whom I've met since I retired, I realize, however, that I am still in the company of courage."

CHAPTER THIRTY-NINE

On November 25, 1987, Anthony Nelson responded to the Fort Hamilton Army base in Brooklyn after receiving a report that a Military Police officer was viciously attacked by an individual with a crowbar. The perpetrator struck the female officer over the head at least twelve times during the unprovoked assault. She was rushed to nearby Victory Memorial Hospital in Bay Ridge with serious injuries.

During the assault, a second female MP, the commanding officer of the Military Police at Fort Hamilton, happened to be exiting the army base and witnessed the attack. Immediately rushing to the aid of the first MP, she was also struck in the head with the crowbar, severely injured, and removed to the hospital.

With the attack in progress, both MPs cried for help, and several soldiers in the area rushed over to assist. They restrained the suspect, later identified as Steven Wavra, and held him until Nelson arrived on the scene.

Nelson placed Wavra under arrest for assault on federal officers and armed robbery. After Wavra waived his constitutional rights against self-incrimination, Nelson interviewed him. "Wavra told me he armed himself with a .22-caliber starter gun and a crowbar," Nelson says. "He also told me he always wanted to commit an attack at the army base and that he'd thrown the starter gun into the leaves on the ground when he was detained by the soldiers."

Wavra then admitted to Nelson that he also tried to steal the MP's gun, but when she fell to the ground, she landed on her side with her gun beneath her leg, touching the ground. A search for the pistol failed to locate it in the extreme darkness and heavy cover of leaves.

"So, I requested the Military Police to secure and guard the area until I could return during daylight with additional FBI agents and a metal detector to perform a proper search," Nelson says. When he returned the next morning with a team of agents, they were initially unable to locate the gun in the leaves.

Then, as Nelson methodically studied the scene, he noticed something unusual—a well-dressed, middle-aged man in a suit and tie, sitting in an abandoned car near the gate to the army base.

"I walked over to question him," Nelson remembers. "He told me it was his car and he was about to drive off to the home of a relative in Bay Ridge."

There was one problem. The car did not have any wheels attached.

"I told the well-dressed but obviously mentally ill man to exit the vehicle, and that was when I found the gun inside the car," Nelson says. "I took the man into custody but was quickly able to determine that he had no connection to either Wavra or the pistol."

Processing Wavra, Nelson checked his criminal history and discovered he'd been released recently from prison after serving several years. "Incredibly, when he was first sent to prison based on that last arrest, he told the assistant district attorney prosecuting his case that when he is released from prison, he is going to steal the gun of a Military Police officer at Fort Hamilton," Nelson says. "He actually kept true to that promise, and it was one of the first acts he committed upon his release."

If the case ended there, it would still be one of the more unusual incidents Nelson investigated.

But it did not end there.

"After a further review of his background, I determined that he was a person of interest in a 1982 unsolved mysterious Sears cookbook bombing in Bay Ridge," Nelson says.

Southern Brooklyn residents of a certain age will clearly remember this case when news hit that Bay Ridge resident Joan Kipp was killed when she opened a package mailed to her home that contained a bomb inserted into a hollowed-out cookbook. The device consisted of a six-volt battery connected with electrical wiring to a couple of metal tubes filled with explosive powder and a trio of .22-caliber rifle shells.

During the investigation of an unrelated case, detectives found bomb-making materials in a residence that was occupied by a male.

That initial suspect was the roommate of Steven Wavra.

At the time, Wavra admitted that the items had belonged to him, but denied involvement. And there was insufficient evidence to charge him with the killing of Joan Kipp since Wavra had an airtight alibi—he was in prison at the time the bomb was mailed and detonated.

Investigators still suspected he was involved, especially once they learned Joan Kipp had been his guidance counselor when he attended Dyker Heights Junior High School. Investigators speculated that Wavra may have held a grudge, given that he'd been held back twice, and theorized that he may have held Joan Kipp responsible.

The theory speculated that Wavra masterminded the plot with an accomplice, but the case fell apart due to a lack of evidence. To this day, Wavra has adamantly denied having anything to do with the bombings, insisting that he has been caught in "a web of circumstantial evidence."

Postal inspectors and NYPD detectives instead focused on a family member of Kipp, whom they arrested but was eventually cleared.

Wavra was a troubled man who fit the profile. In the early 1970s, he briefly served in the Navy but was discharged after being diagnosed as a paranoid schizophrenic. After leaving the Navy, Wavra accumulated a rap sheet including possession of noxious liquids, making bomb threats against postal facilities, and assaulting a military police officer.

Still, investigators could not directly connect him to the Kipp bombing.

The case went cold. Eleven years passed. Then suddenly, a new series of bombings took place with similarities to the earlier attack—five more bombs like the one that killed Kipp were mailed to people, though the victims seemed to have nothing in common.

On October 15, 1993, Anthony Lenza, a retired sanitation worker from Staten Island, opened a blue velvet coin box mailed to him, and projectiles injured three people, including his eleven-year-old granddaughter.

The Kipp and Lenza devices were compared and deemed the work of the same person, from the similar typeface used on the address labels to the design of explosive devices. Both used a pair of six-volt batteries. The triggering mechanisms used a screw inside a ballpoint pen spring. The .22-caliber rounds had double the gunpowder.

On April 5, 1994, Alice Caswell, seventy-five, of Sheepshead Bay, was critically injured by a device in the same type of coin box. It was addressed to her brother, Richard McGarrell, a retired Customs agent who previously lived with her.

Then on June 27, 1995, Stephanie Gaffney was wounded in St. Albans, Queens, by a parcel addressed to "Gilmore or occupant." Gilmore was the name of her grandfather, a former police officer. Her uncle James Gilmore was also a cop who had worked to dismantle a drug gang.

A year later, on June 20, 1996, Richard Basile, seventy-seven, of Bensonhurst, opened a small parcel addressed to his wife, detonating the device packed inside a videocassette. No one was injured. The rounds shattered his kitchen window. He had opened it from a distance, a law enforcement source said.[64]

At this point, the media had begun referring to the maker of these explosive devices as the "Zip Gun Bomber," despite the definition not exactly fitting that of a zip gun (zip guns are generally crude, homemade firearms that use rudimentary materials improvised for a barrel, breechblock, and a firing mechanism, much like today's 3D-printed guns).

---

64. Weir, Richard. "TRACING NEW LEADS TO ZIP GUN BOMBER Cops Eye Con's Links, Victim's Family." New York Daily News. April 9, 2018. https://www.nydailynews.com/2002/05/20/tracing-new-leads-to-zip-gun-bomber-cops-eye-cons-links-victims-family/

Investigators were able to link elements of the devices together based on their designs. However, they varied in key aspects, either using a book, a video cassette or a coin box.

In each case, the creator of the device had removed the firing pins from the projectiles used, which were .22 cartridges, and replaced them with electrical filaments. These were then charged by the recipients of the packages, opening them up. This completed an electrical circuit that the culprit had created through the devices' inner wiring and created enough heat to fire off the projectiles.

Usually, three bullets were fired off at once, which the barrels aimed at what would usually be the victims' torsos.65 Although there had been injuries among the people who opened the five packages, there were no additional deaths.

No motive was ever proven to connect the bombings.

Then the bombings mysteriously ceased and were never solved.

In 1995, Wavra resurfaced as a person of interest in the so-called Zip Gun case after he sent a menacing manifesto to multiple federal courthouses. When authorities apprehended him, he was found carrying a hollowed-out book that concealed knives, along with four .22-caliber rifle cartridges. The discovery constituted a clear parole violation, landing Wavra back behind bars. Once again, investigators attempted to link him to a string of mail bombings—but came up empty.

Wavra was sentenced to ninety months in a federal prison for possession of ammunition while being a convicted felon. He served his sentence in Beaumont, Texas, before being released in March 2005.

He continues to deny any involvement in the crimes attributed to the Zip Gun Bomber, and at one point claimed that he was working on his own account of his ordeal. This has yet to come to pass.

Meanwhile, the Zip Gun Bomber has been referred to by several investigators as the most bizarre unsolved case of the century. Daniel Mihalko, a postal inspector, told the media that his long-lasting investigation struggled to come up with any details that proved helpful. "We can't tie the victims together," Mihalko reported. "We don't have a motive here. So we're not really sure what the zip gun person is trying to show here."

A $100,000 reward exists for any information that may lead to this criminal being identified and detained by authorities.

Until such time, the story of the Zip Gun Bomber remains unresolved.

"The female Military Police officer who was the object of the initial attack in my case was so traumatized that she retired from the US Army, moved to another state, and legally changed her name," Nelson says. "She was so appreciative of what I had done for her in this case that she mailed several pounds of homemade chocolate chip cookies to me at my FBI office every single year since the time of the attack until the year I retired from the FBI."

CHAPTER FORTY

Anthony Nelson.

Regrets?

He has a few.

A career in the Federal Bureau of Investigation, really law enforcement in general, will do that to you. You see things no one should. And you live with things no one can. Sometimes, you wonder how the average person views this sacrifice.

"Since my retirement from the FBI in 2004, I can't count the number of times a friend, an acquaintance, or just someone I met at a social function told me how lucky I was to have a traditional federal civil service pension," Anthony Nelson says.

Sure, a career at the Bureau earns you what some would deem generous retirement benefits.

But the Job also comes with its side effects.

Like an inability to peacefully sleep through the night.

Mid-afternoon, July 25, 1988, about 2:30, Anthony Nelson was enjoying something of a rarity: a Monday off in the summer. With the temperature approaching ninety degrees, Nelson planned to spend the day with his wife, Syndee, and their then four-year-old son, Michael.

That was not to be.

As had happened so many times before, Nelson's phone rang with an urgent call for another case that would haunt him for the rest of his life.

He was called in to respond to a shooting at the Veterans Administration Hospital in the Bronx.

The FBI has the federal jurisdiction to investigate crimes committed at facilities within the vast Department of Veterans Affairs, often partnering with the VA Police. They investigate offenses ranging from financial fraud and threats to patient harm across 170 VA medical centers, outpatient clinics, and 135 national cemeteries. The VA maintains its own uniformed law enforcement service, responsible for protecting its facilities—such as the Bronx VA Medical Center that Nelson was racing toward that July afternoon.

VA Police trace their origins to the National Home for Disabled Volunteer Soldiers, established in 1865 by President Lincoln. Early officers kept order and handled minor offenses like drunkenness and disorderly conduct, turning severe cases over to local authorities or the Bureau of Investigation (now the FBI). Today, VA Police work to deter and investigate crime, maintain order, and ensure the safety of staff and patients on VA property while the FBI steps in for more serious or federal-level offenses.

By the 1970s, violent criminal offenses increased dramatically on VA grounds. Guards were elevated to full police status, and their training and responsibilities increased. Yet despite the more dangerous threats the VA Police faced, they were only armed with mace.

On the afternoon of July 25, 1988, two men walked into the Bronx VA Hospital, the entrance guarded by VA Police Officer Ronald Hearn, forty-nine years old at the time.

By all accounts, Hearn was respected and loved by family, friends, and colleagues alike. Hearn joined the VA Police force eight years earlier and was an Air Force veteran who lived in Flushing, Queens, caring for his elderly mother.

"When I arrived at the crime scene," Nelson recalls, "I learned that Hearn was manning a metal detector at the entrance to the hospital when two young men had attempted to bypass him and gain entry into the hospital."

The men, sporting military-style haircuts, were armed, triggering the metal detector.

"Hearn, who was wearing a personally owned ballistic vest, spotted a gun on one of the two subjects," Nelson says.

Note, the vest was not standard issue. The VA Police were not afforded protective gear or firearms. Despite this clear and present danger, the unarmed Hearn pursued.

"He chased the man with the gun into the vestibule of the entry door and attempted to subdue him," Nelson recounts. "However, Hearn failed to notice the second subject running up from behind."

As *New York Daily News* writer Jerry Capeci reported, "The men, both casually dressed and sporting gold chains around their necks, scaled a fence and escaped on July 25 after one of the men fired five shots from a .380-caliber handgun into Ronald Hearn at point-blank range."[65]

"Three of the rounds were stopped by Hearn's ballistic vest," Nelson recalls. "But the other two rounds slipped past the vest and struck him."

Hearn died shortly thereafter in a second-floor operating room.

"Both subjects ran over the grounds at the VA Hospital, jumped over a high fence, and escaped," Nelson says, fleeing down Webb Avenue and escaping onto Fordham Road. "An intensive investigation by myself and other FBI agents from my squad failed to identify his killers."

Hearn was buried a week later, on August 1, 1988, as "FBI agents began recanvassing the area around the hospital and re-interviewing, along with sketch artists, some of the dozens of witnesses to the midafternoon shooting," Capeci wrote.

"When I attended Hearn's funeral, the pastor publicly acknowledged my presence in the church," Nelson remembers. "I then promised Hearn's mother, Evelyn Skeete, that I was going to find the two animals that killed her son."

This was a promise Nelson was never able to keep.

"It's an unkept promise that has haunted me ever since those bullets struck Hearn," Nelson says. "At least once or twice every

---

65. Capeci, Jerry. "FBI seeking pair in fatal shooting of cop." New York Daily News. April 3, 1986

week for longer than I can remember, Evelyn would call me, and I would give her updates on our investigation. But those updates were never good news."

In the aftermath of Hearn's murder, Nelson appeared on television's *New York's Most Wanted* and in several newspapers pleading for information about Hearn's killers.

"It was unusual for me not to develop any leads in a killing," he explains. "So many times in the past, when more than one subject had committed a crime, someone, somewhere would inevitably get arrested for a crime and then offer up information on some other offense to lessen the charges against them."

Yet as the weeks turned into months and the months into years, no positive information was developed in connection with Hearn's murder.

"It was suspected that Hearn's killer had come to the VA hospital to deliver drugs to either a patient or a VA employee," Nelson says. "But drug use was so rampant in the Bronx and at the hospital, I couldn't narrow it down to any single suspect at the facility."

To this day, the failure to find Hearn's killers has weighed heavily on Nelson.

"It was the most disappointing period of my career in the FBI," Nelson says. "I can still hear the voice of Hearn's mother, Evelyn, asking me if I had any good news about locating the killers of her beloved son. I will forever have to live with images ingrained in my mind of murdered friends, shots being fired, disfigured victims of gunshot wounds and airline crashes, dead children, and other crimes that would shock the conscience of almost everyone. Images that no one should ever have to remember each night of their life."

Anthony Nelson. Regrets?

He has a few.

And sure, when they ask him, Nelson will say he does consider himself fortunate to have good financial benefits for his years of service to the FBI.

"But then again, I'm also not so fortunate," he adds, "to have taken so many vivid memories of evil into retirement with me. And I know I'm not alone."

PostScript

Throughout the 1980s, a series of violent incidents claimed the lives of four unarmed Veterans Affairs Police officers and several other staff members, including the tragic murder of Officer Ronald Hearn.

In part due to outcry, the VA considered arming its police force for the first time. Three years later, Secretary Jesse Brown directed the development of a pilot program to arm VA Police at no more than six facilities. In September 1996, the North Chicago VA Medical Center became the first facility to arm its police officers, followed by Richmond, Bronx, West Los Angeles, and Chicago (West Side). The pilot program proved successful, so around 1998, Secretary Togo West expanded the arming of VA Police at a rate of about sixteen sites per year.

Following the terrorist attacks of September 11, 2001, the arming program was accelerated. By fall 2002, ninety-two VA medical centers had 1,830 armed police officers, and in 2003, the entire force was armed. In 2002, Jose Rodriguez-Reyes, an officer at the San Juan VAMC in Puerto Rico, was the first policeman to be killed after the VA Police became armed. Since 1985, at least seven officers have lost their lives while on duty.

Respectfully, may these brave officers be remembered for their courage, commitment, and ultimate sacrifice, including:

Marvin C. Bland, age thirty-four, was killed in an automobile accident on September 6, 1985, while responding to a fire alarm at the Veterans Affairs Hospital in Bedford, Massachusetts.

Mark S. Decker, age thirty-one, and **Leonard B. Wilcox**, age thirty-seven, were shot and killed on January 31, 1986, while attempting to question a suspicious man at the Brecksville VA Hospital in Brecksville, Ohio. Both Decker and Wilcox were armed only with mace due to administrative guidelines. While the officers were talking with the man, he pulled out a .45-caliber handgun and shot Officer Decker, killing him instantly. Officer Wilcox attempted to run for cover, but the suspect chased him before shooting him as well. The killer was sentenced to two life terms for the murders.

Ronald Hearn, age forty-nine, was shot and killed on July 25, 1988, at the Bronx VA Hospital in New York City.

Garry A. Ross, age forty-one, died from a heart attack on December 24, 1990, at the VA Medical Center in Washington, DC. Ross died after responding to a call of a mentally deranged patient, who assaulted him several times. Ross suffered a massive heart attack after restraining the patient.

Horst Harold Woods, age forty-six, was shot and killed on January 10, 1996, in Albuquerque, New Mexico. Woods had approached a man kneeling beside his patrol car; when Woods approached him from the opposite side of the vehicle, the man stood up, exchanged words with Woods, then shot him in the back of his head as Woods turned away. The man was arrested later the same day. The suspect was arrested a short time later by Air Force security police law enforcement officers, now called security forces, from Kirtland Air Force Base, where he was found with "two extra fully loaded magazines, an eighteen-inch bowie knife and a long-barreled Derringer loaded with two shotgun shells."

Jose Oscar Rodriguez-Reyes, age fifty-three, was shot and killed on April 24, 2002, while stationed at a gate at the VA Medical Center in San Juan, Puerto Rico. Rodriguez-Reyes was attacked by two men for unknown reasons and shot in the head and chest. The two attempted to steal Rodriguez-Reyes' service weapon but were unable to remove it from the holster. Rodriguez-Reyes was the first armed VA Police officer to be killed in the line of duty. Two suspects were arrested by the FBI. Charged with murder, the suspect who shot Rodriguez-Reyes was convicted in July 2006.

Ronald Leisure, age sixty-six, suffered a fatal heart attack while conducting a foot patrol of the VA Medical Center in Livermore, California, on November 14, 2014. He was conducting checks of the large complex when he suddenly collapsed. Medical staff immediately initiated lifesaving measures but were unable to resuscitate him.

Special Agent Gregory Cleveland Holland, age forty-seven, died from complications as a result of contracting COVID-19 as a result of a presumed exposure while on duty at the VA Law Enforcement Training Center in North Little Rock, Arkansas, on Friday, August 13, 2021.

CHAPTER FORTY-ONE

October 18, 1988—one of the darkest days in the history of the New York City Police Department.

That evening, at approximately seven o'clock, Christopher G. Hoban and a fellow undercover narcotics officer, Michael Jermyn, entered an apartment on West 105th Street in Manhattan to make a drug buy, along with two suspects. Hoban was assigned to Manhattan North Narcotics. In less than four years on the job, he received four commendations for his work.

Upon entering the apartment, the undercover officers encountered a third suspect. During the transaction, the drug dealers suspected Officers Hoban and Jermyn were police officers and demanded to search Jermyn, and discovered his service weapon.

Officer Hoban drew his sidearm. In a close-quartered shootout, Hoban was killed by gunshot wounds to the chest and head. One of the suspects was also killed at the scene by Hoban, while a second was apprehended by officers waiting outside the building.

Meanwhile, that same evening, further uptown, in an unrelated incident, another NYPD officer, Michael Buczek, was killed trying to arrest two suspected members of a Dominican drug gang on a narcotics charge in an apartment building at 580 West 161st Street in Washington Heights.

October 18, 1988—that date marked the first time in the history of the NYPD that two officers were killed in separate incidents on the same night.

Hoban and Buczek did not know each other, though a joint funeral mass was held for them at Our Lady of Perpetual Help in Brooklyn on October 22, 1988. Twelve thousand officers and nearly eight thousand civilians attended the joint funeral.

In the wake of the shootings, Anthony Nelson was assigned to locate and apprehend Hoban's killer. NYPD Detective Michael Sheehan contacted him with the formal request to assist in the investigation.

"I knew Michael Sheehan from other investigations," Nelson remembers. A veteran detective, Sheehan spent twenty-five years with the NYPD and worked on several high-profile cases, including as a lead detective on the 1989 Central Park Jogger case. Sheehan also played a role in solving the Robert Chambers' Preppy Murder case in 1986. After retiring from the force, Sheehan joined the media, serving as a popular on-air television reporter for years at FOX 5 before joining PIX11.

Unfortunately, Mike Sheehan died at the age of seventy-one from cancer contracted on September 11, 2001, while covering the terrorist attacks on the World Trade Center.

Nelson had a solid lead in the Hoban case. The NYPD identified Bienvenido Castillo as one of the individuals who was in the apartment at the time of the Hoban murder and was the suspected shooter. The NYPD specifically requested the assistance of the New York Office once word came that Castillo might attempt to flee New York to the Dominican Republic, his homeland.

This was a high-profile, sensitive case. In a later commendation of Nelson, FBI Supervisory Special Agent Richard K. Berry wrote that he assigned the case to him due to his close professional and personal relationships with numerous ranking members of the NYPD, and that Anthony Nelson is considered to be one of the most respected agents in the New York Office.

More leads flowed in.

Numerous associates of Castillo were hunted and apprehended, while raids went down at several of his known hangouts. But Castillo eluded capture in New York City.

Nelson established contact with Lieutenant Doyle of the Major Case Squad, who oversaw the investigation. Nelson determined

Castillo had fled to Puerto Rico and was desperately attempting to get a visa to enter the Dominican Republic.

He dialed the San Juan division, which confirmed this information.

Nelson now faced an enormous problem: he needed to stop Castillo. However, there was no arrest warrant issued, even as it became apparent Castillo was fleeing to Puerto Rico.

New York District Attorneys are, at times, reluctant to pursue warrants, since New York State law prohibits questioning any individual for whom there is an outstanding warrant.

Nelson turned to his contacts in the Manhattan District Attorney's Office, who agreed to obtain a warrant. He personally drafted the text for the warrant. Simultaneously, he reached out to the Southern District of New York US Attorney's Office and dictated the complaint for the unlawful flight warrant.

Fighting the clock, Nelson was able to get the local warrant and then rapidly got it to the US Attorney's Office, where he obtained the unlawful flight (UFAP) warrant in record time: it usually takes four to six hours to get a warrant in the Southern District of New York: Nelson secured both the New York State warrant and the federal warrant within about an hour.

San Juan FBI agents apprehended Castillo approximately one hour after the warrant was issued. Fortunately, Nelson had the foresight to include a drug count in the complaint to eliminate any possibility of Castillo securing a release on bail in Puerto Rico, where the suspected cop killer clearly had associates to aid his escape from justice.

"Anthony was very, very effective at writing search warrants," says George Terra. He would know. Later in Nelson's career, when he joined the King's County District Attorney's Office as an investigator, Nelson reported to Terra. "Obviously, you need to get the warrants right, or you can have issues not just with the investigation and arrest, but with the prosecution. I don't think Anthony has a law degree, but he might as well because he had a talent for writing out warrants for any number of different matters and making sense out of a mishmash of different pieces of information."

This foresight paid off.

Castillo fought extradition and even staged a phony medical episode in the courtroom in San Juan. Since Castillo was not indicted in New York, the US attorney in San Juan had a probable cause hearing, and Nelson was subpoenaed to testify, as were several NYPD detectives.

Nelson was on a plane headed to San Juan within three hours.

In a letter to Assistant Director in Charge James M. Fox, US Attorney Rudolph W. Giuliani stated:

The removal hearing was held on November 2, 1988. After Agent Nelson testified, Assistant United States Attorney Warren Vasquez rested. He did not present the additional evidence he had planned because of the comprehensive presentation made by Agent Nelson. Mr. Vasquez has told us that Agent Nelson was one of the best witnesses with whom he has ever worked.

SA Nelson has been instrumental in getting the Manhattan District Attorney to agree to turn Castillo over to the US Attorney's Office for prosecution once the State trial on murder charges has been completed. Thanks to his insight into this case, SA Nelson has been able to have Castillo and his associates tried under the RICO statute for a drug enterprise and numerous drug-related homicides.

In a painful twist, during Nelson's earlier investigation into the homicide of Ronald Hearn, the VA Police officer murdered four months prior, tips alleged that Hearns' killers were members of Castillo's drug gang.

Following Castillo's takedown in Puerto Rico, the *New York Post* reported the connection and that the NYPD was hoping the increased pressure would produce new leads in that cold case.[66]

It was not to be.

"By sheer chance, I was the same FBI agent from that case, now assigned to hunt down Castillo on federal charges related to Hoban's murder, and we captured him as he attempted to flee to the Dominican Republic," Nelson says. "But unfortunately,

66. Weiss, Murray. "Cop-kill suspect linked to VA hospital slaying." New York Post

there was never enough evidence to connect Castillo to the earlier Hearn homicide."

After Castillo's capture, Michael Sheehan presented Nelson and two FBI agents from San Juan with honorary NYPD detective shields and plaques from the NYPD Detectives Endowment Association during a formal dinner at the Marina Del Rey restaurant in the Bronx.

This was no cause for celebration for Anthony Nelson though, at least in the Hoban murder, the perpetrators were brought to justice.

"Hoban's death was so emotionally upsetting for everyone involved in the investigation and, of course, for everyone who knew and loved him," Nelson says. "So I felt a great sense of satisfaction to be instrumental in the apprehension of Bienvenido Castillo, the drug dealer who shot and killed him."

CHAPTER FORTY-TWO

How large is your family?

There were 720,652 full-time law enforcement officers employed in the United States in 2023, the most recent year for which statistics are available from multiple sources pooled by Statista. This includes officers at the federal, state, and local levels, but not the thousands of law enforcement's civilian administrative personnel.[67]

Like most extended families, they may be located in different places, may not always agree, and may even argue at times. But regardless of jurisdiction, the colors of their uniforms, or the shapes of their badges, they are all united in purpose.

"I can tell you, based upon my life experience, I haven't noticed too many professions that care so deeply about the well-being of their colleagues," Nelson reflects. "There's something about facing danger and mortality each day you go to work, and relying on partners by your side who face those same dangers with you, that creates a real sense of 'family.'"

They collaborate on the same cases. They chase the same crooks. They participate in the same training programs. And they share the same trauma. Most importantly, when one falls, they all feel the grief—especially when those relationships are personal.

The FBI and the DEA are agencies under the Department of Justice. While the FBI has broader jurisdiction over federal

---

67. Statista. "Number of Law Enforcement Officers U.S. 2004-2023." November 14, 2024. https://www.statista.com/statistics/191694/number-of-law-enforcement-officers-in-the-us/

crimes, the DEA specializes in enforcing laws related to controlled substances and combating drug trafficking and abuse. So not surprisingly, the FBI and DEA often work together in joint task forces when drug trafficking intersects with terrorism, organized crime, or financial fraud.

"Early in 1988, I had the honor of meeting DEA Special Agent Everett E. Hatcher," Nelson says. "He had been assigned by the DEA to a Joint Organized Crime Drug Enforcement Task Force located in the New York Office of the FBI at 26 Federal Plaza."

Before joining the DEA, Hatcher spent six years in Germany as a US Army Deputy Provost Marshal and physical education teacher at a military dependents high school. He returned to New York in 1975 to teach in New York City public schools. Hatcher was working for the New York district attorney as an investigator when he was accepted as a Special Agent with the DEA.

Special Agent Hatcher earned a bachelor's degree in physical education from Hampton Institute in Virginia in 1968, a master's degree in education from Boston College with high honors in 1974, and completed advanced graduate studies at Boston College and John Jay College of Criminal Justice in New York.[68] Hatcher formally became a DEA Special Agent in January 1977 at the New York Regional Office. During his twelve years with DEA, he excelled in a variety of investigative assignments throughout the New York Field Division, for which he received Special Achievement Awards in 1982 and 1983. He also served as a firearms instructor and a recruiting officer.

The year before, in 1987, Hatcher received a third Special Achievement Award for his efforts with the DEA's agent recruiting program. But Hatcher was more than an outstanding DEA agent. He was a great guy, admired by his peers.

"Hatcher had such an amiable personality; he was one of those rare people with whom you could develop an instant friendship," Nelson remembers. "Whenever I spoke with him in my office, our conversations after a simple hello would inevitably turn

---

68. DEA Museum. "Everett E. Hatcher." https://museum.dea.gov/wall-honor/everett-e-hatcher

into fifteen or twenty minutes of interesting discussions about everything from organized crime figures to his military service."

In addition to a primary office at 26 Federal Plaza, Nelson also maintained an off-site office at Fort Hamilton in Brooklyn.

A short time after Nelson first met Hatcher, he happened to pass him walking on the street near the Post Exchange (PX) on Fort Hamilton. Hatcher was dressed in his military uniform, and Nelson recalls his pleasant surprise when Hatcher shared that he was still in an Army Reserve unit.

"I also learned that Hatcher had been a deputy provost marshal while on active duty in the US Army," Nelson says. This was right up Nelson's alley. A deputy provost marshal is a senior military police officer who assists the provost marshal, the head of the military police, in overseeing law enforcement and security operations within a specific area or command. They manage daily operations, supervise personnel, and ensure the implementation of policies and procedures.

The two men formed a friendship through their shared experience in the service. "It turned out that Hatcher and I had several army friends in common who were still on active duty at Fort Hamilton, including Major Jerry Wolff, who was the provost marshal at the time," Nelson says.

They crossed paths many times.

In fact, on Saturday, February 25, 1989, Hatcher and his family attended a get-together at the residence of Major Wolff on base.

"I'd also been invited, along with my wife Syndee," Nelson remembers. "We had a delightful time while all of our children played together."

Around this time, Special Agent Hatcher was investigating Gerard A. "Gerry" Chilli, a Bonanno Family captain who ran a violent crew based in Staten Island, as well as illicit Bonanno operations down in Florida's Broward County, based in Hollywood.

Gerry was less volatile than his older brother, Joseph Chilli, another Bonanno capo who rose to prominence in rackets related to rampant corruption at the Fulton Fish Market. He had a reputation as a hothead. In the late 1970s, he was involved in an altercation in a Staten Island bar with Joe "the German" Watts, an associate in the Gambino Family. Though never made, Watts was a close associate of John Gotti and participated in the Gotti-planned assassination of Gambino boss Paul Castellano (Gotti also tapped Watts as a liaison to the Westies gang in Hell's Kitchen).

While the altercation was not physical, Watts felt slighted. He brought his beef to Castellano, who insisted on Chilli's murder, even though Chilli was made and Watts was not. Watts, however, was a major earner for the Gambinos.

Alphonse "Sonny Red" Indelicato, caporegime in the Bonanno Family, brokered a compromise, basically shelving Chilli and demoting him to another smaller crew in the Bronx. In the context of the American Mafia, to "shelve" someone means to remove them from active service and/or strip them of power.

Gerry Chilli, who operated as more of a lone wolf by all accounts, was unfazed by being sidelined. He continued his nefarious ways and spent long stretches in prison.

During his time "away at college," Jerry Chilli met Costabile "Gus" Farace. Chilli unofficially adopted Farace, who was in his late twenties at the time, as a protégé, and stayed in contact after Chilli's release from prison. This was a relationship Chilli would come to regret.

Farace used his contacts with old friends and new ones he met in prison to start a marijuana-selling business, which soon expanded into other drugs.

In early June 1988, Farace was released from prison. Shortly after, Farace had become a partner with Gregory Scarpa Jr., who operated out of the Wimpy Boys Social Club run by his father, Colombo powerhouse Gregory Scarpa Sr.

Farace's drug trafficking and Mob connections drew the attention of the DEA.

Throughout 1989, Hatcher, operating undercover, met Farace on multiple occasions to discuss purchasing cocaine. By late February 1989, Farace arranged a major cocaine deal with Hatcher.

At approximately ten o'clock on the evening of February 28, Farace was to meet Hatcher at a remote overpass on the West

Shore Expressway in the Rossville section of Staten Island to complete the deal.

This section of Highway 440 at night feels desolate, like a forgotten corridor at the edge of the city's reach. Long stretches of pavement unspool in near-total darkness, wetlands flanked by patches of scrub pine, tangled brush, and fenced-off industrial lots.

Heading to the drug meet on the very outskirts of New York City in his unmarked Buick Regal, Hatcher got separated from his surveillance team.

When the team finally found Hatcher, he'd been shot through the head three times. The window was rolled down and the Regal's engine was still running, Hatcher's lifeless foot wedged on the brake.

Police theorized that Farace shot Hatcher from a van as it passed Hatcher's car. That van was found abandoned three days later on a street about two miles northeast of the murder scene.

Farace was familiar with the area, which is why he likely chose it for the ambush. This location was less than half a mile from the Arthur Kill Correctional Facility, where Farace spent the last two years of his manslaughter sentence. Farace pleaded guilty and was sentenced to seven to twenty-one years in prison for an October 7, 1979, gay-bashing incident where Farace murdered a seventeen-year-old boy and brutally beat the victim's sixteen-year-old companion.

It is not known why Farace killed Hatcher; one theory is that Farace had become suspicious of Hatcher from rumors he had heard.

This was four days after Nelson and Hatcher attended, with their families, the affair at Fort Hamilton, where their children played together.

That fateful evening, February 28, 1989, FBI Special Agent Anthony Nelson was at home when his telephone rang. "There was always something about those late-evening telephone calls that had a way of letting me know, before I even answered the call, that I was about to be sent out on some ominous assignment by the FBI," Nelson says. "Those late-evening calls were so common that I knew I'd be gone for the rest of the night."

Yet this call was different.

The call was from the FBI Operations Center.

"I was told that the SAC, the head of the FBI's Criminal Division, wanted me to respond forthwith to the vicinity of Bloomingdale Road and the West Shore Expressway in Staten Island to assist in a crime scene search," he says.

Nelson was briefly informed that a DEA agent had been shot and killed during an undercover narcotics operation, yet he was not told the identity of the slain agent.

"As soon as I arrived at the scene," Nelson says, "I approached the driver's side of the undercover auto and immediately recognized that the dead agent was Everett Hatcher."

The revelation stunned Nelson on the side of that cold, dark Staten Island road.

After so many years in the FBI, and only four months after Nelson had returned from Puerto Rico with Bienvenido Castillo, the drug dealer who had shot and killed NYPD Police Officer Christopher Hoban, Nelson remembers thinking there were not too many crimes that could still shock him.

"But the sight of Everett Hatcher in that vehicle, shot to death, really took an emotional toll on me," he says. "I'm standing there and for a few moments, I just couldn't process the thought that it was him, really *him*, that we'd just spoken, just had a great day with him and his family."

After the crime scene had been cleared, teams of FBI and DEA agents, along with NYPD detectives, met at the 123rd Precinct to map out plans to apprehend his killer. An intensive multi-agency investigation was initiated that included a legal, but no-holds-barred, plan to attack every known organized crime operation in New York City.

Hatcher's death was the first murder of a DEA agent in New York City since 1972. He was also believed to have been the first law enforcement officer killed in the line of duty on Staten Island.

A $250,000 reward was issued; at the time, it was the largest federal bounty ever set. President George H.W. Bush called for the enactment of a federal death penalty in cases in which law enforcement officers are murdered.

It was not long before the investigators identified Farace as the person who set up, shot, and killed Hatcher. A nationwide manhunt for Farace commenced, and he earned a new distinction when the FBI placed him on its Ten Most Wanted list.

In March 1950, a reporter for the International News Service submitted a request to the FBI for a list of the "toughest guys" the Bureau would like to capture. Envisioned as a one-time feature, the story generated so much publicity that it attracted the attention of FBI Director J. Edgar Hoover.

And so was born the FBI's Ten Most Wanted Fugitives program.

Since then, 513 fugitives have been on the Top Ten list, with 481 apprehended or located.[69] The list is compiled by the Criminal Investigative Division and the FBI's Office of Public Affairs, calling upon all fifty-six field offices to submit candidates.

To be considered, the criminal must have a lengthy record of committing serious crimes and/or be considered a particularly dangerous menace to society due to current criminal charges. And it must be believed that the nationwide publicity can be of assistance in apprehending the fugitive. A reward of up to one hundred thousand dollars is offered by the FBI for information that leads directly to an arrest.

Farace was in some pretty bad company. The list included Ted Kaczynski (Unabomber), Eric Robert Rudolph (1996 Atlanta Olympics bombing and attacks on abortion clinics), Dzhokhar and Tamerlan Tsarnaev (Boston Marathon bombing), James "Whitey" Bulger (Boston organized crime boss), Robert Hanssen (FBI agent-turned-spy for Russia), Timothy McVeigh and Terry Nichols (Oklahoma City bombing), Ramzi Yousef (1993 World Trade Center bombing), Saddam Hussein (Iraqi dictator), El Chapo (Mexican drug lord), and many others.

---

69. FBI. "Original Top Ten Ledgers." December 23, 2022. https://www.fbi.gov/history/artifacts/original-top-ten-ledgers

Local and federal law enforcement increased their surveillance of Cosa Nostra members, relentlessly disrupting their operations, stopping them, taking photographs, and asking questions.

As pressure increased on the Bonanno Family (in fact, all Five Families), the Bonanno leadership decided to kill Farace. Everyone was running for cover.

Following the Hatcher murder, Gregory Scarpa Sr. told David Krajcek of the *Daily News* that the Farace and Scarpa families were no longer close. No one from the Scarpa family had gone to Farace's wedding to Toni Acierno a few months earlier. Scarpa feared that a strong connection would send his convicted drug dealer son, Gregory Jr., to a distant federal prison.

Meanwhile, Farace was hiding with friends and criminal associates around the Greater New York area. He first stayed with Margaret "Babe" Scarpa, an old girlfriend who was Chilli's daughter.

Soon after Farace departed that location, the police raided Scarpa's house and arrested her; at the scene, a DEA official told Chilli he could blame Farace.

At this point, an aggravated Chilli wanted Farace dead. A new Mob associate with the Lucchese Family, John Petrucelli, was helping Farace find places to hide. Chilli met with Petrucelli and Lucchese capo Mike Salerno to discuss the situation. Chilli demanded that Petrucelli kill Farace, but Petrucelli refused.

Two months later, Petrucelli was found dead with a hood over his head, which is a Sicilian message for "never keep secrets from the Family."

Law enforcement continued to exert immense pressure, not just on the Bonannos but on all Italian organized crime operations, resulting in massive losses to their gambling income, in particular.

"During the period of the search for Farace, a very close cousin of mine, without my knowledge, had unwisely started to hang out with some Lucchese Family members at the 19th Hole bar in Brooklyn," Nelson remembers.

Nelson had generally seen this cousin fairly regularly. Their families were close; when Nelson was young, his uncle had been like a second father to him while his own father had been on active duty in the Army.

Nelson remembers he'd not seen his cousin for several months, which was rather unusual. During a family event later in the year, with the manhunt underway, Nelson's cousin asked to speak with him privately. "He told me that an FBI agent I knew well had picked him up for questioning in connection with the hunt for Farace," Nelson says. "My cousin had stayed away from me for months because he believed I was the one who suggested he be taken into custody. I told him I had absolutely no idea about what happened to him and that my fellow agent had not even mentioned it to me. It was just another one of the scores of coincidences that seemed to follow me throughout my career in the FBI."

Nelson attended Hatcher's funeral in Boonton, New Jersey. More than four thousand attended the service at St. Christopher's Church in Parsippany, as thousands of DEA and FBI agents and police officers from all over the United States lined the parking lot.

Hatcher was honored at that time by the attendance of representatives from virtually all law enforcement departments in New York, New Jersey and surrounding areas. Also in attendance was former New York Senator Alfonse D'Amato.

"It was an honor that a hero like Hatcher had earned and deserved," Nelson says. "He will always be remembered fondly by those who knew him."

Special Agent Hatcher was survived by his wife, Mary Jane, and two sons, Zachary and Joshua. An annual golf tournament in his honor benefits a charity.

Less than ten months after the Hatcher murder, the manhunt for Farace ended abruptly.

At 11:08 p.m. on November 17, 1989, police dispatchers received a 911 emergency call about a car parked at 1814 81st Street in the Bensonhurst. The car contained one male occupant, with another male lying face down on the sidewalk, both of whom had just been shot. The call came in as "shots fired," no other specifics.

Police rushed to the scene and found the two men, one dead and the other seriously wounded. The dead man was identified as Costabile Farace. He had gunshot wounds to the head, neck, back, and leg. The survivor in the car was identified as Joseph Sclafani, a member of Farace's organization. Sclafani said he fired back two shots at the assailants.

According to witnesses, a van had driven alongside Farace's car and shot the men nine times. This was the same method Farace used to kill Agent Hatcher.

On September 17, 1997, Lucchese Family soldier James Galione and associate Mario Gallo admitted in court to murdering Farace. A third mobster, Louis Tuzzio, slain in 1990, was the third member of the hit team. Daniel "Dirty Danny" Mongelli was convicted of killing Tuzzio in 2004 and was released from prison in 2020 after contracting COVID-19.

CHAPTER FORTY-THREE

The Job takes its pound of flesh.

No matter how hardened a member of law enforcement may be.

Blood-splashed crime scenes. Screaming family members. Mutilated bodies.

There is a toll to be paid.

And the pace can be relentless.

"Rarely a week or two would pass during my career while assigned to the New York Office Criminal Division," Nelson shares, "when I was not challenged to either make critical case decisions, engage in dangerous arrests, execute search warrants, or supervise agents assigned to my squads who were presented with similar stressful situations."

Over time, agents become desensitized to crime scenes. Sure, they're trained to handle trauma and exposure to violence, suffering, and death. But every scene, every arrest, every body chips away at their psyche.

"For me, there was no darker period than 1987 to 1990," Nelson says. "I'd worked dangerous undercover assignments for years, engaged in major narcotics transactions with heavily armed suspects. And I'd seen a lot. But it wasn't until that period of time when I was involved in several separate shooting incidents, two of which were deadly."

The first incident, in December 1987, Special Agent Anthony Nelson fired shots during an operation at an apartment building on 95th Street and Fort Hamilton Parkway in Brooklyn.

Special Agents Michael Falcone and Nelson were covering two cooperating witnesses who were trying to buy several hand grenades that were reported stolen from the Army. The agents converged on the unoccupied building on Fort Hamilton Parkway, where the transaction was set to take place. As the agents waited for the suspect, who never did appear, they noticed a light go on in the window of the upper floor of the abandoned building.

Falcone and Nelson went up the stairs to investigate when someone pointed a handgun directly at them from behind a half-open apartment door. Startled, the agents scrambled back down the stairwell to call in backup, narrowly avoiding disaster. Nelson fired two shots to cover their retreat. The subject escaped, though a handgun was recovered in the hallway.

The second shooting occurred on December 1, 1989. The sequence of events on that Friday evening is well established from testimonies captured from law enforcement personnel involved, and there exists a radio transmission.

At about 7:15 that evening, Mark Alan Geaney, a thirty-year-old resident of Coney Island, Brooklyn, was traveling from Manhattan through the Brooklyn Battery Tunnel (renamed in 2012 as the Hugh L. Carey Tunnel to honor the former New York State governor). For reasons unknown, Geaney attempted to drive through the tunnel toll booths without paying. Note that this was years before the E-ZPass toll payment system was implemented at the East River crossing in December 1996. And it would be decades before open-road cashless tolling started on January 4, 2017. Therefore, the physical toll booths had yet to be dismantled, and drivers were still required to pay cash entering and exiting the tunnel from the Brooklyn side.

As reported in the *New York Times*, NYPD Inspector John Murphy, who led the investigation, stated that several Triborough Bridge and Tunnel Authority officers surrounded the van, with Sergeant Walter Piasecki in front of it, his revolver drawn.[70] The van lurched and knocked the sergeant down, and the he fired four

70. McKinley Jr., James C., "Driver Slain by Officers After Chase Was Unarmed." New York Times. December 3, 1989. https://www.nytimes.com/1989/12/03/nyregion/driver-slain-by-officers-after-chase-was-unarmed.html

times at the van as it sped onto the Gowanus Expressway toward the Belt Parkway.

Confusion ensued about whether Geaney was armed, stemming from a misunderstanding between the tunnel officer, who was hit by the van, and a Highway Division officer, who radioed to a dispatcher that there had been ''a shootout,'' Inspector Murphy said.

Geaney was unarmed. He then led police officers on a six-mile chase eastbound.

Officer Anderson Monro, alone in a patrol car on the Belt Parkway, spotted the van and began pursuing it near the Verrazano Narrows Bridge, Inspector Murphy said.

Murphy said FBI Special Agent Anthony Nelson, who was working in Fort Hamilton at the foot of the bridge and monitoring the police radio, drove his car onto the Belt Parkway at the Bay 8th Street exit.

Other police officers set up roadblocks.

Geaney, now stuck in the traffic jam, pulled onto the shoulder.

Inspector Murphy said Agent Nelson saw the van and started to walk toward it, taking out his .38-caliber revolver. Officer Santoro also approached the van on foot with a 12-gauge shotgun. Officer Monro pulled up behind the van and joined the other officers with his .38-caliber revolver drawn.

At least twelve shots were fired, according to the inspector.

Geaney, hit numerous times, was pronounced dead at the scene.

In a flurry of radio transmissions, dispatchers made it sound as if the driver of the van had shot someone five minutes earlier at a toll booth on the Brooklyn side of the Brooklyn-Battery Tunnel, said a police spokesman, Sergeant Maurice Howard.

That recording is available.

Specifically, the highway officer told the police dispatcher that shots had been fired, and that the van was fleeing, Inspector Murphy said. Then, he said, the dispatcher asked, ''What happened?'' and the officer, Howard Charyn, answered over the air: "I don't know. I heard shots. The supervisor advised me they were just in a shootout."

Radio dispatchers then made it sound as if the driver of the van had shot an officer, Sergeant Howard said.

The two highway officers involved, Anderson Monro, twenty-seven, and Gene Santoro, thirty-two, were placed on modified assignment while the authorities investigated the shooting.

FBI Special Agent Anthony Nelson remained on active duty while the agency conducted an internal investigation, said a Bureau spokesman at the time, Joseph Valiquette.

The investigation cleared the officers and the agent of wrongdoing.

The third shooting was in January 1990 when Nelson discharged his weapon, along with other agents and NYPD detectives, foiling an attempted armed robbery of a storefront branch of the Hamilton Federal Savings Bank.

The FBI/NYPD Bank Robbery Task Force linked a light blue Datsun 210 hatchback to a string of bank robberies. That day, they tracked down the vehicle. Several unmarked cars tailed it as it drove by casing two other Brooklyn banks, though they did not rob them, before heading to the Hamilton Federal branch.

The Datsun stopped on 65th Street, and the two bank robbers, later identified as Joseph Mangine and Joseph Coluccio, both drug addicts, donned masks and caps and entered the branch.

The anti-robbery team sealed off the block, hoping to keep residents away in case of a shooting.

The two suspects emerged from the bank with twenty thousand dollars in a satchel, then defied the FBI agents on scene, who had identified themselves and ordered them to stop.

The lawmen surrounded the light blue Datsun as the suspects attempted to drive through the ring of agents, witnesses later attested.

The car struck an FBI agent, who landed on the hood. Law enforcement, including Nelson, opened fire, and the Datsun crashed less than one hundred yards away: One suspect, still wearing a stocking mask and a ski cap, died at the scene. The other was pronounced dead at Maimonides Hospital. The agent was not seriously injured.[71]

Note that during this same period, Nelson also participated in multiple investigations involving homicides of members of law enforcement. That included the previously mentioned cases of the July 1988 shooting at the Bronx VA Hospital of VA Police Officer Ronald Hearn, the October 1988 murder of NYPD Officer Christopher G. Hoban, and the cold-blooded assassination of DEA Agent Everett E. Hatcher, whom Nelson knew personally.

Moreover, at this same time, Nelson was investigating everything from domestic violence involving families to hostage crises and suicidal veterans.

As cases pile up, agents develop coping mechanisms to dull their emotional responses. This might help them function in the short term, but it can lead to a sense of detachment from their own emotions or the world around them.

And there is a limit.

The FBI, at around this time, recognized these traumatic events as "critical incidents" which have the potential to forever change an FBI agent's life, and perhaps the lives of their family members. Consequently, agents who were involved in critical incidents— such as Nelson, who discharged his weapon on three occasions during that period—especially when there is loss of life, were sent to the FBI Academy at Quantico, Virginia, where they were afforded "peer support."

Very often, law enforcement officers involved in critical incidents are reticent to discuss the emotional impact they experienced. They usually tend to outwardly exhibit a macho attitude and a reluctance to let anyone, especially another law enforcement officer, know that they are hurting or suffering emotionally from the traumatic event. It's only natural for some agents to feel irrationally that if they had only done something a little differently, perhaps their situation might have had a better ending. After all, in many cases, how could it have turned out any worse?

---

71. Barron, James. "Agents Kill Two Linked to Series of Bank Thefts." New York Times. January 19, 1990. https://www.nytimes.com/1990/01/19/nyregion/agents-kill-two-linked-to-series-of-bank-thefts.html

"I found that the FBI peer support program had been an effective tool in getting agents to open up and vent their feelings," Nelson says. "It was an environment where some felt safe enough to admit they are human, and that they had been hurt by life or otherwise adversely affected by what happened to them."

While he found the training helpful, he would face more trauma on the road ahead.

In the mid-morning hours of July 31, 1992, Nelson responded to an armed robbery in progress at the Finance Office of the base at Fort Hamilton.

"It just so happened that I maintained an off-site FBI office with the US Army Criminal Investigation Division (CID) on the army base," Nelson recalls, "so I was only seconds away from the robbery in progress and accompanied by CID Agent Jaime Davila."

Despite Nelson's urgency, upon his arrival, the subjects had just fled the scene and managed to escape.

Within twenty minutes of the Finance Office robbery, a report of a robbery in progress with "shots fired" at the Manufacturers Hanover Bank on 4th Avenue and 51st Street in Sunset Park was transmitted by the NYPD over Nelson's citywide radio.

Two employees of Globe Wholesale Company were about to deposit between six thousand and twelve thousand dollars when they were confronted by several men. The descriptions of the robbers were identical to those of the subjects who had just robbed the Finance Office, and the robbery at the bank was only minutes away.

Upon arriving at the bank, Nelson immediately met up with two NYPD friends, Detectives Anthony "Tony" Angotti and "Billy Jack" Tomasulo, both of whom were assigned to the Brooklyn South Homicide Task Force.

"At the crime scene, I learned that two subjects had just robbed a payroll truck transporting cash from the Globe Tobacco Company to the Manufacturers Hanover Bank," Nelson reports.

Then he learned what no member of law enforcement ever wants to hear—during the robbery, one of the subjects, later identified as Arnold Stover, had shot and killed retired NYPD Lieutenant Robert Nesbitt, now serving as the company's security director, who had been escorting the cash shipment to the bank.

Nesbitt drew his semi-automatic handgun and exchanged fire. Mortally wounded, he bravely fired at Stover. Despite being shot seven times, Stover was transported to Lutheran Hospital in critical condition and later survived his wounds.

The second subject escaped in a white van, which was later recovered. It had been reported stolen. The recovered van was processed for fingerprints, and a latent print was developed on the passenger side door handle.

That print was identified as identical to that of an individual named James Goolsby.

An interview with Stover at the hospital determined that he, Goolsby, and an unknown person with the first name "Jimmy" committed the robbery using the stolen white van that was driven by Jimmy.

Stover was also wearing a wristwatch with an organizer that contained a number and a possible location for Goolsby.

"However, despite this evidence, the Brooklyn District Attorney's Office would not authorize the arrest of Goolsby, even though we developed information that he was about to flee to South Carolina," Nelson says.

The DA's office wanted an additional investigation.

"Detectives Angotti, Tomasulo, and I believed there was sufficient evidence for an arrest, and we did not want Goolsby to escape New York State," Nelson says. He knew he needed to act quickly. "So, on August 5, 1992, I arrested Goolsby and Stover on federal charges since the DA's office had no jurisdiction over my decisions." Nelson was fully aware of the consequences of such an action.

"My actions set off a firestorm of objections and protests by the Brooklyn DA's Office to the US Attorney's Office in Brooklyn," he remembers. The Brooklyn DA's Office wanted the case tried in State court. "Ultimately, we turned the case back over for prosecution by New York State, but at least we had achieved our objective of not allowing Goolsby to flee New York."

Subsequently, Detectives Angotti and Tomasulo, as well as Nelson, received award plaques for their work on this case. The awards were presented in the office of John Pritchard, who at that time was the first deputy commissioner of the New York City Police Department. Pritchard was also a former FBI agent, and he had been Nelson's roommate at the FBI Academy.

"I was also honored during this ceremony to have my dear friend Kenny McCabe in attendance as well as another good friend, Lieutenant Robert 'Bob' Azzinari, the commanding officer of the Brooklyn South Homicide Squad," Nelson says.

Yet this recognition was bittersweet, and it's not what Nelson remembers of the incident.

A police spokesman, Lieutenant Raymond O'Donnell, said Nesbitt was a member of the police department from 1961 to 1980 and was assigned to the 67th Precinct in Brooklyn when he retired because of a disability.

"My personal experience has been that same sense of belonging to a law enforcement family extends even into retirement," Nelson says. "And when I think back, when I look back—look at the plaques, the pictures, the press—that's not what stays with me. No. I remember Robert Nesbitt and so many others we lost, and I remember them like family, like a deep loss, and I think of their families, their fates. And it's a deep sadness that never goes away."

CHAPTER FORTY-FOUR

On June 21, 1989, Special Agent Anthony Nelson responded to a call regarding a suspected poisoning of federal workers. Throughout that day, at the federal Food and Drug Administration offices at 830 3rd Avenue in Sunset Park, Brooklyn, several employees fell ill mysteriously.

"I responded to the FDA complex with my partner, Special Agent Michael Falcone, to determine what transpired at the facility," Nelson recalls.

A year older, Michael Falcone was Anthony Nelson's day-to-day partner on the FBI's Fugitive Squad from 1988 until 1993. Before going on to a distinguished career with the Bureau, Falcone served six years as a police officer in Westchester County, New York. He entered duty with the FBI already with a degree in accounting and later earned a law degree.

"We learned that an electrician immediately became violently ill after taking a drink of water from a PURO Corporation portable water cooler in the building," Nelson says. The electrician was rushed by ambulance to Methodist Hospital in nearby Park Slope, then transferred to Lutheran Hospital for further treatment. "We then learned that several other people began to fall ill after drinking from that same water cooler."

The FDA notified the PURO Water Corporation that its products may be contaminated. This had the potential to be highly destructive for the provider. If the PURO water caused the illness, it would require a recall, possibly setting off a panic with dire financial consequences, not to mention regulatory and brand impact.

It was somewhat of a stroke of luck that this particular crime occurred at an FDA facility.

Many poisons leave telltale signs and are relatively easy to discover. Others, such as cyanide, evaporate or dissipate quickly, making detection of the crime difficult, especially if significant time has passed before investigation. Moreover, cyanide is metabolized quickly in the body, so the detection window is short. If too much time passes after the poisoning, cyanide levels may become too low to accurately detect. Even the ability to detect a substance like cyanide requires specialized forensic equipment, like gas chromatography or mass spectrometry devices.

These are not easily accessible, unless the crime happens to occur at a facility with the expertise and equipment used in "protecting the public health by ensuring the safety, efficacy, and security of human and veterinary drugs, biological products, and medical devices; and by ensuring the safety of our nation's food supply, cosmetics, and products that emit radiation."[72]

"On June 22, 1989, the FDA informed me that they conducted tests on the water in the suspect cooler," Nelson says, "and determined it contained an extremely high amount of cyanide, approximately one and a half to three grams."

Cyanide poisoning is nasty business for an investigator.

For one thing, it can cause a painful death within minutes. By the time symptoms are recognized, the victim may be incapacitated, or even deceased, and unable to respond to questions.

Unlike other forms of poisoning, cyanide doesn't always leave noticeable external marks. The victim may appear to have died from natural causes, especially if death was quick, complicating the initial diagnosis. Cyanide poisoning also shares symptoms with other medical conditions, such as heart attacks, strokes, or

---

72. Office of the Commissioner. "What We Do." U.S. Food and Drug Administration. November 21, 2023. https://www.fda.gov/about-fda/what-we-do

seizures. Criminally speaking, for these reasons, cyanide is often associated with premeditated acts.

"Special Agent Falcone and I determined the cyanide had to have been placed in the water cooler between four and five p.m. on June 21, 1989," Nelson explains. "This narrowed down our list of suspects to just a few people."

After conducting several interviews, Nelson and Falcone concluded that the cyanide was most likely placed in the cooler by an employee of a cleaning service contracted by the FDA. With a bit more legwork, the agents homed in on a suspect, Hector Cabassa.

The agents took Cabassa in for questioning. During the interview, Cabassa admitted he stole the cyanide from a laboratory at the FDA facility. He then poisoned the water cooler in the office of his boss, Frank Cruz, on June 21, 1989.

The motive?

"Cabassa said that he hated his boss, Cruz," Nelson says. "He hated him so much that he wanted to kill him. But he did not intend to hurt any of the other FDA employees or contract staff."

Fortunately, cyanide is water soluble. "If Cabassa had placed the cyanide in the cooler earlier than he did and it had not had the time to dissolve and degrade to some extent," Nelson suspects, "many more people may have consumed higher concentrations and become ill or died."

Nelson placed Cabassa under arrest for reckless endangerment. He was arraigned on the charges in Brooklyn federal court and remanded to prison.

On April 30, 1990, Nelson was given an award by then Director of the FBI William Sessions for not just solving this case and preventing the loss of life, but also staving off financial disaster for the PURO Water Corporation.

Another interesting case Anthony Nelson fielded at a federal facility involved one of the earlier uses of DNA as an investigative tool.

The FBI began widespread use of DNA technology in criminal investigations around 1988, even establishing a DNA Analysis

Unit within its laboratory. In the years prior, the Bureau was still getting its arms around the new technology.

"In the early 1980s, during periodic training, I learned that the FBI was spearheading a scientific effort to identify subjects based upon analysis of human DNA," Nelson says. "However, during that early period, it was an arduous process and required several weeks for examinations to be completed."

For that reason, and others, the FBI Laboratory was limiting requests for analysis to serious violent crimes, such as murders and rapes.

"I had an early 1980s case which I felt was within those parameters," Nelson says. The puzzle he sought to solve through DNA testing was one of paternity. "When I submitted the DNA request to the FBI Lab, a technician called me to say that he couldn't process my request. It was my fault for arguing with him, as I believed he was telling me my case was not important enough to use DNA testing."

The technician then explained he literally could not conduct the examination requested.

"Apparently, the FBI DNA technology during that early period was not perfected enough to conduct such an examination. Today, you could get the results back within hours."

By the 1990s, the Bureau's DNA testing capabilities improved dramatically. In 1994, the FBI launched a national DNA database, CODIS (Combined DNA Index System), enabling the comparison of DNA profiles from crime scenes and convicted offenders. This system became fully operational in 1998.

According to the Department of Justice, "DNA is generally used to solve crimes in one of two ways. In cases where a suspect is identified, a sample of that person's DNA can be compared to evidence from the crime scene. The results of this comparison may help establish whether the suspect committed the crime. In cases where a suspect has not yet been identified, biological evidence from the crime scene can be analyzed and compared to offender profiles in DNA databases to help identify the perpetrator."[73]

"The next time I requested another DNA examination was in 1992," Nelson says. "Ironically, it indirectly resulted in the dismissal of rape charges against a subject who was, in all probability, guilty of multiple sexual assaults, if not rapes."

Nelson received a complaint from a young Latina intern working in the Bronx Veterans Administration Hospital. "She reported she'd been raped by her supervisor, who was very well respected by most officials at the facility," Nelson says.

Kenny McCabe was now working as a criminal investigator for the US Attorney's Office in the Southern District of New York.

"Kenny and I had been out on the street working an organized crime matter, but we diverted to the Bronx VA Hospital to investigate the rape complaint," Nelson says.

After interviewing the victim and sending her to a local hospital, Nelson retrieved the rape kit, which he sent to the FBI Laboratory for DNA analysis. He also asked Special Agent Jason Randazzo to assist with the investigation.

Jason Randazzo—like Jim Murphy and John Pritchard, two other heroes mentioned in this book—was also a former NYPD officer who decided after six years in the NYPD to switch agencies and join the FBI, followed by his time conducting investigations involving bank robberies, fugitives, kidnappings, extortions, and other assorted personal crimes. Now retired, Randazzo enjoys a second career as a successful author with two well-received books to his credit about his years of service, *Just Another Day*, published in 2020, and *The Day After: The Life and Times of a New York FBI Agent*, which made its debut in 2023, in which he writes about this case from pages 168 to 171.

Nelson obtained the assistance of an assistant US attorney named Fran Fragos from the Southern District of New York on the possible prosecution.

---

73. "ADVANCING JUSTICE THROUGH DNA TECHNOLOGY: USING DNA TO SOLVE CRIMES." March 7, 2017. https://www.justice.gov/archives/ag/advancing-justice-through-dna-technology-using-dna-solve-crimes

"Fragos was an outstanding prosecutor who had formerly been an assistant district attorney in the Sex Crimes Unit of the Brooklyn District Attorney's Office," Nelson recalls.

That tireless prosecutor today is now more familiar as Frances M. "Fran" Fragos Townsend, following her 1994 marriage to lawyer John Michael Townsend.

Fran Townsend served as Homeland Security Advisor to President George W. Bush from 2004 to 2007, playing a key role in shaping national security policy during a critical period. She previously held the roles of deputy assistant to the president and deputy national security advisor for combating terrorism. Following her government service, Townsend transitioned into the private sector, becoming executive vice president for corporate affairs, corporate secretary, and chief compliance officer at Activision Blizzard. She held that position until September 2022 when Microsoft acquired the company in a landmark seventy-five-billion-dollar deal.

Townsend also built a media presence, initially joining CNN as a contributor in 2008 before moving to CBS, where she now serves as a national security analyst. In addition, she has served as president of the Counter Extremism Project, an organization focused on combating radicalization and terrorist threats.

"Once the intern filed the rape charge against her supervisor, it gave four more women at the facility the courage to come forward and report they'd also been sexually harassed by that supervisor," Nelson recalls. "Two of those four women also claimed they were sexually assaulted by him."

Randazzo conducted interviews for the case alongside Fran Fragos. "Fran and I were then heading up to the Bronx VA Hospital on a regular basis interviewing potential victims, and eventually the supervisor," Randazzo recalls. "And the guy was actually a rising star in the VA hospital community."

Not everyone was convinced of the suspect's guilt.

"I remember how much the investigation bothered this one supervisor because she couldn't believe he would do something like that," Randazzo says. "She was defensive and actually became offended. But then, as we found other victims, she changed her tune."

The suspect was arrested and charged with one count of rape and nine counts of aggravated sexual abuse.

Then came the surprise.

"The FBI Laboratory did, indeed, find semen in the rape kit specimen," Nelson says. "But the DNA did *not* belong to the subject that Jason Randazzo and I arrested."

Fran Fragos requested the intern meet at Nelson's FBI office; the victim was joined by her mother to discuss the lab results.

"The intern then admitted that she had sex earlier that same day with her boyfriend during her lunch hour," Nelson says. "But she adamantly claimed that her supervisor did, in fact, sexually attack her, penetrating her with his finger."

The victim did not realize that the digital penetration under federal law was just as serious a crime, as she wanted the supervisor to face the most serious charges for what he had done to her.

"All of a sudden, the intern's mother began to repeatedly slap her daughter all around my office in the FBI building until I restrained her," Nelson says. "The worst part of this whole episode was that Fragos had to dismiss the charges against the supervisor."

Jason Randazzo and Fran Fragos did the necessary but uncomfortable task of going up to the Bronx VA Hospital and explaining to the other victims that the case of the original victim could not go forward due to an issue of her credibility, which would compromise her testimony in court. "We were willing to continue with the case involving the remaining victims," Randazzo adds. "However, after initial reluctance, but later receiving wholehearted support from the VA administration, the dismissal of the first victim, coupled with their trepidation of testifying against a former rising star of the hospital staff, they individually decided they did not want to have further involvement in the prosecution.

"He used his position to victimize these women, and unfortunately, the first victim had this dent in her credibility, and that, and other factors, deterred the victims. Unfortunately, this was a case that did not end in a conviction."

However, the predator was dealt with, though not prosecuted.

"The supervisor was dismissed from his job at the hospital," Nelson says, "But as I said, ironically, the DNA technology probably freed a guilty sex abuser."

Today, DNA testing is a key tool in the law enforcement's arsenal.

On April 21, 2021, a significant milestone was reached in one of US law enforcement's most powerful investigative resources—the national DNA database surpassed twenty million profiles submitted through the CODIS software. CODIS enables authorities to match unidentified DNA collected from crime scenes with samples provided by individuals legally obligated to submit their genetic information, helping to connect offenders to previously unsolved crimes.

After the FBI launched the national DNA database in 1998, the program began with only nine participating states. It quickly expanded to include all fifty states, forming the foundation for a nationwide forensic network.

Today, CODIS is in use at 203 federal, state, and local laboratories across the United States. It enables seamless sharing of DNA profiles among all fifty states, the District of Columbia, Puerto Rico, federal agencies, and the Department of Defense. Additionally, fifty-eight countries utilize CODIS software for their own law enforcement needs, though these international systems remain separate from the US national database. The systems are kept separate due to differing laws concerning the privacy of genetic material, data privacy security risks, and variations in legal and ethical standards in the DNA collection process.

Under the amended DNA Identification Act of 1994, CODIS continues to empower public forensic labs to connect crime scene DNA to other investigations or to individuals already convicted or arrested for qualifying offenses. As DNA collection laws have broadened at state and local levels, the reach and effectiveness of CODIS has grown—contributing to a surge in solved cases and successful prosecutions nationwide.

In addition to criminal investigations, a vital component of the national DNA database focuses on identifying missing persons and unidentified human remains, which offers answers to families and helps close long-standing cases. As of June 2025, CODIS has produced over 761,872 hits assisting in more than 739,456 investigations[74]—made possible by the collaborative efforts of the FBI's CODIS Unit, forensic laboratories, law enforcement agencies, and committed partners across the criminal justice system. Statistics are from all fifty states, the District of Columbia, and Puerto Rico, as well as for the DC/FBI Lab, and US Army.

74. Law Enforcement. "CODIS-NDIS Statistics." August 11, 2025. https://le.fbi.gov/science-and-lab/biometrics-and-fingerprints/codis/codis-ndis-statistics

CHAPTER FORTY-FIVE

Dominick Misino could handle pressure.

In fact, if you were held hostage in the New York area in the decades prior to 1995, Misino probably saved your life.

As the primary hostage negotiator for the NYPD's world-renowned Hostage Negotiation Team (HNT), consisting of 120 trained negotiators, Misino worked more than two hundred hostage and barricade incidents.

Not a single life lost.

So no doubt about it, Misino is a legend in law enforcement, following a distinguished twenty-two-year career, during which he served in the high-pressure Special Operations Division for eighteen years. Misino trained law enforcement personnel from over five hundred departments and agencies, including personnel from many foreign countries.

It was Misino who played a pivotal role in resolving the hijacking of Lufthansa Flight 592 without loss of life.

In February 1993, Nebiu Demeke hijacked a commercial flight en route from Frankfurt, Germany, to Addis Ababa, Ethiopia. Brandishing what appeared to be a real firearm—later determined to be a starter pistol—Demeke forced the crew to divert the aircraft to New York's John F. Kennedy International Airport.

The plane touched down around four p.m. and was directed to a remote section of the runway. A specialized three-man negotiation team quickly mobilized: NYPD's Misino, FBI Agent John Flood, and Port Authority representative Carmine Spano. From the airport's air traffic control tower, they established radio contact with the hijacker.

Through calm and strategic dialogue, Misino convinced Demeke to exchange his weapon for the pilot's sunglasses. Demeke surrendered peacefully soon after. Remarkably, all ninety-four passengers and ten crew members emerged from the ordeal unharmed.

After he retired from the NYPD in 1995, Misino trained law enforcement, military personnel, and civilian corporations both in the US and overseas. Law enforcement personnel representing over four thousand agencies were trained by Dominick Misino in the US alone.

He also authored two of the definitive books on the topic, *Negotiate & Win: Proven Strategies from the NYPD's Top Negotiator* and *Negotiating in the Big Apple*, and founded the International Association of Hostage Negotiators (IAHN).

"There was a saying at the time, which I'm sure is still repeated to this day, that 'when someone needs help, they call a cop, but when a cop needs help, he calls ESU,'" Nelson says. The NYPD ESU is New York City's elite version of what most other police departments call their SWAT team. "But I can tell you story after story from my personal experiences in calling upon ESU that they are much more than a SWAT team."

ESU members are a special breed.

Most members have specific skills beyond special weapons and tactics. Some ESU members Nelson worked with were experts in aviation, plumbing, electrical work, carpentry, construction, and other specialized areas. In 1989, Nelson successfully completed the NYPD's Specialized Training—Tactical Operations Course at Floyd Bennett Field in Brooklyn, conducted by Misino.

"Dominick Misino was one of the most talented officers I've known concerning tactical operations," Nelson says. "In fact, at the time, he was one of the inventors of a new door-breaching device that used air bags to remove any reinforced door from its hinges to make a dynamic entry into a location."

Misino gave Nelson one of his new door-breaching devices in the hope the agent would have an opportunity to use it and then be able to attest to its effectiveness. It did not take long to test the device.

At 11:30 p.m. on February 23, 1990, Nelson was notified that an armed robbery had just occurred at the Adams Guest House, a hotel located at Fort Hamilton: a lone man, armed with a 9mm handgun, had entered the lobby of the Adam's Guest House and stolen $1,400 in cash from the evening receipts.

Over the next few days, Nelson interviewed and re-interviewed the hotel desk clerk. She provided such specific information about the robber that Nelson suspected her story was rehearsed and untrue. Upon further questioning, on March 1, 1990, that desk clerk, Renee Neal, admitted to Nelson that her boyfriend, Calvin Thompson, was the perpetrator who robbed the hotel at gunpoint.

Nelson began the manhunt for Thompson.

"I soon learned that he was hiding in a nineteenth-floor safe house apartment on Hopkinson Avenue in Brooklyn," he recalls.

Nelson formulated an arrest plan that included placing a pretext telephone call to the apartment to get Thompson on the phone.

"Since we had only sought the worst of the worst subjects when I was on the FBI's Fugitive Squad," Nelson explains, "it was my personal tactical preference during a planned arrest to completely surround a house and then place a telephone call into the fugitive's residence." Unless Nelson and his team were also looking for evidence that could be destroyed, this approach to initiate contact usually avoided escalation and produced better outcomes.

Nelson would also request the fugitive to look out a window to confirm that he was surrounded by FBI agents and then demand his surrender.

"Without cell phone technology," he adds, "this technique also required giving up an arrest team member to make that landline call from a remote location or a neighbor's apartment."

Seasoned hostage negotiator FBI Special Agent Charles Williams was dispatched to place the call.

During his twenty-three years at the FBI, Williams was a certified assessor, street survival agent, general police instructor, community outreach specialist, and reserve team member of the FBI New York Crisis Negotiation Team. He worked on numerous top ten fugitive investigations: the Crown Heights investigation, the 1998 United States Embassy Tanzania bombing investigation, and the World Trade Center attacks in 1993 and 2001. Following retirement, Williams founded the private firm of HDI Investigation, Inc.

As Williams raced to find a public payphone, he faced challenges uncommon for today's agents.

"The nearest payphone was a couple of blocks away," Nelson recalls. "And by then, I knew to always keep a stash of quarters on hand when needed to give to an arrest team member to make the phone call."

The plan worked. Williams engaged Thompson in a conversation for over ten minutes while Nelson and the arrest team made their way up to the nineteenth floor of the housing project.

Along the way, Nelson lugged Misino's new door-breaching tool, which was extremely heavy.

"When we arrived at the nineteenth-floor apartment, we could hear Thompson through the door, still engaged with Williams on the telephone," Nelson says. "My arrest team consisted of Special Agents Michael Henehan, Barry Higginbotham, Thomas Sinnott, and Michael Falcone." These agents, as well as Nelson and Williams, were seasoned members of the FBI's Fugitive Squad.

"We were used to going out together several times each week to pursue the worst of the worst fugitives, and we completely trusted each other. As a matter of fact, Mike Henehan, in my opinion, was the most proficient FBI agent I had ever known when it came to tactical situations."

A decorated combat veteran of the Marine Corps, Henehan went on to a successful twenty-five-year career with the FBI, where he designed, directed, and managed special operations supporting US foreign counterintelligence interests. He received many awards for his work over the years, including the Director of

Central Intelligence Award as the Outstanding Human Intelligence Gatherer for the Intelligence Community.

"Once we were in place at the apartment door, Williams told Thompson his true identity and further instructed him to open the apartment door for us," Nelson says. Still, it took several minutes before one of the occupants of the apartment let the team inside the building. "Although we knew Thompson had been in the apartment, because we had heard him speaking with Williams, he was nowhere to be found."

It didn't make sense. The team was on the nineteenth floor, and there were no nearby fire escapes that would have allowed the suspect to flee.

Falcone and Nelson then carefully made their way outside onto the balcony of the apartment. It was winter, and it had recently snowed. Falcone noticed footprints in the snow along the three-inch-wide railing of the balcony.

"Falcone and I then realized that Thompson had balanced himself along the railing, somehow bypassed a barrier wall, and forcibly entered an adjacent apartment on the nineteenth floor," Nelson says. "How he didn't fall to his death doing so is beyond my understanding."

Suddenly, the agents heard screaming from the adjacent apartment: Thompson had taken hostages.

Preparing for the worst, Nelson set Misino's new breaching tool in place on the adjacent apartment door, just in case the agents needed to gain immediate access to the apartment where hostages were now being held.

First, however, the agents attempted to engage Thompson in conversation before executing a dynamic entry into the apartment.

A dynamic entry is a last resort. More than just forced entry, it involves a rapid, surprise breach to overwhelm suspects before they can react—often to protect hostages, preserve evidence, or gain control of a space.

FBI field agents are trained to execute these high-risk entries under strict command protocols. While effective, they carry significant danger for officers. Experts suggest dynamic entry is most appropriate in highly vulnerable areas like hallways or stairwells, after which agents should shift to slower, more deliberate clearing methods once the threat level drops.

For more than an hour, Mike Henehan and Nelson engaged Thompson in dialogue, alternately trying to convince him to surrender but to no avail. By that point, Nelson had requested backup from the NYPD ESU and a hostage negotiator.

"Within several minutes of my request, however, noises were coming from the apartment that led us to believe the hostages were being threatened," Nelson remembers.

This is what makes law enforcement different from almost any other profession that needs to make split-second decisions, based on inadequate or non-existent information, when the stakes are life and death.

"Our arrest team decided it was time to make a dynamic entry," Nelson says. "As I inflated the air bags of Misino's tool and the apartment door began to creak, the door suddenly opened and two of the hostages came running out."

Neither of the hostages had been hurt, and the agents quickly escorted them to safety.

This was the kind of split-second decision-making situation that FBI agents dread and most regular people cannot fathom.

"It was not the first time I faced it," Nelson says. "Nevertheless, it's a part of the job. But it's also the part that keeps me awake at night."

By this time, ESU had arrived on scene and had taken positions above and below the nineteenth floor in case Thompson performed another acrobatic trick.

Fortunately, Thompson decided to surrender, revealing the threat was real. He turned over a loaded 9mm handgun, a loaded .32-caliber revolver, hundreds of rounds of 9mm ammunition, and more than one hundred empty crack cocaine vials.

This incident took place a little over a month after Nelson, with other FBI agents and NYPD detectives, was involved in a deadly shooting during the robbery of the Hamilton Federal Savings Bank.

"Both bank robbers were shot and killed during that incident," Nelson says. "I had enough violence etched into my mind, so luckily it wasn't compounded by something going wrong during the standoff with Thompson."

Meanwhile, the Adams House incident demonstrated again how communications challenges made life difficult for agents.

Still, they got the job done.

"Even when we secretly placed a beeper on a subject's vehicle to track its location," Nelson says, "we still had to physically drive around wide areas to locate the signal."

Analog beepers emit a radio signal that can be picked up by directional antennas or receivers. Agents could follow a vehicle discreetly from a distance, minimizing the risk of being spotted in a traditional tail. But there's a limit to the range. The investigative team had to hope the beeper's battery held out, as it lasted only a few days.

"Just think that today, anyone can place a twenty-five-dollar smart tag inside a vehicle and track its location on Google Maps for months," Nelson says.

Like other agents, during everyday investigative work, Nelson was limited to receiving messages over his FBI car radio or portable transceiver to call the office.

"I just accepted that burden as a fact of life, but it certainly was not easy, especially in rough neighborhoods where most of the payphones had been vandalized," he remembers.

Nelson, like most agents, learned to improvise.

"Since I had been an electronics technician with the Bureau," he says, "I still had my handheld telephone installer's clip-on handset, which I kept in my car."

Using this device in apartment buildings on a handful of occasions enabled Nelson to go to the building's telephone company frame, usually located in the basement.

"I would clip my handset onto a working phone line of a building resident and place a telephone call to the subject's apartment," Nelson says. Easier than sprinting for a local payphone, but he admits this was usually not an option. Access to the frame was typically limited.

Despite how arrests are depicted in Hollywood, Nelson avoided forcibly entering whenever he could.

"Fugitives knew the layout of their apartments better than we did," he explains. "They could hide, gain access to weapons, forcibly resist, and you were always at a disadvantage." Instead of kicking down the door, Nelson always preferred calling into the location and talking them into surrender.

"I don't mean to say that every arrest was that dramatic, but it was appropriate for fugitives who were considered armed and dangerous."

Of course, without cell phone technology, this technique was not always easy.

In 1991, Special Agent Anthony Nelson received a call to respond to another crisis unfolding in the apartment of Denise Best, a US Army Sergeant, located at Fort Hamilton.

Sometime earlier, the sergeant's husband, Errol Best, secretly attached a tape recorder to his home telephone, believing his wife had been cheating on him.

Gunshots were reported. The Best family included two young children who lived in the apartment.

Nelson later learned that Best converted a British STEN blowback-operated submachine gun to fully automatic.

FBI Special Agent Jason Randazzo was also on the scene that day.

"As an agent responding, you don't always know what you're walking into, but you've investigated similar crimes, been in similar situations, so you draw on those experiences," Randazzo says. "It takes a lot to get someone to that breaking point, and it's sad, and you feel for them. But as an agent, you need to focus on the crime and the situation. It's not an easy thing to process.

"With this case, the male was on the phone with her family, called the family, shot her dead for cheating, and the body was up against the door just as we're trying to get into the unit," Randazzo says.

"After he shot and killed her, she landed against the inside front door of their apartment," Nelson adds, "so to preserve the crime scene, neither the Military Police nor I nor Special Agent Michael Falcone were able to open the front door."

Ultimately, Nelson, Falcone, and Randazzo, along with Army Criminal Investigative Division officers, commandeered the resident's apartment next door to use the phone, gain access to a fire escape, and then a window to enter the Best apartment.

"Errol Best used that submachine gun to kill his wife, and then he killed himself," Nelson remembers.

He did this in front of his two young children, though he did not hurt them—at least not physically.

"I was always so protective of children," Nelson says. "So walking into this scene, it's something that has stayed with me over the years. But it's not the only one, just one of the many cases I get to relive at night."

This was 1991, and that lack of access to cellular communications technology had other harsh consequences you won't see on statistical reports.

"I can't tell you the number of times that I, and most other FBI agents in the Criminal Division, were diverted to emergency situations while in our FBI cars and could not call home," Nelson says. "Not being able to cancel an everyday dinner, a child's birthday party, an anniversary, a formal affair, or just an expected delay returning home, that causes issues."

This is a reality of law enforcement from that era that they don't show on the screen—the inability to connect when it counts. This disruption and destruction of countless marriages, this slow-burning shattering of families, this damaging of relationships between parents and children, is heartbreaking.

"I've been beyond lucky to have my wife, Syndee, who over so many years has been so supportive, understanding, and accepting of the realities of my job," Nelson says. "It has not been fair to her, and I am sorry on such a deep level, as I am sure she's been disappointed, worried, concerned, on so many occasions, when I did not show up at home, and there were no phone calls, and she just … waited.

"So sure, cell phones just did not exist at the time, so we couldn't miss them. But I have to say, we sure could've used them."

CHAPTER FORTY-SIX

Some call it "choir practice."

Others call it "the Weekly."

Some don't call it anything at all.

And some of them can be legendary.

Like Mama Tury's on Thursdays.

Ever since there's been law enforcement, its members have gathered afterhours to blow off steam, swap stories, and compare case notes.

"Although I found FBI Peer Support to be a worthwhile program, my personal source of validation for any of my feelings had always been my dear friend Kenny McCabe," Nelson says.

It started in the early 1980s. Not long after the two lawmen started their nighttime rides, they began meeting for a working lunch just about every Thursday or Friday, circumstances permitting. They'd update each other on ongoing cases, share the latest intel, and trade photographs of wiseguys who were of interest to them.

"But maybe more importantly, we'd sometimes spend the entire time just discussing what was going on in our personal lives," Nelson says.

So Mama Tury's on 86th Street in Brooklyn became a regular spot.

During one lunch in 1982, McCabe and Nelson walked in on Gambino Crew chief Roy DeMeo. He was sitting at a table with one of the representatives of a Cadillac dealership located a short distance from the restaurant.

"Roy drove a Cadillac, and this meeting may have just been benign and related to his vehicle lease," Nelson speculates.

However, the trained eyes of the two lawmen spotted more familiar faces as several other Gambino Family members were seated nearby, though dining separately from Roy.

Also present, alone at his own table, was a bookie the NYPD labeled as a "KG," meaning "known gambler." For the purposes of this story, let's call this bookmaker "Nicky R."

In a bizarre scene you could only rip out of pages of real-life 1980s Brooklyn, all organized crime figures present were carrying on independently ... until law enforcement strolled into the restaurant.

"As Kenny and I sat down to eat lunch, we were getting sarcastic glares from the Gambino members, so it was obvious we interrupted their plans to have conversations of a criminal nature," Nelson recalls.

Strangely, Roy DeMeo did not acknowledge their presence and even seemed unaware they were seated in the back of the small restaurant.

"Kenny turned his head toward the front of the restaurant and was debating whether he should take out his camera and photograph what he called the 'three faces of the Mafia,'" Nelson relates.

At one table were three Gambino soldiers known for labor racketeering, extortion, and infiltrating operations at the Port of New York and New Jersey.

"In contrast was Roy DeMeo, who conceivably could have just murdered someone, cut him into pieces, stuffed him into garbage bags, and still came to have lunch at Mama Tury's," Nelson says.

Lastly, there was Nicky R., the well-known gambler and bookmaker, reportedly liked by most who knew him, even by some law enforcement officers.

Just as McCabe was describing this only-in-Brooklyn scene from an Italian restaurant unfolding across those three tables at Mama Tury's, Nicky R. abruptly got up from his seat.

He brought a portion of the meal he was eating outside and handed it to a homeless person who was panhandling out on the 86th Street sidewalk.

It was an act of kindness that almost inspired McCabe and Nelson to pay for Nicky R's lunch.

Almost.

"That would have been inappropriate," Nelson clarifies.

So it appears in 1980s Brooklyn, not all gangsters were created equally.

Before long, these lunches at Mama Tury's grew to include members of the Brooklyn Central Robbery Squad as well as a revolving cast of major crime fighters of the era. There was Ron Cadieux, Al King, Tony Angotti, Frank Pergola, and many others.

"Anthony Nelson was close with a number of NYPD heavy hitters," says retired NYPD Detective Tommy Dades, ten years Nelson's junior. "Don't believe what some tell you that it was all about rivalries and there was no cooperation. Anthony—how he and the other agents and supervisors in the BQ office collaborated with the NYPD—was critical in so many cases. It wasn't just about work. These guys had a higher purpose. And for the younger guys, like me, it was important."

As one of these younger guys, Dades was invited to the Thursday lunches. "You'd walk downstairs to this Italian restaurant, and there they'd be, all these legends, just shooting the breeze, comparing notes, discussing cases," he says.

"You name it—the DeMeo case, the Castellano case, the Commission Case, and so many more; these were the guys that everybody wanted to talk to all the time," Dades adds. "And let me tell you, Anthony and the rest of these guys, they forgot more than I know."

In most fields, the next generation is rarely welcome in such an exclusive setting.

"Sure, I went, and remember, I'm still wet behind the ears," Dades says. "You're in awe of these guys, and you'd think they wouldn't be open with a young guy. Picture it; everybody at this table is a living legend. And then there's me. But no, they were all great about it, very welcoming and open. Says a lot about character and the kind of people and professionals they were. That's inspiring for a younger guy. Teaches you something and it stays with you."

Dades was not the only younger attendee to those legendary lunches.

"Throughout much of my earlier life, I just remember Anthony always being around my dad," says Duke McCabe. "I remember those lunches and how they compared notes and cases. My dad would take me every now and then, starting when I was nine or ten years old, all the way up to when I was in college."

Sure, members of the group would frequent other establishments, but it wasn't the same.

"Kenny, Ron, Al King, and I started to eat dinner fairly often at Embers Steakhouse on 3rd Avenue and 96th Street," Nelson recalls. "We knew the owners, Lou and Theresa Rocanelli. The Rocanellis were like family to us."

Less than a mile off the Verrazano Bridge, Embers was frequented by many law enforcement officers, including ranking officers in the NYPD hierarchy.

However, high-level Cosa Nostra members also frequented Embers, sometimes taking seats at the bar or at tables next to off-duty cops who did not know them. "They did this to overhear law enforcement conversations about ongoing criminal activity," Nelson says. "More than once, conversations were picked up on FBI bugs about what some of them overheard at Embers."

McCabe, Cadieux, and Nelson began pointing out wiseguys to Lou Rocanelli so that he could seat them out of earshot of police conversations.

"I was told that the NYPD, at one point, listed Embers as an off-limits premise to local 68th Precinct officers," Nelson says.

This was not a concern at Mama Tury's, and the weekly lunch went on for years.

Then came a fateful lunch that deeply affected Anthony Nelson.

It was a lunch like hundreds of others—until it wasn't.

"It was 1990, during lunch at Mama Tury's that Kenny and I were discussing the involvement of NYPD Detectives Louis Eppolito and Stephen Caracappa in the murder of Eddie Lino," Nelson says.

Edward "Eddie" Lino was a Sicilian-American capo in the Gambino Family and drug trafficker. He was also a cousin of Bonanno Family capo Frank Lino and brother-in-law of Salvatore Scala. Lino was related by marriage to Genovese Family associates Carmine and Francis Consalvo, brothers who worked with Vincent Gigante.

Lino was a close friend of John Gotti, whom he helped to murder Gambino boss Paul Castellano. With Castellano gone, Lino was even more of a force in the Gambino Family as a drug trafficker with ties to African American drug rings in Harlem.

In what was believed to be at least a partial act of revenge for Paul Castellano's 1985 assassination—engineered by John Gotti—Lucchese underboss Anthony "Gaspipe" Casso ordered the murder of Lino.

On November 6, 1990, NYPD Detectives Stephen Caracappa and Louis Eppolito, who were secretly working for Casso, stopped Eddie Lino as he drove his Mercedes-Benz. Moments later, they gunned him down, firing nine shots and leaving him dead at the scene.

Unbeknownst to them at the time, Caracappa and Eppolito were committing crimes on behalf of various crews, but principally for the Luccheses and Gambinos.

They became known as the Mafia Cops.

"Kenny had known much more about the evidence of their involvement than I did, and he was usually right about all of his assessments," Nelson says. "I, on the other hand, had trouble believing that the detectives had shot Lino to death after pulling him over in an NYPD unmarked car."

Nelson knew enough about Louis Eppolito to believe he may have been involved. "But I was having doubts about Caracappa during our lunch," he says.

On one occasion, while Nelson was hunting for Mafia hitman Joseph "Mad Dog" Sullivan, he noticed Eppolito stick his head out of the side employee door of a Chinese restaurant.

Eppolito turned his head quickly back and forth, obviously scanning to see if he was being followed. He then exited the restaurant, smuggling what appeared to be a couple of boxes of lobsters.

"I would've bet anyone at the time that he did not pay the owner for those lobsters," Nelson recalls. "I knew Eppolito could not be trusted, but I was debating with Kenny about Caracappa."

During an investigation, Lucchese associate and government informant Burton Kaplan agreed to testify about his criminal dealings with Caracappa and Eppolito. The two were arrested in March 2005 and charged with racketeering, obstruction of justice, extortion, and eight counts of murder and conspiracy.

These included the homicides of James Hydell, Nicholas Guido, Israel Greenwald, John Heidel, Anthony DiLapi, Bruno Facciolo, Bartholomew Boriello, and Eddie Lino. Kaplan, a businessman and career criminal who served as the buffer between Gaspipe Casso and the two detectives, was the chief accuser and provided two days of riveting testimony at trial. Both were convicted.

Caracappa was initially incarcerated at the United States Penitentiary in Coleman, Florida, before being moved to a federal facility in North Carolina. He died of cancer on April 8, 2017, while serving his sentence.

Eppolito was imprisoned at the United States Penitentiary in Tucson, Arizona. He died on November 3, 2019, while in federal custody at a Tucson hospital. His cause of death has never been disclosed. "I received a letter from Louie Eppolito before he passed away, from a federal correctional facility while he was serving a life sentence plus one hundred years," says Duke. "He referred to my father as the most knowledgeable and respected cop he had ever met. Told me to hold my head up high because I am Kenny McCabe's son."

The case was the subject of a successful *New York Times* bestseller in 2003, *Friends of the Family: The Inside Story of the Mafia Cops Case*, penned by none other than Tommy Dades, with former top Brooklyn prosecutor Mike Vecchione and writer David Fisher.

Yet back in 1990, as Nelson and McCabe debated the case over lunch, the FBI agent noticed something.

Something troubling. "I happened to ask him about a small Band-Aid he had on his ear," Nelson says. "At first, I didn't question him because it just appeared to be a typical shaving cut."

In that fateful moment, McCabe shared with Nelson that he had a small skin cancer growth removed.

The debate about Eppolito and Caracappa then continued without Nelson realizing that Band-Aid would be etched into his memory as deeply as any of the shooting incidents in his career.

"I had no idea at the time that the clock started ticking on the amount of time I had left with my friendship with Kenny," Nelson reflects.

CHAPTER FORTY-SEVEN

In 1993, Special Agent Anthony Nelson responded to a disturbance in Brooklyn where a retired Navy SEAL assaulted federal officers.

Nelson knew from experience that these calls were trouble.

Today, the VA New York Harbor Healthcare System serves hundreds of thousands of veterans annually, including the Brooklyn campus at Poly Place at Fort Hamilton, marked by a massive towering grey monolith that looms over New York Harbor about a mile off the Verrazano Narrows Bridge.

Over the years, Nelson responded to scores of these types of calls, often where suspects are traumatized because of their service. Research shows deployment increases the risk of post-traumatic stress disorder (PTSD); veterans who were deployed are up to three times more likely to experience PTSD than their non-deployed peers from the same service era. Several elements of combat can increase the risk of developing PTSD and other mental health issues, including a service member's role or military specialty, the political climate surrounding the conflict, the geographic location of the war, and the nature of the opposing force.

"It's sad to see so many men and women who go overseas and come back different, harmed mentally, their lives are ruined," says retired FBI Agent Jason Randazzo. "Sometimes they vent those frustrations, and it escalates into an assault. Then it's a tough case. You're interviewing veterans you feel sympathy for, who served our country and are just trying to get the care that they deserve."

Not all veterans seek care through the VA, but those who do are more likely to be diagnosed with PTSD.

According to one study, twenty-three percent of veterans who received treatment through the VA had experienced PTSD at some point in their lives. In contrast, only seven percent of veterans who relied on non-VA healthcare reported the same.[75]

Moreover, specific eras produced more affected veterans, especially those from the Vietnam War, who, at the time Anthony Nelson was assigned to the Bureau's New York Field Office, were increasing statistically in cases reported to the FBI.

This is dangerous work. Former service members, especially combat veterans who suffer from PTSD, may exhibit impulsivity, anger, and difficulties managing stress. These men and women were trained to be on high alert in dangerous environments. They struggle to adjust to civilian life, sometimes reacting inappropriately to perceived threats.

And sadly, many veterans turn to alcohol or drugs to self-medicate to cope with PTSD, anxiety, or depression.

"In some cases, the veterans clearly suffered from PTSD," Nelson says. "Others were addicted to alcohol; others were addicted to drugs. Consequently, I became aware of an increase in drug sales and shylocking taking place among patients, while I was also receiving complaints about some of the vets robbing or conning each other."

In one case, Nelson investigated a group of veterans at the VA hospital who stole another veteran's checkbook and removed a large sum of money from his bank account.

"I interviewed one of the suspects I'd developed who lived in the Six-Eight Precinct not far from where the VA Hospital is located," Nelson says. "It turned out to be one of the worst interviews I ever conducted."

The veteran, a former Navy SEAL, broke down in tears after Nelson confronted him.

Navy SEALs, due to their intense training, high-risk missions, and frequent exposure to combat, are at a significantly increased risk of developing PTSD. And the qualities that make SEALs elite

---

75. Veterans Affairs. "How Common is PTSD in Veterans?" https://www.ptsd.va.gov/understand/common/common_veterans.asp

warriors, not to mention a military culture that stresses strength and toughness, make them unlikely to seek treatment for PTSD.

"He was anything but a criminal," Nelson says. "He'd stolen the checkbook out of desperation. He was penniless, suffering depression and PTSD."

Rather than arrest him, Nelson gave him one of his FBI business cards and told him he would try to resolve the theft issue directly with the victim, who would hopefully just accept an apology and reimbursement.

Later that evening, as Nelson was driving over the Verrazano Bridge, he received a chilling courtesy call from a detective from the 68th Precinct. "She told me that the veteran I had interviewed that same day … just killed himself," Nelson says.

Gripped in the veteran's hand, she added, was Anthony Nelson's business card.

So in 1993, Anthony Nelson knew all too well the volatility to expect when he and Special Agent Michael Falcone responded to the scene while an assault by a former Navy SEAL on federal officers was in progress.

"The veteran had consumed an entire bottle of vodka and the better part of a gram of cocaine," Nelson recalls. "He was struggling with us on a patch of sidewalk ice during a cold January night. As I fell to the ground with him, I literally felt something tear in my back, but Falcone and I managed to subdue him."

When the agents picked up the veteran up for court the next morning, the former service member reported no recollection of fighting them the night before. He was extremely apologetic.

"During my career, I'd always been most protective of children, the elderly, and of veterans who returned to civilian life scarred by the memories of war," Nelson says. "But I could not release this veteran. I did not know if he presented a future danger to anyone. And he obviously needed psychological help."

Anthony Nelson himself would soon need help. He suffered several severe back injuries throughout his career. They were starting to take their toll. Still, he kept on keeping on.

Not much more than a year later, in 1994, Nelson and FBI Special Agent Rodney Davis entered the notorious Red Hook Houses, a sprawling, crime-ridden New York City Housing Authority complex. They sought to apprehend a wanted fugitive.

An address in the Red Hook Houses rented by the fugitive's father surfaced in several background documents Nelson reviewed.

For Anthony Nelson, this was a return to the neighborhood where he'd been born.

But this was no homecoming.

Red Hook was always a rough area. Yet starting in the late 1960s, once shipping containers began to replace bulk shipping, dock workers lost their jobs and the neighborhood fell into stunning decline.

By the 1990s, the Red Hook Houses, the largest public projects in Brooklyn, built in the 1930s as part of the New Deal to house dockworkers, was overrun by rival drug gangs. *Life* ranked Red Hook one of the "worst" neighborhoods in the United States and "the crack capital of America."

Then tragically, the morning of December 17, 1992, popular PS 15 Principal Patrick Daly left school grounds searching for a nine-year-old student who had fled after a fight with another pupil. Daly was slain stepping into a hail of gunfire, caught in the crossfire between rival crack gangs.

The incident drew national condemnation. The school was later renamed the Patrick Daly School in honor of this heroic fallen educator, but it took years before law enforcement and community leaders reclaimed Red Hook.

This was the lethal environment that agents Nelson and Davis entered that morning in pursuit of a fugitive.

Right from the outset, things turned for the worse.

After the agents were permitted entry to the fugitive's father's cramped apartment, the wanted man sprang out from a hiding spot and attacked them in furious hand-to-hand combat.

"We wound up wrestling him down onto a sofa that overturned," Nelson says. "The fugitive, and then Rodney, and then the sofa, all overturned onto me, and I was in an awkward position being crushed by all that weight."

As they grappled with the desperate, violent, well-trained combatant, most likely under the influence of narcotics, the fugitive's father rushed into the room to come to the agents' aid and helped subdue and handcuff his son.

"I was barely able to walk," Nelson recalls. "Rodney broke one of his fingers. We both wound up in Elmhurst Hospital for the remainder of the day."

Unfortunately, that day, just one day of thousands of days as an agent, one arrest out of hundreds upon hundreds of arrests, had lingering, lifelong consequences. Nelson would be plagued by even more severe back issues that he suffers with to this day.

Dealing with incidents involving damaged American veterans takes a physical and mental toll on FBI investigators.

Former FBI Special Agent Jason Randazzo, assigned to Nelson's squad, recalls another haunting case. A teenage girl, a member of a military family stationed at Fort Hamilton, alleged she was sexually abused by a friend of her mother. The assault, she said, occurred on the base after the father was deployed overseas.

"With the father overseas, the female, his wife, and their children, stayed at Fort Hamilton, where she became friendly with a coworker with whom she worked in nearby Bay Ridge," Randazzo says.

The mother invited this coworker to the house on the base to watch the children while she attended to errands. The daughter had two friends come to the house, also from a military family.

Sometime later, when the father came home, they left Fort Hamilton for reassignment to Germany.

However, it later came out through counseling in therapy that the girl, a minor, recounted a sexual assault that occurred that day at Fort Hamilton.

"That must have been about a year after the crime was committed in Brooklyn, and they were now overseas," Randazzo says. "So, obviously, they get army investigators involved, CID (Criminal Investigation Division) at Fort Hamilton gets involved, and then

I'm assigned to work the investigation, which means going to Germany to interview the victim."

Randazzo enlisted an agent from the FBI squad specializing in cases where children are abused. "I called the supervisor, asked to help me out since talking to young females who were victims of sexual assaults is delicate, and they have that experience," he says. "So I worked with that agent and we went to those locations and interviewed, and the victims all recounted the sexual abuse."

Through diligent investigation, Randazzo was able to identify two more female victims, one in a small town in Texas and the other in Nashville.

"So we also interviewed them during successive trips to their new residences," Randazzo says. "By then, the perpetrator was living in Queens, out by Shea Stadium (which is now Citi Field), and fortunately, through these efforts, it resulted in arresting him and getting him to plead."

CHAPTER FORTY-EIGHT

In 1990, after having been involved in the bank robbery shooting incident, Special Agent Anthony Nelson was sent to the FBI Academy in Quantico to attend a Peer Support Critical Incident seminar.

FBI research indicates roughly two-thirds of police officers involved in shooting incidents may experience significant emotional reactions. Line-of-duty shootings, death, suicide, serious injury of co-workers, homicides, and hostage situations are considered critical incidents that may leave agents with an overwhelming sense of vulnerability and lack of control.[76]

Anthony Nelson has been involved in all these scenarios.

The Bureau developed the Critical Incident Stress Management (CISM) program to promote the psychological well-being of FBI employees following traumatic experiences. The CISM program shares techniques for defusing critical incidents, stress debriefings, peer or one-on-one support, family assistance, management support, referral and follow-up services, eye movement desensitization and reprocessing, and post-critical incident management.[77]

The seminar Nelson attended included a speech delivered by retired Navy fighter pilot Captain Charles Plumb.

Plumb described flying a combat mission during the Vietnam War when his aircraft was shot down by the North Vietnamese military.

---

76. "FBI's Critical Incident Stress Management Program | Office of Justice Programs." https://www.ojp.gov/ncjrs/virtual-library/abstracts/fbis-critical-incident-stress-management-program

Ejected from his fighter jet, he was captured by the enemy and held as a prisoner of war for six years. He spent those years in captivity in an eight-by-eight-foot cell. A number of other heroic US pilots were also being held in that prison camp, including former Senator John McCain.

"Charlie Plumb's story was so captivating that I can almost remember every word of it," Nelson recalls.

It's impossible to not be humbled by the heroic humility of Plumb. His memoir is actually titled, *I'm No Hero—A POW Story.*

The theme of his speech that day was entitled "Overcoming Adversity," where Plumb described his ordeal in that prison and reflected upon his life.

"One of Charlie's thoughts, and regrets, centered upon a realization that, despite his many accomplishments, including flying seventy-five combat missions over Vietnam, he'd never fully appreciated some people who supported him in his life and career," Nelson says.

Those of lesser rank, status, and recognition than Plumb, but nevertheless critical to his survival, Plumb affectionately called, "parachute packers." Someone had to have packed his parachute properly, the one that saved him when he ejected from his downed jet. He didn't pack the chute. And he probably passed that person in the halls of his command, not recognizing him for his work, or even to say hello.

Charlie Plumb was a Navy commissioned officer, a graduate from the US Naval Academy in Annapolis, Maryland, and he flew fighter jets.

This enlisted man simply packed the parachute.

"Charlie could not have cared less about thanking him for his work," Nelson recalls, "until he ejected from his downed jet and that parachute flawlessly opened and saved his life."

Listening to Plumb at that seminar, Nelson experienced a rush of clarity.

"I realized that there had been many occasions during my FBI career when I was engaged in special operations, when I too had been in the company of humble, selfless, nameless parachute packers," Nelson says. "And I never properly thanked or recognized them for the heroic work they performed."

During particularly dangerous arrests, the FBI may request New York City Fire Department Emergency Medical Technicians to stand by at the scene if an agent or police officer is injured.

"We also regularly relied on NYPD Emergency Service Units," Nelson adds. "We relied on our radio dispatchers to get us help and on our support employees to get us critical info or perform key duties. Everyone within our organization contributed to our war on crime."

The doctors and paramedics who treat gunshot wounds, plane crash victims, or injuries at mass casualty incidents Nelson calls silent heroes who are rarely identified, recognized, or properly thanked for their efforts. "There's a very small percentage of people who could perform the specialized duties carried out by many of these parachute packers, but their work is essential in assisting front-line law enforcement officers," he says.

Anthony Nelson has many, many examples.

On March 19, 1996, he responded with a team of agents to enter the hull of a bulk container ship named the *Ostfriesland*. Nelson and his squad members joined the Coast Guard to investigate the 496-foot vessel at Pier 11 in Red Hook at dawn.

The ship, registered under a Singapore flag, arrived at a pier in Brooklyn from West Africa. Three men seeking a better life in America suffocated in the sealed hold of that cargo ship after the crew unknowingly fumigated the area where the stowaways were hiding.[77] Their remains were discovered seventeen days after the freighter departed from the port of Abidjan along the Ivory Coast. The men concealed themselves in a dark, damp compartment stacked with massive containers of cocoa beans.

Specifically, roughly a week into the journey, the crew sprayed the hold with phosphine gas—a pesticide routinely used to kill

---

77. "3 AFRICAN STOWAWAYS DIE ON TRIP TO THE U.S." New York Daily News, January 12, 2019. https://www.nydailynews.com/1996/03/20/3-african-stowaways-die-on-trip-to-the-us/

insects such as gypsy moths that threaten US agriculture and storage facilities.

Their bodies were found in a tight space between the ship's bulkhead and stacks of burlap bags in a lightless, sealed compartment.

"An NYPD ESU Unit had tested the air quality for us to make sure it was safe to breathe before myself and the other agents entered the ship to conduct a crime scene investigation," Nelson says.

This was a challenging assignment on many levels.

"We donned Tyvek suits, N95 face masks, and placed a large amount of Vicks VapoRub in our nostrils before we entered the ship's hold," Nelson remembers.

However, the three bodies were in such an advanced state of decay that the smell of death was almost beyond description and impossible to ignore.

"It took about three days of multiple showers each day to remove the smell of those bodies from my nostrils. I suppose the scent may have lingered in my mind rather than on my person, but I could vividly smell it for days."

How foul was the stench? That day, the agents placed just some of the crime scene evidence from the ship into the rear compartment of a relatively new SUV. The vehicle was so contaminated by the odor that it was unusable for weeks and required multiple thorough deep cleanings.

"The real point, though, is not the smell, but that someone had to perform the difficult task of conducting autopsies on those three bodies," Nelson says. "I can't even imagine what those conditions were like for those pathologists. This is one case of many, where real heroic work is being done by dedicated, nameless support personnel who served selflessly in the background without any desire or demand for recognition."

A fourth man, twenty-four-year-old Seth Lawson of Ghana, managed to escape the hold before the gas took effect. Lawson was treated for mild respiratory distress and was taken into custody by immigration officials.

The vessel's owner, Copenhagen-based D/S Torm, repatriated Lawson and the bodies of the deceased.

CHAPTER FORTY-NINE

In mid-1997, Don North, assistant Special Agent in Charge (ASAC) at the Brooklyn-Queens Office, turned to Anthony Nelson and asked him to accept a posting in Manhattan as the acting coordinating supervisory special agent (CSSA) for the FBI's Violent Crimes Branch in New York City.

This vote of confidence was especially impressive, considering the source.

As an ASAC in the New York Office from 1990 to 1997, North supervised a staff of five hundred, including two hundred federal agents and thirty-five police detectives. On his watch, nearly three hundred top and middle-echelon leaders in seven families were convicted on various charges.[78] This included helping convict the slippery Gambino boss John Gotti, as well as the landmark case against the murderous Lucchese head Vittorio Amuso, both in the same year.

Before moving to New York, North helped engineer anti-crime strategies at FBI headquarters in Washington, as chief of the FBI's organized crime unit. James Kossler, retired FBI supervisor, credited North with innovating game-changing techniques in the seizure of mobsters' assets. While in Washington, he also wrote Bureau guidelines for applying RICO, "The Enterprise Theory of Investigation." This seminal work has since been translated into thirty-four languages.

---

78. Martin, Douglas. "Donald V. North, 62, Leader in F.B.I.'s Fight Against Mafia, Is Dead." New York Times. January 29, 2005. https://www.nytimes.com/2005/01/29/obituaries/donald-v-north-62-leader-in-fbis-fight-against-mafia-is-dead.html

North sadly passed away in 2005 following a heart attack.

Accepting the assignment, Nelson now reported to another distinguished FBI leader, ASAC Jack Slicks.

Anthony Nelson was built for this role. A coordinating supervisory special agent leads and oversees investigations, provides technical direction to other agents, and ensures the smooth operation of investigative activities.

In this role, Nelson was tasked with producing the FBI New York Field Office's Crime Problem Assessment Reports. Nelson also left his mark by updating "The FBI New York Strategic Plans for Responding to and Neutralizing Airplane Skyjackings," "The FBI Kidnapping Response Plans," and other operational materials.

By the summer of 1997, Nelson was entrenched in his new assignment, day to day, playing a crucial role in coordinating with various law enforcement and intelligence agencies, when one of the most audacious homicides ever perpetrated by organized crime hit New York.

On August 25, 1997, a Mafia hit squad lay in wait, gunning down twenty-eight-year-old NYPD Officer Ralph Dols outside the Brooklyn home he shared with his wife, Kimberly Kennaugh, and their infant daughter. Kennaugh is the ex-wife of Colombo consigliere Joel "Joe Waverly" Cacace, who ordered the murder.

The assassination of Officer Dols exploded like a bomb.

This was a different type of murder. This was a major investigation with intense pressure and implications.

However, it would take months before investigators firmly established that the Dols murder was a Mob hit. The hit crew escaped the scene, and later, one of the Colombo gunmen, Dino "Big Dino" Calabro, testified that he only became aware Dols was a police officer when news of the assassination splashed across the New York tabloids the next day.

"As we got into the case, there was a big problem with Internal Affairs," says Al King, who later rose to the post of commanding officer of the NYPD's Brooklyn South Homicide Task Force.

"But I didn't have the homicide. I was in the 6-7 [67th Precinct] and Chief Allee called me in from vacation. So I went there and I didn't have the best relationship with some. I was too young, but I tried. The thing is, we found out IAB was all over and the cops weren't saying anything," King remembers.

The reluctance to get officers to talk, to help eliminate some of the massive flow of tips coming in, was problematic.

"The Homicide Task Force is in PSA1, and that's where Ralph Dols worked," Kings says. Police Service Area 1 serves the NYC Housing Authority developments within the confines of Brooklyn's 60th, 61st, 63rd, and 69th Precincts, with duties including patrols, responding to emergencies, and working with the community to address safety concerns.

"I don't look down on cops; like, I was a cop. I get hold of one of the PBA affiliates. He says the guys have things to say, but every time they say anything, it winds up under investigation. No one will talk, but they want to. I said, 'You let me know who wants to talk and we'll meet and everything I get will be anonymous,'" King adds. "And that was how we started finding out things."

Still, it would take months of investigation before the truth came to light.

CHAPTER FIFTY

Shortly after 8:30 on the morning of January 14, 1998, Anthony Nelson, acting FBI coordinating supervisory special agent in the New York Office, fielded a call to respond to an armed robbery.

Some armed robberies are lone-wolf crimes, motivated by desperation, financial stress, maybe even addiction. Things get real messy, real fast.

Some are small-group heists, impulsive, poorly planned, bumbling bank robbers trailing DNA bread crumbs as they spread around all those marked bills. Law enforcement likes those kinds of capers, where at least one crew member folds under questioning.

And then there are well-orchestrated, high-stakes takedowns.

You know, the kind involving penetrating the impenetrable fortress, mind-boggling sums, diabolical kingpins, and bandits blasting through a battery of clandestine safe houses.

That's when they call in the Bureau.

Nelson rushed to the 11th floor of 1 World Trade Center in Lower Manhattan. He was met by members of the FBI/NYPD Joint Bank Robbery Task Force and by William H. Allee, the NYPD chief of detectives at the time.

Allee's presence alone was enough to raise Nelson's eyebrows.

Allee served as the department's chief of detectives from 1997 to 2003, having joined the NYPD in 1963 and been promoted to detective four years later. Before that, he was commanding officer of the 7th Precinct on the Lower East Side, as well as the Midtown

North precinct, and headed detective operations in Staten Island, where he lived.

While a lieutenant at Manhattan South Narcotics, Allee and his team worked tirelessly to rid the Lower East Side of drug dealers during the height of the crack epidemic. He also played a pivotal role in the Midtown South Precinct's epic cleanup and revitalization of Times Square.

After the tragic events of September 11, Allee was in charge of the evidence from the World Trade Center site at the Fresh Kills landfill on Staten Island. In a C-SPAN documentary from January 2002, he said his team was able to identify forty-six victims after digging through the debris at the former landfill. "This is not a dump," he famously said in the documentary. "It's sacred ground."[79]

In the aftermath of the attack, Chief Allee rushed to Ground Zero and worked tirelessly amid the chaos. The thick dust and debris he was exposed to took a serious toll on his health, leading to months of respiratory issues.

Allee retired in 2003 on the fortieth anniversary of his first day on the job. Unfortunately, he developed leukemia as a result of his exposure to the toxins in the air at Ground Zero and passed away.[80]

A year after Allee's death, Police Commissioner James O'Neill and NYPD Chief of Detectives Dermot Shea joined family members at the street renaming ceremony for the fallen hero at the corner of Bascom Place and Collfield Avenue in Manor Heights, Staten Island.

Upon Nelson's arrival at the World Trade Center in Lower Manhattan, he learned that a team of Brink's armored car guards had just delivered $1.6 million worth of US and foreign currency to the Bank of America. The guards had brought the money up to

79. The Officer Down Memorial Page. "Chief of Detectives William H. Allee." https://www.odmp.org/officer/23692-chief-of-detectives-william-h-allee

80. Wassef, Mira. "'A Cop's Cop:' Decorated NYPD Chief Dies From 9/11 Illness." SiLive. June 14, 2018. https://www.silive.com/news/erry-2018/06/e83869d5316135/a_cops_cop_decorated_staten_is.html

the eleventh floor on a freight elevator when they were subdued by three men wearing ski masks.

Enough details emerged to indicate this was a sophisticated heist, likely involving an inside connection.

For one thing, one of the robbers had a World Trade Center employee ID card, which was later found to have been obtained from a corrupt employee of the building. During the heist, the crew was able to pack up the cash and hit the exits within fifteen minutes.

So, a well-orchestrated operation, sure—but they made one big mistake.

"To blend in with the general public," Nelson says, "they had removed their ski masks prematurely, apparently giving little thought to the fact that there were scores of closed-circuit video cameras operational around the World Trade Center."

Cameras were not as commonplace in 1998 Manhattan. In fact, they were only installed as part of the enhanced security put into place following the earlier terrorist bombing.

On February 26, 1993, Al-Qaeda carried out a bombing beneath the North Tower of the World Trade Center by detonating a van packed with explosives in the underground parking garage. The 1,336-pound device, made of urea nitrate and enhanced with hydrogen gas, was designed to topple the North Tower into the South Tower, to destroy both buildings and cause mass casualties.

Although the plan failed to bring down the towers, the blast killed six people—including a pregnant woman—and injured over a thousand others. Approximately fifty thousand people were evacuated from the complex in the aftermath of the attack.[81]

The South Tower reopened to tenants on March 18, 1993, while the North Tower remained closed until April 1 of that year. According to the National September 11 Memorial & Museum, the estimated cost to repair the damage to both towers reached two hundred and fifty million dollars.

---

81. FBI. "World Trade Center Bombing 1993." May 9, 2022. https://www.fbi.gov/history/famous-cases/world-trade-center-bombing-1993

That price tag included new security measures the robbery team overlooked, including surveillance cameras, a barrier rising out of the roadway to stop rogue vehicles, and other enhancements.

It didn't take long to get a break in the case with the thieves unaware that CCTV footage captured their faces.

"A short time after the robbery," Nelson says, "I received a telephone call from an FBI agent who told me that we, the FBI, had an informant who knew the identities of the armed thieves."

However, the thieves were unaware that the FBI knew their identities; in fact, they had their photographs. "They had no reason to hide or even suspect that they were wanted at that point in time," Nelson says. "All we had to do was to go to their homes in Brooklyn and arrest them.

"However, Chief of Detectives Allee decided unilaterally that he was going to release the photos of the unmasked thieves taken from the CCTV cameras to the media," he continues. He advised against the move, fearing the publicity would drive them further underground. Allee released the photos along with an offer of reward money for their capture.

"Releasing their photos, he not only told the whole world who we were looking for, he let the thieves themselves know they were wanted," Nelson says. "So, of course, one of them, Richard Gillette, fled to New Mexico." Meanwhile, more of the pieces fell into place. Investigators learned that the robbery was plotted and executed by Ralph Guarino, an actor and petty criminal with connections to the DeCavalcante Family.

The DeCavalcante Family—often referred to as the North Jersey Mafia or North Jersey crime Family—is a faction of the Italian-American Mafia primarily based in Northern New Jersey. Supposedly the inspiration for the HBO series *The Sopranos*, its operations are concentrated in cities such as Elizabeth, Newark, West New York, and nearby communities.

Guarino received intelligence from a WTC worker named Salvatore Calciano, who told him about the increased security that followed the 1993 World Trade Center bombing and would later give him his employee ID badge from a friend of Calciano. Apparently, he neglected to tip Guarino off to the new cameras.

Calciano also informed Guarino of the scheduled arrival time for a Brink's armored truck to deliver money via elevator to the eleventh floor of the North Tower (Tower One) of the WTC. The two of them planned the robbery and recruited three other criminals to complete the actual robbery: Richie Gillette, thirty-nine, from Windsor Terrace, Brooklyn, as well as his friends Melvin Folk, forty-four, and Mike Reed, thirty-four.

"Luckily, two of the robbers, Michael Reed and Melvin Folk, were picked up at their residences in Brooklyn," Nelson says. "But like I said, the third team member, Richard Gillette, fled to Albuquerque, New Mexico, once his photo was released, but he was captured a couple of days later."

The FBI picked up Guarino in connection with the robbery. "He was brought to an office I had maintained at the Fort Hamilton US Army Base in Brooklyn, where he met with his attorney, Alan Abramson, and Assistant US Attorney David Kelley, who was in charge of Organized Crime prosecutions in the Southern District of New York," Nelson says. "Guarino was given a chance to immediately cooperate with the understanding that he would testify at a later date instead of an immediate arrest."

Abramson was an assistant district attorney in the Kings County District Attorney's Office from 1985 through 1990. Since 1990, Abramson has been a partner in Abramson & Morak, a full-service criminal defense firm specializing in defending clients in high-profile, complex prosecutions and investigations by federal, state and local law enforcement.

"Ralph was an interesting guy and very talented," Abramson recalls. "He could build things, run things, had talents to do extraordinary things in the legitimate world, but for whatever reasons, he was involved most of life on the other side of the law."

However, Abramson does point out this robbery was not flawlessly executed by his former client. "So the robbery went down and it was kind of shortsighted that they robbed a bank, but what they got was not millions in US dollars. It was mostly in foreign currency. And then after the robbery," Abramson adds, "you started seeing, like, all this Japanese yen and Thai baht began making appearances out in Brooklyn."

There were other errors the gang made noted by investigators.

"Like that very week, the United States president was supposed to be at the World Trade Center, and that was publicized, so they should have known there'd be heightened security," Abramson says. "And then, of course, they didn't realize there'd be cameras right outside, so they took off their masks."

To avoid an immediate arrest, Guarino had to tell the FBI where the remaining cash from the robbery was hidden.

And so began a prolonged interrogation/negotiation. "It literally took hours for Guarino to commit to becoming a witness," Nelson remembers. "At one point, it seemed he was going to choose an arrest rather than cooperation when he told his lawyer to hold his watch because he was 'going to jail.'"

Guarino finally relented and agreed to testify. "He told us where the remainder of the $1.6 million was hidden," Nelson says.

FBI Special Agent George Hanna was to oversee directing Guarino's cooperation on the street to take down the DeCavalcante Family.

"Guarino gave us the location of the remaining Brink's cash," Nelson says. "Special Agent George Hanna, Kenny McCabe, and I drove to a house in Upstate New York and recovered what turned out to be only the foreign currency from the robbery."

Then something unplanned happened on the way to recover the stolen money. "On the way upstate to recover the money, our FBI SUV, driven by George Hanna, was pulled over for speeding by a New York State Trooper Canine Unit," Nelson says. "It was obvious from the look on the trooper's face that both he and the dog were suspicious of us."

As the trooper cautiously approached the driver's side window, Hanna told him the occupants of the car were with the FBI.

The trooper then demanded to see some FBI identification. "Hanna started laughing and said he forgot his credentials and driver's license back at the office," Nelson says. "Kenny McCabe and I then also started to laugh because Hanna had turned his head around toward us and asked if Kenny or I had our identification on us. I produced my FBI credentials, and the trooper allowed us to leave. But it was obvious that the trooper didn't think there was anything funny about his car stop."

CHAPTER FIFTY-ONE

After more than a year in Manhattan as an FBI Coordinating Supervisory Special Agent in the New York Office, Anthony Nelson was headed back to BQMRA for a homecoming.

Nelson was officially assigned back to Queens as the permanent supervisory special agent of what was commonly referred to as the Truck Hijacking Squad.

"This designation had been somewhat of a misnomer because virtually all of our pending cases had been related to organized crime," Nelson says.

Special Agents are essentially more sophisticated versions of street-level detectives within the federal law enforcement community.

Supervisory special agents are first-line, front-line supervisors who oversee the investigations of those Special Agents under their command, give assignments, hold briefings, conduct field interviews, oversee overall case integrity, and assume other supervisory roles to ensure integrity and adherence to the law and administrative guidelines. An SSA typically manages a team within a specialized unit, such as counterterrorism, cybercrime, organized crime, or public corruption.

Anthony Nelson was tapped for oversight of not one, but two units.

Specifically, Nelson became the supervisor of the Major Theft—Truck Hijacking Squad, a post he held from 1998 through 2002. In 2002, he transferred to Manhattan to take over the FBI/NYPD Bank Robbery—Violent Crimes Task Force. These were formidable assignments. As with a Special Agent, an SSA is required to be "on call" at all times, though the SSA has supervisory responsibilities for leading the squad and mounting the investigation.

Nelson was now responsible for reviewing and directing investigations, ensuring proper protocols were followed, and guiding agents in gathering evidence. They manage a team of Special Agents, providing training, guidance, and mentorship. He was also responsible for interagency coordination, working with federal, state, and local law enforcement agencies to share intelligence and resources.

Nelson needed to ensure investigations adhered to constitutional protections, FBI policies, and Department of Justice regulations. Nelson led response efforts in hostage situations and communicated findings to FBI leadership or government officials. (Note: Nelson did not routinely lead any response efforts regarding terror threats except for the two-plus months after the September 11, 2001, terrorist attack on the World Trade Center, when every New York-area FBI agent contributed to anti-terrorism matters.)

This new role for Nelson was absolutely critical to maintaining investigative integrity, ensuring cases are built on solid legal grounds, and preventing procedural errors that could compromise prosecutions.

Both assignments were daunting.

The FBI Major Theft Unit is part of the FBI's Criminal Investigative Division. The unit investigates major theft crimes that cross state and international lines, including the major theft of cargo, including vehicles, retail items, and metals, jewelry theft, and the theft of major artwork, including cultural property and looted art. These are typically not crimes of opportunity, but rather calculated thefts orchestrated by organized crime groups and sophisticated rings.

The FBI's Violent Crime unit focuses on the most violent criminals and organizations that pose a significant threat to American society.

Again, as with the Major Theft Unit, the Violent Crimes squads focused on investigating cases with substantial impact, such as armed bank robberies, mass killings, dangerous fugitives, gang violence, and armed robberies—criminal activity that can paralyze communities and stretch state and local law enforcement resources to their limits.

Meanwhile, the Third Colombo Family War was raging, bodies piling up across Brooklyn, and a renegade associate was rampaging across the city, leaving body after body in his wake.

Years earlier, aging Colombo boss Thomas DiBella voluntarily stepped aside. His natural successor was the Family's most influential captain, Carmine "Junior" Persico, also known as The Snake. But Persico's path to leadership was complicated—he had spent ten of the thirteen years leading up to 1985 behind bars, the result of relentless federal prosecutions.

Despite his imprisonment, Persico managed to maintain control over the Family from his cell, delegating authority to his brother, Alphonse, and longtime ally Gennaro "Jerry Lang" Langella. Under their guidance, the Colombo Family focused heavily on narcotics trafficking and labor racketeering.

But as federal authorities intensified their crackdown on organized crime, Persico and Langella were indicted in the landmark Mafia Commission case. Prosecutors used the RICO Act to charge the leadership of New York's Five Families. Representing himself at trial, Persico railed against the charges, shouting in court: "Without the Mafia, there wouldn't be no case here!"

His outrage didn't sway the jury: both Persico and Langella were convicted and sentenced to one hundred years in prison.

Though Persico knew he would never walk free again, he refused to relinquish control. He had ruled from behind bars before and planned to do so again—at least until his son, Alphonse "Allie Boy" Persico, completed his own prison sentence and could take the reins. In the interim, Persico appointed a distant cousin, Victor "Little Vic" Orena, as acting boss.

But Orena quickly grew comfortable in power. By 1990, with support from John Gotti of the Gambino Family, Orena petitioned the Mafia Commission to formally remove Persico and recognize him as the official boss. The Colombo ranks split. Lines were drawn. Loyalties were tested.

The first shots in what became a full-blown mob war were fired by Persico loyalists on June 20, 1991. A five-man hit squad led by Persico consigliere Carmine Sessa arrived at Orena's Long Island home to assassinate him. But the plan fell apart when one gunman opened fire too early, alerting Orena before the others were in place. He narrowly escaped.

The failed hit forced Orena to double down. He turned again to the Commission, seeking recognition as the Family's rightful leader. Meanwhile, Sessa defended Persico's claim to power, painting Orena as a traitor who had turned on the man who gave him everything.

The Colombo Civil War had begun.

After two years of mayhem, the war drew in dozens of gangsters, including a rising drug dealer, John Pappa.

John Pappa was only five years old when his father, Gerard Pappa—a Genovese Family soldier—was executed for breaking Mafia protocol. Gerard had originally aligned himself with the Colombo Family before switching sides to become a soldier for the Genovese Family, where he was connected to notorious figures like Anthony "Gaspipe" Casso and Salvatore "Sammy the Bull" Gravano.

Pappa and Gravano had known each other since their days in the Rampers street gang, growing up in Bensonhurst alongside Casso and Frank DeCicco. But Gerard Pappa's rise through the ranks came to a violent end in 1980, when Vincent "the Chin" Gigante ordered his murder in retaliation for two unsanctioned killings.

As a teenager, Pappa began dealing drugs and soon gravitated toward a Lucchese crew run by James "Froggy" Galione. But Pappa wanted more than street-level hustle—he wanted a name. And during the bloody Colombo Family civil war, he found his opportunity.

Pappa set his sights on Colombo capo Joseph Scopo, a key ally of acting boss Victor Orena in the war against Carmine Persico's loyalists. On October 20, 1993, Pappa and two Colombo associates—John Sparacino and Eric Curcio—headed to Scopo's home in Ozone Park, Queens, with a single goal: take him out.

They found Scopo sitting in his car. Sparacino yanked open the door and unloaded a burst of machine gun fire—missing every shot. Scopo, dazed but unhurt, shouted at them in fury. Sparacino panicked and bolted. Pappa ducked behind a tree, watching for any sign Scopo might be armed.

But Scopo didn't flinch. Instead, he taunted Pappa: "You got balls? Come on, come on. If you're gonna kill me, kill me, you little punk!" Then he hurled his cell phone at him.

That was all Pappa needed. He stepped out from cover, approached the car, and calmly emptied a .380 pistol into Scopo at close range—eight shots in total.

Scopo's murder marked the end of the Colombo War. With their top enforcer dead, the Orena faction crumbled, and the Persico side claimed victory.

For Pappa, the hit meant he had officially made his bones—and a spot in the Family looked all but guaranteed.

But Pappa's thirst for violence didn't stop there. He was linked to several other murders in the aftermath and made no effort to hide his role in Scopo's execution. He and his co-conspirators couldn't stop bragging, each one spinning his own version of events.

At one party inside a social club owned by rising mobster Vincent Basciano, Sparacino vented his frustration. As Pappa and Curcio left, Sparacino leaned over and told Basciano, "They think they're tough guys? Please. They're punks. You remember the Scopo hit? I'm the one who did the shooting. They ran like cowards and left me there."

Afterwards, Pappa believed the trio had been seeking to steal "street cred" for killing Scopo.

At this time, NYPD Detective Tommy Dades caught the case and worked the investigation with the assistance of Anthony Nelson's squad.

"I first met Tommy Dades when he was assigned to the 68th Precinct Detective Squad," Nelson says. "He stood out, positively, among most of the other detectives in the squad. So much so that I personally believed he was not getting sufficient support in terms of resources, manpower, and personal protective backing for the extensive and significant work he was doing to combat organized crime."

"Anthony opened up that BQ office to us and we worked some incredible cases and as a result we developed a really strong working relationship that produced real results, closing cases and getting convictions," Dades says. "Anthony Nelson, I can't say enough good things about him as an agent and FBI supervisor. But more than that, just a great person, with integrity, and actually one of the sweetest guys you'd meet. You wouldn't think that with an FBI agent of his caliber. But a lot of these guys were just really good people."

Tommy Dades retired from the NYPD as a first-grade detective in 2004. Dades' work in the 68th Precinct detective squad as well as the intelligence division helped put away many members of organized crime. After he retired from the NYPD, he worked as an investigator for the Brooklyn District Attorney's Office.

Dades and others in the Brooklyn DA's Office, as well as members of the DEA, including DEA Agents Frank Drew and Timothy Moran, were instrumental in arresting and building a case against the so-called Mafia Cops. Lou Eppolito and Stephen Carracappa died in prison based on the efforts of Tommy Dades and the FBI, the NYPD, and the Brooklyn DA's Office.

Subsequently, Dades co-authored the New York Times bestseller *Friends of the Family: The Inside Story of the Mafia Cops Case* with Mike Vecchione, formerly in charge of the Rackets Division of the Brooklyn DA's Office, and David Fisher, about two decorated NYPD detectives, Louis Eppolito and Steve Caracappa, with access to the department's most sensitive information, who sold their badges to the Mafia—and became murderers for the Mob.

Dades and former partner, retired NYPD Detective Mike Galletta, were also featured in the book *Mob Over Miami* by *New York Daily News* reporter Michele McPhee.

Dades, a former amateur boxer with around thirty-five bouts under his belt—many as part of the NYPD's Fighting Finest—was brought on by the Police Athletic League (PAL) to run the Park Hill Boxing Club when it opened in 2004. The gym, located in Staten Island's Park Hill housing projects, was established in memory of undercover NYPD Detectives Rodney Andrews and James Nemorin, who were killed by gun traffickers in March 2003.

The club quickly gained momentum, becoming a training ground for hundreds of amateur fighters, as well as a launching pad for local pros like light heavyweight Tim O'Neill and rising, undefeated featherweight Gary Stark Jr.

"Tommy Dades is the one who is a legend," Nelson says. "Tommy had an exceptional ability to develop informants, and he developed such rapport with them that most were more than willing to provide critical evidentiary information."

"We had some things, and of course, as the FBI, they had a ton of things we didn't, and Anthony was in the heart of all that, and he had a great team and ran a great team," Dades says. "I also remember Anthony was very close to Buddy Murnane on the NYPD Major Case Squad, and they did a lot of great work together in hijackings and organized crime, which really were closely connected.

"For those who know these names, like Buddy Murnane, you know Anthony just operated at a different level, building relationships with the cream of the crop, which was way above my pay grade," Dades adds. "But Anthony never looked at us like we were anything but partners, never said don't tell them this, or hold his back. He fostered a very welcoming atmosphere, making you feel welcome both around him and the people he supervised.

"Anthony Nelson was the FBI Supervisor of C31, the hijacking squad in the Brooklyn-Queens Office of the FBI. He had George Hanna and Matt Tormey, two amazing FBI agents, working for him, and that's how we met."

Today, Matt Tormey is an accomplished professional with extensive experience in compliance, risk management, and law enforcement. Tormey graduated from law school in 1990 and practiced law until he was accepted into the FBI in July 1991. In January 2000, he left the FBI and joined Health Management Associates (HMA) as the corporate compliance officer.

Currently serving as executive vice president of compliance and risk at Ensemble Health Partners since July 2019, he previously held significant positions, including chief criminal investigator at the Westchester County, New York District Attorney's Office and chief compliance officer at TeamHealth. His background also includes a role as JV basketball coach at Barron Collier High School and vice president of compliance and security at Health Management Associates. Early career experiences encompass serving as a Special Agent for the FBI and practicing law as an attorney in the law office of Joseph Messina. Academic credentials include a master's degree in criminal justice from Florida Gulf Coast University and a Juris Doctor from New York Law School.[82]

"We worked with George Hanna on quite a few things and then me and Matt Tormey started working together on the John Pappa case," Dades says. "Anthony was Matt Tormey's supervisor. I worked the Pappa case for two years with Matt, and throughout that time, both our teams worked closely in the FBI's BQ office. I cannot speak more highly of George and Matt and the rest of the agents in BQ at that time, and especially the leadership of Anthony Nelson. He knew how to support his agents, provide them with what they needed, when they needed, and allowed them to do the work they needed to do.

"The Pappa case went federal," Dades says. "It had to go federal. It was during the Colombo War. So me and Matt worked through all these state homicides to put the case together. This was me and Matt grabbing all these folders and slowly working through it, conducting tons of interviews, which eventually resulted in obtaining numerous informants, and then working to get them ready to testify at the trial. We conducted so much surveillance on known associates. And at the end of the day, we were able to build the case for Amy Walsh in the Eastern District."

Amy Walsh was an assistant United States attorney for twelve years in the United States Attorney's Office for the Eastern District of New York, where she led dozens of investigations and cases on behalf of the government and supervised several sections within the office. Before entering private practice, she was chief of the

82. "Matt Tormey." LinkedIn. https://www.linkedin.com/in/matt-tormey-4974761/

business and securities fraud section in the US Attorney's Office for the Eastern District.

"Jim Walden also played a part in that, and it was a great victory against organized crime," Dades adds.

After serving as an assistant US attorney for the Eastern District of New York from 1993 to 2002, Walden entered private practice, where he has been involved in several prominent cases involving matters of white-collar crime, antitrust law, and government reform.

After two years, that investigation led to a dramatic arrest at a wedding rehearsal in Staten Island. Pappa, arriving for a wedding rehearsal for his pal Salvatore Sparacino, was intercepted by NYPD detectives and FBI agents. They nabbed him for the 1994 murder of the groom's brother, John.

"I remember Pappa went to his front waistband as we yelled, 'John. Police. Don't move!'" Dades says. "Matt and I were only about seven to eight feet away. Pappa raced toward the church doors, but never pointed the gun at us. He threw the gun to the right, and we handcuffed him, recovering a Taurus 9mm, fully loaded with one round in the chamber.

"Police, John," Detective Tommy Dades yelled as Pappa walked up the marble stairs of the church with his girlfriend. "Stop! Police!"

Pappa spun and scowled. He bent over, clutching his stomach, and stood straight, pointing a fully loaded 9mm pistol.

"Put the gun down, John!" FBI agent Matt Tormey said.

Pappa ran into the church amid the stunned wedding party. He hurled his gun to the floor and kept running, weaving in and out of the pews with cops in pursuit.

"Hey, you guys are unbelievable," the infuriated groom growled. "Show some respect."

"Respect?" answered a detective. "This mutt killed your brother."

Pappa was arrested feet from the altar. No shots were fired.[83]

83. "GANGSTER'S RISE CUT SHORT." New York Daily News. January 10, 2019. https://www.nydailynews.com/2001/04/09/gangsters-rise-cut-short/

John Pappa's rapid ascent in the Mob ended abruptly on the steps of St. Ann's Church on Staten Island on September 26, 1997.

"I just loved having Tommy and Mike Galletta working with us every day on Squad C-31," Nelson says. "Pappa's arrest by Tommy Dades and Matt Tormey was something right out of a movie script. If I'm not mistaken, when Tommy and Matt chased Pappa through the church, Pappa's loaded handgun fell and skidded under several pews as the arrest team raced to get it.

"As a matter of fact, I had been in the Queens area with my wife, Syndee, son Michael, and my daughter Marissa, and I stopped at my office with them on a weekend," Nelson remembers. "When I brought them into my squad area, all three of them remarked about a giant photograph that was hanging above a desk used by Tommy Dades and Matt Tormey. It was a photograph of Pappa's entire back with the Italian tattooed inscription, '*Morte Prima del Disonore,*' which in English translates to 'Death Before Dishonor.'"

The Colombo War claimed the lives of twelve people, including three innocent bystanders. Eighteen others—associates tied to the losing faction—simply vanished. In the aftermath, more than eighty made men and associates were indicted, imprisoned, or flipped.

John Pappa stood trial in Brooklyn Federal Court for the October 20, 1993, murder of Joseph Scopo, along with three additional homicides committed in the year following the final killing of the Colombo Family Civil War.

Pappa was ultimately found guilty of racketeering, drug trafficking, and four murders—including the last slaying of the brutal Third Colombo War. He received a sentence of two life terms plus sixty-five years. In June 2025, Judge Pamela Chen of Brooklyn Federal Court denied his request for compassionate release. Pappa is currently fifty years old.

CHAPTER FIFTY-TWO

Throughout 1998, Ralph Guarino was the gift that kept on giving for the FBI, as life with the cooperator got very interesting.

The Truck Hijacking Squad, now led by Supervisory Special Agent Anthony Nelson, managed Guarino and the many leads he threw off. Before Guarino, Special Agent Steven Braus had already made substantial headway conducting a major organized crime undercover truck hijacking operation.

Special Agent George Hanna, working with Special Agent Eileen O'Rourke, was also using Guarino and coordinating with another organized crime squad to take down the New Jersey/New York DeCavalcante crime Family. Hanna's case particularly gained momentum once Guarino was drawn into the FBI fold, following the Brinks robbery at the World Trade Center. However, he was a handful.

"Guarino was a master manipulator who could get most people to like and trust him within a matter of minutes," Nelson recalls.

"At the time I first met Guarino, I'd already spent so many years as an FBI agent, among so many bad people, that I had come to distrust just about everyone and everything, even good and decent people," Nelson says. "Yet even I became amused by Guarino. I'll admit I enjoyed listening to some of his stories about his life on the streets of the city."

To ensure that Guarino was committed to testifying in the future, Hanna wired him up to capture evidence.

So, the first plan was for Guarino to tell the wiseguys in his crew that he had a contact in the telephone company who could get him free cell phones with unlimited phone and text messaging.

At the time, all the major cell phone companies were charging for phone calls by the minute, and phone bills started to get exorbitant.

"Even if the phone billing was not expensive, you could always count on the wiseguys for trying to get something for nothing," Nelson says. "It was just part of their nature."

Since Guarino had urgent meetings scheduled with DeCavalcante Crew members, Hanna took one of the cell phones used by FBI agents in Nelson's squad for daily investigative work.

"Although the phone was subscribed to a fictitious name," Nelson says, "it was nevertheless one of several phones that were in general use by the agents on my squad and were on the same billing invoice."

Guarino, in turn, gave that cell phone to DeCavalcante soldier Joseph "Joey O" Masella so the team could monitor what telephone numbers he was dialing to prepare for a Title III (federal wiretap warrant).

"I had told Hanna to get that cell phone back from Masella by having Guarino tell him it was obsolete and that he would get him a newer and better phone," Nelson says.

However, before Hanna was able to get the phone back, on October 10, 1998, Masella was lured to the Marine Park Golf Course in Brooklyn.

When Masella arrived at the golf course parking lot, he was shot to death with the FBI cell phone in his pocket.

This was a touchy situation requiring discretion, as once NYPD homicide detectives linked that phone to the FBI, it could possibly expose Guarino as a cooperating informant and destroy his value in many ongoing investigations.

The next day, NYPD Lieutenant Al King appeared at Nelson's office with First Grade Detective Tony Angotti. "I first met Anthony Nelson not long after I arrived as the new commander for the Brooklyn South Homicide," King recalls. "Anthony is a man of honor. What you see is what you get, never withholds info, and is very upfront, and a man of integrity whom I hold in the highest regard."

However, that morning, the agent and commander were just meeting, with a touchy situation to resolve.

"I'd already known Tony Angotti for the last twenty years," Nelson says.

"Kenny McCabe and I would often meet with Angotti while he was in uniform, assigned to the 62nd Precinct, and after he became a detective in the Homicide Task Force," Nelson adds. "Angotti was not only a friend. He was also one of the most knowledgeable police officers about organized crime activities and subjects in Brooklyn."

Angotti requested assistance with the Masella homicide, and he told Nelson that he could trust Lieutenant Al King completely. "I told George Hanna that I was going to let Al King know that Masella was carrying an FBI cell phone," Nelson says. This decision did not sit well with one of the prosecutors in the Southern District of New York.

"However, despite the prosecutor's objections, I told Hanna that even the least capable NYPD detective working on the Masella homicide would figure out in no time at all that Masella had some connection to the FBI after reviewing the general billing records of the phone found on Masella's body. So, notwithstanding the objections of the SDNY prosecutor, I told Al King what was going on with Masella and the cell phone."

And then he held his breath.

Ultimately, King agreed to help conceal Masella's FBI connection, vital to furthering the investigation into the DeCavalcantes.

"I remember Masella was murdered on a golf course and had a cell phone, issued by the FBI, which Anthony told me," King says. "From the beginning, I knew Anthony was a team player, as was George Hanna, and we really melded. There was no bullshit, no hiding information, so we were able to build up a level of mutual trust that carried forward in working the cases against the DeCavalcante Family."

Guarino produced case after case for the government that ultimately led to the cooperation of other members in the DeCavalcante Family, including Vincent "Vinny Ocean" Palermo, the head of the Family.

In the aftermath of Masella's murder, Palermo and the DeCavalcante leadership inducted Guarino into the Family. But by 1999, with serious charges looming—including crimes that could carry the death penalty—Palermo chose to cooperate with federal authorities and turn informant.

"Once Palermo was on board as a cooperator, I took Al King, Tony Angotti, and other detectives from the homicide squad to a safe house where they were able to debrief Palermo and clear many unsolved homicides," Nelson says. "Very often, even cooperators or informants did not know the last names or true identities of those with whom they did business."

"So I headed to the FBI safe house with Anthony Nelson, and I brought along the entire Brooklyn South Homicide log," King says. "And I sit with Vinny Palermo, and we go through the log, and he starts providing details on all of these open homicides.

"We get to one homicide, and Vinny says, 'I did that one, shot the guy in the head,'" King recalls.

Then, Palermo not only told the investigators the body was buried—he provided the address.

"He tells us to go to this house, and says for us to 'move a picture to the side and see what you find,'" King says. "And sure enough, behind the picture was a bullet hole with the bullet from the gun used in that murder. That day, we got a lot of information to work on, and as a result, we closed quite a number of open homicides."

On a lighter note, King remembers something else about his collaborations with the FBI.

"That George Hanna, great agent, but he was famous for not calling my detectives back," King says. "In fact, I was talking to a detective and Hanna's name came up." King laughs. "He said he polled all the homicide detectives and every single one— that's fifteen detectives retired—who said they never got a call back from George Hanna. But all kidding aside, I had a great relationship with George Hanna and Anthony Nelson and cannot speak more highly of them."

"By 1998, Al King and I had now developed a working relationship," Nelson says. "I provided him with two very experienced FBI agents from my squad to help his task force working on the murder of Officer Dols.

"I also supplied Al's squad with FBI vehicles and cell phones," Nelson says. "Special Agents John Anticev and Michael Ferrandino reported to Al King's office daily in an attempt to develop evidence against Dols' killers.

"Look closely," says retired NYPD Detective Ron Cadieux. "This tells you what kind of guy Anthony Nelson is. When that case broke, he had his people help, really cooperating, and then he gave the team that had the case and the boss of the homicide office a new car and new radios to help with the investigation. All that came out of the FBI budget."

CHAPTER FIFTY-THREE

Soon after Anthony Nelson met Al King and established a working relationship, the Ralph Dols homicide investigation picked up steam.

"We ran down so many bad leads until we started looking at his ex-wife, and that's when it started to come together," King says.

At the time he was killed, Ralph Dols was working with Police Service Area #1 in Brooklyn and was married to Kim Kennaugh, former wife of Colombo captain Joel "Joe Waverly" Cacace. Prosecutors would later claim that Cacace ordered the hit out of resentment, believing it was a personal insult that his ex-wife married a police officer and had a child with him.

Initially, Kennaugh was hesitant to assist investigators, and when subpoenaed to testify at Cacace's trial, she declined to take the stand, citing her Fifth Amendment right against self-incrimination: according to Kennaugh, her refusal stemmed from fear that federal prosecutors didn't trust her and might accuse her of perjury if they doubted her testimony.

However, dogged investigators were able to make headway and soon had suspects.

"We got someone in prison who told us the whole thing and worked closely with the FBI squad, because it had to go federal. The intel wasn't strong enough for a State indictment. The FBI did a great job."

Once it was clear the Mafia captain ordered the assassination of a New York City police officer, and a hit team stalked Ralph Dols for days before murdering him in cold blood, it marked a turning point, at least on the streets: the Mafia was now on the run like never before and would never operate as obviously as it had.

As the case developed, there was a sense on the street that this crime was different, intolerable.

While the string of high-profile Mafioso trials, including the landmark Commission Case, did much to dismantle organized crime's grip on New York, at the street level, the Dols homicide also severely damaged the Italian-American Mafia.

"This was a terrible thing, out of bounds, and you knew it was just an outrage," remembers retired NYPD Detective Tommy Dades. "When that happened, the Chief of Department Anemone wanted search warrants for all the gambling places and the clubs."

Louis R. Anemone was the chief of department for the New York City Police Department from 1995 to 1999, the third-highest position in the department. He is known for his role in developing and implementing the CompStat system, which significantly contributed to reducing crime in NYC.

In the days and weeks that followed, law enforcement across the region descended on scores of organized crime locations that Nelson and McCabe had long surveilled as social clubs and bars throughout New York were shuttered.

"We called in the FBI, the DEA, Brooklyn South Homicide," Dades says. "We took down Billy's Cutolo's club, George DeCicco's club, Joey Flowers' club, and so many more. We got the warrants and seized money we vouchered, which we need to do for asset forfeitures. We put up posters all over the place, putting pressure on them. We got warrant after warrant and went in, as a joint effort across the board—the NYPD, the feds, and the Brooklyn DA. Even Chief of Detectives William Allee came down to a couple of these raids." Eventually, the FBI Colombo Squad indicted Cacace and Colombo associates for Dols' murder.

A sweeping twenty-four-count federal indictment was later filed against several members and associates of the Colombo Family, among them former acting boss Thomas Gioeli, ex-consigliere Cacace, captain Dino Calabro, and soldier Dino Saracino. The charges against Cacace, Calabro, and Saracino specifically included their alleged roles in the 1997 murder of NYPD Officer Ralph Dols.

In disturbing testimony later delivered in Brooklyn federal court, Calabro, by then a cooperating witness, described the calculated ambush, recounting how Dols, unaware of the danger, casually greeted his killers with a simple "What's up?" moments before being shot.

"He had no idea," Calabro told jurors, describing how he and his cousin, co-defendant Dino "Little Dino" Saracino, stalked their victim, before tailing Dols back to his residence. As soon as the off-duty officer parked his Oldsmobile Cutlass, the pair sprang into action.[84]

Dols stumbled back, collapsing onto the hood of his car as the bullets tore through him.

"I shot him. My cousin shot him. We both did," Calabro said, his voice steady as he described the cold-blooded execution.

According to Calabro, the murder wasn't spontaneous. He and Saracino hunted Dols for weeks, tracking his routines and looking for the right moment to strike. At one point, more than a week before that fatal night, they followed him home and nearly carried out the hit—only to be thwarted when Dols made it through a yellow light, leaving them stuck behind at a red light.

Calabro testified against his former associates—Saracino and Thomas "Tommy Shots" Gioeli—both charged with murder and racketeering as part of a sweeping federal case targeting the Colombo crime Family. The testimony marked another grim chapter in a case that reveals how personal vendettas and Mafia codes of honor can end in deadly consequences—even for a police officer just living his life.

---

84. Maddux, Mitchel. "Mob Turncoat Details the 1997 Slaying of NYPD Cop Ralph Dols." New York Post. March 27, 2012. https://nypost.com/2012/03/27/mob-turncoat-details-the-1997-slaying-of-nypd-cop-ralph-dols/

CHAPTER FIFTY-FOUR

During Anthony Nelson's tenure as the supervisory Special Agent of the Major Theft—Truck Hijacking Squad, he was in almost daily contact with Sergeant Francis "Buddy" Murnane of the NYPD Major Case Squad.

Murnane was another legendary detective of the NYPD, and not just because by then he was the department's longest-serving officer, first appointed in 1973, according to NYPD statistics.

In 2010, the City Council honored Murnane, who, at the time, had not called out sick to work during his entire thirty-seven-year career. "If you are the bad guy, the worst of the worst, for the last thirty-seven years Buddy Murnane has been part of the team looking for you to bring you to justice," then Councilman James Oddo said during the 2010 ceremony at City Hall in Lower Manhattan. "He has truly put community, city, and country above all." As a supervising sergeant with the NYPD's Major Case Squad, Murnane played a key role in solving thousands of high-stakes investigations, ranging from kidnappings and hijackings to bank heists and major commercial burglaries.[85]

He also led a homicide unit within the New York City Housing Authority Police, overseeing cases across Staten Island, Brooklyn, and Queens. Throughout his career, Murnane earned numerous honors, including Staten Island Officer of the Year, the NYPD Combat Cross, the Medal of Exceptional Merit, the Commendation

85. D'Anna, Eddie. "NYPD Loses Its 'Iron Man'; Sgt. Francis Murnane Dies at 62." September 11th Families Association. March 16, 2015. https://911families. org/nypd-loses-its-iron-man-sgt-francis-murnane-dies-at-62/

Medal, five Meritorious Police Medals, and fourteen Excellent Police Duty Medals. His work was also formally recognized by multiple law enforcement agencies and prosecutors' offices across state lines.

"Buddy was my counterpart in the NYPD regarding truck hijacking crimes," Nelson says.

Coincidentally, Murnane's office was just down the hall from Lieutenant Al King in Coney Island.

"Since Al King's office and Buddy Murnane's office were only feet away, I would often meet with both of them at the same time," Nelson says. These meetings, without fail, would always turn comical. "Al King has such a great sense of humor; he is the type of person who could read a telephone directory to you and make you laugh."

King had a nickname for everyone, but in a good-natured way; the names were never meant to be hurtful.

Buddy Murnane, like Kenny McCabe, was solidly built and not someone you would want to tangle with physically.

"Al King would exaggerate Buddy's physique during our get-togethers by referring to him as 'Belly' Murnane," Nelson says. "But everyone knew it was all in good fun. These are the kind of things that only happen when you work closely with people you respect, not rivals. And they do much to help alleviate the tension and stress of the day to day."

Many of the truck hijackings Nelson's squad investigated originated from the ports and trucking companies in New Jersey, and the thefts were generally reported rather quickly to the Newark FBI Office by the trucking companies or by local New Jersey police departments.

Many, if not most, of the hijacked trucks would also find their way into Mafia "drops" in the New York City area.

"So, I would always let Buddy know if an informant had alerted us to a hijacked truck coming our way," Nelson says. In turn, Buddy would reciprocate and update Nelson regarding any trucks hijacked in New York City. This level of collaboration was key, especially as the US Attorney Offices in both the Eastern and

Southern Districts of New York had prosecutorial policies referred to as "blanket declinations."

In other words, if a truck was hijacked and no gun was displayed and the driver was not kidnapped during the theft, the federal government generally opted to decline federal prosecution in favor of turning the case over to the NYPD for New York State prosecution.

"In addition, if the financial loss, absent an armed hijacking, was relatively low in value, we would also give the case to Buddy's squad," Nelson adds.

There were also many instances where both squads would go out in the field together, particularly when a hijacking was suspected or a search warrant was intended to be executed.

"So you can see, under those circumstances, and the prosecutorial guidelines, there was rarely a reason for there to be conflict," Nelson says. "Except, once again, for the few individuals who just had inexplicable feelings of hatred for one or the other of our organizations."

During one of the last cases Anthony Nelson worked with Buddy Murnane before he transferred to 26 Federal Plaza to take over the FBI/NYPD Joint Bank Robbery Task Force, involved backing up George Wright, an FBI agent assigned to Nelson's squad who was acting in an undercover capacity and dealing with a Queens hijacking crew.

"Buddy was in my FBI car and we were about to arrest one of the hijackers," Nelson says. However, as Nelson drove directly up to the vehicle occupied by Wright and the hijacking subject, the hijacker spotted the car and several other FBI vehicles approaching and fled on foot. "George Wright ran in between two cars in an attempt to stop him and wound up running into a jagged and damaged car bumper. He ripped a massive hole in his leg while the rest of our team chased the subject down Junction Boulevard."

A young, new agent fresh out of the FBI Academy was the first agent to catch up to the subject.

"As the new agent grabbed him, the subject turned and punched the agent directly in his face," Nelson says. "By that time, we had all arrived on the scene and made the arrest."

The agent who caught him was not seriously injured, but George Wright required multiple stitches and was brought to the hospital.

"By a stroke of luck," Nelson adds, "an available ambulance was right at the corner of the street where we made the arrest." The ambulance crew was quickly able to treat George Wright's injury on scene before taking him to the hospital. "This case was just a typical example of Buddy Murnane's squad working alongside mine."

CHAPTER FIFTY-FIVE

It was a cold winter day in 1999 in an old abandoned railway yard out in Staten Island, and FBI Special Agent Anthony Nelson had a problem.

In the World Trade Brink's Robbery Case, DeCavalcante soldier Ralph Guarino provided the FBI with information on scores of crimes, including a tip on some stolen property and cars.

As supervisor of the Truck Hijacking Squad, Nelson worked the case with Buddy Murnane on the NYPD Major Case Squad. They tailed a convoy of trailers to that desolate old yard in spitting distance from the Kill Van Kull, a tidal strait between Staten Island, New York, and Bayonne. They waited in the distance for the trailers to be offloaded into a massive industrial warehouse. With a warrant in hand, they returned to the site later, not a soul in sight.

They gained access to the warehouse, and what they saw stunned the two lawmen—it was filled to the rafters, brimming with all kinds of stolen merchandise from automobiles to consumer electronics.

This presented a problem beyond even the capabilities of the FBI.

See, seizing the millions of dollars in stolen merchandise that day was of secondary consideration.

More importantly, realizing they'd uncovered a major crime ring, they needed to take down the thieves. And they needed to move quickly.

Nelson knew precisely who to call.

1-800-HARVEY

That's not an actual phone number. It's more of a reputation for how in-the-know members of law enforcement referred to the one, the only, Harvey Pincus.

Harvey Pincus, proprietor of Model Garage in Sunset Park for decades now, developed a sideline specializing in solving the unsolvable for law enforcement.

Not crimes.

Problems.

Like the one Nelson and Murnane faced on that cold winter morning.

"Anthony and Buddy wanted to get the merchandise out of there fast," Pincus recalls. "That way, when the hijackers come back for the merchandise and then see it's not there, they could follow them and make a bigger arrest."

Nelson admits he was skeptical. Maybe, finally, he'd found a problem even 1-800-HARVEY couldn't solve.

"I worked that job two and a half days straight, with a full crew with five box trucks and trailers," Pincus remembers. "I set up a relay. We'd get as much on the trucks as we could going fast back and forth, then make transfers from the trucks to larger trailers at another location, then run the trailers back to my warehouse on 39th Street in Brooklyn to unload and store."

Racing against the clock, knowing any moment the hijackers could return, Harvey and his crew kept going. "So, we're doing this nonstop, more than two days," Pincus explains, "and Anthony and Buddy just couldn't believe it, telling me over and over, 'Harvey, I don't know how you keep this up.'

"I mean, these are tough guys. Buddy was an ex-Marine who started out in Housing Authority Police before it merged with the NYPD, went on the Major Case Squad, and was famous for never taking a day off in his career. So that's high praise coming from him, may he rest in peace," Pincus concludes.

"There was so much hijacked property stored in that Staten Island warehouse that it took Harvey, his workers, and my entire squad of agents all through a cold winter's night and into the following days to recover all of it," Nelson says. "I even invited Al King down because the recovery of the merchandise, which even included several stolen cars, resulted from information provided by Ralph Guarino. Since I had already involved Al in the DeCavalcante case to debrief Vinnie Oceans about the Brooklyn murders, I invited him along on other developments in the case."

"Anthony says he didn't know if I would be able to clear it out in time," Pincus says. "But I knew I would. After all, I'm 1-800-HARVEY."

Harvey Pincus is one of those unforgettable supporting characters you only find in New York's law enforcement landscape.

"My mother and father had a business, Model Garage, and I started working for my father, actually hanging around the garage, starting about ten or eleven years old," Pincus says. "It was just a garage; we stored vehicles and commercial cars, provided repair service, had lifts, and in addition to service, we washed cars and fixed flats."

Pincus was drafted into the Marine Corps, where he served for two years. Upon his return, he went back to work with his father at Model Garage. Then one day, Harvey got a call from the FBI.

The Bureau had a problem—the FBI needed to vacate a building on East 69th Street in Midtown Manhattan. The lease on a full garage in the building was expiring. The landlord wanted them out.

The FBI leased a new space downtown in Tribeca. But they had to vacate by a specific time or incur severe financial penalties.

Pincus made an appointment.

"To make a long story short, they had a lot of these vehicles that had been seized and stored there, and over time, many of them had been cannibalized for parts," Pincus says. "Some were missing wheels, doors, engines, and some were completely stripped down. Basically, you had so many cars dead in the water that had to either be towed or, if they couldn't be towed, put on a flatbed and transported."

It was a big, demanding job; nothing was easy about it. Harvey presented a deal.

"Now this guy, Tom Lee, he's gun-shy, very skeptical, didn't think I could get it all done, and I could see in his face he felt that I was not going to live up to my end," Pincus says. "I said, 'Give me the benefit of doing what I said I could do.'"

Harvey and his crew worked around the clock for seven days.

The following Monday, Tom Lee returned.

"I had the entire garage cleaned out, broom swept, all the vehicles relocated into their new building," Pincus says. "Then Tom went down to the garage on North Moore Street in Tribeca, an elevated building with five floors, and it was all straightened out."

Harvey submitted the bill. Then, Tom Lee asked for his business card.

And so a legend was born.

Word started to get around.

An administrator for the US Attorney for the Southern District of New York office when Rudolph Giuliani held the post called Harvey once, asking if he could store a couple of cars.

Harvey responded to a warehouse on Little West 4th Street in Manhattan's Meatpacking District.

"Sure, the building's garage had these cars, but they'd not been cared for, so they had flat tires, wouldn't start, and all needed to be transported on flatbeds," Pincus remembers. "She said, 'Just get the cars out of there,' so I did."

These were vehicles seized as part of the investigations that led to the Pizza Connection, a large-scale international heroin trafficking and money laundering operation conducted by the Sicilian Mafia and American organized crime families, primarily in the 1980s. The operation involved using seemingly legitimate pizza parlors as fronts for the distribution of heroin and the laundering of the proceeds.

"I took these five cars, towed them, cleaned them up—high-end cars, Mercedes, Cadillacs, a Lincoln Town Car," Pincus says. "So we started with five cars, and it became a regular thing. At one point, I was storing more than one hundred and twenty cars for the FBI. And this was way before computers. I had everything organized on index cards, and we billed them once a month for towing, services, and storage.

"I got friendly with different squads in the Bureau, basically in Manhattan," he continues. "Then, when they opened up an office on Queens Boulevard in Forest Hills, I became friendly with different squads and started to store their evidence."

Before long, Model Garage got the call for anything the agents couldn't carry with their left and right hands.

"Then I got started with Car Squads, the C15 Taskforce, and grew my fan club with more agents because I worked with them on a lot of major cases, as one case led to another led to another, and it just started to escalate."

About this time, Harvey Pincus first crossed paths with Anthony Nelson.

"Anthony was actually an agent on the Major Theft Squad, that's how I met him," Pincus says. "Anthony left the squad, went to bank robberies, and then to CID, and went to Fort Hamilton, and all along the way, I worked with Anthony.

"Whenever Anthony needed services, he'd call, say, 'Harvey, I got a problem, I got this and this and this,'" Pincus says. "So I started doing recovery jobs for the Bank Robbery Squad; you know, the getaway cars and the holdup cars, and I grew my reputation as 1-800-HARVEY. So I grew with the squad."

That reputation was earned, not given lightly.

"Usually these things were after hours, middle of the night, Saturdays, Sundays," Pincus says. "I had a telephone book of agents. I knew everyone, and as agents transferred, I always went with them. That's how Model Garage got involved with the FBI to start, and then the Queens DA, the Brooklyn DA, the DEA, the US Marshals, Customs, all of them. You do good work, you don't turn down the hard jobs, one thing leads to another, and then another."

"I'm still close friends with Harvey to this day, and he still owns the garage." Nelson laughs. "I'd call upon Harvey for services so often, in fact, I saw Harvey as almost another agent on my squad."

Pincus was more than a tow operator. "He had the talent, ability, and equipment to help us accomplish tasks that would be worthy of a James Bond movie," Nelson says.

And whenever presented with impossible, even dangerous requests, the unflappable Pincus had one response: "No problem."

Not only did the FBI task Pincus with running at least five dig-site operations to recover the bodies of victims slain by organized crime figures, but he was also trusted to physically relocate cooperating witnesses.

Once a criminal makes that decision, for security and safety, the family needs to leave the house immediately, and the home needs to be cleared out.

"I'd get those calls and I'd have to respond at the drop of a hat," Pincus says. "It all had to be done within twenty-four hours. So I'd get to the house and move them out, maybe use a couple of trucks to get in and get out, then go to another location to load it all into a large truck and then relocate them, sometimes on the other side of the United States."

Over the years, Nelson and Pincus bond over crime scenes, some that went way beyond hijackings and witness relocations, and truly tested the resolve of 1-800-HARVEY.

In 1992, Pincus responded to a call from Nelson on a Saturday, asking to meet him at Fort Totten in Queens. Fort Totten is a former active Army installation on the north shore of Long Island. While much of the fort has become a public park and the property is now owned by the City of New York, the Army Reserve continues to maintain a presence, and it is used for NYPD and FDNY training.

"There was an event being hosted on the grounds, the Lawrence Carr Carnival," Nelson remembers. "You know, one of those travelling carnivals whose workers were complete transients, most with no verifiable identification, just wandering the country, from city to city."

Nelson needs Pincus to pick up a Porta-John—this was a curious request until Pincus learned one gruesome detail.

"Someone went into the Porta-John and had a baby, and then left the baby in there," Pincus says. "So I had to get the cleaning service to come down. The way they clean these things out is through a big suction pipe. We did it at my building in Red Hook."

"It was not a pleasant scene to see a fetus with an umbilical cord still attached being sucked out of the portable toilet," Nelson says. The mother was never identified. "The NYC Medical Examiner's office buries unclaimed bodies of deceased individuals on Hart Island, or at least did during my era. The island was, and probably still is, used for that purpose. It's often referred to as Potter's Field. I believe the burials were handled by prisoners who volunteered for work details."

Today, Hart Island, located at the western end of Long Island Sound, in the Northeastern Bronx, still serves as the final resting place for New Yorkers who are indigent, poor, or whose bodies go unclaimed, with estimates that likely more than one million people have been buried on the site.[86]

The following year, the Lawrence Carr Carnival returned to New York City.

Once again, Anthony Nelson was called in.

And once again, he pulled in Harvey Pincus.

"Despite my less-than-stellar personal opinion of their operation, they came to me for help because they were being extorted for large amounts of money by members of the Colombo Family," Nelson says.

Following an investigation, Nelson arrested a Colombo Family associate on federal extortion charges. "When I arrested him, I did a cursory search of his vehicle and did not see anything of evidentiary value," he says. "However, I seized his car and had Harvey Pincus tow it for me."

---

86. Data Team. "Hart Island." https://council.nyc.gov/data/hart-island/

Back in Sunset Park, Harvey later conducted a thorough search of the vehicle to inventory any property. He found a large stash of US currency in a hidden compartment.

Nelson laughs. "Just another great job by 1-800-HARVEY."

In 1996, FBI Special Agent Anthony Nelson was wrapping up a crime scene investigation in the parking lot of the Brooklyn VA Hospital in Fort Hamilton when he called Harvey Pincus.

"Anthony calls me from the VA, says a guy pulled into the parking lot in a small car, took out a gun and put a bullet through his jaw and into his head," Pincus says. "I said, 'I'll be there within the hour.'"

"I was there with a few other agents from my squad, and I was placing paper bags on the hands of that veteran who'd just shot himself," Nelson remembers. "The bullet entered under his chin, went through his brain, and lodged somewhere within the headliner of the car he sat in."

That day in 1996, as Harvey arrived on scene, the deceased veteran was still in his car, with Nelson examining his body.

Nelson waved Pincus through VA security.

"The coroner was there and I watched Anthony take two paper bags, put them over the victim's hands, and take masking tape and tape the bags closed around his wrists, as if he was putting his hands in gloves," Pincus remembers. "When he was done, I asked why he did that. He said that's for the gun residue for later when they test the gun versus powder, and the hole in the roof of the car. So Anthony knew how to improvise.

"I take the car, put it up on the flatbed, do an inventory, take pictures with a Polaroid, which was a very big thing at the time," Pincus says. "They give me an EV number—or Evidence number—I tag the car, take pics, fill out the form, and pass it along to the evidence department." As Pincus wrapped up, he noticed something was off with his friend.

"How can you keep doing this?" he asked Nelson.

The agent did not have a ready answer. But it made him think about his career.

"Perhaps it was time to gain that sense of contribution I had always sought by other means," Nelson says. "Perhaps it was time for me to consider applying for a supervisory position and imparting some of my knowledge to newer agents who needed experience."

Nelson had not been interested in promotions. For him, the FBI was a calling. "I was in a rare position, or at least I was during my era, where I was evaluated on my ability to perform my assignments with minimal supervision," Nelson attests.

Comparatively speaking, police departments are, by nature, paramilitary organizations. Officers are strictly supervised, their movements and actions closely monitored. In contrast, at least within the Criminal Division of the FBI, most agents operate with more autonomy.

For the most part, absent joint, unusual, or dangerous investigative activity, FBI agents chart their own course. They have the flexibility to change work shifts, traverse the city several times a day, meet with informants, collect evidence, conduct interviews—basically solve crimes without someone looking over their shoulder.

"Agents are expected to make supervisors aware of their work schedules and investigative activities," Nelson says. "They must also be available to assure their safety, emergency assignments, and other needs of the Bureau."

Nelson never seriously considered applying for promotion.

That's not to say opportunities did not arise.

"By 1984, I was being urged by several of my superiors to apply for supervisory vacancies," Nelson says. "Even my friend and boss at the time, ASAC Jim Murphy, had urged me to think about career advancement."

Promotions for most people, especially within the business world, are usually exciting and coveted events in their lives. They come with increased prestige and financial benefits.

"I wasn't interested in either at the time," Nelson says. "I knew I would never have everything I ever wanted in life, but I also knew I already had everything, if not more, than I needed."

So Nelson did not have a response for Pincus. But it did make him think.

Just days after that investigation, Nelson processed the scene of another veteran who died while injecting himself with heroin in a VA Hospital bathroom.

That scene, plus another one soon after, again gave him pause.

"I'd taken a new female FBI agent with me to recover a completely decayed body floating in the waters off Fort Hamilton," Nelson says.

Over the years, that stretch of water has seen more than its fair share of floaters. Due to the frequency of suicides at the Verrazano, construction of twenty-eight thousand feet of stainless-steel mesh prevention fencing was completed in 2023. But it's not just jumpers.

The Narrows is in the aptly named Gravesend Bay tidal strait separating the boroughs of Staten Island and Brooklyn, connecting Upper New York Bay with Lower New York Bay and forming the principal channel to the Hudson River, the maritime gateway to New York City and the Northeastern United States.

The Narrows' dark and unpredictable undercurrents have a habit of drawing more than driftwood to the shores of Southern Brooklyn.

"The new female agent who helped me with the floater was also assigned to help me prepare for the trial of two subjects who planned a prison escape plot at the Metropolitan Correctional Center in Manhattan," Nelson says. "She did a great job in both dealing with the floater and with the trial preparation. I also felt rewarded for guiding her and giving her the on-the-job experience in just one day. It reinforced my thoughts about applying for a supervisory position."

Meanwhile, Nelson and Pincus had become good friends. And after all, it can't hurt to have a friend in the FBI.

Model Garage opened nearly eighty years ago in Sunset Park on 39th Street behind Greenwood Cemetery. Pincus has since added a Red Hook facility.

"In Red Hook, I got a building that was thirty-three thousand square feet on the waterfront, fit an aircraft carrier in there," Pincus says. "Whatever I couldn't put in 39th Street—like the takedown of vehicles from a chop shop, whatever—I put it in there. I formed my own system and then went to computers and incorporated all that. And Anthony was always there, another trailer load of cigarettes, liquor, whatever, and I had the forklifts, the trailers, the trucks ... I fit the Bureau's program, 1-800-HARVEY."

Under Pincus, the Sunset Park facility has grown to overtake the entire block, spanning from 8th to 9th Avenues.

However, this was a very different area in the 1980s and 1990s.

Sunset Park was once a bustling hub of manufacturing and shipping, home to a vibrant working-class community. But in the 1950s, the neighborhood began a long decline as major employers shut down or relocated, eliminating more than thirty thousand jobs and leaving behind vast, empty factories. Rows of brownstones and modest apartment buildings fell victim to a national housing scandal that saw low-income families—many of whom couldn't afford the costs—lured into purchasing poorly renovated homes backed by federally insured mortgages. The fallout was swift and devastating.

By the early 1970s, Sunset Park was dotted with abandoned properties. Many were left vacant by owners—often Hispanic immigrants—unable to keep up with mortgage payments. These buildings became targets for arson and vandalism, accelerating the neighborhood's decline. The federal government officially labeled Sunset Park a "poverty area."[87]

Over time, Sunset Park experienced a dramatic turnaround. By February 2016, its western section had become a symbol of urban renewal, featured in the *New York Times* as one of "New York's Next Hot Neighborhoods."

But back in the 1980s, Pincus was lucky to have such close ties with law enforcement. "We were always very fortunate, almost never had a break-in, never had burglaries, never lost vehicles," Pincus says. "However, there was an incident, this local guy who lived on 7th Avenue, married to a Spanish girl, and he was one bad hombre.

87. Maitland, Leslie. "Despair in Sunset Park and Hope, Too." New York Times. December 8, 1978. https://www.nytimes.com/1978/12/08/archives/despair-in-sunset-park-and-hope-too-reclaiming-the-neighborhood.html

"He broke into my garage, actually came down through the skylight, so when I walked in at seven a.m., the place was upside down," Pincus says. "It could've been much worse. I had seven hundred dollars in cash saved to buy rugs for my house. They found the envelope and left."

Pincus shared the troubling news with Nelson.

"Anthony responded immediately when he heard the call and got the Bureau to install alarm systems that were wired to the command center at the Javits Center," Pincus says. "So, if an alarm went off, the duty officer would call me, and I'd come down from Bay Ridge, where I was living by then. Maybe it was a mouse or a rat or the wind or whatever, but I'd check buildings and call back to cancel the alarm. But really, we never had any problems after that, and Anthony was responsible."

Harvey Pincus was later involved in another major case with Anthony Nelson and his squad.

A confidential informant provided a tip concerning the hijacking of a United Parcel Service truck as it headed to the Verrazano Bridge.

Retired Special Agent Jason Randazzo was part of the operation.

"I remember that hijacking; the UPS truck contained two and a half million dollars in jewelry," Randazzo says. "They must've had an informant who gave them the information that either the head of the crew or one of the crew members had moved part of the stolen merchandise to a vehicle outside his home in Mill Basin."

The truck, with half the load, was parked on Ralph Avenue across from a strip mall near Avenue J. The rest of the loot was offloaded into a van and sat in front of a home in Mill Basin, according to the informant.

Nelson did not want to rush the arrest and confiscate the vehicle.

Instead, he wanted to steal it.

And he knew just who to call.

"So, Anthony calls me, tells me about the merchandise in the van, and asks me if I can go out to Mill Basin and grab the van," Pincus says. "Of course I said I could do it. I grabbed a bunch of guys and we headed over there in the middle of the night. We went in with an unmarked flatbed, grabbed the van, and took off."

But there was a complication.

"They had tail cars and plenty of agents for cover," Pincus recalls. "But they told me later, the guy actually came out and took off looking for me. By then, I had shot out of there fast, so I didn't know."

"So Anthony has Harvey, at about two a.m., steal the stolen load," Randazzo recalls. "A short while, we're talking maybe a minute or two, one of the subjects, Glenn Schaeffer, comes out, finds the truck missing. He goes completely ballistic. Jumps in his car, does three complete high-speed screeching U-turns while screaming to himself out the window of his car, then takes off looking for a van.

"Mill Basin was like a Howard Beach West, if you will, notorious as a stronghold for organized crime, so I guess this guy felt pretty confident leaving all of that stolen property just sitting in a van in an area of Brooklyn where there was no really no thru traffic, surrounded by water and not a clean exit," Randazzo says. "You have to have a reason for going in there.

"So Harvey jacked up the van in the middle of the night and drove it out of there," Randazzo adds. "But then this guy comes out in his underwear, yelling like a maniac, so angry, ranting. "I remember Kevin Butt was there in a tail car and he's driving behind Harvey, but in front of this guy, who's trying to find Harvey, who had the van on the tow." Kevin Butt was a detective assigned to the NYPD Major Case Squad under Buddy Murnane.

"And now I'm driving behind this guy, and the big thing is we have to control the situation, and we do not want to expose ourselves as law enforcement," Randazzo says.

There was a substantial level of risk developing.

"This guy knows someone in the know ripped him off, but he doesn't know it's law enforcement," Randazzo continues, "and we want it to stay like that so then we can see how he reacts, what he does next, who he's conspiring with, so we can build the case. Fortunately, that's how it played out.

"It shows that even under controlled circumstances, it can get to be a bit of a Wild West situation very quickly."

"Sure, this was serious business, but I trusted these guys," Pincus says. "I knew I had these guys on my back all the time. I was part of the squad, and it was like a family. They look out for me and I look out for them."

Pincus managed to slip away into the Brooklyn night.

The FBI later arrested Shaeffer and recovered the jewelry.

"Number one: Anthony Nelson is a unique person, a very unique human being," Pincus says fondly. "What he says is what you see and what you receive. Anthony Nelson is very knowledgeable about many things; he inspires confidence, and he is very, very capable. He has a steady speed for doing things, doesn't have a high speed or a low speed, but a steady speed, and that speed is right below the radar."

CHAPTER FIFTY-SIX

J. Edgar Hoover, legendary director of the Bureau, was many things.

However, a champion of women's rights was not one of them.

Even by 1969, when Anthony Nelson entered on duty as a support employee with the Bureau, there were no female FBI Special Agents.

Sure, when Hoover started at the Bureau in 1924, he inherited two female agents: Jessie B. Duckstein and Alaska P. Davidson. But both resigned within months. And sure, in 1924, Hoover grudgingly changed the status of Lenore Houston from "special employee" in the New York Office to "special agent." But he only did that to appease a congressman. Houston resigned at the end of 1928.[88]

"Hoover held a firm belief that the position of FBI Special Agent was much too dangerous and arduous a position for women," Nelson says. "Hoover's misguided—and by today's standards, misogynistic—belief was also shared to a great extent by the US military that did not assign women to frontline combat."

Following Hoover's death in May 1972, Acting FBI Director L. Patrick Gray announced the FBI would be accepting applications from female candidates.

On July 17, 1972, Susan Roley Malone and Joanne Pierce Misko were officially sworn in and became the first two female Special

---

88. FBI. "Female Special Agent's Briefcase." December 21, 2022. https://www.fbi.gov/history/artifacts/female-special-agent-briefcase

Agents of the FBI. By the end of 1972, eleven women would be sworn in.

Two years later, in 1974, the first female FBI Special Agent was assigned to the New York Office.

"Her name is Margot Dennedy," Nelson says. "Margot immediately became inundated by requests from the male agents in the office who requested her help in major criminal investigations.

In 1977, after Nelson had graduated from the FBI Academy and returned to the Truck Hijacking Squad of the New York City Office, he couldn't help but notice that Margot was spreading herself thin by the overwhelming number of requests for her help.

"My desk was located nearby," Nelson says. "It would've been wrong to view her as somewhat of a novelty. The truth was that J. Edgar Hoover was wrong by not recognizing the essential need for female FBI agents."

Margot Dennedy did significant undercover work in major kidnapping cases, including the 1974 kidnapping of businessman Jack Teich in Kings Point, New York, which resulted in the largest ransom paid in the United States up to that point.

Teich was kidnapped by radicals sympathetic to the Palestinian liberation political cause. Teich was thirty-four years old when he was abducted at gunpoint in his driveway on November 12, 1974. He was reported missing by his wife, Janet, after he failed to return home from work.

The kidnappers began contacting his family the following night and demanded $750,000 in ransom ($4.78 million in today's money).

In 2013, this crime was listed as one of the most notorious on Long Island. The Teich case was also cited in a 1975 *New York Times* article, indicating kidnappings had increased over the previous ten years. Teich's older brother, Buddy, was the original target of the abduction.

The ransom was paid, with Teich's wife and brother following instructions to leave the money in a locker in Pennsylvania Station.

During the week he was held, Teich was bound in chains and kept in a closet. His kidnappers made anti-Semitic and anti-wealth comments and accusations, and threatened to rob him. Although he was told he was being taken to Harlem, it is believed he was held in the Bronx. Teich was told the money would "go out of the country to feed hungry people, Palestinians, and poor Blacks."

"After delivering a $750,000 ransom, Teich was dumped from a car on the Belt Parkway near Kennedy Airport," Nelson says. "Margot Dennedy was an essential part of covering the ransom drop."

One of the subjects involved in the kidnapping was subsequently identified as Richard Williams. He was tracked down and arrested in California in September 1976, where money tied to the ransom was used to buy groceries and supplies. He was found with thirty-eight thousand dollars of the ransom money in the walls of a mobile home he shared. He was convicted of several charges and sentenced to life imprisonment for the kidnapping.

"Women Special Agents became an essential part of the FBI's workforce and many, if not most, of the FBI's investigative successes could not have been accomplished without them," Nelson attests. "Special Agent Eileen O'Rourke was one of my most effective agents when I took over as the supervisor of the Major Theft—Truck Hijacking Squad in 1998."

"Eileen was perhaps the only Special Agent I ever met who had the unique ability to perfectly balance the demands of the job with her foremost job as a mother," Nelson adds. "She was, and still is, one of the kindest, most thoughtful people I've ever known. Her kindness and caring were such evident qualities that she became one of the few females who was able to win over even the most vicious Mafia figures."

In fact, Eileen O'Rourke, along with FBI Agents Nora Conley and Courtanae Druker, successfully conducted some of the most important debriefings of Vincent "Vinnie Oceans" Palermo, head of the DeCavalcante Family, who became a witness for the government.

"Eileen O'Rourke was also highly thought of by the detectives of the NYPD, including my friend Lieutenant Al King, the commanding officer of the Brooklyn South Homicide Task Force," Nelson says. "Although Eileen was tall, thin, and physically fit, she had a voracious appetite whenever our squad had dinners. Al King, in fact, coined a nickname for her: Two Fork O'Rourke."

"Sure, I had nicknames; I tried to break the tension, it's important," King says. "That's something I picked up in Vietnam, and it is much needed because the tension will crush you." But no, Anthony Nelson never had a nickname, King laughs.

"I personally will never forget Eileen's kindness and efficiency," Nelson says. "To this day, Eileen O'Rourke has never forgotten my birthday, and she calls me each year to wish me another great year."

Eileen O'Rourke followed in the footsteps of her father, Edward Thomas O'Rourke, who recently passed away, enjoying a distinguished career at the Bureau, especially investigating organized crime. In October 2008, she was recognized by then US Attorney General Michael B. Mukase as part of a team of law enforcement members in New York who received the Attorney General's Award for Distinguished Service for their work during the investigation and trial of Bonanno Family acting boss Vincent Basciano and the prosecution of the gangsters who served him.

"Basciano's conviction was the product of a lengthy investigation into the Bonanno family, which has resulted in the incarceration of every major leader of this violent criminal enterprise," the press release read announcing the commendation. After O'Rourke retired, she was later appointed associate director of Global Security Group at Merck.

While women still represent a minority of special agents (around twenty-four percent in 2024), they are more numerous in other roles, such as intelligence analysts and professional staff. And more and more women have risen to admirably serve prominent roles at the Bureau.

Mary E. Galligan served as a senior special agent and supervised the FBI's probe of the 9/11 terrorist attacks.

Cassi Chandler served as the FBI's first African American female special agent assistant director as well as the Bureau's first female national spokesperson and director of public and community affairs.

Kathleen McChesney served as the first woman special agent supervisor in the Los Angeles Field Office and executive assistant director at FBI headquarters.

And My Harrison served as a law enforcement officer for ten years before joining the Bureau and ended her career as an assistant director at FBI Headquarters.

If women in general faced an uphill climb in law enforcement, that slope was even steeper for women of color.

For Anthony Nelson, Sylvia Elizabeth Mathis stands out as not just an outstanding female colleague but an exceptional Special Agent, regardless of gender.

Mathis was the first African-American woman to become a Special Agent for the FBI. She joined the Bureau not long before Nelson, arriving at the FBI Academy on February 17, 1976. She was a pioneer at the time—only forty-one of the Bureau's 8,500 agents were women.

After completing her training, Mathis received her badge and credentials as an FBI Special Agent on June 2, 1976. Her first posting was at the FBI's New York Field Office, where she would join the organized crime squad.

"Silvia literally sat at a desk directly in front of mine in NYC," Nelson recalls. "She was working on counterfeit credit card cases with Herbie Goldstein, the American Express investigator we worked closely with on many of the organized crime-related credit card cases." This led to other high-profile assignments.

"She was later sent by the FBI to conduct interviews in the infamous Jim Jones massacre case in Guyana," Nelson adds.

In 1979, Mathis left the FBI to work as an attorney in New York. In 1982, she returned to Florida to care for her family. Sadly, Mathis died in a car accident at age thirty-four on October 22, 1983.

In an interesting side note, a new crime thriller series, *Duster*, created by J. J. Abrams and LaToya Morgan and starring Josh Holloway, Rachel Hilson, and Keith David, premiered on the streaming platform HBO Max on May 15, 2025. The show is set in 1972; Hilson portrays a fictional version of the FBI's first Black woman agent, and Holloway plays a getaway driver. It ran for one season.

Today, more than 2,600 female special agents are serving on and leading counterterrorism squads, cyber squads, counterintelligence squads, and criminal squads. They lead field offices, divisions, and overseas offices. They work as firearms instructors and in all other specialty fields.[89]

The FBI now has a goal to increase the percentage of female special agents to thirty percent by 2030.

"These women helped pave the way for many who came after and exemplified the very best qualities of what it takes to be successful as an FBI Special Agent," Nelson says. "I am honored to have served alongside them and regret that, even today in this modern era, they often do not get the recognition they so greatly deserve."

CHAPTER FIFTY-SEVEN

In the winter of 1999, an agent assigned to Anthony Nelson's squad received informant information about a plan by a known criminal group to hijack a truck at gunpoint in Maspeth, Queens. With the hijacking set to take place within the hour, the squad geared up and headed out to the area.

Local news reported it to be the coldest day of the year, with an ice storm expected to hit the city later that night.

Nelson thought little of the bitter winds ripping through him and his squad that January morning as they set up surveillance of the area. They remained onsite for the rest of the afternoon.

The bitter cold day wore on. The armed hijacking never took place. The squad returned to the Brooklyn-Queens FBI Office in Kew Gardens. But just as Nelson was taking off his ballistic vest and packing up his gear, he received an urgent call from the FBI Operations Center.

The Coast Guard reported a mutiny aboard a Russian ship, the *Banner of October*.

"They also told me that the ship was moored within US territorial waters, just off the coast of Sandy Hook in New Jersey, and that the ship's crew had murdered the captain," Nelson says.

During pleasant weather, Sandy Hook is a picturesque barrier spit about six miles in length at the north end of the Jersey Shore, enclosing the southern entrance of Lower New York Bay south of New York City, guarding it against the rough open waters of the Atlantic Ocean.

For more than four hundred years, ships have run aground along this coast from Sandy Hook down to Cape May, with its shifting shoals and many sand bars. Beneath the surface, some 3,700 vessels met their fate off these treacherous shorelines.

Owned by the federal government, most of it is managed by the National Park Service and its rangers as the Sandy Hook Unit of Gateway National Recreation Area.

"I mobilized my squad back at the BQ FBI Office and directed Special Agent Ted Otto to coordinate with the Coast Guard to take us out to board the ship," Nelson says. "Otto notified me a short time later that the Coast Guard refused my request because the weather, especially out at Sandy Hook, made it too dangerous."

Rough winter seas and the approaching ice storm brewing made boarding the ship treacherous, and to get aboard, agents had to climb a "Jacob's ladder," nothing more than ropes with unstable wooden slats for steps. Even in ideal conditions, a Jacob's ladder is a challenge.

Nelson had other issues to deal with besides finding transportation out to the *Banner of October*. "For one thing, I had no direct communication with anyone aboard the ship and, according to the Coast Guard, no one aboard could speak English," he explains.

Nelson was able, however, to reach a representative of the US-based company that had a contract with the owners of the *Banner of October* for shuttling cars between the United States and the Dominican Republic. This representative assured him there was no mutiny aboard the ship and that the captain was not murdered.

Instead, the situation was one of despair.

"The ship's crew had not been paid in months," Nelson says. "They had no current work to perform, and they had run out of food."

There was only a limited supply of fuel, and from what the company rep was able to determine, the captain of the ship died by suicide. Nelson also learned the vessel was under the jurisdiction of the Ukrainian government, not Russia.

"Whether the ship was Ukrainian or Russian made little difference to me other than the fact that whatever law enforcement actions I took could create a diplomatic issue with either country," Nelson adds. This was a delicate situation.

"I certainly was not going to create even a slight chance of danger for any of my squad members by totally relying upon the little information I learned from the US shipping company," Nelson says. "But I also didn't want to assault the Ukrainian ship with an FBI SWAT team and really create a diplomatic incident if the overwhelming force was unnecessary."

Later in the evening, the shipping company advised Nelson that there was a qualified pilot aboard the *Banner of October* who could, and would, maneuver the ship to a position near the Verrazano Narrows Bridge directly across from Fort Hamilton.

Nelson set up a command post, directing his entire squad over to Fort Hamilton, where he'd brief them on a tactical plan for boarding the ship.

Still, Nelson lacked transport to the ship.

"But I always knew when I needed help, I could rely upon my friends in the New York City Police Department," Nelson says. "So, I started making my calls."

Nelson contacted the NYPD Harbor Unit and they were willing to take the FBI agents out.

"My next call was to my dear friend, Lieutenant Al King, commanding officer of the NYPD Brooklyn South Homicide Squad," Nelson adds.

"The *Banner of October*, what a mess that was," Al King recalls. "Anthony calls me up, and then of course I head to the scene, and I'm in a suit and tie. I remember that night clearly, and it was cold, so very cold."

The *Banner of October* was now positioned near the Verrazano Bridge and within Al King's area of jurisdiction. He agreed to meet Nelson at Fort Hamilton to help in any way possible.

"When Al King arrived at Fort Hamilton, he found me feverishly working the phones, still speaking with the shipping company," Nelson says. "I was also contacting our Evidence Response Team, headed by Special Agent Stan Ragan."

Ragan spent twenty-nine years with the FBI, where he held a range of critical roles. He served on the SWAT team, led the Evidence Response Team (ERT) as its coordinator, and handled crisis management operations in both investigative and supervisory capacities. Ragan played a role in numerous high-profile investigations led by the FBI's New York Office, often overseeing the Bureau's international crisis response efforts. His work included coordinating deployments to major incidents such as the El-Khobar Towers bombing in Saudi Arabia, the downing of TWA Flight 800 off Long Island, EgyptAir Flight 990 near Rhode Island, the *USS Cole* attack in Yemen, and the US Embassy bombings in Kenya and Tanzania, as well as the September 11th terrorist attacks. Domestically, he also contributed to the FBI's response to Hurricane Marilyn, the emergency landing of U.S. Airways Flight 1549 on the Hudson River, and Hurricane Sandy.

Before retiring, Ragan served as a senior advisor to New York Field Office executives, developing continuity of operations plans and procedures.

As the weather worsened, Nelson had one more knot to unravel.

"I needed to locate a Russian-speaking FBI agent to go along with us," Nelson says. But after a few calls, he was able to locate a translator. "I was also lucky, and grateful, to have Special Agents Jason Randazzo and Peter Kohn with me. Both of these agents were assigned to my squad, and I always felt secure when I had them with me. They were not only Special Agents, they were also Special People, two of my best agents, and I could always rely upon them for total support during tactical situations or any other types of assignments."

Randazzo grew up in the Richmond Hill section of Queens and, like Nelson, had several friends who decided to pursue "that life."

"For Jason and me," Nelson says, "it was endemic in our respective neighborhoods. Euphemistically speaking, you had your cowboys and you had your Indians."

One of Jason's closest friends from childhood was John Alite, later confidant to John "Junior" Gotti Jr., who briefly took over as acting head of the Gambino Family when his father was imprisoned in 1992. On their little league team, Randazzo batted fourth in the lineup, Alite third.

"When I first came back to New York, I hoped, actually prayed, that I wouldn't be assigned to the Gambino Squad because I didn't want to use my personal relationship with John [Alite] in my professional arena," Randazzo recalls.

Randazzo spoke to the case agent for John Gotti Sr., George Gabriel, and advised him of his prior relationship with Alite, including that although the FBI Special Agent had not spoken to him on the phone and would not be found on a wiretap, Randazzo ran into Alite on occasion, as his mother still lived in Richmond Hill. Although by this time, Alite had relocated to a compound in Cherry Hill, New Jersey, his family still lived in the adjoining town of Woodhaven.

"From that point moving forward, whenever I would inadvertently meet John on the street or, later on, receive phone calls from him through the years, I would inform George or the case agent," Randazzo says. "These calls included a question from John in which two Special Agents from the squad paid him a visit to advise him that there was a contract on his life initiated by the husband of John Sr.'s daughter. John had contacted me wanting to know the veracity of the information."

In 1999, Junior Gotti pled guilty to racketeering charges and went to prison until 2005. Between 2004 and 2009, additional federal charges were filed against the Mob scion, and Alite became a cooperating witness for the government.

Alite had been the best man at Junior Gotti's wedding, and he committed several murders on behalf of the Gambino Family. However, Alite was eventually arrested and decided to testify against Gotti Jr. in federal court. Junior was tried on four separate occasions for a variety of federal crimes, but each time, the government was unable to convict him. Following his fourth trial, which ended in a hung jury, the government decided not to try him again.

Randazzo and Kohn set about gathering all the weaponry and equipment Nelson and team anticipated would be needed for the developing operation.

"Peter Kohn was one of the most low-key, quiet, and unassuming agents I had ever met," Nelson shares. "But Pete was built like a professional football player and could easily take down most doors during a tactical entry into a premise without the use of a battering ram."

"I actually knew the duty captain who responded that night," Randazzo says. "I got in touch with him through his brother. I knew his brother, who was an agent on one of the other teams. When I did SOG, he was on another SOG team, Dennis Collins. I still see him over the years. His brother was the duty captain responding to the dock the night of the incident, so that just goes to show what a small world law enforcement can be sometimes."

Meanwhile, as Nelson made telephone call after telephone call, his immediate supervisor was calling him with scores of questions he needed answered in anticipation of being asked those same questions by his bosses as well as officials at FBI Headquarters in Washington, DC.

"I could not blame him for asking so many questions," Nelson says. "It was necessary information he was seeking. But while Al King was listening to my end of the conversation, he asked me about the color of the ship and exactly how many feet it was in length. I told him I didn't want to be rude but I had to hang up. I was trying to get this ship into New York Harbor. I was also trying to find a Russian-speaking agent, a harbor unit to get me onsite, and an arrest team to board. I had no way of knowing the color of the ship nor did I care."

Around midnight, the squad was ready to go. "We headed to the Harbor Unit's base in Bay Ridge." They soon learned they would have to limit the number of people who could board the harbor launch.

"We then headed out with my boarding team carrying heavy weapons, as well as myself, the Russian-speaking agent, Al King, Detective Anthony Angotti, and the NYPD Duty Captain Tim Collins, whose brother Denis was an FBI agent," Nelson says.

When they arrived at the *Banner of October* in rough seas, the crew threw the Jacob's ladder down the side of the ship as waves were rocking the harbor launch and ice pellets were falling at an alarming rate.

"Once the ladder was lowered for us to board, I felt much more at ease," Nelson says. "At that point, I fully expected there would not be any resistance to our boarding."

Immediately, the tactical team, which included Pete Kohn, climbed the ladder.

The evidence team, Russian interpreter, Al King, and Tim Collins followed.

As each person went up the ladder, the Harbor Unit backed away from the Ukrainian ship. Then it approached again, repeatedly, a maneuver designed to allow each climber to fall into the water rather than onto the launch if they lost their balance.

"So we're out on the water and it's rough, real rough, and real cold," King remembers. "You've got to jump from the Harbor boat onto this Jacob's ladder, and they keep backing the boat up, saying, 'If you go under the boat, that's it,' so I just had to laugh. I got these gloves on, and my gloves actually froze on the rope of the Jacob's ladder, so I had to climb up barehanded, and I thought I'd lost my hands, had the skin ripped up."

The chances for survival were better if one of the climbers hit the water rather than the hard deck of the launch. "But the truth was either way, the climber would probably have died if he fell," Nelson says.

As Nelson went to put his first foot on the ladder, one of the Harbor pilots pulled him back by the shirt collar. He showed Nelson that one of the airbags used to cushion the boat from the ship had broken open due to the rough seas. He then told Nelson, "If you fall into the water, you will be dead in less than a few minutes. You can't go up, and we can't get your team back down until the seas calm. I think your friends are going to be having breakfast with the Russians."

Anthony Angotti and Nelson then stayed on the harbor launch until the investigation was completed.

King conducted several interviews using the FBI Russian interpreter. He also examined the captain's body and determined he had died by suicide, finding he felt responsible for the terrible conditions his crew was enduring.

"I'll never forget; we got aboard and the ship stunk, absolutely awful," King says. "We boarded with an interpreter and we go in, finding the captain's body in the cooler. Once I saw the ligature marks, I realized nobody did this to him. It turned out he couldn't feed his crew. They were trapped. He was just so ashamed of himself."

The investigators completed the interviews and assessment of the scene onboard the ship, then prepared to leave.

"We get done with what we had to do, but by then, the storm's so bad, we can't return to shore," King says. "So now we're stuck on the ship overnight, and there's nothing to eat."

The storm passed by the next morning, and the investigators were able to return to shore.

"When the Russian interpreter returned down the ladder to the launch, he told me the captain gave his last glass of orange juice to a crew member just before he hung himself," Nelson says. "He also told me the ship's crew pleaded with us to circle the *Banner of October* three times while the crew stood at attention in the freezing cold and saluted their beloved captain from the railing. After we lowered the captain's body down from the ship, the harbor launch did what the crew requested. It was quite an emotional tribute."

Just one week later, Nelson had his squad report to his office at Fort Hamilton for a squad conference and a lecture on homicide investigations. Al King's detectives gave part of the lecture. Nelson then spoke about homicides before discussing crisis management issues.

The lecture was also attended by Nelson's immediate boss, who, the week before, had asked him about the color and length of the ship during the middle of the crisis. There were also a couple of other executive management agents present.

During the session, Nelson brought up the issue of "white-shirt syndrome."

"It is a term that refers to the constant stream of bosses who show up and pepper you with questions during a crisis," Nelson says. "I had said that white-shirt syndrome then becomes the primary crisis while the actual crisis becomes secondary."

At that point, Al King yelled out from the back of the room, "Yeah, like the asshole during last week's crisis who was asking you about the color and exact length of the ship."

"I turned every color in the color chart because Al King didn't know that my supervisor, who had asked me those questions, was sitting in the front row," Nelson says.

Everyone laughed, not knowing what Al King was referring to.

"Al is one of the funniest people you could ever meet and did not intend that comment to be hurtful," Nelson says. "It didn't matter anyway at the time because only Al and I knew the significance of his joke."

The *Banner of October* remained stranded in New York Harbor for months.

News that the twenty-six crew members stuck aboard were running low on food and without fuel for air conditioning prompted a wave of sympathy and support from New Yorkers.[89]

"The good people of Bay Ridge began contributing food and clothing to them until they were finally able to get another shipping assignment," Nelson says.

A New York Fire Department vessel arrived with much-needed relief, delivering four hundred pounds of meat, four hundred gallons of drinking water, and forty cases of fresh produce.[90]

News emerged that the 3,900-ton ship was stuck in legal and logistical limbo due to financial troubles facing its owner, Azov Shipping International, a Ukrainian state-owned company. Ukraine's consul in New York, Bohdan Yaremenko, acknowledged

89. "METROPOLITAN REPORT UKRAINIANS TO SHIP OUT." New York Daily News. January 11, 2019. https://www.nydailynews.com/1999/08/12/metropolitan-report-ukrainians-to-ship-out/

90. "CITY BRINGS FOOD, WATER TO STRANDED UKRAINIAN CREW." New York Daily News. January 11, 2019. https://www.nydailynews.com/1999/08/04/city-brings-food-water-to-stranded-ukrainian-crew/

that bureaucratic hurdles had delayed funding for the vessel's upkeep, but said the issues had since been resolved.90

The NYC medical examiner concluded that the ship's captain had, in fact, died by suicide.

For four months, the Ukrainian cargo ship sat idle in New York Harbor until August, when it was finally loaded with two hundred and sixty used cars and trucks at the Howland Hook Container Terminal on Staten Island, bound for the Dominican Republic and Haiti.[91]

91. "Ship Stranded off New York Finally Gets Orders and Cargo." New York Times. August 11, 1999. https://www.nytimes.com/1999/08/11/nyregion/ship-stranded-off-new-york-finally-gets-orders-and-cargo.html

CHAPTER FIFTY-EIGHT

On November 1, 2000, FBI Supervisory Special Agent Anthony Nelson was notified by the Federal Bureau of Prisons that a top co-conspirator of Al-Qaeda leader Osama Bin Laden, the terror kingpin behind the September 11, 2001, terrorist attacks, was trying to escape from the Metropolitan Correctional Center (MCC).

Since Congress established the Federal Bureau of Prisons (BOP) within the Department of Justice in 1930, it's grown from a handful of penitentiaries to more than one hundred and twenty federal institutions, incarcerating over 150,000 federal inmates convicted of drug offenses, violent crimes, white-collar crimes, immigration violations, and more.

The BOP today employs around thirty-six thousand staff, including correctional officers, healthcare providers, and administrative personnel, in its prisons, detention centers, and halfway houses classified into security levels ranging from minimum security (work camps with dormitory housing, limited fencing, and community work programs) to maximum security.

These can be dangerous places for all those who enter. Yet few are as notorious as the MCC.

Ominously looming over the Thurgood Marshall Courthouse in Lower Manhattan since 1975, the MCC has hosted some of the most infamous criminals of the twentieth century, held over for trial in pending cases in the United States District Court for the Southern District of New York.

Bernie Madoff, the disgraced financier convicted of carrying out the biggest Ponzi scheme in history, spent time there before being transferred to a North Carolina prison to serve out his one hundred and fifty-year sentence.

Gambino Mob boss John Gotti might be the most notorious inmate to have been housed at the MCC, but he's one of hundreds of Mafiosi who have made their way through its seven stories of cells and holding pens. And that includes Gotti's turncoat underboss Salvatore "Sammy the Bull" Gravano.

More recently, Mexican drug lord Joaquin "El Chapo" Guzman was housed there before being convicted in federal court and later sent to the supermax prison in Colorado. Paul Manafort, President Donald Trump's one-time campaign manager, was moved to the Manhattan facility after he was sentenced in March 2025 to seven and a half years for federal tax fraud, bank fraud, and foreign lobbying violations.

And this was where Jeffrey Epstein was found unresponsive in his cell from an apparent suicide while awaiting trial on federal charges that he had sexually abused scores of women and girls, including some as young as fourteen.

At times, Special Agents in the Federal Bureau of Investigation, the principal investigative arm of the DOJ, are called in to investigate crimes committed at BOP facilities.

When that happens, you know it's serious business.

Nelson rushed to the MCC to investigate an escape attempt by Mamdouh Mahmud Salim, a founding member of Al-Qaeda who helped manage Bin Laden's businesses. He was arrested in Germany in 1998 after the bombings of two American embassies in East Africa and extradited to the United States, where he was awaiting trial on broader terrorism charges at the time of the assault.[92] Those embassy bombings in Kenya and Tanzania killed 224 people, including twelve Americans.

---

92. Weiser, Benjamin. "Salim, a Reputed Bin Laden Adviser, Gets Life Term." New York Times. September 1, 2010. https://www.nytimes.com/2010/09/01/nyregion/01salim.html

As Nelson would learn, this incident involved the high-stakes notoriety of investigating suspected terrorists as perpetrators in a crime at a federal facility.

It also involved a deadly assault on fellow members of law enforcement.

Nelson has always been particularly sensitive and deeply sympathetic to the plight of the victims of the crimes they investigate. However, investigating despicable crimes against fellow law enforcement officers comes with an extra layer of emotional trauma.

And this was a dastardly crime.

Salim and fellow terrorist Khalfan Khamis Mohamed planned to hold federal Correction Officer Louis Pepe hostage as part of the escape plot and then kill him.

During the escape attempt, Salim threw hot pepper sauce in the face of Pepe. He then kicked and punched him repeatedly, before stabbing him in his left eye with a sharpened comb so violently that the comb not only pierced Pepe's left eye, it went into his brain.

As Nelson and his fellow agents rushed to the MCC, Pepe was barely hanging on in critical condition, in a coma.

"I immediately dispatched my entire squad to respond to the ongoing events at the MCC," Nelson recalls. "Upon my arrival, I requested the Bureau of Prisons lock down the entire facility and not let anyone leave the building, including a horde of defense attorneys who had been visiting their clients on unrelated matters.

"When I entered the high-security ward where Pepe had been stabbed, there was blood and debris everywhere, including on all the walls. It was a large crime scene, so I requested the assistance of additional FBI agents, some of whom had been trained in crime scene processing and evidence recovery."

One of those FBI Special Agents was Leonard W. Hatton, whom Nelson had known from the FBI/NYPD Bank Robbery Task Force. Hatton took charge of the crime scene processing for Nelson. At the same time, the supervisory special agent assigned the rest of his agents to conduct interviews of possible witnesses, including defense attorneys who had been visiting with their clients.

Nelson also assigned an agent to retrieve the videotape from the recorder within the crime scene area and to bring the tape across the street to the FBI's headquarters. "I had wanted an immediate review of any video recordings so that I would have an accurate understanding of how the escape attempt and stabbing had occurred," he says.

Unfortunately, it turned out that the VCR had reportedly malfunctioned or was not appropriately operated, and the videotape was blank.

Nevertheless, there was enough evidence to charge Salim with attempted murder and conspiracy to commit murder.

In 2002, Salim admitted to stabbing Pepe and was sentenced to thirty-two years in prison for the attack, even though US Attorney James Comey requested a life sentence. However, in 2008, a federal appeals court overturned the sentencing, agreeing with prosecutors that the original judge had not applied a terrorism-related sentencing enhancement that could have resulted in a harsher penalty. After a resentencing in 2008, Salim was handed life imprisonment.

Judge Deborah A. Batts of the Federal District Court in Manhattan resentenced Salim to life in prison, describing the assault on Officer Pepe as "exceptionally cruel, brutal, and a gratuitous act of violence."93 Salim appeared at the hearing via video link from the high-security supermax prison in Colorado.

Playing out in court was a heart-wrenching drama of the aftermath of this despicable crime.

Accompanied by his mother, Margaret Pepe, and sister, Eileen Trotta, Louis Pepe listened as Salim spoke defiantly, declaring, "If Mr. Pepe wants to take my eye, let him take it. My hand, my leg—he can take whatever he wants."

Salim insisted he was "not a criminal," even as his attorney Richard B. Lind conceded the attack was "ghastly" and "despicable," though he argued that a life sentence would be "completely unjust." Lind urged the judge to reinstate the original thirty-two-year term and announced plans to appeal the new ruling.

Prosecutor Jonathan S. Kolodner emphasized the calculated nature of the attack, noting that Louis Pepe had endured a decade of surgeries and rehabilitation, trying to regain even a fraction of the abilities he lost that day.

Judge Batts, in delivering the life sentence, called the act "appalling," remarking on the deliberate force with which Salim drove the sharpened weapon into the eye of a defenseless man—words she had echoed during the original sentencing six years earlier.

US Attorney Preet Bharara said the life sentence offered "at least a small measure of vindication" for Pepe and his family.

The attack left Louis Pepe blind in one eye and severely impaired in the other. He suffers from speech difficulties, right-side paralysis, and requires near-constant care—sixteen hours a day—for even basic tasks. From his wheelchair, he addressed the Court slowly but with conviction. "Salim, how are you doing?" he began. "I can't talk anymore. Or walk. Or anything. That's what you did, Salim."

Believing Salim had hoped to die as a martyr, Louis Pepe added, "Guess what, Salim? You're not going to be a martyr. You're going to hell. That's where you're going."

Before concluding, he pulled a small paper bag from his lap and dropped a doughnut onto the table. "This is for you, Salim," he said.

His sister, Eileen Trotta, later explained that her brother had been known for treating inmates fairly—including Salim. The doughnut, she said, was meant as a biting reminder of that irony.

Corrections Officer Pepe is one of the many victims who haunt Nelson.

Moreover, in another horrible twist of fate, Leonard Hatton, the FBI agent Nelson assigned to take control of the crime scene at the MCC, was killed on September 11, 2001, when he was crushed in the destruction of the World Trade Center terrorist attack.

"Hatton died a hero trying to save people during the attack," Nelson reflects, "but he had already deserved to be considered a true hero for all that he had accomplished during his career in the FBI."

CHAPTER FIFTY-NINE

It was a Tuesday morning like every other.

Until it wasn't.

And afterwards …

Leaving home that September as the sun broke over the Mill Basin rooftops, Anthony Nelson took extra care not to wake Syndee.

He'd not sleep beside her again until the end of November, right before a low-key Thanksgiving.

Early morning traffic was light as Nelson drove west towards Manhattan, flipping on the radio. It was a beautiful early autumn morning, even as meteorologists were tracking the first hurricane of the 2001 season.

It wasn't a particularly busy news cycle.

Barry Bonds hit his sixty-third home run on his way to breaking the record for most home runs in an MLB season. Michael Jordan had come out of retirement, while Michael Jackson was mounting a comeback.

Time Warner and America Online were completing their merger, while Tom Cruise and Nicole Kidman were ending theirs. Democrats and Republicans were squabbling (Bush tax cuts), while sharks were gobbling (East Coast swimmers).

Jeepers Creepers still owned the box office. The US Justice Department was still trying to break up Microsoft. And Capitol Hill intern Chandra Levy was still missing.

Nelson arrived at his off-site office in the US Army Criminal Investigation Division (CID) building at the Fort Hamilton. This office was a little more than eight miles from Lower Manhattan.

Then shortly after 8:46 that morning, Nelson heard an NYPD unit transmit over the citywide radio channel: an airplane had just struck the North Tower at the World Trade Center.

"Even though my first thought was that it had been an accident, I got into my FBI car and responded to the plane crash," Nelson says.

Seventeen minutes after the first strike, Nelson heard the report on the radio that a second plane had now hit the South Tower. At that moment, as he headed to Lower Manhattan, Nelson, like so many others in law enforcement, knew America had likely suffered a massive terrorist attack.

Of course, on this day of all days, Nelson's siren on his FBI vehicle failed and he was having mechanical problems. Rush hour traffic on the Brooklyn-Queens Expressway—on a good day a crawl—was now clogged. Instead of continuing, Nelson veered off and headed to the Brooklyn-Queens (BQ) Office of the FBI to get another emergency vehicle.

Nelson arrived at the BQ Office in time to watch the Towers fall.

"I'd been so close to the Towers when I had both car trouble and my siren failed," Nelson reflects, "that I suspect I would have been in the Towers when they fell."

Nelson marshalled up his squad of agents at the BQ Office, directing them in a convoy to the office at Fort Hamilton to establish a temporary headquarters to provide whatever support was needed, as close as possible to Ground Zero.

"In what seemed like minutes after arriving, although it was actually a little longer, all of our telephone service at the army base started to fail," Nelson recalls. "Even our two-way radio service began to fail because the repeaters that were part of our radio system no longer functioned."

The telephone lines that ran through Lower Manhattan had been severed during the terrorist attack.

Nelson took roll call to ensure all the agents under his supervision were accounted for and available.

He then instructed Special Agents Jason Randazzo and Peter Kohn to physically begin setting up the temporary headquarters with any long-term supplies that were needed, especially personal protective gear.

Nelson then drove to the Ground Zero zone to reestablish contact with other supervisory personnel. After a couple of visits to Lower Manhattan, Nelson remained at Fort Hamilton to coordinate with the Army and to handle all leads that developed in the Brooklyn area.

"In just a short amount of time, my squad and I were sent out at a furious rate to multiple locations suspected of having some involvement in terrorist activity," Nelson says. "And my dear friend, Lieutenant Al King, the commanding officer of the NYPD Brooklyn South Homicide Squad, had come to Fort Hamilton to assist me along with his squad of detectives."

Earlier that morning, King was also sitting in his office, the NYPD Homicide Office, which covered thirteen precincts, when he heard the same call come over citywide.

"I tell one of my guys to throw on the TV," King remembers. "I'm thinking it's one of those Cessnas or Pipers. I really did not expect it to be a commercial airliner … and then we see the second airliner hit."

The morning 9/11 hit, King says his detectives were the first on the scene. "I gathered up all my detectives and we rushed to the World Trade. And we got there just as people were jumping from the windows.

"I've been a police officer for decades, and before that I was in Vietnam, in-country for two years, and even having lived through all that, I can say that I've never seen anything as terrible as I saw that day as all those bodies were leaping from the Towers," King says. "In those moments, there was nothing for a detective to do, so I decided we'd go to the local hospitals."

As he and his detectives raced from hospital to hospital, it dawned on him that this was unlike any other crisis.

"I went to St. Vincent's, then Cabrini—I think four hospitals—and right away we knew something was wrong, that this was different than any other crisis or disaster," King says. "At the hospitals, in the immediate aftermath, there were no bodies, no victims. So, we went back down to the Trade Center ... to help organize the body parts."

FBI Special Agent Jason Randazzo remembers coming across a friend looking for the admitted patient hospital lists. "We played high school baseball together, and we later frequently went to bars during our college years, and were in sister companies in the NYPD academy. His brother was at Cantor Fitzgerald, so he asked about the list of hospitals, grasping for anything. Like so many people in the aftermath of the attacks, looking for people missing, it turned out that his brother never got out of there," Randazzo says.

As for the lists of admitted patients to hospitals?

"There were none," Randazzo says. "There were no survivors from the collapse of the Towers."

Meanwhile, the US Army Post Commander had shut down the Guest House (Hotel) on base and provided Nelson with five rooms to use for agents and other law enforcement personnel. In addition, he ordered the Post Exchange (PX) to supply the agents with whatever items were needed to function on a long-term basis.

"I remember vividly after 9/11, we went to Fort Hamilton to assess and follow up on leads in Brooklyn, so I was with the squad there every day," Jason Randazzo says. "I remember as the days and weeks wore on, you heard about this guy or that one who died that day; some you knew directly and others you kind of knew and then remembered how you knew them.

"I remember Sergio Villanueva, a former NYPD detective who later joined the FDNY, who perished at the WTC," Randazzo remembers. "I also remember John Tipping, who I met at Hunter Mountain on a ski trip through a mutual friend. Great guy. We'd see each other at various bars and clubs during several summers. He later joined the FDNY and was stationed at the firehouse under the FDR Drive. He also died on 9/11. You meet so many members of law enforcement, so as weeks wear on, you see their pictures, hear their names, and it hits you every time."

Nelson lived in the Fort Hamilton Guest House from that fateful day through late November.

Meanwhile, King and his detectives would spend the next six months working with the Medical Examiner's Office.

"You know, I really hand it to all of those young women and men in the ME's Office who I feel went so underappreciated," King says. "There were no bodies—just parts, body parts, sometimes just pieces. That was the thing with 9/11; I don't remember seeing a single body, intact. It was all pieces, all body parts, that had to be processed, identified if possible, and that's not easy work."

King says that this time, the aftermath of 9/11, is even hard for him to think about now.

"My wife recently reminded me that those nights I would come home with it, the body and the matter, caked into the soles of my shoes," King says. "I would take them off and leave them in the hallway, and then come back later, and there'd be maggots crawling all over those shoes. And you get some sleep, but you don't *sleep*. Then you go back, and you go back, and you go back.

"I remember dealing with a chest, just a chest, where someone else's hand had been blown into that chest and we had to work with ME to make those identifications," King says. "It was hard work, terrible work, especially for those MEs. I remember a police shield blown into another body, and that was the only identification of that officer. Torsos transported to the Medical Examiner's Office, so burnt, like sides of beef ... I remember the partial remains of one Black gentleman, every bone was broken in his face that there was no structure, so when the ME lifted up what was left of his face, it changed shape, reshaped; there was no blood, it was just all so unbelievable. Every day you saw things … just terrible things.

"But I knew these investigations were important, very important," King reiterates. "Families were suffering, and they deserved answers; they deserved some closure."

While the heroism of the New York City Fire Department, the NYPD, and the Emergency Medical Service was on full public display, the evil aspect of human nature also began to rear its ugly head.

"Many of the tips and leads that my squad pursued, some with the help of Al King's detectives, turned out to be from people who were sending in fictitious reports to get the homes of people they hated raided by us," Nelson says.

"I remember all of these investigations at that time focusing on this section of Bay Ridge, 2nd and 3rd Avenues in the '60s and '70s, that we started getting a lot of leads, most of them either names of suspects," says Jason Randazzo. "Then there were reports of people supposedly dancing on the rooftops or in the streets, celebrating after the planes hit the buildings. So there was a lot of running around for nothing."

"We broke down many doors of innocent people who were reported to be making bombs," Nelson says. "But all of them turned out to be victims of malicious reports. Some of the people we detained had, at most, simply been in the country illegally."

One report in particular stands out for Jason Randazzo.

"We got the call on this guy, Mohamed Atta, who lived in Canarsie off the Belt Parkway, and I had to interview him," Randazzo says. "He had the same name as the hijacker, and it was tough on this guy because of his name. No connection. He just shared the name with one of the hijackers. Lost his job, was constantly harassed, and was just having a real tough time in the weeks after 9/11."

The next event was the mailing of white powder, some containing the deadly anthrax virus, through the US Postal System.

The reports of anthrax were coming in at a rapid clip, and Nelson found himself responding to many reports of suspicious white powder at government facilities throughout the days and into the nights. Reports of suspicious white powder were even received in the housing areas of Fort Hamilton and at the adjacent VA Hospital.

As if these two historical events taking place simultaneously were not enough to deal with, Nelson received an early morning call on November 12, 2001, to respond to the Rockaways.

American Airlines Flight 587, bound for the Dominican Republic from New York City, had just crashed, and the possibility of terrorism was initially suspected.

"It was horrible; again, burnt bodies everywhere," King says. "Blood running down the street. Really, blood was literally running down the street. So much blood. It was so bad that I remember piling sandbags to stop that flow of blood. And then, again, you're processing body parts to identify victims for their families, and it's terrible. But you got a job to do and the investigation is important and you try to focus, but it's just so unbelievable."

"It only took a short amount of time to determine that the plane crash was accidental," Nelson says. "But I was asked to assist in calling my contacts with the US Park Police to use an airplane hangar as a temporary morgue and evidence retrieval location."

It was an assignment Nelson came to regret.

He assured the Park Police that he would have an approved biohazard floor laid down in the hangar so that it would not be contaminated by blood and hazardous materials. "But since the crash had been determined to be accidental, the NYPD took over the hangar and disregarded my request that the floor be protected," he says. "I then had to apologize to my contacts at Floyd Bennett Field and explain to them that I had lost control of the temporary morgue. The biohazard cleanup costs were astronomical."

Back at Fort Hamilton, Nelson and his fellow agents were joined at our temporary headquarters by members of two Nassau County police departments, as well as the NYPD Brooklyn South Narcotics Squad, headed by Lieutenant Dave Campbell.

Throughout this time, in addition to several ground trips Nelson took to Ground Zero to obtain situation updates, he also accompanied Dave Campbell on an NYPD helicopter into the area.

"It was sickening to watch the remnants of the Twin Towers still burning as we approached the area from the air," Nelson says.

"Since I was not equipped with the proper footgear to stand on the pile during the helicopter visit, I had to radio Pete Kohn to give me a ride back to Fort Hamilton by car."

The terrorist attack on the World Trade Center caused an immediate and drastic change in the core mission within the FBI. Resources were taken in an inordinate amount from the Criminal Division and were redirected to the counterterrorism mission.

CHAPTER SIXTY

On October 2, 2002, a sniper's bullet struck a fifty-five-year-old man in a parking lot in Wheaton, Maryland. By ten o'clock the next morning, four more people within a few miles of each other had been similarly murdered.

The initial investigation soon linked the attacks, and a massive multi-agency investigation was launched. The case was led by the Montgomery County (Maryland) Police Department, headed by Chief Charles Moose, with the FBI and other law enforcement agencies playing a supporting role.

"Chief Moose had specifically requested our help through a federal law on serial killings," says Nelson, who was serving as the supervisory special agent of the FBI's Joint Bank Robbery Task Force at the time. This squad of FBI agents and NYPD detectives based in 26 Federal Plaza in Manhattan was perhaps the most active with respect to fighting street crime.

"My squad not only had the investigative responsibility for responding to armed bank robberies but also, at the time, we were charged with apprehending dangerous fugitives, investigating kidnappings, extortions, arson, and crimes on government reservations," Nelson says.

Within hours, Anthony Nelson was en route to Montgomery County to supervise a team of New York FBI agents.

"We all met at my house and traveled in a convoy," Nelson says. "When we arrived, we were each given a special identification card and a discreet sticker that we had to place on the rear license plate of our FBI vehicles. We did not know if the shooter was a member of law enforcement, so we needed the vehicle stickers to identify ourselves as part of the task force searching for the shooters."

Within days, the FBI alone had some four hundred agents around the country working the case, providing support in several key specialized areas.

"We set up a toll-free number to collect tips from the public, with teams of new agents in training helping to work the hotline," Nelson says. "Our evidence experts were asked to digitally map many of the evolving crime scenes, and our behavioral analysts helped prepare a profile of the shooter for investigators." He and his squad also helped set up a joint operations center to help Montgomery County investigators run the case.

The big break in the case came, ironically, from the snipers themselves.

On October 17, a caller claiming to be the sniper phoned in to say, in a bit of an investigative tease, that he was responsible for the murder of two women (actually, only one was killed) during the robbery of a liquor store in Montgomery, Alabama, a month earlier.

That set in motion a chain of events that led to the capture of a pair of snipers.

Investigators soon learned that a crime similar to the one described in the call had indeed taken place—and that fingerprint and ballistic evidence were available.

"An agent from our office in Mobile gathered that evidence and quickly flew to Washington, DC, arriving Monday evening, October 21," Nelson says. "While the ATF handled the ballistic evidence, we took the fingerprints to the FBI Laboratory, then located at our headquarters."

The following morning, the FBI database produced a match—a magazine dropped at the crime scene bore the fingerprints of Lee Boyd Malvo from a previous arrest in Washington State.[93] The

93. FBI. "Beltway Snipers." April 17, 2022. https://www.fbi.gov/history/famous-cases/beltway-snipers

arrest record also provided another significant lead, mentioning a man named John Allen Muhammad.

"One of the FBI's agents from Tacoma recognized the name from a tip called into that office on the case," Nelson says.

The collaboration with ATF agents revealed that Muhammad had a Bushmaster .223-caliber rifle in his possession, a federal violation since he had been served with a restraining order to stay away from his ex-wife. This enabled law enforcement to charge him with federal weapons violations. And with Malvo clearly connected, the FBI and ATF jointly obtained a federal material witness warrant for him.

Meanwhile, on October 22, the FBI continued to search its criminal records database and found that Muhammad had registered a blue Chevy Caprice with the license plate of NDA-21Z in New Jersey.

That description was given to the news media and shared far and wide.

"On the morning of October 24, the hunt for the snipers quickly came to an end when a team of Maryland State Police, Montgomery County SWAT officers, and special agents from our Hostage Rescue Team arrested the sleeping John Allen Muhammad and Lee Boyd Malvo without a struggle," Nelson says.

Just a few hours earlier, just before midnight at approximately 11:45 p.m., the dark blue 1990 Chevy Caprice with New Jersey license plate had been spotted at a rest stop parking lot off I-70 in Maryland.

Within the hour, law enforcement swarmed the scene, setting up a perimeter to check out any movements and make sure there'd be no escape.

The evidence found by experts from the FBI and other police forces was both revealing and shocking. The car had a hole cut in the trunk near the license plate so that shots could be fired from within the vehicle. It was, in effect, a rolling sniper's nest.

Also found in the car were the Bushmaster rifle used in each attack, a rifle's scope for taking aim, a tripod to steady the shots, and a backseat that had the sheet metal removed between the passenger compartment and the trunk, enabling the shooter to get in the trunk from inside the car.

Moreover, investigators recovered the Chevy Caprice owner's manual with—the FBI Laboratory later detected—written impressions of one of the demand notes. They also found the digital voice recorder used by both Malvo and Muhammad to make extortion demands, and a laptop stolen from one of the victims containing maps of the shooting sites and getaway routes from some of the crime scenes.

That was the end of the attacks, but not the FBI's role in the case. FBI agents spent many more hours gathering evidence and preparing it for court—work that ultimately paid off.

Both Malvo and Muhammad were convicted at trial or pleaded guilty in multiple court cases in Maryland and Virginia. And both were sentenced to life without parole. Muhammad also received the death penalty in Virginia and was executed on November 10, 2009.

The Beltway Snipers case marked a turning point in Nelson's career in more ways than one.

After the perpetrators were apprehended, Nelson returned to New York City and was designated as the acting assistant special agent in charge of the FBI's Violent Crimes Branch.

This was a significant assignment.

The second-line supervisors are known as assistant special agents in charge (GS-15) or ASAC. They are responsible for managing multiple investigative units, reporting to either the special agent in charge (the highest-ranking criminal investigator in each region) or the deputy SAC (responsible for enforcing discipline and executing SAC orders).

"I had the supervisory oversight responsibility for all violent crime matters within the jurisdiction of the New York FBI," Nelson explains. "This position entailed oversight of ten squads addressing, among other things, bank robberies, kidnappings, extortions, fugitives, violent street gangs, auto crime, major theft, and crimes against children.

"During my time as supervisor, I often requested that brand new FBI agents be temporarily assigned to my squad to assist us with pending cases. It provided all of them with a great deal of criminal investigative experience. I had found that many of the new agents, unlike new NYPD police officers, had hailed from small towns in various parts of the country.

"Once again, I gained that sense of contribution by exposing them to real life in New York City," Nelson says, adding that some of them had what he describes as "culture shock" when they were exposed to death scenes and evil on the streets and housing projects of New York City.

"During raids, I had to explain to many of them about even small safety concerns, navigating the streets and the projects of the city," he says.

Not surprisingly, quite a few of the temporarily assigned new agents had asked if they could be transferred to his squad once their temporary assignments ended.

"I know now, many years later, that some of those same agents have gone on to become the current supervisors of the FBI's New York Office," Nelson says.

Unbeknownst to most, Nelson suffered silently with debilitating back pain that had flared during the Beltway investigation, but somehow continued to work.

"I went to dozens of physical therapists, chiropractors, acupuncturists, surgeon visits, and even tried holistic seminars," he says. "I was close to the mandatory retirement age, which is fifty-seven now but had been fifty-five when I first joined the FBI. It was time for me to leave and allow a new generation of agents to carry on with the noble work of the FBI."

Nelson served for more than a year in that capacity; however, his back pain had become so severe, he could no longer function safely while dealing with violent crimes.

"Although I'd been designated as the acting assistant special agent in charge of the FBI Violent Crimes branch, I could not have remained in that position longer than I did," Nelson adds. "And I could not have qualified for the permanent ASAC because I was not willing to fulfill the requirements. To become the permanent ASAC, I would have had to spend two years at FBI Headquarters in Washington, DC, and travel the country to participate in approximately twelve inspections of other office operations. That just wasn't going to happen.

"I was placed on sick leave for an extended period and ultimately retired from the FBI in November of 2004," Nelson says.

CHAPTER SIXTY-ONE

Throughout the rest of 2004 and into 2005, Nelson received aggressive treatments to try to reduce the debilitating back pain he'd suffered for years. Ultimately, he required seven procedures under anesthesia over three years. Anthony Nelson was at a crossroads, unsure of what the next chapter of his life would bring.

Then one evening in early 2005, he received a telephone call out of the blue from none other than George Terra.

"It would take an entire book to describe George Terra and his many accomplishments," Nelson says. "He's still one of my closest friends."

Terra spent twenty years with the NYPD. In 1982, while assigned to the NYPD Auto Crime Unit, Terra was selected to join a newly formed NYPD/FBI Auto Crime Task Force based in the Brooklyn-Queens FBI Office.

"This task force was actually formed based upon the recommendations of Jim Murphy to combat the enormous auto-theft crime problem at the time," Nelson remembers. "And George was not only one of the most accomplished detectives in auto crime, but any type of investigation, particularly if it involved La Cosa Nostra."

Terra's case work spans weapons and narcotics trafficking, financial crimes including mortgage and insurance fraud, human trafficking, child exploitation, Medicare, Medicaid, and Social Security fraud, trademark and intellectual property crimes, identity theft, political corruption, and organized crime.

Upon his retirement, Terra was recruited as a supervising detective investigator for the Brooklyn DA. "In 1989, I was actually the first retired police officer hired by the Brooklyn DA," he says.

At the time of this phone call, Terra was the assistant chief investigator in the Special Investigations Unit of the Kings County District Attorney's Office, also known as the Brooklyn District Attorney's Office (as the county and borough cover the same geography). The Office includes three principal divisions: Investigations, Trial, and Gender-Based Violence.[94]

"George was among the best undercover operatives ever," Nelson says. "But one of his strongest talents was as a manager and a leader."

In the Brooklyn DA's Office, Terra had fifty investigators under him, including retired members of law enforcement from other agencies.

"We had a really busy shop," he recalls. "I'd say, on average, every investigator had at least two open cases, and many were significant. We even investigated three corrupt (New York State) Supreme Court judges."

Nelson's phone call with Terra then turned into somewhat of a reunion. "George placed the call on speaker and, to my surprise, he was calling from a restaurant while in the company of my friend, Jim Murphy," Nelson says.

Terra and Murphy called to say hello and to get an update on Kenny McCabe's declining health. At the time, McCabe's condition was a source of concern for many.

As the three lawmen caught up, Nelson had an idea. "It occurred to me that with George's help, I might have the opportunity to join the Brooklyn DA's Office, the very place my relationship with Kenny McCabe began," he says.

"Anthony already had a soft spot for the Brooklyn DA's Office because he worked on so many cases with Kenny McCabe," Terra says. "With Anthony, it's in his blood to do investigations. We had a conversation, and as he was retired from the Bureau, expressed a desire to come over.

---

94. "BUREAUS & UNITS." https://www.brooklynda.org/bureaus-units

"I said, 'let's be clear, this is not a favor,' as in me doing Anthony a favor." Terra laughs. "Anthony would be doing the office of the Brooklyn DA a favor by coming to work as an investigator. And once it was clear Anthony did want to join the Brooklyn DA, obviously, it was not a hard sell at all to Joe Ponzi."

In the Brooklyn DA's Office, George Terra was second in command to Joseph Ponzi, a highly regarded member of law enforcement who spent thirty-six years on the job. As chief investigator in one of the most prominent prosecutor's offices in America, Joe Ponzi commanded a squad of over one hundred detectives and personally worked on some of New York's most notorious cases, including the prosecution of multiple sitting state Supreme Court judges and the Mafia Cops case.[95]

"I took the same career trajectory that Kenny McCabe had taken, only in reverse," Nelson adds. "When I first met Kenny, he was an NYPD detective assigned to the Brooklyn District Attorney's Office. Upon his retirement, he was recruited to be a federal criminal investigator. I was now, on the other hand, retired from the FBI and contemplating taking a detective position in the Brooklyn DA's Office."

In 2005, within just a few months of that phone call, Nelson was assigned to the Special Investigation Unit (SIU), a detective squad within the DA's Office that handled investigations within the Rackets Bureau.

"I felt right at home when I started to work there," Nelson says. "I already knew Joe Hynes through Kenny McCabe from several meetings before he was the district attorney."

Flatbush native Charles "Joe" Hynes served as Kings County District Attorney from 1990 to 2013. On the New York City Fire Commission from 1980 to 1982, Hynes also notched successful prosecutions in the notorious racial attack in Howard Beach, Queens, as special state prosecutor for the New York City Criminal Justice System, a position to which he had been appointed by then Governor Mario Cuomo in 1985.

---

95. CBS News. "Brooklyn DA: The Prosecution Teams." May 28, 2013. https://www.cbsnews.com/pictures/brooklyn-da-the-prosecution-teams/25/

Hynes also initiated the landmark Drug Treatment Alternative-to-Prison Program (DTAP) and a variety of public safety programs, including ComAlert, which helped aid individuals on probation or parole as they reentered their Brooklyn communities. He also helped implement a citywide program to monitor convicted domestic violence offenders in collaboration with former Mayor Rudy Giuliani. This was an important issue for Hynes, whose mother was a victim of domestic violence.[96]

Hynes passed away in 2019 at the age of eighty-three.

In the Brooklyn DA's Office, Nelson joined former NYPD Detective Doug LeVien, who was one of Hynes' executive assistants for many years. LeVien was a twenty-year veteran of the NYPD. Eight of those years were spent undercover.

Detective LeVien's most celebrated cases include the 1972 sting called Operation Gold Bug, centered on wiretapping a Canarsie junkyard trailer in which known Mafiosi planned a spate of crimes, resulting in 1,200 police officers fanning out to serve subpoenas. He also played a two-year role as a drug-dealing millionaire in an operation that snared Enzo Napoli of the Sicilian Mafia who served the Gambino and Lucchese Families. In fact, in the 1970s, LeVien was placed in federal witness protection when his life was threatened by the Mafia. In later years, LeVien's investigative work aided prosecutions in the ABSCAM federal corruption trials, the fatal Howard Beach racial attack of 1986, and the Mafia Cops case of the 2000s.[97]

LeVien passed away in 2015 at the age of sixty-eight following a heart attack.

"Talk about being in the company of courage," Nelson reflects. "George provided me with a desk that still contained numerous documents within it. When I opened the first drawer, I realized it

96. Alexander, John. "Former Brooklyn District Attorney Charles 'Joe' Hynes Dead at 83." Queens Daily Eagle. January 30, 2019. https://queenseagle.com/all/2019/1/30/former-brooklyn-district-attorney-charles-joe-hynes-dead-at-83

97. Fox, Margalit. "Douglas LeVien, New York Detective Who Infiltrated the Mafia, Dies at 68." New York Times. August 8, 2015. https://www.nytimes.com/2015/08/09/nyregion/douglas-levien-new-york-detective-who-infiltrated-the-mafia-dies-at-68.html

had been Tommy Dades' desk. Tommy had just resigned from the DA's Office, and I replaced him."

Tommy Dades also joined the Brooklyn DA after a career in the NYPD, including work in the 68th Precinct and the Intelligence Division, helping to put away many members of organized crime.

"That's right. I worked for Joe Ponzi in the Brooklyn DA's Office before Anthony Nelson arrived, and he did get my old desk," Dades says. "I loved Joe. We all did, God rest his soul. Joe was the most decent human being anyone had the pleasure to meet, educated, street-smart, the voice of reason, and he never had a bad word to say about anybody.

"But for you to know who Joe trusted and respected, you'd have to pay attention and see who he associated with on a steady basis. And Joe adored Anthony Nelson. He was thrilled to have Anthony join the team. When you have someone like Joe Ponzi react and respond like that, it tells you all you need to know about Anthony Nelson."

Alan Abramson, the criminal defense attorney from the Brink Robbery in 1998 and other cases investigated by Anthony Nelson, previously served in the Kings County District Attorney's Office from 1985 through 1990. As an assistant district attorney in the Rackets Bureau, Abramson investigated and prosecuted fraud, bribery, extortion, narcotics trafficking, tax fraud and racketeering.

"I had the pleasure and honor of working with George Terra, a magnificent undercover and investigator," Abramson recalls. "So just think of it: Anthony Nelson, Joe Ponzi, and George Terra working cases in the same office. Now that's the gold standard.

"In the Brooklyn DA's office, Anthony and Joe Ponzi showed me how cases got put together the right way," Abramson says. "And they showed me the right way to conduct an investigation. And Anthony taught me in this business that it's not always the good guys or the bad guys, but there can be so many different shades of grey."

Sadly, Joseph Ponzi succumbed to cancer and passed away. He served the Kings County District Attorney's Office for thirty-seven years, overseeing more than fifteen hundred investigations and producing one hundred and twenty-five murder confessions.

He was also heralded for organizing many gun buybacks throughout the years and was a responder at both Ground Zero and the landfill.

Today, Joseph J. Ponzi Way memorializes the former lawman's contributions at the intersection of Dawson Circle and Arlene Street in Staten Island.[98]

"Joe Ponzi was just a wonderful individual who left us all way too early," Terra adds. "So Anthony came over and settled in, and I had the pleasure of working with him for six years.

"Anthony Nelson was a good fit, highly intelligent and academically inclined, but he also had that common sense and street savvy," Terra continues. "I think that's what made him so successful in law enforcement. But it also helped that the guy was modest, sincere, and just an all-around genuine article. Anthony Nelson is not in it for himself, but for God and country."

When Anthony Nelson landed at the Brooklyn DA, there was plenty of work to go around.

"We worked on everything and locked up all kinds of crooks," Terra says. "We did corruption, locked up judges, rogue law enforcement, attorneys, locked up LCN members and drug dealers, gun sales—just about the whole gamut. And many of the cases involved multiple categories of crime because the people involved in narcotics were involved with murders, so cases were always expanding."

Nelson started to notch win after win. He personally drafted the search warrants for pharmacies engaged in a multimillion-dollar scam to redeem rebate coupons. He foiled a gang that used motorcycle helmets to disguise themselves while illegally withdrawing money from ATM machines. Nelson even supervised an undercover operation to take down a New York State court officer who was selling cocaine while on duty.

He also led a successful investigation into a New York State judge involved in a fraudulent real estate scam in the Jewish Community, wiring up a Hasidic Jew as a cooperating witness.

---

98. New York City Council File #: Int 0968-2024. April 18, 2022

Then there was the investigation into cigarette bootlegging schemes, as New York State began heavily taxing sales. In a clever twist, Nelson applied for and received a grant from Philip Morris, which funded the operation.

"All these cases Anthony worked on in the Brooklyn DA's Office totally impressed me," Terra says. "He could take the most complicated matters, with complex facts, unusual circumstances and conflicting interviews, and capture it all on paper in an understanding and clear format.

"Sure, we'd sit down and talk, because being the professional he was, he wanted to keep the boss apprised," Terra adds. "But I always knew Anthony knew what he was doing."

CHAPTER SIXTY-TWO

In August 2005, an unusual case strolled into the Kings County District Attorney's Office that would explode across the front pages of all the major New York tabloids.

"This case came to us from a female police officer who came into the Kings County DA's Office and gave me a set of facts and circumstances," George Terra remembers. "She was a uniformed police officer who just happened to be talking to someone about some strange things that were going on at this funeral parlor. And basically, she was looking to have someone investigate."

Former dental surgeon Michael Mastromarino was the owner of Biomedical Tissue Services (BTS), a New Jersey company that shipped bones, skin, and tendons to tissue processors such as Regeneration Technologies Inc., LifeCell Corp., and Tutogen Medical Inc.

The bodies came from funeral homes throughout New York, Pennsylvania, and New Jersey, and about ten thousand people received tissue supplied by BTS.

Unbeknownst to both the loved ones of the deceased and the recipients though, the organs and tissues were harvested without consent. Moreover, many of the tissues removed unlawfully and transplanted into live patients may have been contaminated, some harvested from cancer victims. News reports at the time even raised the possibility of tissue being infected with HIV.

Once the media got wind of the case, the villainous Mastromarino was splashed across front pages nationwide as a "body snatcher."

"I remember knowing my office would love to have this case and we had very qualified people, including Anthony, to bring it to a logical conclusion," Terra says. "If Anthony Nelson was dealing with an issue, I never would have to or want to look over his shoulder. I knew I could stake my life on the fact that his work was one hundred percent accurate and effective. Sure, I read his reports and we had case reviews, but these were more conversations. Honestly, I was Anthony's supervisor, but he could have and should have been my supervisor."

But as the case quickly drew notoriety, the Kings County DA would not serve as the lead investigative agency on the case. "When they ran it up to the police department chain of command," Terra says, "they must have realized this was a noteworthy case and they stayed involved in it."

Kings County DA's Office Detective Investigators Anthony Nelson, Michael Seminara, and Patrick Lanigan assisted in the investigation under the supervision of Supervising Detective Investigator Robert Intartaglio.

"I know I've thrown around a lot of accolades to describe many of the NYPD detectives with whom I worked, but Lanigan and Seminara were truly two of the best," Nelson says. "If you were to imagine a family member needing the police, you could only hope that Lanigan and Seminara were the ones assigned to help."

Patrick Lanigan, a twenty-year veteran of the NYPD, earned widespread recognition for his work solving cold cases before transitioning to the Kings County District Attorney's Office. On September 11, 2001, Lanigan was among the first officers to respond to the World Trade Center attacks.

At the time the first plane hit the North Tower, Lanigan was in a Brooklyn precinct with Detective Dennis Bootle. The two were immediately dispatched across the Brooklyn Bridge and arrived at the scene just as the second plane struck the South Tower.

In the aftermath of the attacks, Lanigan took a key role at the Bereavement Center on Pier 92. There, he helped coordinate efforts to identify victims, collecting personal items such as hair brushes and toothbrushes from grieving families to assist with DNA matching.

Michael Seminara also brought years of distinguished service as an NYPD detective to the Kings County DA's Office, where he continued his commitment to justice.

Following an exhaustive investigation, the team gathered enough evidence to mount a 122-count indictment. Due to the insidious nature of the crimes, the case quickly became a tabloid sensation.

Mastromarino and his cabal forged death certificates and organ donor consent forms to create the appearance that the tissue was harvested legally.

Though tissue transplant guidelines set age limits and health requirements for donors, the defendants falsified the ages of their victims, so in one case, a ninety-five-year-old cancer victim was listed as a healthy eighty-five-year-old who died of heart failure.

It is illegal for people to sell their tissue or other body parts. They can only be donated, and only with the expressed written consent of the donor before the person dies.

However, on the open market, one body can bring in as much as a quarter million dollars for harvesting and transplant companies. Mastromarino and co-defendant Joseph Nicelli allegedly paid funeral home directors up to one thousand dollars per body, masking the payments as fees for services.

Mastromarino, a former oral surgeon, got into the tissue business after losing his dentist's license.

Nicelli, of 49 Clifton Avenue, Staten Island, owned Daniel George & Son funeral home at 1852 Bath Avenue, Brooklyn, before partnering with Mastromarino in BTS and another sham company, BioTissue Technologies. The companies were licensed in New Jersey but had offices in Brooklyn. Lee Crucetta and Christopher Aldorasi both worked with Nicelli and Mastromarino, removing body parts.

The investigation began after people who bought Daniel George & Son from Nicelli found numerous inconsistencies in the bookkeeping. They came to the Brooklyn District Attorney's Office to complain that money paid in advance for future funerals was missing from the business's accounting records. The investigation that followed uncovered a scheme to steal bones from unwilling donors.

In a secret room in Daniel George & Son, Mastromarino would remove bones, tendons, heart valves, and other tissue from recently deceased people. When the bodies were of people who had not consented to the procedures or were too old or ill to donate tissue, Mastromarino and Nicelli doctored their death certificates and forged consent forms, according to the indictment. In those cases, Mastromarino replaced the bones with plastic polyvinyl chloride (PVC) piping, and repaired the incisions so they would not be noticed at the funeral.

Nicelli also owned a business transporting bodies to funeral homes and would be notified of deaths. This enabled him to supply Mastromarino with more corpses.

During the successful investigation, Nelson was promoted to assistant deputy chief in the Special Investigation Unit, with Lanigan and Seminara assigned to his unit.

District Attorney Charles "Joe" Hynes stated at the time, "What happened here—stealing tissue from the dead and selling it for transplant without consent of a family member and without taking any medical precautions to ensure that transplants were free from disease or defect is like something out of a cheap horror movie. But for the thousands of relatives of the deceased whose body parts were used for profit, and the recipients of the suspect parts, this was no bad movie. It was the real thing."[99]

Mastromarino was sentenced to eighteen to fifty-four years behind bars.

Christopher Aldorasi, a so-called "cutter" in the plot, was sentenced to nine to twenty-seven years in prison.

Lee Cruceta was sentenced to six and a half to twenty years in prison in 2008. His was a reduced sentence in exchange for testifying against the ringleaders.

And Nicelli was sentenced to eight to twenty-four years.

---

99. Daily Mail. "'Bodysnatch' Ring Plundered BBC Veteran's Remains." February 24, 2006. https://www.dailymail.co.uk/news/article-378175/ Bodysnatch-ring-plundered-BBC-veterans-remains.html

In a touch of karmic coincidence, Mastromarino died in 2013, five years into his sentence, due to complications of metastatic liver cancer that had spread to his brain and bones.[100]

Meanwhile, Anthony Nelson's transition to the Kings County DA's Office was relatively seamless, although it presented some challenges. "On the day I had arrested one of the tissue theft subjects in the Bones case, Joe Ponzi contacted me and wanted me to head up the investigation of retired FBI Agent Lin DeVecchio," Nelson remembers.

DeVecchio worked for the FBI during law enforcement's assault on the Mafia in New York during the 1980s and 1990s, rising through the ranks of the FBI, eventually taking charge of the Bureau's squad tasked with monitoring the Colombo Family. Among his key responsibilities was managing Gregory Scarpa Sr., the longtime Colombo who had operated as a confidential FBI informant since the 1960s.

Scarpa's 1993 guilty plea to racketeering charges triggered new scrutiny. That same year, former Colombo consigliere-turned-government witness Carmine Sessa alleged to prosecutors an unusually close—and potentially compromising—relationship between Scarpa and DeVecchio.

Prosecutors later presented circumstantial evidence suggesting DeVecchio had allegedly passed sensitive law enforcement information to Scarpa, possibly enabling violent acts.

An internal FBI investigation spanning two years ultimately concluded without charges. However, the controversy tarnished DeVecchio's standing, and he retired from the Bureau in 1996.

Though officially exonerated by FBI leadership, the fallout was significant: courts overturned or dismissed charges against nineteen members of the Colombo Family's Orena faction after defense attorneys argued that DeVecchio's conduct undermined the integrity of the cases against them.

---

100. "Funeral Parlor Owner From Staten Island Sentenced in Body Parts Scheme." SiLive. January 26, 2009. https://www.silive.com/news/2009/01/former_staten_island_funeral_p.html

Brooklyn District Attorney Hynes was now reengaging the prosecution.

Nelson declined the assignment. "I told Ponzi that I cannot do that," he says. "First of all, I did not believe that DeVecchio had committed any crimes. I believe he was caught up in how the FBI handled informants."

The FBI's strategy for managing informants long term to continually provide intel to tackle larger objectives, such as dismantling organized crime groups, did not jive with other agencies' approaches, which instead saw informants more as short-term sources to support prosecution of current crimes.

"The differences in the way we operated could easily give rise to the appearance of wrongdoing, even when there was not any," Nelson says. "Secondly, if I took over DeVecchio's case, I would be accused of impropriety by one side or the other, regardless of what facts and evidence were developed."

Nelson also had another, less consequential, reason for stepping aside on the DeVecchio investigation: DeVecchio and Nelson were both sued for several million dollars in 1980 by four "mercenary soldiers" who intended to hijack a cruise ship and hold it for two million dollars ransom.

"These four bananas put an ad in *Soldier of Fortune* magazine trying to recruit others into their insane plot," Nelson remembers.

The ad was answered by an undercover FBI agent, and Nelson and DeVecchio arrested the subjects in Staten Island.

"These four mopes had less than a dollar among them," Nelson says. "At arraignment, when the judge asked if the defense wanted to make an argument regarding the size of the bail, one of the defense attorneys told the judge that if he set bail for more than a dollar, it would be a moot issue."

In any event, Nelson recused himself from any part of the case against DeVecchio.

"And I was quite resentful and vocal that he was even indicted," Nelson says. "I had told Patrick Lanigan that it appeared to me from day one that the office already made up its mind to charge him. Although, admittedly, I was not privy to all the evidence at the time."

In 2006, Brooklyn District Attorney Hynes indicted DeVecchio on charges that he allegedly supplied confidential FBI information to Scarpa that led to the gangster murdering four people in the 1980s and early 1990s. The case was based almost entirely on the testimony of Scarpa's longtime girlfriend, Linda Schiro.

However, the case imploded in the fall of 2007 when Tom Robbins of the *Village Voice* came forward with an interview he and Mob expert Jerry Capeci had conducted with Schiro in 1997 in which Schiro denied DeVecchio had been involved in most of the murders.

Robbins and Capeci had interviewed Schiro for a book they planned to write, and had promised Schiro that her revelations would not appear in a news article or be attributed to her. However, Robbins said, the prospect of DeVecchio facing life in prison trumped any promises they had made to Schiro.

This forced prosecutors to move for a dismissal of charges against DeVecchio, which was granted on November 1, 2007.

A retired judge was appointed special prosecutor in 2008 to examine whether Schiro had committed perjury; his report concluded that her interview tape was insufficient to prove she had perjured herself.

DeVecchio co-authored a book, published in 2011, about his experiences.

At the time though, Nelson had plenty of cases to investigate, including working with Lanigan on the tragic homicide of Dominick Masseria.

The case was one of those senseless crimes that truly shook a community to its core. Masseria was a popular Brooklyn youth fatally shot outside a Bensonhurst church just before midnight on Halloween, two hours after he was embroiled in a row that started when a group of teenagers threw eggs at a passing limousine, the police said at the time.

Masseria was not a member of organized crime. He was just a teenager.

Masseria, only seventeen years old—young, handsome, popular, with a bright future ahead—was shot in the back as he stood in front of Our Lady of Guadalupe Roman Catholic Church at 15th Avenue and 73rd Street. The shots were fired from a passing white stretch limousine with Florida license plates, the police reported. Masseria died at the scene.[101]

The Masseria case had a related but legally collateral issue to the case against DeVecchio.

"Patrick Lanigan and I went out to Staten Island and found Reyes Aviles, the limo driver, who was a witness and participant, along with Linda Schiro's son Joseph, in the homicide of Masseria," Nelson says. "Joseph Schiro was Linda's son with Gregory Scarpa."

The New York Post reported it was the renewed investigation into DeVecchio helped crack the 1989 Halloween night drive-by. Investigators linked DeVecchio to the murder of Patrick Porco, a key witness in the Masseria probe. DeVecchio, a fixture at the 62nd Precinct in the late '80s, allegedly tipped Scarpa that Porco was cooperating with police. A week after he met with detectives, Porco was shot five times in the head in Canarsie. DeVecchio was cleared and vehemently denied the allegations.[102]

Porco had been one of four men in the white limo during the shooting. The group included driver Reyes Aviles, who served time, Joey Scarpa (the mobster's son), and an unidentified "Craig," rumored to be the shooter. Porco's murder derailed the case.

Years later, prosecutor Noel Downey revisited the case while investigating DeVecchio and Scarpa's connection to multiple murders. In old files, he found a note with the name Craig Sobel.

Aviles, wired up, approached Sobel, now a boat captain in Florida. He casually reminisced and admitted to his role in the murder.

101. "Brooklyn Youth Slain After Halloween Fight." New York Times. November 2, 1989. https://www.nytimes.com/1989/11/02/nyregion/brooklyn-youth-slain-after-halloween-fight.html

102. Ginsberg, Alex. "MOLE PROBE SOLVES SENSELESS '89 MURDER - B'KLYN TEEN'S KIN: IT'S JUSTICE AT LAST." New York Post. March 30, 2006. https://nypost.com/2006/03/30/mole-probe-solves-senseless-89-murder-bklyn-teens-kin-its-justice-at-last/

Sobel had been in trouble before. Records show he spent three years in a New York prison for wounding an off-duty court officer at a cafe in Queens in October 1990, a year after the Halloween murder. Sobel fired a shot that grazed the officer's face, then was shot by another officer at the cafe.

However, by the early 1990s, Sobel had moved to Florida, married, had kids, and bought property in Odessa and Hudson. He started a plumbing business and impressed people with his work. He also founded Reel Crazy Charters. On local fishing websites, he advertised using the moniker "Captain Scupperz."[103]

The team moved quickly on its new information. Once Nelson and his team contacted Aviles, the limo driver, he agreed to cooperate as a witness.

Investigators flew to Hudson and watched Sobel's movements at home and at work on a construction site. When they had his patterns down, they flew in Aviles and arranged for him to bump into Sobel at work. Aviles wore a wire. "What are the chances?" Sobel said of their meeting, Downey said.

On March 27, 2006, a Pasco sheriff's deputy arrested Sobel. Three days later, prosecutors announced Sobel's indictment in Masseria's killing.

"It was rewarding for me to ultimately receive a thank you letter from the Masseria family to all of us who worked on the case," Nelson says. "I still have a copy of the letter."

---

103. Jenkins, Colleen. "Pasco Fisherman Held as Suspect in Slaying." Tampa Bay Times. December 10, 2019. https://www.tampabay.com/archive/2006/04/10/pasco-fisherman-held-as-suspect-in-slaying/

CHAPTER SIXTY-THREE

After Anthony Nelson fully retired from the FBI, Kenny McCabe continued to work at the Southern District of New York, doggedly pursuing the remnants of the once powerful Cosa Nostra that he, more than anyone, helped dismantle.

By the beginning of 2001, all Five Families of the Italian-American Mafia were in disarray, reeling from devastating blows thanks to the concentrated efforts of the FBI squads and many other agencies dedicated to eradicating them. The successes achieved in the war against the Mafia could not have been realized without the joint cooperation of the Federal Bureau of Investigation, the New York City Police Department, and many other groups.

The formation of joint task forces between the FBI and the NYPD took the fight beyond reacting to street-level crimes such as gambling, drug dealing, and extortion, attacking the upper echelon of organized crime. And now they were targeting the remnants of the traditional Italian-American Mafia, assaulting emerging international criminal networks, and pursuing a next generation of narcotics traffickers and cartels.

The story continues, with new chapters, new players.

The criminal prosecutions and appeals in both the Southern and Eastern Districts of New York of some of the more high-profile, colorful, media-darling mobsters like John Gotti and company were either completed or were winding down.

But the job itself was not complete.

This next generation of not-so-wiseguys was hatching new schemes when they were not ratting each other out, and Kenny

McCabe remained a crucial weapon for the federal government to continue the battle.

"Kenny McCabe was continuing to provide critical intelligence and testimony in major pending organized crime prosecutions," Nelson says. "He was also traveling the country to meet with, and debrief, high-level mobsters who were now in the Witness Security Program and cooperating with the federal government."

Although the majority of Nelson's time was now devoted to supervisory duties at the Brooklyn DA's Office and he was no longer working the streets either formally or informally with McCabe, the two of course continued to meet for a working lunch each Friday whenever possible.

"I still had lunch with Kenny, as well as with Detectives Tony Angotti and Ron Cadieux each week, whenever possible," Nelson says. "Both Angotti and Cadieux had also been retired by the time I left the FBI. Detective Angotti has also since passed away."

The seasons were changing. Nelson now watched with concern as the once powerful McCabe slowly faded during those lunches as cancer gradually began to take its toll on his friend, his hero.

"I'm grateful that I was able to visit with him and hold his hand in the hospital in his last days, even though he didn't know I was there," Nelson says. "It eased the emptiness I felt. Kenny was such a heroic figure to me that never did I ever think, not for a moment, that one day I'd be going to his funeral.

"I suppose," Nelson adds, "I believed that superheroes never grew old, nor did they ever pass away."

In the bleak winter, Special Agent Anthony Nelson received the heartbreaking news he knew was inevitable. "On February 19, 2006, at the age of fifty-nine, my best friend Kenny McCabe passed away after a heroic fight with brain cancer."

It's impossible to gauge the seismic impact McCabe had on the landscape of law enforcement during his years of working at the NYPD and later at the Manhattan US Attorney's Office.

In the days that followed, report after report lauded McCabe for his many contributions.

"McCabe had direct involvement in virtually every celebrated Mafia case in New York—from the 1980s takedown of the mob's ruling body, 'The Commission,' to the arrests of Paul 'Big Paul' Castellano and John Gotti," hailed Murray Weiss from the *New York Post*, recognizing McCabe as "the nation's foremost organized-crime investigator" who "had the singular distinction of not only being respected by his peers but also by mob bosses and wiseguys—including some who sent him Christmas greetings after they began cooperating with authorities."[104]

Douglas Martin from the *New York Times* heralded McCabe as "an investigator who became a quiet legend among crime fighters by spying on and testifying against mobsters to help topple godfathers," and added "Mr. McCabe was known for his careful observations of Mafia chieftains at their social clubs, weddings and funerals. Then he testified at their trials with such detail that few defense lawyers dared question him for fear of surprises."[105]

McCabe was a legend long before he passed, so it was not surprising when news emerged that even after illness forced his retirement just months earlier in December, he still provided assessments on evidence and open cases.

A member of the New York Police Department for eighteen years, most of that time as a detective assigned to the Brooklyn District Attorney's Office, and then for twenty years as an organized crime investigator for the United States Attorney's Office in Manhattan, McCabe was a giant among men, and not just for his towering height.

Reporters, lawmen, prosecutors, judges, even criminals he helped convict, so many across both sides of the underworld divide paused when they heard the news of his passing.

"During Kenny's sickness," Nelson recalls, "a high-level Mafia cooperating witness wrote a letter to the government, and to

104. Weiss, Murray. "MOB-BUSTER MCCABE DIES." New York Post. February 22, 2006. https://nypost.com/2006/02/22/mob-buster-mccabe-dies/

105. Martin, Douglas. "Kenneth McCabe, 59, a Dogged Investigator of the Mob, Dies." New York Times. February 27, 2006. https://www.nytimes.com/2006/02/27/nyregion/kenneth-mccabe-59-a-dogged-investigator-of-the-mob-dies.html

Kenny, stating that if he did not have such a sick criminal brain, he'd be willing to donate it to save Kenny McCabe's life."

In the weeks and months after his passing, everyone seemed to have their own Kenny McCabe story.

"Kenny McCabe was just this big strapping guy, a physical presence, but as humble and as friendly as a guy could be, very approachable," says retired NYPD Detective Tommy Dades. "But make no mistake, he was an absolute legend. Kenny McCabe was a walking, talking database of intelligence on organized crime. He knew everything and everyone, and had the pictures and intel you only get by putting in thousands of hours of surveillance.

"They actually put a statue up for him," Dades says. "I attended his funeral and the unveiling outside the Southern District, and those were just such profound experiences because of his career and his extraordinary service. But for those who knew Kenny McCabe and knew how humble and polite, no ego at all, and how dedicated he was, you're left in such awe of the man."

Outside family members, few felt the heartache of McCabe's passing as intensely as the FBI agent who accompanied this legendary lawman on so many of those night rides.

"Kenny was the most instrumental weapon the US government had in the fight against organized crime," Anthony Nelson attests. "Throughout the years, he testified against countless members of La Cosa Nostra from every crime family. Kenny's photographic memory allowed the government to connect the dots with respect to the disruption and dismantling of all five organized crime families operating in the New York area and elsewhere."

Ironically, for the lawman acclaimed as "La Cosa Nostra's unofficial photographer," there is little entered in the public record of McCabe's actual physical presence, aside from countless testimonies captured by court reporters and a single image from 1984 during the arrest of Paul Castellano.

"Kenny was never one to grab the microphone," Nelson says. "It just wasn't in his nature. He never wanted to be photographed, avoided interviews, shunned the spotlight, even as others sometimes claimed much of the credit that was his due. That would've bothered any other person, but Kenny shrugged it off, never promoting himself, instead looking to the next case. That alone tells you much of what you need to know about Kenny McCabe."

Nelson is not alone. There are more than a few members of law enforcement who, to this day, do not believe Kenny McCabe has received the credit due.

"Kenny McCabe was a remarkable individual and investigator, just one of a kind," says George Terra. "And I have to say, being honest, there were a few guys riding Kenny's coattails. I won't mention any names, but that really used to annoy me. You know, the hang-arounds and the fakers."

But that lack of photographs and press conference clips has made it challenging to recognize the contributions of Kenneth McCabe Sr.

"If anyone in the history of law enforcement deserves to be recognized in books and film, it's Kenny McCabe, but sadly that's not been the case to date," Nelson reflects. "His son, Kenny Jr., has done a remarkable job over the years curating and championing Kenny's legacy, and I do hope, more than anything, he succeeds in getting the type of recognition that my dear friend deserves."

"There is no doubt that my father was light years ahead of every investigator when it came to organized crime," says Duke McCabe. "That's not just Kenny McCabe's son talking, but a universally held opinion. And I have the interviews and testimonies to prove that a hundred times over. They all knew, all the other investigators. But my father wasn't arrogant, didn't jump in front of the cameras or try to show anybody up. He avoided the spotlight. His fingerprints are all over every major Mafia case from the 1970s up through the 2000s, and that's no exaggeration. Pull any case and I'll show you where he contributed.

"He just didn't have a peer in the OC world, head and shoulders above everyone, and everyone knew it; literally in a league of his own," Duke says. "He never got his due because he didn't promote himself or talk about himself in that way. It was only about the work, the cases, the investigations, the trials.

"Inside the game, everyone had the utmost respect for my dad," he adds. "But as far as the general public goes, there's very little, if any, recognition or realization of the dramatic impact this single man had on the war against organized crime."

His aura even affected the people he arrested. By all accounts, cooperating witnesses were more likely to be forthcoming and willing to testify when they were in the company of, or being debriefed by, Kenny McCabe.

Kenny was called as a witness in so many major cases against La Cosa Nostra that there were very few defense attorneys who didn't know him or who dared to challenge his expertise or testimony on the witness stand.

"In my opinion, Kenny McCabe was the government's nuclear weapon that contributed most substantially to the destruction of the Mafia," Nelson says. "Its existence today is only the remnants, the ashes left behind in the wake of the firestorm that was Kenny McCabe."

For now, today in the lobby of the United States Attorney's Office in Lower Manhattan, a plaque exists erected to the memory of Kenny McCabe and his contributions. It's one of the highest honors a law enforcement officer could receive. Yet it's not enough.

"Rest in peace, my dear friend," Nelson says. "Gone, but never forgotten by so many lives you touched."

EPILOGUE

In December 2012, Anthony Nelson retired as the assistant deputy chief of the Special Investigations Unit in the Brooklyn District Attorney's Office, ending his active career in law enforcement.

"I am often asked how it feels to be retired from the Job," Nelson reflects. "I must say that it is unusual not to feel like I've been given a shot of adrenaline several times a week for the past thirty years. But it was time for me to go.

"A new and even better generation of men and women have stepped forward to take over where I had left off. The only thing I miss about the Job is the sense of contribution it gave to me. The sense that my life had counted for something."

Anthony Nelson has much to reflect upon.

"Of course, what gratification I get from remembering the accomplishments of my career comes with a sadness realizing they came at a high cost to my dear wife, Syndee," he reflects. "She'd been left all those years taking care of my children and bringing them to sporting events, parties, and other school and social events. It just tears at me to remember how some of her friends would tease her by saying that they didn't even believe she was married."

Anthony Nelson remains active in the American Legion. "I spend much of my time now with military veteran friends, including Russell Holman and his brother Ken Holman, both of whom have been designated Hometown Heroes," Nelson shares. The Holman brothers served our country as US Marines and fought in the jungles of Vietnam during 1965 and 1966, respectively. "They experienced some of the same types of critical incidents that I endured in the FBI during my thirty-five-year career. But their traumas were condensed into one year each. So really, even in retirement, I'm still in the company of courage."

Like many retired members of law enforcement, Nelson struggles with the physical and emotional damage he absorbed over the decades; wounds that fade but never fully heal.

From time to time, media coverage closed chapters and tied off loose ends. News reports with old mugshots that may be casual viewing for most elicit flashbacks for someone like Anthony Nelson. Names, faces, violent crimes, victims … all can come flooding back in an instant.

Years after Nelson retired, during the first week of March 2015, Buddy Murnane called.

"Buddy was approaching the mandatory retirement age, and he invited me to attend his retirement party that was planned for May of 2015," Nelson says. "I was looking forward to it."

Then suddenly, the following week, on March 15, the Ides of March, Nelson received a call from an NYPD detective friend with news—Francis "Buddy" Murnane had just passed away from natural causes.

"Buddy never got to enjoy his retirement," Nelson says. "Maybe Buddy would have preferred it this way. See Buddy, in my opinion, lived for the job, not for the prospect of retirement. He is remembered by so many, not just for the legendary police officer he was, but also for being such a remarkable person and friend."

From time to time, names appear from the past to drag Anthony Nelson back.

Roy DeMeo's son, Albert, died by suicide in 2017. Roy's final victim.

Dominick Montiglio died of natural causes on June 27, 2021.

Joseph Testa and Anthony Senter, the so-called Gemini Twins, were sentenced to life in prison, plus an additional ten years after their convictions in federal court on eleven counts of murder only to be released on parole in the spring of 2024.

Someone retires, makes parole, passes on—a slow, steady drumbeat of reminders of a past better left buried.

"I have to tell you a story, not a story for the book, just a quick story," Nelson shared in October 2024, not long after we'd first met in a New Jersey bagel shop.

"I have no business experience, nor do I have any concept of which new stocks, bonds, products, or ideas would be worthy of financially pursuing as an investment opportunity," Nelson said that day. "But this morning at the bagel store where you first met me, two older gentlemen who come in fairly often were discussing the hostages being held by Hamas in Gaza."

One of those men stated he would never want to negotiate for their release because of the likelihood he'd be blamed if something went wrong.

The other man responded that he still hadn't even emotionally recovered from having his car stolen recently after leaving his car keys in the cup holder of his vehicle.

"He said it was the most traumatic thing that had ever happened to him," Nelson added. "I happened to tell them about the Hopkinson Avenue hostage situation. It was fresh in my mind, as I had just written the account out for you for the book."

These two gentlemen at the bagel store were absolutely amazed.

And in true Anthony Nelson style, he was amazed that they were amazed.

Of course, he did not tell them it was also part of a book in development on his career in law enforcement.

"They were not only amazed," Nelson says. "They were actually mad at me and told me I never confided in them about anything like this, and they now felt embarrassed that they so often complained about small things while I never told them anything. It's a good thing I didn't tell them any additional stories or about the book."

Now it all started to make sense for these two gentlemen.

"Little did I know they noticed, even discussed, some of my small quirks, like always insisting I sit at a table with my back against the wall." Nelson laughs. "They also noticed that I'd never enter the bagel shop without first stopping to look through the front glass to see if anything unusual was going on inside before I entered."

Now they knew.

And, of course, like most who get to know Anthony Nelson, they cared.

"They thought about it for a bit, and then shared how they felt it was a terrible way for me to live, suspicious of everyone and everything wherever I go," Nelson says. "Sometimes, when you see how others see you, it gives you a perspective you didn't have. What's normal for me is not normal. What other members of law enforcement accept every day, on the job, in retirement, maybe it's not acceptable. But it is what it is."

Then something happened.

As Anthony opened up, that group in the bagel shop that morning grew from two to four to more, hanging on every word as he shared the details of that single critical incident, the hostage crisis at Hopkinson Avenue described earlier in this work.

"You know, after I left there, it was the first time I thought you may actually have some success with your book sales if those people were so enthralled about hearing just one true story," Nelson told me.

"It was that strange coincidence, those two men talking about the Gaza hostages at the same time I was writing to you about negotiating the release of hostages in Brooklyn so long ago," Nelson says. "I probably could have sold a bunch of books right on the spot."

A career in law enforcement comes with challenges that are underappreciated or not well-known by the general public. Over time, the emotional and psychological strain, the accumulation of these experiences can lead to severe emotional stress, PTSD, anxiety, and depression. The long, unpredictable hours, the lost nights, the weekends and holidays without family, the sleep deprivation, the violent scenes.

There's that habit members of law enforcement develop, remaining ever vigilant. They're always on edge, hyper aware, teeth grinding, eyes never stopping, prone to sudden starts. That must be exhausting, never being able to relax, the threat of violence always right on the other side of that door.

But again, members of law enforcement have always dealt with these challenges in one form or another.

It's just part of the Job, right?

These days, though, something has changed.

"It seems that lately law enforcement officers are constantly being subjected to verbal, physical, and legal attacks, even when they have performed their jobs in good faith, often flawlessly," Anthony Nelson reflects.

It's a new era, and law enforcement is always under the microscope. Even routine decisions made in high-pressure situations are second-guessed. Officers are openly mocked and vilified by the communities they protect and serve.

"I have to commend the newest generation of law enforcement officers whose actions and conduct are always recorded by body cameras or the cell phones of the general public," Nelson says. "They have stepped forward to perform a job that often seems to have little or no rewards.

"A job that can not only imperil their lives but also embroil them in criminal and civil jeopardy by simply making the slightest, even though well-intentioned mistakes, or perhaps even no mistakes. Then they are criticized by their superiors or by politicians seeking to score political points. But the most hurtful attacks are those that come from the members of their own communities, who just don't understand the nature of their work. Or maybe they just don't care."

There were times in Anthony Nelson's career, some shared in this work, many not, where he held the lives of people in his hands. "But unlike the surgeon who claimed to be immune from feelings of guilt if something went wrong," Nelson explains, "I would have felt intense pain if I failed to protect the life of an innocent person or a member of law enforcement.

"I could only imagine how police officers in today's environment must feel, having to defend their actions, and often being deemed by their communities to be evil and hateful," Nelson says, "even when they act according to the law and, more importantly, according to their own conscience."

Not everyone feels that way.

We can do better.

PICTURES

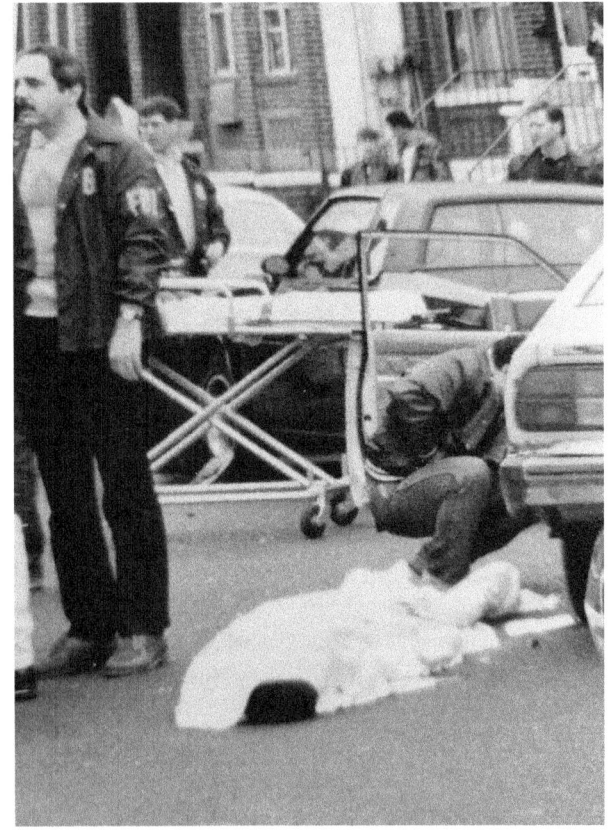

*Anthony Nelson at Hamilton Federal Saving
Bank Robbery Shooting Crime Scene*

*Anthony Nelson's photo for staged mugshot
to support undercover operation*

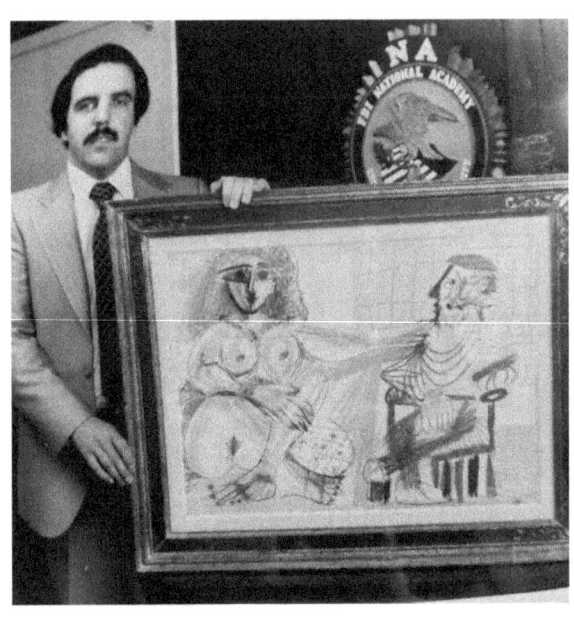

Anthony Nelson with recovered Picasso painting

*Anthony Nelson counting ransom payment Feb
1978 for the Klein kidnapping case*

Anthony Nelson Christmas Photo with NYPD Detectives Ron Cadieux and Anthony Angotti (2003)

Anthony Nelson and Others Recieve Award for Nesbitt Murder Case

Anthony Nelson in 1978 FBI Surveillance
Photo With ATF Dominick Polifrone

Surveillance photo of Gambino Family,
DeMeo crew attending a vistation

Anthony Nelson with FBI Director Louis J. Freeh in 1999

Anthony Nelson with Sydnee Nelson

ACKNOWLEDGEMENTS

This work would not have been possible without the tremendous support of the following people.

Anthony Nelson would like to recognize the following.

I wish to acknowledge the following people who have contributed directly to this work or who have inspired me to make this work possible through the positive and profound influence they have had on my life. I will remember them forever.

I would first like to acknowledge my beautiful wife, Syndee. There are no words eloquent enough to describe her. Syndee chose to forgo a potential career in modeling to literally devote every minute of her life to motherhood and to her concerns for my well-being.

I also could not be more proud of my children, Marissa and Michael, as well as my grandchildren, Emily Nelson, Kylie Nelson, and Ryan Nelson. To be in their presence is a constant reminder of the most fortunate life I have lived.

My beautiful and loving daughter, Marissa, of whom I am so proud, is one of the smartest, creative, kindest, and most caring people one can ever meet. Sahas Apte, my daughter's husband, is like a son to me, and I enjoy every conversation I have with him— usually about the most complex topics of science and cosmology.

My son, Michael, is a sergeant with the elite New Jersey State Police. He has been cited and commended several times for courageous acts in difficult and dangerous situations, and I am very proud of his decision to also commit his life to the service of others. Jenna Nelson, my son's spouse, like Syndee, also manages to successfully deal with the demands of being married to a law enforcement officer.

In as much as this book chronicles more than thirty-five years of my career as a law enforcement officer, some of the individuals I wish to acknowledge next are no longer with us. However, they have nevertheless contributed to the completion of this book. Many of them literally had my back during the execution of dangerous arrests and search warrants or just everyday tactical police actions on the street.

Foremost, I want to acknowledge the late Kenny McCabe for being such an important part of my life. He was like a brother to me and was always there when my life, safety or general wellbeing depended upon him. Kenny's son, Duke, is a clone of his father. No one among us has any way to know for sure if our lives continue in some form beyond our earthly existence. But if it does, I know that Duke's father is looking down upon him and is so very proud of the son he brought into this world.

It is beyond my ability, and not practical, for me to describe the affection I feel for each of the following law enforcement officers or attorneys who have contributed, directly or indirectly, to this book.

Al King, Ron Cadieux, Alan Abramson, Harvey Pincus, Tony Angotti, Jason Randazzo, Frank Pergola, Janine Pergola, George Terra, Leo Farrell, Louis Randazzo, Saul Rodriguez, Carl Schroeder, Joseph Sciarrino, Steven E. Braus, Michael Francis, Lewis Schiliro, Joseph Ponzi, Tommy Dades, James F. Murphy, Eileen O'Rourke, George Hanna, Michael Falcone, Rodney M. Davis, Walter Mack, Paul Shechtman, Patrick Lanigan, Greg DeBoer, Michael Seminara, Robert Intartaglio, Francis "Buddy" Murnane and Bob Azzinari.

I also want to acknowledge the following people who inspired me to assist in writing this book. Their friendship, values and advice cannot be overstated.

Kathy McCabe, Barbara King, Harold and Maxine Pincus, Emily Sabatella, Nitin and Varsha Apte, John and Beth Napoli, Frank and Stella Shamy, Giuseppe and Ornella Iaccarino, Ramzi and Wafaa Zahreddine.

It has been an absolute privilege for me to have worked with Craig McGuire. Without his expert abilities as an established author in addition to his initiative, enthusiasm, and encouragement, I may never have had the opportunity to tell not just my story but, more importantly, the stories of so many heroic members of the law enforcement community with whom I worked.

Lastly, I wish to honor the memory of my parents, Catherine and Edward Nelson, as well as the memory of Syndee's parents, Bernard and Bernice Liemer.

Craig McGuire would like to recognize the following.

First and foremost, Anthony, I am grateful for the privilege of sharing these remarkable stories. From that very first conversation, I knew this was a special project with a higher purpose.

To Syndee Nelson, for helping convince Anthony to participate and for adding so much value. This work would not have been possible without your contributions and encouragement.

To Marie McGuire, my ma, whose unwavering support and sacrifices shaped the person I've become. The example you set lit the path that I still follow. And to Francis X. McGuire, my dad, who first opened the door to the wonderful word of the written word. I carry deep sorrow that you couldn't see this next chapter of the story you helped begin.

Those individuals who allowed me to call upon them for advice and consolation, including Billy Malone, Mike Deliso, Bill and Liza Donnelly, Greg and Trisha Janvier, Marisa and Kevin with Baby AK, Maria Scopello, Ron Valdes and Gina Marie, Sean Lawler, Anthony Ibelli, Rob Bolstad, Danielle Fasano, Kristen Valdes, Ivan Avelancio, Amy Kovar, Cindy Wen, Steven Matt, Dori Bright, Robert Sales, John Manbeck, Catia Deliso and Paul, Enza Deliso and Sara Beck, Angela and Gianluca Baccaro, Marina Deliso and Xena and Poky, Santino Deliso and Gemma, Christopher Bayer, Brittany and Tyler Bell, Alexis Petty, Matt Schweikert, Shannon Smith, Rich Ponce De Leon, Joe and Cheryl

Pupo, and so many more. I beg forgiveness from those I have failed to mention.

Special thanks to the most wonderful in-laws a man can have, Tony and Maria, for their patience, their support, and their firecracker of a daughter. Also Susan McGuire, Bailey, Eddie, and Sophie, as well as Bryan, Barbara and John Ambre, Mary Ellen and Robert McGuire, Carol and Dennis O'Connor, MaryAnn and Billy Grey, AJ McGuire, Terry McGuire, Colleen McGuire, Kieran and Michelle McGuire, Erin and Jeff Tupper, Anthony Muscarello, Joseph and Jennifer Muscarello, Donna and Mark Sokolowski, Robert and Nancy Grey, Michael and Stephanie Grey, Chrissy and Jesus Fernandez, Luca Reed, Marco Reed, Antonio-Santino Deliso, Antonio-Michael Deliso and Marina, Zander Deliso, Enza and Joseph Delise and Tommy Leli, Marta and Joseph Carvo, Lisa and Tim Amass, Enza and Vinny Curatolo, and so many others.

Finally, and especially, my wife, my rock, my everlasting love, my reason for living, my Anna, for inspiring me in so many ways, keeping me honest and true; and my three sons Frank, Jace, and Antonio, for their support and honesty. You remind me daily what truly matters, and your belief in me has meant more than you'll ever know.

Joint List of Acknowledgements

To our publisher, WildBlue Press, for taking a chance on this work and nurturing it in its long march to market, especially Steve Jackson, Michael Cordova, Elijah Toten, and editor Jenn Waterman, as well as the rest of the crew. There is something amazing going on at WildBlue Press. If you support independent publishing and the arts, support WildBlue Press.

Last, but certainly not least, retired NYPD Detective Tommy Dades, for bringing us both together at the start of this long road, making the time to guide us along the path when needed, and inspiring us to complete the journey.

SOURCES

"History & Mission | Sesquicentennial." https://www.downstate.edu/about/our-history/sesquicentennial/history.html#:~:text=The%20Long%20Island%20College%20Hospital,clinics%20were%20used%20for%20teaching

"The Rise and Fall of LICH: America's First Teaching Hospital – Cobble Hill Association." https://cobblehill.nyc/knowledge_base/the-rise-and-fall-of-lich-americas-first-teaching-hospital/

Silver, Nate. "The Most Livable Neighborhoods in New York." *New York Magazine*. https://nymag.com/realestate/neighborhoods/2010/65374/

"A Brief History." https://www.fbi.gov/history/brief-history

"History - Federal Bureau of Investigation." https://irp.fas.org/agency/doj/fbi/fbi_hist.htm

US Office of Personnel Management (OPM) Handbook.

"Eligibility and Hiring." FBI Jobs. https://fbijobs.gov/eligibility

New Utrecht High School Alumni. https://newutrechthighschool.org/

"How Can You Become an FBI Agent?" Tulane University School of Professional Advancement. https://sopa.tulane.edu/blog/how-can-you-become-fbi-agent

"Special Agent Overview." FBI Jobs. https://fbijobs.gov/special-agents?gad_source=1&gad_campaignid=22295396297&gbraid=0AAAAADd8NODrELmFXMJh-q0T6u-w93hXC&gclid=Cj0KCQjwoZbBBhDCARIsAOqMEZW0gjqnAze4AIIdRaB-

TQ3w9m6oWgSSiEns3JAs68TUdjhww51Pb-UaAh42EALw_
wcB

Meacham, Andrew. "Phil McNiff Served the FBI, Then George Steinbrenner's New York Yankees," *Tampa Bay Times*. August 25, 2019. https://www.tampabay.com/news/obituaries/fbi-agent-phil-mcniff-worked-major-cases-then-helped-george-steinbrenner/2218046/

Kihss, Peter. "BRONFMAN'S SON RESCUED IN CITY AFTER A PAYMENT OF $2.3 -MILLION; MONEY RECOVERED, 2 SUSPECTS HELD." *New York Times*. August 18, 1975. https://www.nytimes.com/1975/08/18/archives/broafmans-son-rescued-in-city-after-a-payment-of-23million-money.html

DeBlasio, Peter E. *Let Justice Be Done: A New York Trial Lawyer's Odyssey Through the Last Half of the 20th Century.* 2020

Roberts, Sam. "John Pritchard III, Tenacious Law Enforcement Leader, Dies at 75." *New York Times*. September 17, 2018. https://www.nytimes.com/2018/09/17/obituaries/john-pritchard-iii-tenacious-law-enforcement-leader-dies-at-75.html

Dienst, Jonathan, and Valiquette, Joe. "Forty Years Later, FBI Agent Who Shot Bank Robber Recalls '*Dog Day Afternoon.*'" *NBC New York*. August 23, 2012. https://www.nbcnewyork.com/news/local/dog-day-afternoon-forty-year-anniversary-fbi-agent-interview/1955404/

"The FBI National Academy's Yellow Brick Road — 40th Anniversary." FBI: Law Enforcement Bulletin. February 8, 2022. https://leb.fbi.gov/bulletin-highlights/additional-highlights/the-fbi-national-academys-yellow-brick-roads-40th-anniversary

"Becoming an Agent: Firearms Training." Federal Bureau of Investigation. June 11, 2021. https://www.fbi.gov/video-repository/becoming-an-agent-series-firearms-training.mp4/view

Shenon, Philip. "F.B.I., AFTER SHOOTOUT, ORDERS AGENTS TO USE VESTS." *New York Times*, June 16, 1986. https://www.nytimes.com/1986/06/16/us/fbi-after-shootout-orders-agents-to-use-vests.html

BulletSafe Bulletproof Vests. "The History of the Bulletproof Vest." https://bulletsafe.com/pages/the-history-of-bulletproof-vests

"Truck Hijacking in City Is a $4.2-Million Business." *New York Times*. May 20, 1974. https://www.nytimes.com/1974/05/20/archives/truck-hijacking-in-city-is-a-42million-business-truck-hijacking-in.html

Farber, M.A. "TRUCK HIJACKING: A HIGHLY ORGANIZED AND SPECIALIZED CRIME IN NEW YORK." *New York Times*. December 16, 1983. https://www.nytimes.com/1983/12/16/nyregion/truck-hijacking-a-highly-organized-and-specialized-crime-in-new-york.html

Historica Wiki, "Thomas Carbonaro," https://historica.fandom.com/wiki/Thomas_Carbonaro

"How a Simple 'Hello' Became the First Message Sent via the Internet." PBS News. February 9, 2015. https://www.pbs.org/newshour/science/internet-got-started-simple-hello

Zukin, Sharon. 2011. *Naked City: The Death and Life of Authentic Urban Places*. OUP USA

Justice, Peter. "The Life and Times of Monte's Venetian Room." *Carroll Gardens-Cobble Hill, NY Patch*. September 7, 2011. https://patch.com/new-york/carrollgardens/the-life-and-times-of-montes-venetian-roo

Edwards, Benji. "Inside the Commodore 64." *PCWorld*. November 4, 2008, https://www.pcworld.com/article/531679/comm64.html

"BODY IN CAR IDENTIFIED AS BROOKLYN WOMAN, 19." *New York Times*. July 26, 1977. https://www.nytimes.com/1977/07/26/archives/body-in-car-identified-as-brooklyn-woman-19.html

"Organized Crime: Issues Concerning Strike Forces." https://www.ojp.gov/ncjrs/virtual-library/abstracts/organized-crime-issues-concerning-strike-forces

Gage, Nicholas. "Organized Crime Reaps Huge Profits From Dealing in Pornographic Films." *New York Times*. October 12,

1975. https://www.nytimes.com/1975/10/12/archives/organized-crime-reaps-huge-profits-from-dealing-in-pornographic.html

US District Court Federal Complaint – Joseph 'Joe Priest' Calder – Adam and Eve Extortion

"5 LINKED TO GAMBINO FAMILY SENTENCED IN a CAR-THEFT RING." *New York Times.* April 10, 1986. https://www.nytimes.com/1986/04/10/nyregion/5-linked-to-gambino-family-sentenced-in-a-car-theft-ring.html

Smothers, Ronald. "GAMBINO TRIAL HEARS CAR THIEF DESCRIBE WORK." *New York Times.* October 16, 1985. https://www.nytimes.com/1985/10/16/nyregion/gambino-trial-hears-car-thief-describe-work.html

"Rodney M Davis." FBI Retired | Signature Directories. https://fbiretired.com/agent/xg-consultants-group

McFadden, Robert D. "Police Call the Klein Kidnapping Spontaneous and Poorly Planned." *New York Times.* February 6, 1978. https://www.nytimes.com/1978/02/06/archives/police-call-the-klein-kidnapping-spontaneous-and-poorly-planned.html

Federal Bureau of Investigation. "FBI New York History." August 8, 2016. https://www.fbi.gov/history/field-office-histories/newyork

Federal Bureau of Investigation. "Field Offices." June 27, 2025. https://www.fbi.gov/contact-us/field-offices

Maitland, Leslie. "3 Held as Brink's Plotters." *New York Times.* June 8, 1979. https://www.nytimes.com/1979/06/08/archives/3-held-as-brinks-plotters-assault-charge-possible.html

"The Brink's Job DVD (1978)." Movie Buffs Forever. https://moviebuffsforever.com/products/the-brinks-job-1978-movie-dvd?_pos=1&_sid=5f78ba260&_ss=r

"Old-school mob man may be headed back to a familiar haunt." *Las Vegas Review-Journal*

Capeci, Jerry. "The Romeo Barfly with a Sting." *New York Post.* April 22, 1980

Rifkin, Glenn. "Thomas Verdillo, 77, Dies; Restaurateur Went From Red Sauce to Blue Ribbon." *New York Times.* January 11,

2021. https://www.nytimes.com/2021/01/11/obituaries/thomas-verdillo-dead-coronavirus.html

Jacobs, James B. *Mobsters, Unions, and Feds: The Mafia and the American Labor Movement*. NYU Press. 2006.

Reuter, Peter. *Disorganized Crime: The Economics of the Visible Hand*. MIT Press (MA). 1983.

Federal Bureau of Narcotics (1950s-1960s). Reports on Organized Crime and Narcotics Trafficking.

Harrell, Adele, and Peterson, George E. *Drugs, Crime, and Social Isolation: Barriers to Urban Opportunity*. The Urban Institute. 1992.

Smith, Dwight C. *The Mafia Mystique*. 1975.

Madeo. "Anti-Drug Abuse Act Creates Racially Biased 100 to 1 Crack/Powder Disparity." https://calendar.eji.org/racial-injustice/oct/27#:~:text=Oct%2027%2C%201986-,Federal%20Anti%2DDrug%20Abuse%20Act%20Signed%2C%20Creating%20Racially%20Biased%20100,people%20incarcerated%20in%20federal%20prison.

Messing, Philip. "Cops Smash Giant Credit Card Ring," *New York Post*

McPhee, Michele. "She Married Three Mobsters and a Cop. Two Husbands Died Violently. Now the 'Black Widow' Breaks Her Silence. NOWHERE TO TURN FOR THE ex-MOLL Shunned by MAFIA – and NYPD." *New York Daily News*. April 9, 2018. https://www.nydailynews.com/2004/08/24/she-married-three-mobsters-and-a-cop-two-husbands-died-violently-now-the-black-widow-breaks-her-silence-nowhere-to-turn-for-the-ex-moll-shunned-by-mafia-and-nypd/

Marzulli, John. "Widow Seeks Vindication as 2 Mobsters Go on Trial in Murder of Her Husband, Officer Ralph Dols." *New York Daily News*. January 10, 2019. https://www.nydailynews.com/2012/03/19/widow-seeks-vindication-as-2-mobsters-go-on-trial-in-murder-of-her-husband-officer-ralph-dols/

FBI. "SPECIAL AGENT FAQ." https://fbijobs.gov/sites/default/files/2023-03/Special_Agent_FAQ.pdf

Indeed Editorial Team. "The Pros and Cons of Being an FBI Agent (Plus FAQs)." Indeed Career Guide. June 9, 2025. https://www.indeed.com/career-advice/finding-a-job/pros-and-cons-of-being-fbi-agent

O'Neill, Jim, and Williams, Stephen. "Death on Rte. 110: A Chase, Bullets," *Newsday*, April 20, 1979

The Associated Press. "Ex-mob Hit Man 'Mad Dog' Sullivan Dies in NY State Prison." *The Seattle Times*. June 16, 2017. https://www.seattletimes.com/nation-world/ex-mob-hit-man-mad-dog-sullivan-dies-in-ny-state-prison/

Office of the United States Inspector General, 2017

United States v. DiNome, Salvatore Mangialino, Anthony Senter, Joseph Testa, Ronald Ustica, Carlo Profeta, Douglas Rega, Judith May Hellman, Wayne Hellman, and Sol Hellman; Docket Number: Nos. 9, 7, 8, 11, 10, 15, 13, 12 and 14, Dockets 89-1458, 89-1459, 89-1527, 89-1537, 89-1550, 89-1556, 90-1229, 90-1230 and 90-1263

Smothers, Ronald. "A PROTECTED WITNESS IN THE GAMBINO TRIAL IS TERMED a SUICIDE." *New York Times*. February 19, 1986. https://www.nytimes.com/1986/02/19/nyregion/a-protected-witness-in-the-gambino-trial-is-termed-a-suicide.html

Capeci, Jerry. "Hot Art from Coast Turns Up in Queens." *New York Post*. 1982

U.S. GAO. "From Quantity to Quality: Changing FBI Emphasis on Interstate Property Crimes." https://www.gao.gov/products/ggd-80-43

"Daily News From New York, New York." June 12, 1990. https://www.newspapers.com/newspage/406768394/

Justia Law. "United States V. Castellano, 610 F. Supp. 1359 (S.D.N.Y. 1985)." https://law.justia.com/cases/federal/district-courts/FSupp/610/1359/1469411/

Blair, William G. "A FEDERAL ATTORNEY HELD IN DRUG THEFT AT NEW YORK OFFICE." *New York Times*. May 31, 1985. https://www.nytimes.com/1985/05/31/nyregion/a-federal-attorney-held-in-drug-theft-at-new-york-office.html

UPI. "Former Federal Prosecutor Sent to Hospital for Psychiatric Evaluation." June 5, 1985. https://www.upi.com/Archives/1985/06/05/Former-federal-prosecutor-sent-to-hospital-for-psychiatric-evaluation/5680486792000/

FBI. "A New FBI Focus." https://archives.fbi.gov/archives/news/testimony/a-new-fbi-focus

Weir, Richard. "TRACING NEW LEADS TO ZIP GUN BOMBER Cops Eye Con's Links, Victim's Family." *New York Daily News.* April 9, 2018. https://www.nydailynews.com/2002/05/20/tracing-new-leads-to-zip-gun-bomber-cops-eye-cons-links-victims-family/

Capeci, Jerry. "FBI seeking pair in fatal shooting of cop." *New York Daily News.* April 3, 1986

Weiss, Murray. "Cop-kill suspect linked to VA hospital slaying." *New York Post*

Statista. "Number of Law Enforcement Officers U.S. 2004-2023." November 14, 2024. https://www.statista.com/statistics/191694/number-of-law-enforcement-officers-in-the-us/

DEA Museum. "Everett E. Hatcher." https://museum.dea.gov/wall-honor/everett-e-hatcher

FBI. "Original Top Ten Ledgers." December 23, 2022. https://www.fbi.gov/history/artifacts/original-top-ten-ledgers

McKinley Jr., James C., "Driver Slain by Officers After Chase Was Unarmed." *New York Times*. December 3, 1989. https://www.nytimes.com/1989/12/03/nyregion/driver-slain-by-officers-after-chase-was-unarmed.html

Barron, James. "Agents Kill Two Linked to Series of Bank Thefts." *New York Times*. January 19, 1990. https://www.nytimes.com/1990/01/19/nyregion/agents-kill-two-linked-to-series-of-bank-thefts.html

Office of the Commissioner. "What We Do." U.S. Food and Drug Administration. November 21, 2023. https://www.fda.gov/about-fda/what-we-do

"ADVANCING JUSTICE THROUGH DNA TECHNOLOGY: USING DNA TO SOLVE CRIMES." March 7, 2017. https://

www.justice.gov/archives/ag/advancing-justice-through-dna-technology-using-dna-solve-crimes

Law Enforcement. "CODIS-NDIS Statistics," August 11, 2025. https://le.fbi.gov/science-and-lab/biometrics-and-fingerprints/codis/codis-ndis-statistics

Veterans Affairs. "How Common is PTSD in Veterans?" https://www.ptsd.va.gov/understand/common/common_veterans.asp

"FBI's Critical Incident Stress Management Program | Office of Justice Programs." https://www.ojp.gov/ncjrs/virtual-library/abstracts/fbis-critical-incident-stress-management-program

"3 AFRICAN STOWAWAYS DIE ON TRIP TO THE U.S." *New York Daily News*, January 12, 2019. https://www.nydailynews.com/1996/03/20/3-african-stowaways-die-on-trip-to-the-us/

Martin, Douglas. "Donald V. North, 62, Leader in F.B.I.'s Fight Against Mafia, Is Dead." *New York Times*. January 29, 2005. https://www.nytimes.com/2005/01/29/obituaries/donald-v-north-62-leader-in-fbis-fight-against-mafia-is-dead.html

The Officer Down Memorial Page. "Chief of Detectives William H. Allee." https://www.odmp.org/officer/23692-chief-of-detectives-william-h-allee

Wassef, Mira. "'A Cop's Cop:' Decorated NYPD Chief Dies From 9/11 Illness." *SILive*. June 14, 2018. https://www.silive.com/news/erry-2018/06/e83869d5316135/a_cops_cop_decorated_staten_is.html

FBI. "World Trade Center Bombing 1993." May 9, 2022. https://www.fbi.gov/history/famous-cases/world-trade-center-bombing-1993

"Matt Tormey." LinkedIn. https://www.linkedin.com/in/matt-tormey-4974761/

"GANGSTER'S RISE CUT SHORT." *New York Daily News*. January 10, 2019. https://www.nydailynews.com/2001/04/09/gangsters-rise-cut-short/

Maddux, Mitchel. "Mob Turncoat Details the 1997 Slaying of NYPD Cop Ralph Dols." *New York Post*. March 27, 2012. https://

nypost.com/2012/03/27/mob-turncoat-details-the-1997-slaying-of-nypd-cop-ralph-dols/

D'Anna, Eddie. "NYPD Loses Its 'Iron Man'; Sgt. Francis Murnane Dies at 62." September 11th Families Association. March 16, 2015. https://911families.org/nypd-loses-its-iron-man-sgt-francis-murnane-dies-at-62/

Data Team. "Hart Island." https://council.nyc.gov/data/hart-island/

Maitland, Leslie. "Despair in Sunset Park and Hope, Too." *New York Times.* December 8, 1978. https://www.nytimes.com/1978/12/08/archives/despair-in-sunset-park-and-hope-too-reclaiming-the-neighborhood.html

FBI. "Female Special Agent's Briefcase." December 21, 2022. https://www.fbi.gov/history/artifacts/female-special-agent-briefcase

"METROPOLITAN REPORT UKRAINIANS TO SHIP OUT." *New York Daily News.* January 11, 2019. https://www.nydailynews.com/1999/08/12/metropolitan-report-ukrainians-to-ship-out/

"CITY BRINGS FOOD, WATER TO STRANDED UKRAINIAN CREW." *New York Daily News.* January 11, 2019. https://www.nydailynews.com/1999/08/04/city-brings-food-water-to-stranded-ukrainian-crew/

"Ship Stranded off New York Finally Gets Orders and Cargo." *New York Times.* August 11, 1999. https://www.nytimes.com/1999/08/11/nyregion/ship-stranded-off-new-york-finally-gets-orders-and-cargo.html

Weiser, Benjamin. "Salim, a Reputed Bin Laden Adviser, Gets Life Term." *New York Times.* September 1, 2010. https://www.nytimes.com/2010/09/01/nyregion/01salim.html

FBI. "Beltway Snipers." April 17, 2022. https://www.fbi.gov/history/famous-cases/beltway-snipers

"BUREAUS & UNITS." https://www.brooklynda.org/bureaus-units

CBS News. "Brooklyn DA: The Prosecution Teams." May 28, 2013. https://www.cbsnews.com/pictures/brooklyn-da-the-prosecution-teams/25/

Alexander, John. "Former Brooklyn District Attorney Charles 'Joe' Hynes Dead at 83." *Queens Daily Eagle*. January 30, 2019. https://queenseagle.com/all/2019/1/30/former-brooklyn-district-attorney-charles-joe-hynes-dead-at-83

Fox, Margalit. "Douglas LeVien, New York Detective Who Infiltrated the Mafia, Dies at 68." *New York Times*. August 8, 2015. https://www.nytimes.com/2015/08/09/nyregion/douglas-levien-new-york-detective-who-infiltrated-the-mafia-dies-at-68.html

New York City Council File #: Int 0968-2024. April 18, 2022

Daily Mail. "'Bodysnatch' Ring Plundered BBC Veteran's Remains." February 24, 2006. https://www.dailymail.co.uk/news/article-378175/Bodysnatch-ring-plundered-BBC-veterans-remains.html

"Funeral Parlor Owner From Staten Island Sentenced in Body Parts Scheme." *SILive*. January 26, 2009. https://www.silive.com/news/2009/01/former_staten_island_funeral_p.html

"Brooklyn Youth Slain After Halloween Fight." *New York Times*. November 2, 1989. https://www.nytimes.com/1989/11/02/nyregion/brooklyn-youth-slain-after-halloween-fight.html

Ginsberg, Alex. "MOLE PROBE SOLVES SENSELESS '89 MURDER - B'KLYN TEEN'S KIN: IT'S JUSTICE AT LAST." *New York Post*. March 30, 2006. https://nypost.com/2006/03/30/mole-probe-solves-senseless-89-murder-bklyn-teens-kin-its-justice-at-last/

Jenkins, Colleen. "Pasco Fisherman Held as Suspect in Slaying." *Tampa Bay Times*. December 10, 2019. https://www.tampabay.com/archive/2006/04/10/pasco-fisherman-held-as-suspect-in-slaying/

Weiss, Murray. "MOB-BUSTER MCCABE DIES." *New York Post*. February 22, 2006. https://nypost.com/2006/02/22/mob-buster-mccabe-dies/

Martin, Douglas. "Kenneth McCabe, 59, a Dogged Investigator of the Mob, Dies." *New York Times*. February 27, 2006. https://www.nytimes.com/2006/02/27/nyregion/kenneth-mccabe-59-a-dogged-investigator-of-the-mob-dies.html

For More News About Craig McGuire,
Signup For Our Newsletter:

http://wbp.bz/newsletter

Word-of-mouth is critical to an author's long-term success. If you appreciated this book please leave a review on the Amazon sales page:

https://wbp.bz/empirecityr

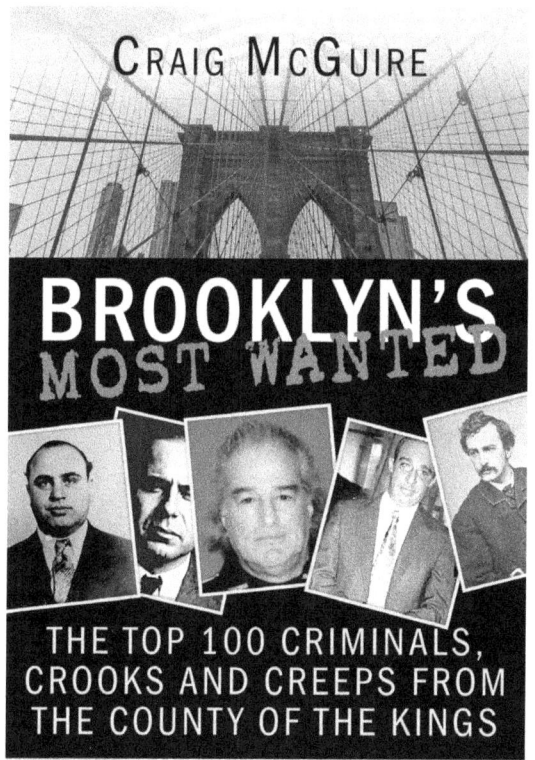